A Devotional G

DAILY BREAD 2013

365 Days of Discipleship Formation

Editor: Lu Mountenay

2013

Community of Christ

Herald Publishing House

Independence, Missouri

Produced by Community of Christ
1001 W. Walnut St.
Independence, MO 64050-3562

Herald Publishing House
P.O. Box 390
Independence, MO 64051-0390

Printed in the United States of America
ISBN: 978-0-8309-1564-4

Cover painting by Jack Martin

Library of Congress has cataloged this serial publication as follows:

Daily Bread
Independence, Mo., Herald Publishing House

v. 18cm

Annual.
"A devotional guide for every day of the year."
Key Title: Daily Bread, ISSN 0092-7147
1. Devotional calendars
BV4810.D23 242'.2 74-640475 MARC-S

Library of Congress 74 [8205]

Welcome to *Daily Bread* 2013
A Companion for your Journey

Daily Bread is just that—spiritual food for your daily walk with God. *Daily Bread* helps you get to know people in Community of Christ through their stories. It also gives you an opportunity to share your testimony. You can use *Daily Bread* as a personal devotional or use it in corporate worship.

Daily Bread helps you reflect on the lectionary scripture readings. *Daily Bread* also connects with the Daily Prayer for Peace at the Temple by including short prayers for peace each day (see Peter Judd's article on page 5).

Daily Bread includes Spiritual Practices to accompany your lifelong formation as a disciple. We added new practices for the five Mission Initiatives, and we've included four new practices for Advent. New to this volume is the inclusion of texts that will be in the new hymnal, *Community of Christ Sings.* Catch an inside look at how writers of these hymns were inspired. Look for more poetry from our community, as well.

Daily Bread is a companion for your spiritual journey and for your role in Christ's mission. Our hope is that *Daily Bread* gives expression to your stories that reflect the Enduring Principles and Mission Initiatives lived out every day—365 days a year. Enjoy!

- New Revised Standard Version is used for all Bible references.
- Revised Authorized Version is used for all Book of Mormon references.
- You can find the complete Daily Prayers for Peace at *www.CofChrist.org/PrayerPeace.*
- You can invite your friends and family to read the *Daily Bread* online at *www.CofChristDailyBread.wordpress.com.*

Acknowledgments

I appreciate the writers who sent their inspirational, informative, and touching stories, articles, testimonies, and poetry. I thank those who contributed in other ways:

- Carolyn Brock and the Spiritual Formation Team, for the Spiritual Practices.
- Sandra Ferguson of the Presiding Bishopric's office, for her help with many stories for Saturdays.
- Pam Robison and Karen Moreland, for their help with the daily scripture readings.
- Jack Martin, who designed the beautiful book cover.
- And thanks to the editorial and production team that helped with the details of placing *Daily Bread* in your hands: Patty Wilson, Pam Evans, Steven L. Shields, Judith Yager, Greg Clark, Jack Martin, Jane M. Gardner, and Barb Harmon. Online production: Cathy Loving, Kathleen Morton, and Jenn Killpack.

—Lu Mountenay
Daily Bread Editor

Future *Daily Bread* Submissions

If you wish to submit stories for consideration in the 2014 *Daily Bread*, send them to

E-mail: *lmountenay@CofChrist.org*

Or you can mail it to:: *Daily Bread* Editor
Community of Christ
International Headquarters
1001 West Walnut Street
Independence, MO 64050-3562
USA

I'll be waiting…Lu

Photo by Jack Martin

The Countries We Pray for Daily

By Peter Judd

> The Temple shall be dedicated to the pursuit of peace. It shall be for reconciliation and for healing of the spirit.
>
> —Doctrine and Covenants 156:5a

The Daily Prayer for Peace is a powerful witness of Community of Christ's commitment to peace. Such regular, public expression symbolizes the church's unrelenting pursuit of peace as God's vision for a bruised and divided world.

Since 1993, the Daily Prayer for Peace has been offered in the Temple Sanctuary. There the spoken voice of prayer rises almost 200 feet into the Temple spire, reaching to the international community. The Sanctuary always has room to symbolically accommodate others around the world who join in the prayers, as well as those for whom we pray. Each day we offer a prayer for a specific country based on the World Council of Churches' ecumenical prayer cycle, which joins our prayers with those of even more Christians throughout the world.

The service begins at 1:00 p.m. (CST) each day. Around the world, interested people know we are praying for peace at the Temple and can pause for a moment of silent prayer.

The Daily Prayer for Peace has impact far beyond the church, its members, and the people who gather each day to worship and pray. The congregation at the Temple is joined by many others wherever they live, and the entire world listens as this Temple becomes known as a place where each day the concern for peace is upheld in prayer.

Many Community of Christ congregations include a prayer for peace in their weekly worship services. We encourage all people throughout the world to pray daily for peace. By including in *Daily Bread* the list of countries prayed for each day in the Temple, those who wish to make this an element of their daily devotions can feel more fully a part of the worldwide focus on peace. Please see those countries listed on the next pages.

DAILY BREAD 2013

Daily Prayer for Peace Countries

December 2012

1 Somalia
2 Sierra Leone
3 Tunisia
4 Liberia
5 Singapore
6 Finland
7 Sudan
8 Romania
9 Senegal
10 Guinea
11 Cape Verde
12 Kenya
13 Malta
14 The Gambia
15 Guinea-Bissau
16 South Africa
17 Kazakhstan
18 Benin
19 Spain
20 Côte d'Ivoire/ Ivory Coast
21 Togo
22 East Timor
23 Ghana
24 Monaco
25 World Peace
26 Tanzania
27 Paraguay
28 Nigeria
29 Malawi
30 Switzerland
31 Palau

January 2013

1 All Nations
2 Egypt
3 Syria
4 Lebanon
5 Jordan
6 Israel
7 Palestine
8 Saudi Arabia
9 Kuwait
10 Bahrain
11 Qatar
12 United Arab Emirates
13 Oman
14 Iran
15 Yemen
16 Iraq
17 Cyprus
18 Turkey
19 Greece
20 Algeria
21 Libya
22 Morocco
23 Antigua and Barbuda
24 Tunisia
25 Botswana
26 Costa Rica
27 Denmark
28 Ecuador
29 Finland
30 Iceland
31 Norway

February 2013

1 Mauritius
2 Sweden
3 El Salvador
4 Ireland
5 Grenada
6 Kiribati
7 Marshall Islands
8 United Kingdom
9 Guatemala
10 Belgium
11 Luxembourg
12 Netherlands
13 Vatican City
14 Indigenous Peoples of Europe
15 Honduras
16 Macedonia
17 Nauru
18 Guyana
19 Portugal
20 Spain
21 Italy
22 Malta
23 New Caledonia
24 Mauritania
25 Germany
26 France
27 Haiti
28 Moldova

March 2013

1 Panama

2 Saint Kitts and Nevis
3 Bulgaria
4 Austria
5 Liechtenstein
6 Switzerland
7 Saint Lucia
8 Andorra
9 Monaco
10 San Marino
11 Saint Vincent and the Grenadines
12 Senegal
13 Slovakia
14 Myanmar
15 Hungary
16 Thailand
17 Cambodia
18 Seychelles
19 Laos
20 Solomon Islands
21 Tajikistan
22 Vietnam
23 Suriname
24 Argentina
25 Ghana
26 Tonga
27 China
28 Tuvalu
29 Hong Kong
30 Macao
31 Australia

April 2013

1 Brunei
2 Malaysia
3 Samoa
4 Bosnia and Herzegovina
5 Singapore
6 Slovenia
7 Sierra Leone
8 Uzbekistan
9 Philippines
10 East Timor
11 Indonesia
12 Vanuatu
13 Liberia
14 Japan
15 Mexico
16 Korea
17 Taiwan
18 French Polynesia
19 Afghanistan
20 United States of America
21 Democratic Republic of Congo
22 Djibouti
23 Belarus
24 Armenia
25 Equatorial Guinea
26 Somalia
27 Comoros
28 Indigenous Peoples of Africa
29 Eritrea
30 Benin

May 2013

1 Indigenous Peoples of North America
2 Algeria
3 Bahrain
4 Ethiopia
5 Bangladesh
6 The Gambia
7 Sudan
8 Russian Federation
9 Greece
10 Uganda
11 Cape Verde
12 Kenya
13 Tanzania
14 Chad
15 Human Family
16 Guinea
17 Cyprus
18 Jordan
19 Malawi
20 Mongolia
21 Zambia
22 Madagascar
23 India
24 Romania
25 Burkina Faso
26 Bhutan
27 Botswana
28 Maldives
29 Côte d'Ivoire/ Ivory Coast
30 Morocco
31 Yemen

June 2013

1 Zimbabwe
2 Guinea-Bissau
3 Lesotho
4 Nepal
5 Egypt
6 Namibia
7 South Africa
8 Swaziland
9 Angola
10 Denmark
11 Mozambique
12 Pakistan
13 Iran
14 Nigeria
15 Qatar
16 Togo
17 Tunisia
18 United Arab Emirates
19 Brazil
20 Iraq
21 Niger
22 Libya
23 Uruguay
24 Argentina
25 Indigenous Peoples of South America
26 Cambodia
27 Kuwait
28 Luxembourg
29 Paraguay
30 Rwanda

July 2013

1 Canada
2 Bolivia
3 Turkey
4 Syria

5 Chile
6 Peru
7 Sweden
8 Colombia
9 Spain
10 Ecuador
11 Venezuela
12 São Tomé and Principe
13 Portugal
14 France
15 Costa Rica
16 El Salvador
17 Nicaragua
18 Oman
19 Panama
20 Netherlands
21 Laos
22 Guatemala
23 Honduras
24 Belize
25 Mexico
26 Italy
27 Antigua and Barbuda
28 Dominican Republic
29 Grenada
30 Cuba
31 Dominica

August 2013

1 The Bahamas
2 Guyana
3 Haiti
4 Barbados
5 Saint Kitts and Nevis
6 Jamaica
7 Saint Lucia
8 Trinidad and Tobago
9 Saint Vincent and the Grenadines
10 Suriname
11 Canada
12 United States of America
13 Australia
14 New Zealand
15 French Polynesia
16 Samoa
17 New Caledonia
18 Fiji
19 Kiribati
20 Marshall Islands
21 Micronesia
22 Nauru
23 Palau
24 Papua New Guinea
25 Solomon Islands
26 Tonga
27 Tuvalu
28 Vanuatu
29 Latvia
30 Estonia
31 Lithuania

September 2013

1 Myanmar
2 Israel
3 Lebanon
4 Czech Republic
5 Poland
6 Slovakia
7 Kosovo
8 Macedonia
9 Bosnia and Herzegovina
10 Croatia
11 Slovenia
12 Albania
13 Montenegro
14 Serbia
15 China
16 Romania
17 Bulgaria
18 Andorra
19 Hong Kong
20 Hungary
21 Switzerland
22 Korea
23 Belarus
24 Paraguay
25 Moldova
26 Russian Federation
27 Liechtenstein
28 Ukraine
29 Armenia
30 Norway

October 2013

1 Malta
2 Azerbaijan
3 Germany
4 San Marino
5 Georgia
6 Afghanistan
7 Kazakhstan
8 Kyrgyzstan
9 Mongolia
10 Tajikistan
11 Turkmenistan
12 Uzbekistan
13 Vietnam
14 Bangladesh
15 Zambia
16 Thailand
17 Bhutan
18 Uganda
19 Nepal
20 Children of the World
21 United Kingdom
22 Pakistan
23 India
24 Indigenous Peoples of Asia
25 Sri Lanka
26 Brunei
27 Comoros
28 Madagascar
29 Mauritius
30 Seychelles
31 Maldives

November 2013

1 Saudi Arabia
2 Indigenous Peoples of Oceania
3 Singapore
4 Burundi
5 Somalia
6 Rwanda
7 Democratic Republic of Congo

8 Sudan
9 Taiwan
10 Republic of Congo
11 Zimbabwe
12 Gabon
13 Austria
14 São Tomé and Principe
15 Mozambique
16 Belgium
17 Cameroon
18 Djibouti
19 Philippines
20 East Timor
21 Central African Republic
22 Ethiopia
23 Equatorial Guinea
24 Burkina Faso
25 Niger
26 Chad
27 Mali
28 Nicaragua
29 Palestine
30 Mauritania

December 2013

1 Swaziland
2 Sierra Leone
3 Finland
4 Liberia
5 Ireland
6 Kenya
7 Lesotho
8 Macao
9 Guinea
10 Guinea-Bissau
11 Cape Verde
12 Malaysia
13 Senegal
14 The Gambia
15 Benin
16 South Africa
17 Monaco
18 Namibia
19 Côte d'Ivoire
20 Togo
21 Angola
22 Venezuela
23 Eritrea
24 Iceland
25 World Peace
26 Japan
27 Peru
28 Ghana
29 Trinidad and Tobago
30 Nigeria
31 Tanzania

1
Tuesday
January

Next...

By John Bonney of Springfield, Oregon, USA

> *Grace to you and peace from God our Father and the Lord Jesus Christ.*
>
> —1 Corinthians 1:3

During the winter months where I live, the trees are dark, stark, and bare, standing bleakly against the winter sky. They show their naked, gnarly bones. It is a sight with which I never grow bored. On any unadorned winter morning I see the imaginative, creative gifts of the Eternal Presence who made those trees.

I see creativity in the trees themselves as they stand waiting for the summons to fulfill their purpose.

Then spring unfolds, and those same unadorned trees find another season of expression. The leaves appear in their small light-green, almost yellow, cloaks. In time, those same leaves become full, darker green, and glorious. They dress the tree in a verdant robe and sing their silent praise of the Presence who created them.

What often enters my thinking on a morning walk is the passage of time. I see the trees, in early summer, decked in lush and deep green at the height of their splendor. They display their leafy tresses as if they were the only specimen. They are gray-green, blue-green, and more greens in-between.

In autumn the cycle comes to another completion. Not an ending, but a continuance to the next cycle. The leaves find the completion of their purpose, and they turn into a varied and glorious palette that seems to express wonder at creation. So the leaf falls and finally understands the purpose, the conclusion of this journey on Earth.

We, too, as humans see the journey. Each season includes joy and pain. We see the passing of those we have known, those close to us—parents, siblings, classmates. It hurts, and we find relief in the memories of cycles past. We are left to watch others move on.

It is like standing on the shore and watching the waves on the sea stretched before us. We imagine the places the waves have been, where they will go, and then we imagine the waves coming back to us. We also imagine the new year stretched before us.

Where will we go? Who will we see? We look back on the previous year and remember those who shared their lives with us. We remember the life and peace Christ shared with us.

Prayer for Peace

Eternal Presence, Creator of rainbow colors, we look to you season after cherished season. We look to you for what is next on our journey and for ways to share Christ's peace.

Spiritual Practice: Connecting with God as Center

Open yourself to God's presence and share what flows from your heart and mind. Your "communication with God" might include thoughts about the cycles of life, about the seasons. Try to write or meditate at least five minutes each day. Are you aware of your connection to God in one season more than another? What deepens or changes in your relationship with God?

Peace Covenant

Today, God, I will not long for other seasons. I will cherish the season in which I find myself.

2
Wednesday
January

Different, but the Same

By Talitha Pennington of Sterling Heights, Michigan, USA

...they shall beat their swords into plowshares, and their spears into pruning hooks; nation shall not lift up sword against nation, neither shall they learn war any more.

—Isaiah 2:4

If we were alike,
perhaps we would greet each other
with a bored, "ho-hum" and hurry on by.
I am glad we are so
delightfully different.
I won't hurry by—I must get to know you.

—Peggy Michael
Cantonment, Florida, USA

I recall one of the most powerful images I have from a recent trip. I remember my 3-year-old granddaughter, Anna, holding hands with another little girl exactly her size as we toured an ostrich farm in Curaçao. The two were physically different: Anna has fair skin and long, blonde hair; her companion had darker skin and long, dark hair.

They spoke different languages, so all communication with each other was non-verbal. Yet they connected instantly and radiated pure joy in being together, hand in hand, every chance they had.

Watching them brought me joy. How much greater must be divine joy when God sees humans holding hands, literally or figuratively, and celebrating our "being together" despite our differences.

Prayer for Peace

God of every nation, every planet, thank you for the diversity of people. Thank you for our unique features and gifts. May we use them to share Christ's peace.

Spiritual Practice: Honoring the Worth of All Persons

Read Psalm 139:13–18. Sit quietly and let the words sink deeply into your mind, heart, and body. Imagine God watching you grow in your mother's womb. What thoughts and feelings do you have about being "fearfully and wonderfully made" (Psalm 139:14)?

Sense the intimate knowledge God has of you and every child. Be aware of the sacred worth of each person. How are you invited to notice, protect, heal, and affirm the spiritual identity of all God's beloved people today? Pray for God's compassion.

Peace Covenant

Today, God, I will look beyond outward appearance to discover similarities I never imagined.

3
Thursday
January

Everyday Heroes

By Kenneth McLaughlin of Independence, Missouri, USA

> *"Here is my servant, whom I have chosen, my beloved, with whom my soul is well pleased. I will put my Spirit upon him, and he will proclaim justice to the Gentiles. He will not wrangle or cry aloud, nor will anyone hear his voice in the streets. He will not break a bruised reed or quench a smoldering wick until he brings justice to victory. And in his name the Gentiles will hope."*
>
> —Matthew 12:18–21

I struck up a conversation with the sacker at our grocery store. A woman in her late 40s, she shared that she also held a second job and was a student at a community college. Her younger brother had died the year before, and she found herself (a single woman) guardian of his children, as well as mother to her own. As if that weren't enough, she was a survivor of breast cancer, now in remission.

"How do you do it?" I asked. She quickly described her various sources of income and the fact the kids were well behaved and expected to contribute to the well-being of the family. And she had the support and respect of an extended family and circle of friends.

"You are my hero," I declared. She found my statement odd, particularly as I asked her if I could mention her in my future sermons, classes, and writings. "Sure," she said, "but all I'm doing is what I have to do—one day at a time."

Each day, everyday heroes are all around us. These are ordinary women and men, boys and girls, who simply are doing what they feel called to do.

They are the salt of the Earth, and the ones who not only talk about the will of God, but do it.

May we each do what we have to do to bring justice for all of God's creation.

Prayer for Peace

God of all, may we look for heroes. May we show appreciation for how they share Christ's peace through their work.

Spiritual Practice: Welcoming Unity in Diversity

Meditate on Unity in Diversity. Create a large circle with your arms. See and feel the diverse people God invites inside the sanctuary of Christ's peace represented by this circle.

Who is easiest to welcome? Whom do you struggle to include? Confess the dividing walls between you and people too different or "dangerous" to invite into your spiritual home. Ask God to forgive and heal barriers that keep you and others from being one in Christ's peace.

Peace Covenant

Today, God, I will look past the uniforms of invisibility and take interest in someone's life.

4
Friday
January

Community of Christ

By Steven L. Shields of Lee's Summit, Missouri, USA

> *"Community of Christ," your name, given as a divine blessing, is your identity and calling. If you will discern and embrace its full meaning, you will not only discover your future, you will become a blessing to the whole creation. Do not be afraid to go where it beckons you to go.*
>
> —Doctrine and Covenants 163:1

We talk a lot about "community." Although we are not always successful, when we do it well we excel at creating the community envisaged by prophets both ancient and modern, the community envisaged by the mission of Christ. Testimonies abound about lives changed at family camps, retreats, World Conference, and in congregations.

Worship is an important facet of discipleship, but the shared community at the meal table after the worship service feeds my soul even more.

A few years ago, when my mother died, members of my faith community rallied and brought food for my family—siblings, spouses, nieces, and nephews (at least 30 people)—that fed us for several days. Only my son and I are members of Community of Christ. I appreciated the support of "my" community; it is a powerful testimony of unconditional love.

Our challenge as disciples of Jesus Christ gathered in his community, is to "embrace the full meaning" of our identity and calling as "Community of Christ." We must extend the boundaries of our comfortable group, which gathers each week. We must embrace those on the "outside." Who those "others" are will be different for each congregation. God prepares the way and assures us so we need "not be afraid to go" wherever our future calls.

Prayer for Peace

Creator God, I am thankful as I continue to sense your self-revealing nature. I praise you. May I reach out and embrace others as part of the call to be part of a signal community that shares Christ's peace.

Spiritual Practice: Praying for Leadership of the Church

An important spiritual practice for disciples is praying for members of the body of Christ, particularly those who carry leadership responsibilities. Ask God to guide your awareness to persons who lead the community of faith at congregational, mission center, and World Church levels. See or sense these persons and ask for insight into any particular physical, emotional, or spiritual needs they may have. Pray for God's outpouring of grace on each servant leader who comes to mind.

Peace Covenant

Today, God, I will open myself to your Spirit. I will listen and follow.

5
Saturday
January

Tsunamis and Poor Choices

By Candy Brayton of Independence, Missouri, USA

> *This covenant entails sacramental living that respects and reveals God's presence and reconciling activity in creation. It requires whole-life stewardship dedicated to expanding the church's restoring ministries, especially those devoted to asserting the worth of persons, protecting the sacredness of creation, and relieving physical and spiritual suffering.*
>
> —Doctrine and Covenants 164:9c

"Why does God let tragedy happen?" After natural disasters and other life-changing events, we often ask this question. People desperately need to make sense of the loss of life, health, safety, and property caused by these events. The answers are not always clear, and many struggle in the aftermath.

Violent, natural events are a part of our living Earth; just as free will is a precious gift from our Creator. Whether it is a tsunami or a poor choice, the resulting tragedies are not because of the action or inaction of a vengeful or disinterested deity.

Our loving God calls us to respond with the capacity of faith, love, compassion, and generosity with which the Divine has blessed us. By responding wholeheartedly to the community, we become a blessing to others in their time of great need. Neighbor digs neighbor out of the rubble. Compassionate people from miles away rally to give aid. Young adults choose to devote their vocations to helping victims of violent crime. People give their tithes to Abolish Poverty, End Suffering. In others' welfare, lies our welfare. We give because we love.

This is Christ's message of peace, justice, and love. It is a wonder when separating walls disappear; when there is no ethnic, gender, or political bias; when there is only humankind.

As disciples of Christ, we can rise to the challenge of embodying Christ's mission and message in our lives. We can embody Christ's mission not only when life-changing events happen, but in our day-to-day living.

Prayer for Peace

God of the storm, God of the calm sea, help us understand the ways of the Earth. May we make choices that help others share in Christ's peace.

Spiritual Practice: Tears of Compassion

Offer a silent prayer for the gift of God's compassion. Ask God to make you aware of the suffering that causes the Earth and its people to groan and weep. Be open to feelings of connection with those who suffer. Discern any invitations to respond to those who weep.

Peace Covenant

Today, God, I will help someone in need "dig out" from darkness to light.

6
Sunday
January

Follow the Star

By Barbara Carter, Council of Twelve Apostles

> *Then Herod secretly called for the wise men... "Go and search diligently for the child; and when you have found him, bring me word so that I may also go and pay him homage." When they saw that the star had stopped, they were overwhelmed with joy. On entering the house, they saw the child with Mary his mother; and they knelt down and paid him homage...And having been warned in a dream not to return to Herod, they left for their own country by another road.*
>
> —Matthew 2:7–8, 10–12

The wise men who followed the star were seekers. A new star had appeared, and they believed its appearance was the sign of a spectacular event. Their seeking eventually led them to Jesus.

The story in Matthew tells us that after finding Jesus, they returned home a different way. This passage describes the original plan to go tell King Herod where the child was.

But I like to think of it this way. After the wise men encountered Jesus, could they go home untouched? They traveled for many years, and once they found Jesus, they would never be the same. That meeting changed their lives and had an impact on them in untold ways.

Isn't this the same for us? After meeting and learning of Jesus, his teachings, his compassion, his love for all people, his message of justice and peace for the world today, can we go back to who we were? In this meeting, our lives have experienced a touch of grace that allows us to see the world through different eyes. Even if we traveled the same road that brought us to this place, we would never see or experience it as before.

It is that way with Christ. Once you have had an encounter, you cannot return home the same.

Prayer for Peace

Creator God, as we search for your star anew, may we encounter your life-changing Spirit. May we pay attention to our journey on the outward path. As the love of Christ touches us, may we return as new and vibrant disciples of peace.

Spiritual Practice: Encountering Scripture as Continuing Revelation

Read and pray with Doctrine and Covenants as Continuing Revelation of God's vision for the church and creation. Choose a favorite section or focus on counsel in Sections 156—164. Read a few selected paragraphs slowly three or four times. Pause to pray for deep understanding after each reading.

Pray for the opening of your heart and emotions. Prayerfully ask to hear the phrase or word that speaks to you or touches your life. Stay with this word or phrase. Listen as fully and openly as you can. What sense of divine presence or invitation comes? What is revealed?

Peace Covenant

Today, God, I will awaken to Christ's mission and discern a new path.

7
Monday
January

Epiphany of Peace

By Donna Boyd of Independence, Missouri, USA

> *...Let the Temple stand as a towering symbol of a people who knew injustice and strife on the frontier and who now seek the peace of Jesus Christ throughout the world.*
>
> —Doctrine and Covenants 161:2b, adapted

He is a war veteran. I watched sadly as depression and flashbacks gobbled him up and spit out a shell of a man. He had no hope, no joy, little love, and visibly no peace. We took him to the Temple, where he found a peace he had never known. But he did not know how to carry that peace on his outward journey.

He struggled with depression for many months in a veterans hospital. He spoke to the chaplain about how much his experience at the Temple meant. The chaplain said my friend had an epiphany, a new understanding of himself.

He later shared one experience that stayed in my heart to share at every opportunity. Officials at the hospital told him they could not help him. He was angry. He went into the restroom before beginning his long journey home.

A man in a wheelchair was at the sink. He insisted he did not need help. My friend asked him over and again. The man finally admitted he wanted to shave but could not reach the sink.

The man had a week's worth of scraggly beard. My friend put paper towels around his neck, put the chair beside the sink, and began to shave the man. He finished, removed the towels, dried the man's face, and prepared to leave. The man asked, "Why did you do that for me?"

My friend answered, "What would Jesus have done if he were here?"

With a smile the man said, "He would have shaved me."

When my friend returned to his wife, who had been waiting for him, she asked what had happened. When he told her, she smiled and tearfully hugged him. She joyously proclaimed that her husband was himself once more!

Prayer for Peace

Binder of wounds, you are with us in our darkest nights. You bring peace to our troubled souls, so we may share peace with the world.

Spiritual Practice: Healing for Broken Spirits

Begin with quiet prayer. Ask God to help you discern "sore places" in the body of Christ and in God's creation. Become aware of people who feel separated, wounded, or left out. Reflect on or write a short journal entry of healing words to at least one person who comes to mind. Ask God for words that will touch this person's broken spirit like healing ointment. Keep this person in your heart and prayers today and act on any ideas that come to bring blessing and wholeness.

Peace Covenant

Today, God, I will find someone who needs the hands of Jesus. I will be those hands.

8
Tuesday
January

Here Be God

By Vera Entwistle of Forster, New South Wales, Australia

So he came and proclaimed peace to you who were far off and peace to those who were near; for through him both of us have access in one Spirit to the Father. So then you are no longer strangers and aliens, but you are citizens with the saints and also members of the household of God.

—Ephesians 2:17–19

There is a map in the British Museum of North America's east coastal area. The map was drawn by a seafarer in the 1500s. The man who drew the map added some ominous notations: "Here be fiery scorpions." "Here be giants." "Here be dragons."

Over two centuries later Sir John Franklin, himself an explorer from England, saw this map and quickly changed these inscriptions. Across the map he wrote, "Here be God."

If I could have traveled with either of these men, I am sure Sir John would have been my first choice.

I wonder what the journey was like for those traveling with the man who drew the first map. Those on the ship might have seen the comments and been afraid of what was ahead.

When we were preparing to go to China, many family members and friends questioned why we would travel to a country perceived by many to be anti-Christian. A few times I found myself questioning our reasoning.

Looking back on the three years we were there, I have precious memories. We made many friends, saw some sad places, and saw places of sheer beauty. We met no "dragons" or "scorpions," but we did meet people who cared enough to struggle to communicate with us. With Sir John, we could say, "Here be the people of God. Here be God."

Prayer for Peace

Pilot God, steer us in the direction where we are needed. Give us courage to face the unknown. There may we find people with whom we can share Christ's peace.

Spiritual Practice: Making Responsible Choices

Prayerfully seek God's guidance in your choices. Discernment invites us to orient our lives toward God and God's vision for us and creation. Begin by reviewing the responsibilities and opportunities in the day before you. Take these choices into prayer, asking God for wisdom and insight about what matters most.

Offer yourself to God with the prayer of Teresa of Avila: "God, what do you want of me today?" Sit prayerfully with this question as you review the day again. Be aware of images, thoughts, names, or actions that come to you. Ask for a blessing to live this day responsibly and compassionately in the spirit of Christ.

Peace Covenant

Today, God, I will have faith that when your people are here, "Here be you."

9
Wednesday
January

Superannuation—a Loss?

By Velma Ruch of Lamoni, Iowa, USA

> *...By the grace of God, you are poised to fulfill God's ultimate vision for the church. ...and steadfastly hold to God's covenant of peace in Jesus Christ.*
>
> —Doctrine and Covenants 164:9a–b

Last week was an epiphany week for me. What had been so rich a time in writing my latest book suddenly was over, and I struggled with what it all means. That is when my superannuation came into the picture, as well. Another ending?

I went through, I think, the worst struggle of my ministry, and there was much I still didn't understand.

I did some thinking about the experience of emptiness I was going through. Primarily it was about the dark night of the soul—why I experienced it and then *discovering that I was in no sense abandoned by God.*

I came to better understand what was meant by "the loss" felt at superannuation. It is indeed a loss—a loss we would avoid if we could. But it is going through "the shadow of the cross." If we persist, as on the Worshiper's Path in the Temple, we come out on the other side in the light. We see ikebana: the balance of Earth, humanity, and the Divine.

I always had thought of the Worshiper's Path as a perfect example of the development of the mystic life. I discovered the path to be the delineation of the whole process of superannuation, both the loss *and* the joy.

Before going to my superannuation service, I reread a paragraph of Doctrine and Covenants 164. It begins with my favorite phrase, "Beloved children of the Restoration..."

I was looking for assurance that the cost of discipleship could be borne if we accepted God's grace. I copied the scripture: "By the grace of God, you are poised to fulfill God's ultimate vision for the church." We are called to live consecrated lives as we "steadfastly hold to God's covenant of peace in Jesus Christ."

I put the paper in my pocket and kept it with me throughout the service.

Prayer for Peace

Use us, God. We are yours. May we change *endings* to *completions*. Let our sorrows fade as we leave the dark behind and walk in the light.

Spiritual Practice: Examining God's Call to Me and to All

Reflect on the ministry of your life. Begin by prayerfully asking to recall particular moments when you have experienced God's presence and invitation. Write in your journal or quietly reflect on images and insights that come. How and when has God called you to use your energies and gifts? When have you felt disconnected or unable to serve? How do your gifts and callings connect with the call of God you notice in your family, friends, congregation, or community? Reflect on God's light in your life.

Peace Covenant

Today, God, I will not regret—I will remember the joy.

10
Thursday
January

Keep on Shuffling...

By Lu Mountenay of Independence, Missouri, USA

Then Jesus told them a parable about their need to pray always and not to lose heart.

—Luke 18:1

When my 5-year-old granddaughter, Samantha, was babysitting me, she decided we would play cards. After about 30 games of "Go Fish" I was beginning to lose focus. My eyes were glazing, and I went into a daze with a fixed smile on my face.

Soon I heard Sama give a deep sigh and patiently say, "You know Grandma, if you keep shuffling those cards, they'll be right back where they started!"

She was perfectly serious, but the humor of what she said jolted me back to reality. I began thinking about what Sama had said and how true it might be. I thought of other situations where her "theory" could apply.

Have you ever seen people attempt to parallel park a car with perfection? They pull into the *spot* and decide they are too far from the curb. They pull out and try again. The next time they might be a little crooked, so they pull out again. They get a "yo-yo" thing going. On the last attempt they are satisfied (or give up), and—you guessed it—they are back in the same position where they started! And it really doesn't matter, after all.

There is a time when it *does* matter. When I pray, I often start with, "...here I am again, God...same old sinner, right back on my knees where I started."

I have to begin every prayer with an apology because I haven't talked with God in a while. God is patient with me, like my granddaughter. And you know, if I didn't know before my prayer that I am forgiven, would I ever come back to that same place? But I do know, and I do come back. And it's like a new and awesome place.

My friend, John Bonney, said, "How many corners can one turn before coming back to where one started? It depends on the *degree* of turning, I would guess."

> ...What we call the beginning is often the end and to make an end is to make a beginning. The end is where we start from...We will not cease from exploration and the end of all our exploring will be to arrive where we started. And know the place for the first time...
>
> —T. S. Eliot
> *Little Gidding*

Prayer for Peace

Eternal God, here we are again, back where we started. May we grow in your Spirit as Christ's disciples. We pray we have matured to where we can share Christ's peace.

Spiritual Practice: Your Relationship with the Divine

Contemplate where you have been in your relationship with the Divine and where you want to be. Are you surprised by the depth of your connection?

Peace Covenant

Today, God, I will return only to what matters most.

11
Friday
January

Be a Refuge

By Eleanor St. Clair of Oak Harbor, Ohio, USA

And the peace of God, which surpasses all understanding, will guard your hearts and your minds in Christ Jesus.

—Philippians 4:7

The Peace Covenant in one day's *Daily Bread* devotion read, "Today God, I will be someone's refuge. They will know by my actions that you are with them."

This inspired me.

Maria, an immigrant from Peru who was a new Community of Christ member, called and sounded frantic. Because of health issues, she feared losing her job and home. Adding to her stress, her sister, who provided for their mother, was diagnosed with cancer.

Maria was to leave work for a medical examination. She requested I remember her in prayer. She became incoherent, so I said, "Wait a minute" and began to pray. Toward the end of the brief prayer, I felt the need to rebuke the spirit of fear as well as bring words of comfort to Maria. The next words came with authority, telling her that she would go in trust and faith in God. God would go with her. "Look to your Savior and have faith in the redeeming peace of Jesus Christ."

Life can be daunting, and can sidetrack us until we allow the peace of Christ to calm us. We are called to be with others in their discipleship struggles, help them refocus, and remind them whose they are.

After the "amen," Maria was transformed and went on her way in confidence that she was not alone. Praise God!

Prayer for Peace

Ever-present God, may we be ever-present also, for those who need your blessing. Let those in need of your peace know they are not alone.

Spiritual Practice: Embodying God's Shalom

Find a way to express and embody God's shalom. Begin by prayerfully listening to your longing for peace. Become silent and imagine you can hear the groaning of the Earth's people, nations, and creatures. Prayerfully open yourself to God's yearning for peace and the divine vision of shalom.

What images, feelings, and words come to you? What prayer for peace comes to you from your time of listening? Speak or write this prayer. What small act of justice, kindness, healing, or peacemaking does God invite you to consider this day?

Peace Covenant

Today, God, I will be a living sanctuary, aware of those in fear.

12
Saturday
January

Hands of the Steward

By Carolyn Brock of Redmond, Oregon

God is calling for a prophetic community to emerge, drawn from the nations of the world, that is characterized by uncommon devotion to the compassion and peace of God revealed in Jesus Christ. Through divine grace and wisdom, this faith community has been given abundant gifts, resources, and opportunities to equip it to become such a people…

—Doctrine and Covenants 163:11a

They don't pass an offering plate at church in Africa. You get up and dance your way to the basket, clutching your nira, or shillings, or kwacha tightly. Then you bow graciously as you let the money drop from your folded hands into the container.

On some days and in some places in Africa, you bring your cassava, fruits, or vegetables to share with those in need.

Think of all the hands sharing their substance on any given Sunday morning in our global family. Bones and tissue covered with skin of every shade from deep browns and mahogany to pinks and tans, amber and cappuccino blends. They are wrinkled, soft, calloused, scarred, arthritic, worn from hoeing, harvesting, hauling, and simply holding on.

How do daily life, the realities of our work, our bodies, our wealth, or poverty connect with what we share within Community of Christ? Some of us give abundantly, painlessly, with generous amounts left over.

For others their offering is that of the widow's two copper coins, and they clap and sing all the way around the church. How then shall we be stewards in a world of diminishing resources and increasing interdependence? What will restore spiritual depth and energy to sharing, whether it be our money, the skills and energies of our bodies, or our hearts and souls?

Prayer for Peace

May we use our hands, God, for your purposes. Whether they are young and smooth or old and wrinkled, we would employ them in Christ's mission to share his peace.

Spiritual Practice: Hand Ministry

Place your hand on a piece of paper and trace around it to create an outline. Add details of fingernails, wrinkles, or skin color if desired. Look at your hand and meditate on what you do with your hands each day. Ask God to direct your thoughts to a person in need of blessing, kindness, or healing touch. Pray for wisdom about the specific act needed by this person and discern how and when you will use your hands to complete this ministry.

Peace Covenant

My mission of compassion today, God, is to abolish poverty and end suffering.

13
Sunday
January

Descend, Holy Spirit

By Susan Oxley, Council of Twelve Apostles

> *...when Jesus also had been baptized and was praying, the heaven was opened, and the Holy Spirit descended upon him in bodily form like a dove. And a voice came from heaven, "You are my Son, the Beloved; with you I am well-pleased."*
>
> —Luke 3:21–22

Most of my life I have thought of the descending of the Holy Spirit in relation to a specific moment, for a specific purpose, with a specific result. I can point to events and say, "The Holy Spirit was present." Or, "There! That's when I experienced the Holy Spirit!"

A defining change has occurred in the last few years. I have become more aware of the flow of the Holy Spirit in all of life, continuous and pervasive. Yes, it has always been there; but now, I can see it more clearly.

- An angry man intended to disrupt the World Conference legislative session. Later, he told me, "I couldn't do it. The presence of the Spirit changed me."
- Creative solutions emerged from distrust at a mission center conference. Spirit-imbued communication triumphed.
- Three women wrestling with the idea of joining our faith community heard of the new policy on church membership at a congregational meeting. They chose to be baptized anew.
- A congregation threatening to leave the church met with church leaders. The result was recommitment to Christ and this church. Baptisms resulted.
- Families in conflict mended their relationships, extending love and forgiveness. Spirit-filled discipleship formation works.
- New understandings of diversity allowed people to embrace one another and confront differences. Communication allows the Spirit to work.

The Spirit is changing the fabric of our church, bringing us in alignment with God's work through Mission Initiatives and sharing. We are living in challenging times, drawing on the Spirit to meet the challenge. Receive the Holy Spirit now, and now, and now—each moment, every day, continuously given. God is waiting for our response.

Prayer for Peace

God, who is always with us, make us aware of the work of your Spirit in our daily lives. Inspire us to join in the work with glad and faithful hearts, sharing Christ's peace.

Spiritual Practice: Being Present with the Spirit

Be still and focus on your breathing. With each inhalation think, "God's Spirit fills me." With each exhalation think, "God's Spirit fills the Earth." If stray thoughts occur during this time, exhale them and give them to God. Simply be present with the Spirit as you breathe in and out for several minutes. Close with a brief prayer of thanks.

Peace Covenant

I am ready to receive your Spirit, God. I am ready to respond.

14
Monday
January

♫ Hymn of the Month: A Great Find

Introduction by Barbara Howard of Independence, Missouri, USA

...let all of us speak the truth to our neighbors, for we are members of one another.

—Ephesians 4:25

"Why Should the Earth Disclose a Face" was written by the late Geoffrey F. Spencer. He wrote it for a worship service about justice. It's never been published. Geoff was one of the most compassionate people I've ever known, and his compassion included the aching Earth as well as those who suffered from neglect and war.

His humility was such that he was rarely in the limelight...This hymn reflects the time in which we live and the call to us to become God's people in the world.

Why should the earth disclose a face
distraught by pain and anguish?
And how can hearts that beat with ours,
in tortured bondage languish?
Should men despair, or women weep,
in cruel deprivation;
or haunted eyes in children mock
the bounties of creation?

Oh, may our hearts be tuned to hear
their cries of quiet weeping;
and may the echoes of distress
disturb our restful sleeping.
The rich resources of the earth,
a table set for sharing;
are bread and wine for humankind,
a sacrament of caring.

The Word made flesh in Christ declares
our lives belong to others;
so let us take our stand beside
our sisters and our brothers.
Let heart and hand reach out across
the walls of tribe and nation;
till every voice on earth shall raise
a hymn of jubilation.

Prayer for Peace

As you weep with us, compassionate God, may we weep with those who are in pain and anguish and do not know Christ's peace.

Spiritual Practice for Today: Contemplate this hymn as a poem.

15
Tuesday
January

Your Mission (Should You Choose to Accept It): Make a Child Happy

By Shirley Van Riette of Independence, Missouri, USA

> *For you shall go out in joy, and be led back in peace; the mountains and the hills before you shall burst into song, and all the trees of the field shall clap their hands.*
>
> —Isaiah 55:12

For several years a group of young men and women from Independence, Missouri, and surrounding communities brought ministry through music and testimony to many congregations. They called themselves Mission Possible.

They sang, played instruments, and shared testimonies of how God blessed them. They were young and eager to offer ministry. The group ended some time ago. On the day of its final concert, passion and pure joy filled the music and testimonies.

Two-year-old Drew was playing quietly in the children's corner of the sanctuary. He did not seem much interested in the service, but as we know with children, he was listening.

Mission Possible chose the African-American spiritual, "Kum Bah Yah," as offertory music. The group sang the verses, accompanied by several instruments.

Then the drums began to beat out loudly. The young men began to boom out a vocal accompaniment: "OOH, OOH, AAH, AAH." The young women sang the words. Drew jumped up from his playing and stood on tiptoes to see what was happening.

His mama lifted him so he could see. But he wanted down. He began dancing, smiling, and singing, "Kum Bah Yah"—a song he knows. Then it was over. The music stopped.

But Drew did not. In his loud voice he blared, "Do it again! One more time! Please! Do it again!" His joy reverberated throughout the sanctuary. The congregation, caught up in the Spirit, continued singing. That is joy—pure joy. That is what the world needs.

Prayer for Peace

God of music and mountains, we clap our hands in joy. We sing and dance in praise to you. May we follow the children and share the joy of Christ's peace.

Spiritual Practice: Listening to Children

Sit in your quiet place and center your heart and mind on God's presence. Spend several minutes asking God to bring into your awareness the names and images of children in your life. You may see their faces or hear their voices as you receive these impressions. Listen deeply to the unique gifts and needs of the children who come to mind. Offer a prayer of blessing for each child and the needs you perceive. If you feel led, you also may want to write a note or card and give a message of affirmation and love to each child.

Peace Covenant

Today, God, I will sing with children. If I can't sing, I will hum. If I can't hum, I will listen with joy.

16
Wednesday
January

God's Love—Tender and Firm

By Sara Parkin of Midland, Michigan, USA

> *How precious is your steadfast love, O God! All people may take refuge in the shadow of your wings. They feast on the abundance of your house, and you give them drink from the river of your delights. For with you is the fountain of life; in your light we see light.*
>
> —Psalm 36:7–9

On a cold, snowy day in winter a lot of noise was coming from the garage below my room. New noises brought me immediately to the world of the awakened. Still in my pajamas, I rushed downstairs.

My father was kneeling beside a newborn calf, wiping it off with a towel. "His mother dropped it in the south pasture, then went off to the barn without it. He would have died if I hadn't been there to shelter and comfort him. Please bring some milk."

A black and white Holstein calf stood on wobbly legs. It was beautiful. The calf was one of our first since buying a farm and moving from the city. It was the firstborn during the winter months. The calf took to the milk bottle right away with his tail expressing pleasure.

All during the experience my father spoke to the calf in soft, comforting words. He gently worked the calf's muscles, warm and tender. The calf's eyes reflected gratitude and trust.

God cares for us in this way—with faithful, reconciling love, breaking down the walls of mistrust. We are blessed by a Living God who moves in and through all Creation and guides us through the Holy Spirit.

Prayer for Peace

Guide us, God, with your tenderness. Lead us, Lord with your gentle Spirit. Teach us how to share Christ's peace.

Spiritual Practice: Develop Disciples to Serve

Read and reflect on Psalm 42:1–2. As disciples of Jesus Christ, we are called to respond to people and their needs. The call to journey inward can restore us in times of physical or spiritual depletion. Imagine you can feel a vessel at the center of your being (a clay jar, a crystal vase, a metal bucket, or other container). Imagine drawing something from the vessel to share with another person, but as you reach inside you find only a tiny pool of stagnant liquid. You are thirsty and dry. Empty.

Listen prayerfully again to the psalm, "As a deer longs for flowing streams, so my soul longs for you, O God. My soul thirsts for God, for the living God." As you feel restored, thank God for the opportunity to be a responding, serving disciple while you move into the outward journey. Remember this exercise as you drink water throughout the day.

Peace Covenant

Today, God, as I willingly receive your love, I also will willingly receive your guidance.

17
Thursday
January

Pick up Your Pen

By June Russell of Independence, Missouri, USA

O Lord, you have searched me and known me. You know when I sit down and when I rise up; you discern my thoughts from far away. You search out my path and my lying down, and are acquainted with all my ways. Even before a word is on my tongue, O Lord, you know it completely. You hem me in, behind and before, and lay your hand upon me. Such knowledge is too wonderful for me; it is so high that I cannot attain it.

—Psalm 139:1–6

One day I picked up a journal I had written in about 20 years earlier. It covered three or four years of my life. It was during a time when I experienced the deaths of my sister, my parents, my husband's mother, and an aunt. It was a dark time for me. The writing was therapeutic.

I often spent time reading and writing whatever "spoke" to me from the scriptures, especially Psalms and Proverbs. I wrote about memories and burdens. Time spent in the scriptures and in prayer was a lifeline for me, helping me through those difficult times.

As I reread my journal, I saw on the first page I recorded the last two verses of Psalm 139. I remember praying this often as I tried to listen deeply to God's voice and to my role in Christ's mission.

The first page also contained a list of what I felt were my shortcomings at the time. Pondering my present life, I am so thankful for any growth I might have made.

Today I sense I again need to spend time reading and reflecting in pen on these scriptures. I pray it won't be 20 more years before I pick up my journal again.

Prayer for Peace

Search us, O God. Reveal to us what you find. May we always be aware of your presence and that we need not be alone. May the words of our mouths and pens be those that share the peace of Christ.

Spiritual Practice: Psalm Writing

The psalms are prayers of honesty and trust. The psalmist trusts God's presence in times of fear and failure, joy and plenty, growth and change. Write a short psalm-prayer, expressing to God the truth about your physical, emotional, and spiritual state. What are your deepest feelings, longings, and needs? What prayer of praise, intercession, or petition flows from you as you consider your life and the life of God's world?

Peace Covenant

Today, God, I will open my heart so your light will reach the dark places.

18
Friday
January

A Flourish and a Flutter…

By Jim Hannah of Independence, Missouri, USA

Are not five sparrows sold for two pennies? Yet not one of them is forgotten in God's sight. But even the hairs of your head are all counted. Do not be afraid; you are of more value than many sparrows.

—Luke 12:6–7

Josh knew something wasn't right. Years of bird-watching had taught him that cardinals are ground-feeders. But this one wasn't eating—or even moving. It just huddled in the snow, a bright red patch in an otherwise-white landscape.

Josh watched from the window for a few moments, concerned that one of the many neighborhood cats might happen by. But the bird remained there in the late afternoon sun, without the usual signs of timidity and fluttering of cardinals coming to feed.

Curious, Josh donned his coat and went out. He walked slowly on the snow crust toward the birdfeeder, trying not to cause alarm. Not until he was nearly upon the creature did it seem to recognize Josh's presence and only then to start, flutter weakly, and collapse.

Josh knew he had witnessed the cardinal's last breath. He picked it up gently to examine it more carefully. So amazing! The brilliant red plumage, iridescent gray highlights, and orange beak contrasted with a black face and a saucy, pointed crest. Its eyes were closed—cold, slate-gray lids. Josh spread the wings and marveled at the wonderful symmetry.

The earth beneath the snow was surprisingly soft and loamy. With a few strokes of the shovel, Josh hollowed out a shallow grave. He lifted the small bundle of cloth and feathers, marveling again at its lightness as he placed it gently in the earth. Is it true, he wondered, that not a bird falls from the sky without the Creator's knowledge? And as he tamped down the earth and covered it with snow, he wondered if the Creator, too, weeps for the fragility of life and its passing beauty—a flourish and a flutter, then silence and cold.

Prayer for Peace

Creator God, we know you see us when we stumble. We know you weep for us when we fall. Lift us with your healing light, God, that we may continue in Christ's mission; that we may share his peace.

Spiritual Practice: Caring for God's Sacred Creation

Choose a way to notice, give thanks, and care for God's sacred creation. Prayerfully consider one of the following practices or create your own. Walk in nature with a spirit of gratitude while looking and listening for God in all things.

Learn about and engage in an act of Earth-keeping such as recycling, simple living, or fasting from over-consumption of resources. Notice the diversity of the planet's creatures and be gentle to plants, birds, trees, and people! Fall in love with the vast, intricate wonder of God's creation and give thanks.

Peace Covenant

Today, God, I will walk without fear, knowing your loving eyes are on me.

19
Saturday
January

Broken Hands

By Barbara Howard of Independence, Missouri, USA

> *Open your hearts and feel the yearnings of your brothers and sisters who are lonely, despised, fearful, neglected, unloved. Reach out in understanding, clasp their hands, and invite all to share in the blessings of community created in the name of the One who suffered on behalf of all.*
>
> —Doctrine and Covenants 161:3a

> When I pray for the world, I become the world. I realize that compassion is not mine to give, but God's gift to me. I cannot embrace the world, but God can. When God became as we are, it became possible for us to share in God's infinite compassion.
>
> —Henri Nouwen,
> adapted from *Genesee Diary*

Paul Brand, noted surgeon of leprosy patients in India and acclaimed for his work restoring their damaged hands, describes a worship service in which he shared, following an intensive day in surgery.

He was tired and distracted when the service began. As he stood to address the lepers, he noticed they all hid their hands—their horribly misshapen hands. He spoke to them:

"I would like to have known Jesus. I would like to have seen his hands." Brand described to the lepers the scarred hands of Jesus that were torn by the nails on the cross—the hands misshapen from such abuse.

As he further spoke of the abiding love and power of the risen Christ he noticed the lepers began to hold up their hands, to wave them in the air as an act of praise.

This story reminds me of the power of Christ's suffering on behalf of the neglected, despised, and cast out. The people to whom Christ brought ministry were those who suffered society's rejection. Jesus offers to all the hand of promise. All of us are outcasts in some way, and Jesus comes to us as welcoming friend.

We clasp his hands, and the promise of new life begins. We open our hands and share that life generously with others.

Prayer for Peace

Take our hands, God. Let them work for you. Touch us with your Spirit. Make us kind like Jesus, sharing peace with all.

Spiritual Practice: Open Hands

Stand or sit with your hands extended in front of you. Prayerfully ponder all the things you hold in your hands that make you feel too full, busy, drained, or tight. Spread your hands up and apart to release these things, then hold them open and empty them again. Thank God for relationships that fill and feed your spirit. Pray for a generous heart and open hands that reach out to make room for all in the circle of Christ's community.

Peace Covenant

Today, God, I will clasp a lonely hand with a hand of friendship.

20
Sunday
January

Believe in Christ

By Michele McGrath of Mission Viejo, California, USA

> *Jesus did this, the first of his signs, in Cana of Galilee, and revealed his glory; and his disciples believed in him.*
>
> —John 2:11

I officiated at the wedding of a friend. On the day of the wedding, the agenda was predictably chaotic: Groomsmen donned cummerbunds upside down, stockings snagged, and despite a successful rehearsal, the correct lineup for the wedding party became impossibly confusing. At least a quarter of the guests lost their way to the reception. If there had been wine at this wedding, it's possible the wine would have run out.

But there was no wine because the bride, groom, and several of their closest friends were recovering alcoholics. I remember sitting at the reception, watching the alternating seriousness and silliness that occurs on every wedding reception dance floor and realizing how this new family had beat the odds.

The bride and groom had found sobriety where there once was drunkenness, had found healing where there once was brokenness, had found community where there once was loneliness. They found love and family where there once was pain and separation.

As I watched the smiling newlyweds dancing forehead to forehead, I suddenly was overwhelmed by the revelation of God's incredibly generous love in that moment, in this couple, right before my eyes.

John's gospel tells the story of a wedding at Cana where Jesus worked his first sign: turning water into wine, which was running short for the celebration. For those disciples with eyes to see, Jesus revealed God's glory in his actions.

Are your eyes open to how God reveals love and generosity through the life of Christ? Believe.

Prayer for Peace

Ever-present God, we will not fear brokenness or separation. We have faith in Christ whose yoke is easy, who responds to our needs, whose peace we share.

Spiritual Practice: Table Ministry

Imagine or write a journal description of a banquet for your congregation and community. Envision rich sharing among diverse groups as people plan, cook, eat, share stories, sing, or pray together. Prayerfully consider this question: "Is there a way for me to transform this vision into a real event?" What does the table ministry of Jesus look like in your personal and congregational life?

Peace Covenant

Today, God, I will look for the sacred in the mundane, the holy in the everyday.

21
Monday
January

Lament...Response...Gratitude

By Peggy Michael of Cantonment, Florida, USA

Make a joyful noise to the Lord, all the earth; break forth into joyous song and sing praises. Sing praises to the Lord with the lyre, with the lyre and the sound of melody. With trumpets and the sound of the horn make a joyful noise before the King, the Lord.

—Psalm 98:4–6

Lament

Lord, I hang my head in shame so you cannot see my tortured soul. How I yearn to have you lift my face and wipe it clean as I do for my child. Do you still love me when you see me... just as I am?

Response

My child, stop weeping bitterly over your foolish mistakes. Place them in my hands, and I will cast them away. I will free you to sing, to shout the news of your salvation to those who are still ensnared. Return unto me, O my people, for I yearn to forgive you...just as you are. I yearn to make you whole.

Gratitude

My burden has been lifted. Do your shoulders grow tired under the extra load, O Shepherd? If they do, I do not see you falter, nor do you rest until each cry is answered.

Faithful Guardian of us all, you give so much yet take so little. How I yearn to invite you in to share the warmth of a fire and touch your bleeding wounds with my unworthy, yet forgiven, hands.

Prayer for Peace

Tender Shepherd, as the hills sing together with joy, accept our humble lament. We are thankful for your grace and love, which lighten our burden. As we have acknowledged our inner yearnings for peace in our soul, may we also acknowledge our desire to share Christ's peace.

Spiritual Practice: The Jesus Prayer of Mercy

The Jesus Prayer is an ancient spiritual practice from Orthodox Christianity. It is a way of connecting with the gracious spirit of Christ as we ask to receive his mercy. The prayer comes from the scripture of the blind man calling Jesus to heal him.

Silently enter prayer and let your breath become slow and even. Greet God and then take up the prayer phrase: *Lord, Jesus Christ* (as you breathe in)...*have mercy on me* (as you breathe out). Prayerfully repeat these words for several minutes (or 40 times). Breathe the presence of Christ into your mind, heart, and body. Be transformed as you receive the compassionate, peaceful heart of Jesus.

Peace Covenant

Today, God, I will turn my yearnings into actions.

22
Tuesday
January

Extend Yourself

By Janné Grover of Lee's Summit, Missouri, USA

> *...let all of us speak the truth to our neighbors, for we are members of one another. ...and live in love, as Christ loved us...*
>
> —Ephesians 4:25, 5:2

As the result of an unsettling break-in at our home, the outpouring of concern and assistance from our neighbors was a blessing. Going through this ordeal and seeing the response of those who live around us has caused me to think about my call as a member of my neighborhood community. I'm a friendly neighbor when I have the opportunity, but I admit I do not reach out and freely extend hospitality.

I was content to be a pleasant member of the community without extending myself into the lives of my neighbors. I chose to know them on a superficial level. I love to welcome people into my home, but the invitation often goes to my extended family and church family. After years of recognizing the need to reach out and share Christ with those in my neighborhood, I have realized I simply need to make myself receptive to opportunities waiting right outside my door.

One night I decided to step out of my comfort zone and try to nurture neighborhood relationships. Going even further, I listened again to the story of Mary and Martha. My house was far from clean and tidy, and the dinner dishes were not yet washed, but I put a cobbler in the oven, and there was plenty to share.

I spontaneously called our neighbors and invited them over. We had a wonderful opportunity for laughter and conversation and allowed ourselves to be receptive to the blessings that come from being fully present in community.

Prayer for Peace

God of hospitality, may we always extend the invitation to gather in community, to live in love and share Christ's peace.

Spiritual Practice: Offering Blessings of Community

Receive and share Blessings of Community. Begin with a prayer of gratitude for the relationships in your life. See and feel connections with family members, spiritual friends, people in your congregation and community, and people and creatures in God's sacred web of life. What blessings flow to you from these circles?

Reflect, pray, or write in your journal about the call to be "Community of Christ." Go deeper each day as you discern what act of blessing you are invited to complete.

Peace Covenant

Today, God, I will not clean my house. I will invite people to Christ.

23
Wednesday
January

Listening Friend

By Dorene Kilburn of Stratford, Ontario, Canada

"Come to me, all you that are weary and are carrying heavy burdens, and I will give you rest. Take my yoke upon you, and learn from me; for I am gentle and humble in heart, and you will find rest for your souls. For my yoke is easy, and my burden is light. …And remember, I am with you always, to the end of the age."

—Matthew 11:28–30

It is indeed a blessing to have a friend who listens when we need to talk. We need friends who forgive us when we say something hurtful, who overlook our shortcomings. Friends want to share both our joys and our sorrows. But sometimes those special friends cannot be with us when we need them most.

We do have a friend who said, "…I am with you always." That friend is Jesus. Though he is not visible to us, the friendship we develop with him is real. When we are overwhelmed by the day's tasks or dragged down by doubts and fears, we can talk to him, for he has told us to come to him if we are burdened. He will give us rest. When we feel inadequate, when our self-esteem is damaged by insensitive remarks, we can turn to Jesus, who teaches us to see the Worth of All Persons.

As we pursue a closer friendship with Jesus, he will encourage us by the power of his Spirit—he will make us new creatures! This new day he beckons, "Follow me." How much more can we do and be in his service, if we respond to his call?

Prayer for Peace

Ever-present God, we are thankful to have a friend like Jesus who we can share our burdens with. May we come to you often and pour out our hearts to make room for joy. May we then share that joy and the peace of Christ with others.

Spiritual Practice: Chalice Prayer

The chalice prayer is a form of intercession. Create a cup or chalice with your hands in front of your heart. Open your heart to God's concern for the Earth and human family as you hold them in your chalice. See beauty and suffering as you lift the chalice and release the creation (open hands) to be blessed and healed by God.

Form the chalice again and hold persons who have particular needs—friends, loved ones, even enemies. Lift them and release them for God's blessing. Place yourself inside the chalice as you confess your deepest needs. Lift and release yourself to God for healing. "Thank you and amen."

Peace Covenant

Today, God, I will cherish your presence with me.

24
Thursday
January

A Continuing Prayer

By Mary Twinn of Collinsville, Illinois, USA

"Humble yourselves, and continue in prayer to him; cry to him when you are in your fields, and over all your flocks; cry to him in your houses, and over all your household, morning, midday, and evening..."

—Alma 16:219

When I was a young mother, I prayed God would grant my children all that they would ever desire, protect them from unhappiness, all pain and sorrow. Foolish! How little I understood.

Today my prayer for my children is quite different. I pray God will speak to the hearts and minds of my children and lead them through their decisions, choices, and experiences.

I pray they will find in whatever life holds for them a developing desire to know and serve God.

I pray they may grow and be strengthened for the work that is theirs to do. My continuing prayer is that my children may discover God's will in their lives and their role in Christ's mission, thus fulfilling the purpose of their creation.

Prayer for Peace

Listening God, hear us when we pray for our families. Hear us when we pray for peace.

Spiritual Practice: Making Responsible Choices

Prayerfully seek God's guidance in your choices. Discernment invites us to orient our lives toward God and God's vision for us and creation. Begin by reviewing the responsibilities and opportunities in the day before you. Take these choices into prayer, asking God for wisdom and insight about what matters most.

Offer yourself to God with the prayer of Teresa of Avila: "God, what do you want of me today?" Sit prayerfully with this question as you review the day again. Be aware of images, thoughts, names, or actions that come to you. Ask for a blessing to live this day responsibly and compassionately in the spirit of Christ.

Peace Covenant

Today, God, I will pray morning, noon, and night.

25
Friday
January

Move Out in Faith

By Evelyn Herron of Lexington, Kentucky, USA

> *Lift up your eyes and fix them on the place beyond the horizon to which you are sent. Journey in trust, assured that the great and marvelous work is for this time and for all time.*
>
> —Doctrine and Covenants161:1a

I was driving along a freeway one evening in a community where I had lived only three months. My husband was out of town on business, and my children were with me. Suddenly something went wrong with the car, and I pulled to the side of the busy road.

The engine died, and I was unable to start the car again. We were about halfway between exits, and I didn't know where the nearest service station was. Cars whizzed by in the darkness. Thick woods and fences separated me from the houses of a nearby subdivision.

Which way should I go for help? Who could I call? I knew only a few people in this city. I sat for several minutes, paralyzed by panic and indecision. Then I realized that my children depended on me to seek a solution. I decided on a direction, and we began walking toward one of the exits.

To my relief, I found a service station just off the freeway whose helpful owner towed my car with his truck. When he heard my plight, he was kind enough to take us home.

Sometimes we find ourselves in fearful situations—alone, with our lives broken down around us. A solution may be near. However, we must move out and seek it. God is there to guide us on our faith journey. God ensures we have the courage to determine our course and to take the first step of our journey.

Prayer for Peace

Tender Shepherd, may we have the courage to walk unknown paths with a faith that goes beyond our present vision. Calm our doubts and uncertainties and give us confidence to step boldly into the future. Give us the faith to share Christ's peace with others who may be in fear.

Spiritual Practice: Intercessory Reflection

Sit quietly with your eyes closed as you enter intercessory reflection and prayer. Ask God to bring persons to your mind and heart who need prayer. Be open to images of the persons or spiritual insight into their needs. Listen for signals from their lives and let the depth of God's love for them become powerful and real to you. Write, speak, or think a prayer of blessing and healing for these much-loved disciples and friends. Ask God to help you see ways to affirm and support them when you meet them in daily life.

Peace Covenant

Today, God, I will see with eyes of faith, where I am to go and how I can serve.

26
Saturday
January

Under the Microscope

By Doug Haden of Calgary, Alberta, Canada

> *Now as you excel in everything—in faith, in speech, in knowledge, in utmost eagerness, and in our love for you—so we want you to excel also in this generous undertaking.*
>
> —2 Corinthians 8:7

This has been a great week for me because of a friend, a magazine article, a microscope, and our global community.

Dr. Gudush Jalloh is from South Africa and is the only private veterinarian in Sierra Leone. I've heard there is a direct link between the health of people and the health of the animals that live in our communities.

A geologist friend, Shaun, put me in touch with Dr. Jalloh, who was in desperate need of a binocular Zeiss microscope. I found one on the Internet, ordered it, and had some local vets make sure it was in good working order. Then I mailed it to the doctor. Within the week he received it and let me know by e-mail of its arrival.

It's gratifying to make a small effort to help someone. I am glad for the opportunity to help others throughout the world make an impact on people's lives.

This simple act of reading an article and connecting the dots through the influence of the Holy Spirit will bring relief to many. Through the skills and giftedness of one lone veterinarian, the citizens of his community will be blessed through his healing ministry to their pets and farm animals.

Christ has promised us that if we respond to those in need, all will be blessed and will sense his peace. This day, I feel privileged for the small part I had in meeting the needs of one doctor, his unique patients, and their owners' holistic health. I praise God for giving me a passion for microscopes and the blessings that these instruments can give to others in towns and villages around God's amazing world.

Prayer for Peace

God of the great and God of the small, help us see beyond our narrow world. Help us focus on needs that might be overlooked and to share Christ's peace.

Spiritual Practice: Generous Offerings

Spend time meditating on the act of giving an offering. Begin by asking God for the spirit of generosity. Pray and reflect with these questions: How do I feel when I bring my offering to a worship setting and share it? What deep reasons motivate me to give? What is my best understanding of A Disciple's Generous Response? Considering my financial circumstances, do I feel I am giving to my true capacity? In other words, am I giving the amount I am capable of giving without jeopardizing the needs and well-being of my family? Is God asking me to be more generous? How will I respond?

Peace Covenant

Today, God, I will try to discover a need and respond.

27
Sunday
January

Christ's Mission Is Our Mission

By Rick Maupin, Council of Twelve Apostles

> *"The Spirit of the Lord is upon me, because he has anointed me to bring good news to the poor. He has sent me to proclaim release to the captives and recovery of sight to the blind, to let the oppressed go free, to proclaim the year of the Lord's favor." Then he began to say to them, "Today this scripture has been fulfilled in your hearing."*
>
> —Luke 4:18–19, 21

Splat! I didn't see it coming until it had splattered on my windshield. It was a wet sponge thrown by a young man several yards away. He and other impoverished boys in this particular country stand at traffic-light intersections, washing windshields. Motorists do not always appreciate their "marketing" technique. Desperate to earn a few pesos a day, they toss their sponges in hopes of "tagging" the windshields of generous drivers.

This young man is among the poor and oppressed spoken of in Luke 4:18. However, when that sponge hit my windshield my first thoughts were not about his plight, but about mine. Someone was invading my privacy, trying to take advantage of my good nature, and trying to get a few pesos from me.

I still have some concern with the method the young men use to secure clients. However, the greater concern is my attitude, how my first thoughts were not about the poor and oppressed. They were about me: *my* space, *my* agenda, and *my* needs. Being a disciple of Jesus requires me to look beyond *my* selfish view of splats on my windshield.

Many living in desperate conditions don't even have a "sponge" with which to draw attention to their problem. Hidden in dark corners, those victimized by poverty and oppression often go unnoticed. If Christ's mission is our mission, we will be aware of those people and generously share our resources to support ministries that will bring good news into their lives.

Prayer for Peace

Compassionate God, help us to engage in Christ's mission. We would abolish poverty and end suffering with Christ as our teacher. We would share his justice and peace.

Spiritual Practice: The International Community

Find (or imagine) a globe or map of the world. Look at all the nations and find a country other than your own. Notice the geographic distance between your homeland and this one. Picture a person living there. Pray for this person. Sense God's love connecting you just as the oceans connect the continents. Thank God for the spiritual connection you have with all of God's people around the globe. Ask a blessing on the church as a community sharing Christ's peace, drawing all into the family of God.

Peace Covenant

Today, God, I will respond to the needs of at least one impoverished person.

28
Monday
January

Purr More…Hiss Less

By Suzanne McMillan of East Sandwich, Massachusetts, USA

If it is possible, so far as it depends on you, live peaceably with all.

—Romans 12:18

Abby has bounded into our lives and hearts. She is a 10-week-old Labrador retriever. Our family has never experienced puppyhood before, so we've been especially charmed by her enthusiastic tail-wagging, and constant puppy antics. She likes dragging bags of groceries down the hall, chasing butterflies (and her tail), hiding shoes, and biting the heads off daffodils.

Then there are the endless attempts to befriend the cat.

Ah...the cat! On Abby's arrival the cat quickly adopted a look of "We are not amused" on her delicate face. Close encounters have not been successful. We are vigilant about their meetings, as the kitty is assertive in her swats. Despite our attempts at diplomacy, hope seemed to be fading for a furry friendship until our oldest daughter made an unusual discovery.

Walking into the house in the wee hours of the morning she found the cat and the puppy sitting close together, seemingly enjoying each other's company. No barks, no hissing, and no evident trauma. Skeptics would say the kennel door wasn't latched properly that night, but we like to think the cat rose to nobler purpose and let the puppy out so they could work things out.

Can pets forgive one another? Can they mediate? Perhaps not. But we still can learn from them a lesson of Unity in Diversity.

If cats and dogs can live together peacefully, why can't we?

Prayer for Peace

Creator God, we realize peace depends on us. Teach us the lessons and give us the courage to live peacefully with all.

Spiritual Practice: Peace Action

Community of Christ is called to ministries of peace, reconciliation, and healing of the spirit. PeacePathways is a church-sponsored website that shares justice and peace ministries, resources, and opportunities.

Visit *www.peace-pathways.org* and prayerfully discern one ministry that speaks to you or captures your attention. Offer a prayer of blessing on the peace ministry you have selected. Listen quietly to see if God is calling you to additional responses to this ministry or another ministry of peace, reconciliation, or healing. If you cannot visit the website, offer a prayer of blessing on all peace ministries.

Peace Covenant

Today, God, I will purr more and hiss less.

29
Tuesday
January

The Embodiment of Christ

By Jeanne Davis of Kansas City, Missouri, USA

> *Jesus Christ, the embodiment of God's shalom, invites all people to come and receive divine peace in the midst of the difficult questions and struggles of life. Follow Christ in the way that leads to God's peace and discover the blessings of all of the dimensions of salvation.*
>
> —Doctrine and Covenants 163:2a

Does the scripture passage say *after* the difficult, or *before* the difficult? Look again…

We all have various struggles. Usually we think of peace as something that could happen *after* the "struggle" part is past. But that's not miraculous—that's understandable and even visible. The invitation is to hope *in the midst* of the difficult, where we will receive peace is *in the midst* of the struggle. That is salvation!

"…discover the blessings of all the dimensions of salvation." As an artist, I work in two dimensions, sometimes three, but there are more dimensions than these—let's add time. The dimensions of salvation include the now. Salvation is *in the midst* of the difficult. How am I saved? How can I see hope in the midst of despair?

I am saved by the peace of Jesus Christ through redemptive relationships—saved from despair, loneliness, rage, and fear. What does this look like?

I was saved from melting into a crazy puddle-of-a-mom with three babies far away by a redemptive relationship with Leslie Skoor and JoAnn Fisher. Saved from the depression and despair of a suicidal teenager through the redemptive relationship of Lisa Lowry and our congregation praise band. Saved from oppressive loneliness by the redemptive relationships of my office colleagues and the healing touch of Dana Speigle.

These people were the embodiment of Christ for me. Relationship with them saved me *in the midst* of my difficulties and brought me peace *in the midst* of my despair. These were ordinary people who became holy through their acts of kindness, through listening—just being there and spilling a bit of themselves with me, and me with them.

What are we not seeing?

Let's open our eyes to see the opportunity to be in redemptive relationships. Who needs our listening ear? Who is it that needs to feel the loving acceptance of Christ's family?

Prayer for Peace

Comforting God, we want to be as Christ, the embodiment of your shalom. We want to be there for one another. We want to be in the midst of sharing Christ's peace.

Spiritual Practice: Embodying God's Shalom

Find a way to express and embody God's shalom. Begin by prayerfully listening to your longing for peace. Become silent and imagine you can hear the groaning of the Earth's people, nations, and creatures. Prayerfully open yourself to God's yearning for peace and the divine vision of shalom.

Peace Covenant

Today, God, I will put on my listening ears and open my embracing arms.

30
Wednesday
January

"Someone" Showed Up

By Karen Fultz of Atwater, California, USA

We know love by this, that he laid down his life for us—and we ought to lay down our lives for one another. How does God's love abide in anyone who…sees a brother or sister in need and yet refuses help?

—1 John 3:16–17

It was the phone call no parent ever wants to receive. Our daughter, Sierra, was in a car accident in Missouri. I flew from California and was at her hospital bedside within 24 hours. After six months, two surgeries, many doctor and physical-therapy visits, I could go home for Christmas. She was on the road to full recovery.

Sierra suffered two broken legs, a fractured foot, an infection, and a gash on her knee that left a scar like a shark bite. There were many blessings amid her trauma. We experienced the sacrificial generosity of friends and church members!

My daughter's friend picked me up from the airport and drove me to the hospital—an eight-hour drive for her!—so I didn't have to rent a car. Sierra's boss heard about the accident and spent the entire night in the emergency room until I arrived the next day. Many of her friends were in and out of the hospital to visit, help Sierra, and make sure I had food, company, and whatever I needed.

Sierra asked the hospital staff to call the local Community of Christ congregation. They asked for a person's name, and she said, "No name. Just call. They'll send someone." The "someone" they sent was the pastor, who knew her family from youth camps. A church member let me stay at her home as long as I needed.

I could go on, and on, and on with many stories of people who blessed us along the way: the friend who took care of all four of Sierra's pets, the woman and her son who saw the accident and pulled Sierra from under the truck, the family of the friend she was in the accident with. God showed up in her life through many lives, and we have been blessed and touched by each action of friends and the congregation.

Prayer for Peace

Thank you, God, for our communities at home and far away. Thank you for the spirit of kindness and generosity that spans the miles. Thank you for people who sacrifice for the needs of others.

Spiritual Practice: Experience Congregations in Mission

Read and reflect on Doctrine and Covenants 164:9a–d. Reread the sentence, "If you truly would be Community of Christ, then embody and live the concerns and passion of Christ." Make a list of the issues you feel mattered most to Christ. Make another list of issues that matter to your congregation. Reflect on the similarities and differences. How can you help align the lists? Throughout the day, as issues arise, ask yourself, "Would this matter to Christ?"

Peace Covenant

Today, God, I will *show up* when needed.

31
Thursday
January

Last-Place Finish, First-Place Medal

By Jim Cummings of Columbus, Ohio, USA

> *He sat down, called the twelve, and said to them, "Whoever wants to be first must be last of all and servant of all." Then he took a little child and put it among them; and taking it in his arms, he said to them, "Whoever welcomes one such child in my name welcomes me, and whoever welcomes me welcomes not me but the one who sent me."*
>
> —Mark 9:35–37

I finished last in a five-kilometer race but received a first place medal!

Sounds funny, but it's true. Let me explain. My niece, Rachel, is a first-year schoolteacher in a poor area of Kentucky. She loves her students and her job. In her first year she has helped to raise her students' educational level by two grades, but they still are behind the national average.

The school needs equipment to help the students, so Rachel organized a race with sponsors to raise the funds. There were about 50 participants, and as I said, I finished last. Rachel gave first-place medals to the winners in each age category. I was the only runner over 60, so I received a medal.

Though I lost the race as a whole, I felt like a winner. Not because I received a medal, but because I helped the children. I could be a servant.

As we approach God in prayer, let us keep in mind the importance of servanthood.

Prayer for Peace

God who calls us, thank you for your Son, who showed us how to be a servant. We praise you for sending us the true peacemaker. May we share his peace with others.

Spiritual Practice: Honoring the Worth of All Persons

Read Psalm 139:13–18. After each reading sit quietly and let the words sink deeply into your mind, heart, and body. Imagine God watching you grow in your mother's womb. What thoughts and feelings do you have about being "fearfully and wonderfully made" (Psalm 139:14)?

Sense the intimate knowledge God has of you and every child. Be aware of the sacred worth of each person. Weep with God over the soul-wounding forces and events that rob people of dignity and worth. How are you invited to let others go before you, to be God's servant?

Peace Covenant

Today, God, I will let others go before me.

1
Friday
February

Stages of Age and Sage

By John Bonney of Springfield, Oregon, USA

> *You are a good and faithful people, but sometimes you fail to see the power that is resident in your own story and fellowship. Look carefully, listen attentively, and sense the Spirit among you.*
>
> —Doctrine and Covenants 162:8a

An old school friend recommended *From Age-ing to Sage-ing* by Zalman Schachter-Shalomi and Ronald Miller. He saw a need in my life. As pitted as we are, with weaknesses and brokenness, there is still a valuable resource for the community within each of us.

After I completed my term of church service as an administrative officer, I intended to continue working where needed. That plan didn't work out. I just couldn't function as I once did. I became depressed. I couldn't do the physical tasks I used to do. Sometimes I thought I wasn't needed anymore and that I didn't have anything left to offer.

I then went through a transformation. I came to terms with my aging. I now recognize who I am. Not only who I am, but who I allow myself to be. All of this unfolded over many months. I gradually realized I *was* needed, I *did* have something to offer, and I *was* of value in this results-and-production-oriented society.

I have moved, in an ungraceful way, from aging into "sage-ing." I thank God for others who have been part of my journey, and I hope that I have been a positive part of theirs. Now I am more accepting of who I am and what I have to offer. I like myself and am willing to offer my service to the community once again.

It helps to put into words what has been going on in my life in recent years. I increasingly find value in my ministry. If there is anything I wish to have said about me when I'm gone, it is that I was one who knew God's love. I don't know just how that will play out in the years ahead. I look forward to exploring this question.

Prayer for Peace

Help us see, God, the value of our journey. May we share a story that encourages others. May we listen closely to their stories. May we share the peace of Jesus Christ with one another.

Spiritual Practice: Weaving a Life

Hold (or imagine holding) a piece of patterned cloth. Examine it carefully. Notice the overlapping of threads, the mingling of colors to form the design. Write a journal entry or meditate about the threads and patterns of your life. What design do you see? How does the life pattern you are weaving create justice and wholeness in God's world? What new patterns is God calling you to weave?

Peace Covenant

Today, God, I will value the ministry I am able to give at this stage of my life. I know it is needed.

2
Saturday
February

Small Deed? Large Dividend

By Jeanne Hough of Clare, Michigan, USA

> *For if the eagerness is there, the gift is acceptable according to what one has—not according to what one does not have.*
>
> —2 Corinthians 8:12

I enrolled at Graceland College in 1945, just after the end of World War II. I lived in a small cottage dorm in Royce Hall that housed nine girls. Two of my roommates were young women of Japanese heritage. They recently had been released from relocation camps.

My other roommates and I loved our new friends, Sets and Audrey. We were outraged by the stories of deprivation and unjust treatment they endured. Audrey's family was taken from its home and left penniless. She had meager clothes but never complained.

In those days we always wore dresses or skirts to class. My mother was an experienced seamstress who made dresses and sent them to me. When she told me she had bought some fabric for a new dress, I asked her to make it smaller than usual. Audrey wore a smaller size.

When the dress arrived, I asked Audrey if she would like to have it. She was delighted. I still can see her in my mind's eye when some boys visiting the dorm teasingly picked her up and set her on the fireplace mantel, wearing that dress. She was smiling from ear to ear.

What joy it gave me to be able to share my mother's love with that sweet young woman. Such sharing was a small act for me, but it meant so much to another.

Prayer for Peace

Reconciling God, inspire us with ways we can minister to others. Help us keep in mind the worth and dignity of all people. Help us share peace where it was compromised or denied before.

Spiritual Practice: Joy of Gratitude

Stand, if possible, with arms outstretched. Imagine God filling your arms with all that you have: family, friends, and possessions. Hold out your arms until they feel tired. Now, bring your arms across your body. Place your hand over your heart and thank God for the abundance that fills your life. Sit for a time, aware of that abundance. Then ask God to help you open your heart in gratitude and share freely with others.

Peace Covenant

Today, God, I will offer an act of kindness.

3
Sunday
February

Challenged by the Truth

By Rick Maupin, Council of Twelve Apostles

> *... "Do here also in your hometown the things that we have heard you did at Capernaum." And he said, "Truly I tell you, no prophet is accepted in the prophet's hometown."*
>
> —Luke 4:23–24

I have rarely experienced feeling like an outsider, not accepted. In some ways, by birth, I have been most often on the "inside," one who has been accepted.

A few years ago while traveling in Africa, a colleague and I visited one country, and then traveled to another country. Two weeks later, we tried to reenter the first country. On arrival, we learned our visas were not valid for reentry. So immigration officers escorted us to the immigration office. They questioned us for a long time. It was obvious I was not welcome. I was an outsider.

That feeling intensified when the lead immigration officer told me—in a less than friendly manner—they were deporting me from their country. I was not allowed in. I was disappointed and hurt that I would not be allowed to visit an area significant to the life of the church. I felt like an outsider.

Deportation required me immediately to arrange to fly from that country to South Africa. I arrived, dejected and disappointed. I was met by Apostle Bunda Chibwe, who surprised me by saying that later that day we would be traveling to Zambia. I had no visa to enter Zambia.

However, a few hours after applying for a Zambian visa, a representative of the Zambian government handed me a multiyear, multiple-entry visa. He smiled and said, "Welcome to my homeland!" I felt accepted, on the inside.

Let us all see the Communion table this morning in ways that say, "We are all accepted. There are no outsiders." Let this sacrament and Jesus' words in Luke encourage us to be about taking down walls that create exclusion.

Prayer for Peace

God of no borders, help us break down forbidding walls. Help us invite and welcome all into the community. May we see the opportunities we have to share the peace of Christ.

Spiritual Practice: Daily Prayer for Peace

The Daily Prayer for Peace is a spiritual practice that takes place year-round at the Temple in Independence, the Kirtland Temple, and many Community of Christ congregations throughout the world. Each day we pray for a different country. Go to the front of this book and identify the country for today. Listen and ask God for images and insights about the people, environment, and needs of this country. Speak or write a prayer of blessing and peace for this part of God's world.

Peace Covenant

This day, God, I will hold up another country to your healing light.

4
Monday
February

Overwhelming Assurance

By Karen Smith of Ludington, Michigan, USA

> *Sustain each other in peace, and ye shall be blessed with my Spirit, in comforting and strengthening you for my work.*
>
> —Doctrine and Covenants 117:13

Many years ago my good friend, Kathy, called me from the hospital to ask for prayers for her newborn. The doctors expected that he might not live through the night. I prayed, and as I did I became aware with an overwhelming assurance the baby would be OK.

Recently my family suffered a near catastrophe involving our severely autistic son. Alex, who will soon be 26, lives in an assisted-living home where he is well cared for and happy. The staff members adore him, and we work together for his welfare. That happy home life was threatened. My boy's future suddenly filled with unknowns and anxieties. I had never felt so helpless, so unable to protect him. I sent an urgent prayer request to everyone I knew.

A few days later I heard from Kathy. She told me that as she prayed for Alex, the Spirit assured her with overwhelming strength that everything would be OK. I clung to this assurance. However I knew it might be awhile before everything would settle and be done.

Today I have received official word; it is over, and all is well. Alex is still in his home, still happy and well-cared for.

Through my troubles my faith has been strengthened. I have always believed, but that deep-down assurance that God is with us is something else altogether. Faith is something that must take seed and grow over time and with experience. Now I not only have faith, but I know God is with us.

Prayer for Peace

Strengthen us for your work, God. Strengthen our faith that we may call on you in times of trouble. Strengthen our gratitude also, that we may praise you in times of joy and peace.

Spiritual Practice: Intercessory Reflection

Sit quietly with your eyes closed as you enter intercessory reflection and prayer. Ask God to bring persons to your mind and heart who need prayer. Be open to images of the persons or spiritual insight into their needs. Listen for signals from their lives and let the depth of God's love for them become powerful and real to you. Write, speak, or think a prayer of blessing and healing for these much-loved disciples and friends. Ask God to help you see ways to affirm and support them when you meet them in daily life.

Peace Covenant

Today, God, I will call on you for strength to share Christ's peace.

5
Tuesday
February

"...Not a Single Bit of Talent Left..."

By Norma J. Cross of Independence, Missouri, USA

How beautiful upon the mountains are the feet of the messenger who announces peace, who brings good news, who announces salvation, who says to Zion, "Your God reigns." Listen! Your sentinels lift up their voices, together they sing for joy; for in plain sight they see the return of the Lord to Zion.

—Isaiah 52:7–8

When I look at ordinary stream or lake fish, they all look the same to me. I'm sure they're different, but I don't notice distinguishing features or qualities. Looking at people, however, I see how different they are from one another. Each person is unique, with diverse qualities, gifts, and talents given by the Creator.

It gives me pause to feel there's just one me. God designed and gave me giftedness to be used for Christ's mission. I can help others understand how loving the Creator God is.

As I ponder these *specs* of mine, I don't feel I should look and wish for more, and yet I sometimes do wish for a beautiful voice to sing God's praises. Nor must I concern myself with the gifts of others. As I listen to those who bring comfort and joy by lifting their voices in praise, I admire those who have musical gifts. Sharing those gifts inspires my compassionate response to God in worship and the community.

Jesus had his work to do here on Earth, and with love he gave us the Comforter to help us be disciples. So with his help we carry out Christ's mission with all the gifts and talents each of us has. His blessing of peace will follow as we follow him. Then one day we can say, as the late satirist, Erma Bombeck, said, "When I stand before God at the end of my life I would hope that I would have not a single bit of talent left and could say, 'I used everything you gave me.'"

Prayer for Peace

Thank you, God, for feet to climb mountains and uplifted voices to announce Christ's peace. May we use all our abilities to share love and peace.

Spiritual Practice: Music for Meditation

Identify a form of music for meditation. If hearing music is not an option, choose a song you can sing or play on a musical instrument. Choose music that carries a soulful, spiritual, or healing quality for you. Sit quietly and soak in the melody and resonance. Allow healing waves of sound to pierce body, spirit, and emotions. What do you feel or see as you listen? Does the music have colors? What spiritual message comes? How are you being restored, nurtured, healed, or moved to compassionate response?

Peace Covenant

Today, God, I will rejoice in the gifts of others and join them on the path of the disciple.

6
Wednesday
February

Just More Stuff

By Peggy Young of Independence, Missouri, USA

> *The Lord has bared his holy arm before the eyes of all the nations; and all the ends of the earth shall see the salvation of our God.*
>
> —Isaiah 52:10

On the morning after the 2011 tornado in Joplin, Missouri, I was watching a news show. It interviewed a woman who lived in New Orleans, Louisiana, before Hurricane Katrina. She had lost everything to the fury of the hurricane and moved to Joplin. Now she had lost everything to the fury of the tornado.

Her response surprised me. She said, "After Katrina I had to learn what I lost was just stuff. What I've lost now is just more stuff."

The loss of something important or precious often causes us to question our priorities. So many times, following a natural disaster, I have heard people say, "I'm just glad I still have my loved ones." Such an event makes us realize the importance of material possessions pales in contrast to the people we love.

Relationships are, indeed, one of the most meaningful aspects of life. Our first exposure to life is the relationship between parent and child. Hopefully, as we grow we learn to trust that our parents care for and nurture us.

Then, as awareness grows that there is an unseen sacred nature underlying life itself, we develop a relationship with God. Hopefully, we don't have to lose everything we have before we're ready to depend on God. But there is a saying: "When you get to the end of your rope, that's where God is."

Events like the Joplin tornado remind us how quickly life can change and how temporary our possessions can be. But the Divine is ever present and ready to wrap us in arms of love. Hopefully, it doesn't take a disaster to persuade us to turn to God. God is there for you when needed—trust me. Better yet, trust God.

Prayer for Peace

God of the hurricane and the warm, calm beach; God of the tornado and soft, cooling breeze, we lean on you for strength when burdens are heavy. We turn to you, and we know you are there.

Spiritual Practice: Caring for God's Sacred Creation

Choose a way to notice, give thanks, and care for God's sacred creation. Walk in nature with a spirit of gratitude while looking and listening for God in all things. Write or pray a psalm of praise for the Earth's beauty or a prayer of healing and blessing for its wounds.

Learn about and engage in an act of Earth-keeping such as recycling, simple living, or fasting from over-consumption of resources. Notice the diversity of the planet's creatures and be gentle to plants, animals, trees, and people! Fall in love with the vast, intricate wonder of God's creation and give thanks.

Peace Covenant

Today, God, I will turn to you to find balance in my life.

7
Thursday
February

Still Able to Bless

By Candy Brayton of Independence, Missouri, USA

For you shall go out in joy, and be led back in peace; the mountains and the hills before you shall burst into song, and all the trees of the field shall clap their hands.

—Isaiah 55:12

I was working in the bookstore at the Temple in Independence, Missouri, when Jack walked in. My family had known him for years. He was an evangelist and had a gifted ministry.

Greeting him by name, I expected recognition. He looked puzzled, so I reminded him who my parents were. The confusion didn't abate, and he seemed hesitant to speak. He turned to the woman who had accompanied him for help. She was his daughter. We discussed how I had come to know him.

She explained that he had Alzheimer's disease. It had progressed to where it affected his ability to speak. I told him I understood, and it was OK he didn't remember me. He gave me a shy smile and reached out to give my hand a reassuring squeeze.

As his daughter looked around the store, he stayed at the counter. He showed interest in a display of wooden boxes, and pewter pieces. I showed him how to open the box, and we discovered how five pieces would fit in it. There were words written on the pieces, and he spent some time picking out ones he liked.

The daughter returned to the counter with her purchase and asked Jack if he wanted the box and pieces. He shook his head, and purposefully pushed them toward me. Neither she, nor I, understood what he was trying to say.

After they left, I was putting the items back in the display. I finally noticed the writing on the ones he had chosen. The pieces in the box said, *hope, love, faith,* and the last said *healing* and had a picture of an eagle on it. Finally understanding his message, I bought them.

That was the last time I saw Jack. Despite his failing health, he still was able to bless others with his ministry.

Prayer for Peace

Tender Shepherd, heal our spirits. Even when we are experiencing disabilities, may we continue to bless as we are blessed. May we continue to share Christ's peace.

Spiritual Practice: Honoring God's Call to Others

Reflect on God's call in your life. Quietly reflect on the moments when you have experienced God's presence and invitation to expand your gifts. Write in your journal or quietly reflect on images and insights that come. When have you experienced God through the calling and gifts of others? How do your gifts connect with the call of God you notice in your family, friends, congregation, or community?

Peace Covenant

Today, God, I will recognize the blessings of others and express my appreciation.

8
Friday
February

A Healthy Dose of Grace

By Janné Grover of Lee's Summit, Missouri, USA

By contrast, the fruit of the Spirit is love, joy, peace, patience, kindness, generosity, faithfulness, gentleness, and self-control. There is no law against such things.

—Galatians 5:22–23

I am constantly amazed at how much I learn from the ones I am most trying to shape and nurture. I wish I could say these lessons come in quiet and intimate moments with my kids. However I am humbled to admit they usually reach me when I'm at anything but my best.

Such is the lesson of grace…

During the craziness of getting a young family ready for bed, we try to wind down from a busy day, yet the kids rev up as we get closer to bedtime. Coupled with tired parents it makes for some frustrating times.

One night I had reached the end of my sometimes-short fuse. I allowed my angry self to replace my patient self. As a result, I let my kids know how I was feeling—in a way that was much less than loving and nurturing. I stepped back, put myself in check, and we had a conversation about why I acted with frustration. We talked about how I ought to have reacted.

One of my kids responded, "We understand, Mom, and we still think you are the best mom ever." Although I felt like the worst mom ever, I responded by saying, "You are God's grace to me."

I recognize how frustrated God must feel sometimes, but I know personally how it feels to experience God's presence and grace in our ordinary daily routine. Dr. Mom recommends a healthy dose of grace. Good medicine.

Prayer for Peace

Patient God, may we be gentle and patient, too. May we learn from those who share grace that it comes from you. We need this remedy most, when we are overcome and frustrated, so we can share this grace and peace with others.

Spiritual Practice: Growing a Gracious, Generous Heart

Open your heart to God's grace and generosity with a "breath prayer." Let your breathing slow and deepen. Be aware of God's breath moving in and out of your heart. Spend several minutes focusing on breathing in God's generosity. With each breath, silently name one gift for which you are thankful. Let your heart expand to contain God's gracious outpouring. With each breath out, name one gift you want to share from the overflow of your heart.

Peace Covenant

Today, God, I will extend my self-control fuse to a gentler length.

9
Saturday
February

You Do the Math

By Ron Dawbarn of Manchester, Tennessee, USA

Do not be fearful of one another. Respect each life journey, even in its brokenness and uncertainty, for each person has walked alone at times. Be ready to listen and slow to criticize...

—Doctrine and Covenants 161:3b

Because of the U-boat blockade of England during the Second World War, few ships could bring supplies. Food was scarce. We used ration books that assured any available food would be distributed fairly.

One evening at church we had a party. To the surprise of everyone, a bowl of oranges was on the table. I had seen pictures of oranges, but seeing them for real fascinated me. I counted them and the number of people in the room.

I figured if they cut each orange into four pieces, each person would get one piece, with five pieces left over. Five children were there, and I figured each would get an extra piece.

The time came for cutting the oranges, and as I expected, they cut each into four. We got our piece, and I ate mine, peel and all. Then I sat, waiting for them to give the rest to us children. To my disappointment, a young woman went to the table, picked up all five pieces, put them in a bag, and started to leave.

I couldn't stay quiet. I blurted, "It's not fair. She's taking all the oranges." I began to say more, but my mother had me by the ear and dragged me from the room.

My mother told me the young woman had brought the oranges. They had been a gift to her, and she had shared them with us. I then felt badly about what I had said. I felt even worse when my mother told me I was to apologize the next time I saw the woman.

Each time I went to church I dreaded meeting her. I put it off until the last moment, when one day she was walking out the door. I rushed to her and blurted out how sorry I was. She laughed, took my head in her hands, and kissed my forehead.

Suddenly the burdens of the world lifted. The sun shined brighter, and I floated home. God blessed me with wise parents who helped me develop as a disciple with Grace and Generosity.

Prayer for Peace

Generous God, may neither pride nor fear keep us from mending broken relationships.

Spiritual Practice: Develop Disciples to Serve

Read and reflect on Psalm 42:1–2. As disciples of Jesus Christ, we are called to respond to people and their needs. The call to journey inward can restore us in times of physical or spiritual depletion. You are thirsty, dry, and empty. Listen prayerfully again to the psalm. As you feel restored, thank God for the opportunity to be a responding, serving disciple while you move into the outward journey. Remember this exercise as you drink water throughout the day.

Peace Covenant

Today, God, I will accept what is offered to me with grace.

10
Sunday
February

In God's Hands

By Susan Oxley, Council of Twelve Apostles

> *Just then a man from the crowd shouted, "Teacher, I beg you to look at my son; he is my only child...I begged your disciples to [heal him] but they could not." Jesus...healed the boy and gave him back to his father. And all were astounded at the greatness of God...*
>
> —Luke 9:38, 40, 42–43

Laurence Song, at the age of 21, was a basketball champion and the hope of New Caledonia. She contracted a rare disease and flew to Australia, where doctors implanted a device in her brain. The device broke, and the doctors removed it.

Her parents brought her home comatose, unable to speak, move, or respond.

They built an addition on the house for her hospital bed and added air-conditioning. Her mother quit work to feed Laurence liquid food, move her unresponsive limbs, and talk to her.

A family friend told a Community of Christ minister about the Song family. Priesthood members began to visit, offering prayers and the sacrament of laying on of hands for the sick. Nothing helped, but the Songs refused to give up.

I met them in 2008, about three years after the tragedy began. The parents received me with quiet joy and greeted my colleagues—Kareva, Ralph, and Moana—like old friends. Once again we administered to Laurence. The years continued with no sign of improvement.

In 2011, I returned with Kareva to the Song home. Laurence lay still, mouth open, eyes unseeing. But her parents told us with great joy that she was improving. She had moved her leg and hand slightly. They praised God for the tiny signs of progress.

Laurence's future is still uncertain. Our priesthood members continue to visit and administer to her. Laurence's family continues to give her care, hope, and faith. They celebrate her existence, and speak lovingly to her. No one knows whether she understands. But we do know that God is with her, because we have placed her in God's hands.

Laurence and her faithful, dedicated parents belong to the Lord.

Prayer for Peace

Healing God, we hold the suffering of the world in your light. We have faith that you are with them always. We have faith that they will know peace.

Spiritual Practice: God's Loving Hands

Take a few deep breaths and quiet your mind. Imagine God's hands surrounding you, offering grace and healing. Now think of someone you love, and pull their image gently into God's loving hands, to stand with you. Just hold that person in God's love for a minute or two, without asking for anything specific. Then thank God and let the person go. Be still for another minute and then close your devotion.

Peace Covenant

Today, God, I will comfort the uncomforted.

11
Monday
February

♫ Hymn of the Month: "The Peace of Jesus Christ"

By Kenneth McLaughlin of Independence, Missouri, USA

> *...to loose the bonds of injustice, to undo the thongs of the yoke, to let the oppressed go free... to share your bread with the hungry, and bring the homeless poor into your house... Then your light shall break forth like the dawn... Then you shall call, and the Lord will answer; you shall cry for help, and God will say, Here I am...*
>
> —Isaiah 58:6–9, adapted

When it became clear Community of Christ would be using the phrase "the peace of Jesus Christ" regularly, I asked myself, "What does that mean?" I have come to realize this question is all-important.

Without answering it thoughtfully, this phrase—or any phrase—becomes a meaningless set of words. This hymn text is my answer to that question, designed to help us understand who we are and what we are called to do.

I did not create the text in a musical vacuum. I already could hear in my mind a melody with a lively Latin beat. I could hear piano, guitar, maracas, and tambourine. With the tune in mind, Pam Robison used her musical skill to create harmony and a simple-to-play tune.

The name of the tune is "Celebration." It is the same word in English, Spanish, and French—three primary languages used in Community of Christ.

The peace of Jesus Christ makes us whole,
gives us life, restores our souls,
brings us grace, sets us free.
God's liberty!

We open heart and hands,
we hear the call
that no child on earth shall fall.
Warfare cease!

Justice for the lost and least.
No walls of hate shall stand,
no words divide
as we journey side by side
making earth one sacred home.

At last!
God's sweet shalom
The peace of Jesus Christ still alive
in each nation, home, and tribe.
God's intent—world rebirth.
All are of worth.

We shall pursue this peace
and share our wealth,
feed the starved, restore lost health.
Dignity,

love for all humanity.
Be brave, be strong, be bold!
We are not frail. Side by side,
We shall not fail
to make earth one sacred home.

At last!
God's sweet shalom.

Prayer for Peace

Working side by side, God, may we bring about your sweet shalom. May we share the peace of Christ.

Spiritual Practice

Contemplate the hymn as a poem (or sing to "CELEBRATION" tune).

12
Tuesday
February

Never Stop Watching

By Sara Parkin of Midland, Michigan, USA

> *...the challenge before a prophetic people is to discern and pursue what matters most for the journey ahead.*
>
> —Doctrine and Covenants 163:11b

"What are you doing son-of-mine?" He was standing over a pot of water, which sat on a hot burner. He was watching the water intently as I entered the kitchen.

"Watching" he responded. "What are you watching?" I asked. "Water" he said.

"Why are you watching the water, son-of-mine?" I queried further. "Because," he responded.

In case you are wondering, my son is a teenager and therefore knows all he ever will need to know in life. In addition he recently graduated from high school and has honed his language to a finely tuned instrument of communication. He now speaks in monosyllables whenever possible. As a parent it is my role to play the 20 questions game.

"Would you please explain...your rationale for standing over a hot stove watching water in a pot."

My son believes patience is a virtue and constantly provides opportunities for me to practice it. At this *reasonable* question he spoke.

"Do you remember the cliché, 'A watched pot never boils?' Well, I'm going to prove that theory false..." Half a second later, as he turned his attention back to the pot of water, "Arrrrrgggghhh! No fair! You distracted me!"

The water had begun to boil while he wasn't watching. He did not disprove the theory.

God has created abundance for us to watch and enjoy. Sometimes we get stuck looking at, dealing with, listening to, and working for the mundane, manufactured, shallowness of everyday life.

We forget to look further. We forget to be aware of and watch for the creations that God has placed right in front of our eyes.

Look now—before they fly away, scurry off, fade, dry up, sink in the west, drop their leaves, or just disappear. Discern and pursue (and watch for) what matters most.

Prayer for Peace

Patient God, help us move away from the mundane. Help us shun the shallow. Open our eyes to what may disappear before we know it.

Spiritual Practice: All That Lives

Take a walk and find a tree where you can sit (or imagine walking and sitting beneath a tree). Lean against the tree and feel the texture of the bark. Listen to the wind move through the leaves. Sit quietly and sense God's presence flowing through the tree and all creation. Offer a prayer of gratitude for your connection to all that lives.

Peace Covenant

Today, God, I will pursue Christ's mission without distraction.

13
Wednesday
February

Sackcloth and Ashes

By Carolyn Brock of Redmond, Oregon, USA

O my poor people, put on sackcloth, and roll in ashes; make mourning as for an only child. . . ."
—Jeremiah 6:26

Ashes for most of us are signs of what is lost, destroyed, consumed—the remnants of what used to be. At times we have lost what is sacred and irreplaceable. We regret what we have done to one another.

Consider the ashes of Jews, the family of Jesus, spewing into the air over Auschwitz. Think of the bodies of those named heretics and infidels, burned at the stake by the church of Christ. Reflect on the villages of Viet Nam, Bosnia, and other places where scorched-earth polices have been employed.

In olden days the Hebrew people covered themselves with sackcloth and ashes in times of mourning and repentance. Some Christians still have their foreheads marked with ashes as a sign of remembrance and repentance on Ash Wednesday at the beginning of Lent.

In her book, *Traveling Mercies*, Anne Lamott talks about the cremated ashes of her friend, Pammy, sticking to her fingers, hair, and clothing as she and Pammy's family tried to spread them on the waters of San Francisco Bay. But the ashes would not cooperate and romantically drift away. Lamott found that ashes "cling and haunt" and they reminded her Pammy would always be an intimate part of her.

Maybe the ashes of past human pain, injustice, genocide, holocaust, and suffering need to cling to *us* like glue. Not so we can be weighed down by sorrow and guilt, but so we can remind ourselves that we continuously need healing, repentance, transformation, reconciliation.

Jesus wept over Jerusalem, grieved over human suffering and oppressive systems. His compassion also moved him to healing words and reconciling actions. Should it not be also with us?

Prayer for Peace

God of the repentant, heal us. Reconcile us to one another. May peace be all that exists between us. May Christ's peace be what we share.

Spiritual Practice: An Offering of Ashes

God promises healing for our wounds and losses. Hold (or imagine holding) a pinch of ashes in your hands as you become aware of situations in your life, family, congregation, and world that are broken, lost, or falling apart. Be honest with God about the fear, sadness, or burden you feel. Offer the ashes to God in prayer. Ask God to create beauty, peace, and healing in the places and people who now experience the ashes of despair and grief.

Peace Covenant

God, I will not brush away the ashes of compassion; I will let them cling until I take healing action.

14
Thursday
February

Pause and Refocus

By Talitha Pennington of Sterling Heights, Michigan, USA

Shun youthful passions and pursue righteousness, faith, love, and peace, along with those who call on the Lord from a pure heart.

—2 Timothy 2:22

A whole series of books and games has developed around the theme of "Where's Waldo?" The challenge to young people is to find Waldo among all the images and colors in a picture. One has to train the eye to look for the right image and identify it among all the others.

In a world that is "erupting" everywhere, either because of natural forces or disasters caused by humans, we might be tempted to ask, "Where's God?" in all this.

Yet, if we train the eye of our souls to look for the image of Christ amid the chaos, we will find God.

The more we make a conscious effort to set frivolous pastimes aside, the easier it becomes to find God. In some ways, Lent offers a good time for such training. Beginning yesterday with Ash Wednesday, we're challenged to pause and refocus on the holy. Then, over the next 40 days, we can refine our searching skills through prayer, fasting, listening, and looking for God in each day's events. Where's God? Look closer.

Prayer for Peace

Ever-present God, help us refocus our search through faith, love, and peace. May we see each day's events clearly through Christ's mission of what matters most. May we pass our time sharing the peace of Christ.

Spiritual Practice: The Ashes of God's World

Hold an imaginary or real bowl of ashes. Let it represent the losses, sufferings, and injustices in the global community. Name things in the bowl that particularly grieve you. Pray a blessing on Community of Christ as it responds to the ashes of God's world with healing words and reconciling actions.

Peace Covenant

Today, God, I will pray, fast, listen, and search for you in my heart.

15
Friday
February

Imaging

By Dorene Kilburn of Stratford, Ontario, Canada

For as the earth brings forth its shoots, and as a garden causes what is sown in it to spring up, so the Lord God will cause righteousness and praise to spring up before all the nations.

—Isaiah 61:11

Recently I had the not-so-pleasant experience of spending 45 minutes in a magnetic resonance imaging (MRI) machine. Not my first time, but my fourth, and still an overwhelming experience. The body-length cylinder is about 24 inches in diameter, and it would be easy to panic in such a confined space. A washcloth over my face and visualization exercises kept me calm each time.

The MRI process was barely under way when I became aware of an itchy spot on my left eyebrow. I did not dare move a muscle! To stop from scratching my eyebrow was difficult, but necessary. Such a small annoyance caused such enormous frustration!

It occurred to me then that often we allow small aggravations to keep us from enjoying the wonders of God's world all around us. Most little issues that annoy or frustrate us pass quickly, but because we have allowed ourselves to focus on them, we have missed opportunities to enjoy something beautiful.

Do we miss, perhaps, a breathtaking cloud or a little child waving to us from across the street? Those precious moments will never come again!

Surely it delights our Creator to see us striving to be aware of all that is presented to us, not only for our pleasure, but also to bring us closer to God.

Prayer for Peace

Creator God, may we take time to stop often and make ourselves aware of the beauty of your creation. We are thankful for the diversity of life we behold. When we are close to your creation, we are close to you. When we are at peace, we are able to share Christ's peace.

Spiritual Practice: Caring for God's Sacred Creation

Each day this week choose a way to notice, give thanks, and care for God's sacred creation. Prayerfully consider one of the following practices or create your own. Walk in nature with a spirit of gratitude while looking and listening for God in all things. Write or pray a psalm of praise for the Earth's beauty or a prayer of healing and blessing for its wounds.

Learn about and engage in an act of Earth-keeping such as recycling, simple living, or fasting from over-consumption of resources. Notice the diversity of the planet's creatures and be gentle to plants, animals, trees, and people! Fall in love with the vast, intricate wonder of God's creation and give thanks.

Peace Covenant

Today, God, I will not let busyness prevent me from seeing the garden you have caused to spring up before my eyes.

16
Saturday
February

Right out of the Font—Inviting People to Christ

By Greg Savage of Lee's Summit, Missouri, USA

Open your hearts and feel the yearnings of your brothers and sisters who are lonely, despised, fearful, neglected, unloved. Reach out in understanding, clasp their hands, and invite all to share in the blessings of community created in the name of the One who suffered on behalf of all.

—Doctrine and Covenants 161:3a

The mission of the church is to proclaim Jesus Christ and promote communities of joy, hope, love, and peace.

When I heard church President Stephen M. Veazey outline the Mission Initiatives that will help members and friends give to their true capacity according to their passions, I sensed the Spirit gently guiding Community of Christ into new opportunities.

From the Chattanooga Congregation in Tennessee we heard of a 10-year-old boy who loved the companionship at church. It was the safest place in his neighborhood. The congregation treated him with respect and loved him for who he was with all his humanness.

He was challenged to consider his potential. He sensed God's call in his young life to become a disciple of Jesus, and he asked for baptism.

He looked forward with great expectation to the event. On the blessed day, he couldn't contain his joy.

The moment he rose from the water, he climbed from the baptismal font and ran from the church, dripping wet.

He ran down the street toward his house, but he didn't go in.

Instead, he went next door to his friend's house and pounded on the door until the friend came out. Then they went to another house and did the same. He led all the friends back to the church so they could experience the same joy of hope.

This child was willing to invite his friends to share in the Blessings of Community. Thank you for your generous response, which enables the witness of the community.

Prayer for Peace

In the name of the One who suffered for all, God, we ask your forgiveness for times we did not invite people to Christ. Grant us further opportunities to share his peace.

Spiritual Practice: Invite People to Christ

Read and reflect on Doctrine and Covenants 162:3b and 163:2b. Pray to be aware of people who might be receptive, and therefore blessed, by your sharing the message of the Living Christ. Imagine being in relationship with them and inviting them to Christ. In preparation, discover your personal testimony of Christ. "Be persistent in your witness and diligent in your mission to the world." Repeat this mantra throughout the day: Christ's mission, our mission, my mission.

Peace Covenant

Today, God, I will extend the invitation that matters most.

17
Sunday
February

Give Your First Fruits

By Jim Poirier, Presiding Bishopric

> *"So now I bring the first of the fruit of the ground that you, O Lord, have given me." You shall set it down before the Lord your God and bow down before the Lord your God. Then you...shall celebrate with all the bounty that the Lord your God has given to you and to your house.*
>
> —Deuteronomy 26:10–11

When I was a young boy, we celebrated Lent in our home. Lent was a big deal in the Roman Catholic faith because it prepared us for the Easter event that comes at the end of the 40-day period after Ash Wednesday. I remember those times because it strengthened my relationship to God. It was a time of seeking, thirsting, listening, and committing.

On Ash Wednesday, weather permitting, we would close the school and march as a group to the church. There we were anointed with ashes on our foreheads in the shape of the cross. This was a sign of our humanity.

The act placed me in a connection with God as creator and source of my being. Like Jesus, during this 40-day period, we were in a wilderness of sorts. We would follow certain rituals to help us reflect, repent, and prepare. We would make sacrifices to make more room for God—give our first fruits to God.

This was the time in my life when I first can remember developing any kind of relationship to God. This relationship continues to develop to this day.

During my daily walks to church, I was alone with God. I remember thinking about who I was. This God who seemed so far away walked with me. I felt that God was pleased with what I was doing. As I worshiped, I talked to God. God responded with a challenge to live my life for others.

The winters were long and cold in northern Ontario. The snow was beginning to melt, and the days were noticeably longer. I felt new life. God accepted my sacrifice and heard my prayers. My relationship to God grew strong. As I ran home God would run with me, through the puddles of melting snow.

Lent for me symbolizes going into the wilderness. But it isn't so bad there—for it was there that I experienced a loving God who assured me that I was not alone. By sharing in the feast of creation, I knew God loved me. I was forgiven and renewed.

Prayer for Peace

Loving God, may we always be open to a deeper connection with you. By committing our first fruits and through our sacrifices, may we see how rich our lives can be as we share the peace of Christ with others.

Spiritual Practice: Spiritual Hunger

Jesus discerned hungers of body and spirit, and he fed them through a physical, verbal, spiritual ministry of presence. In a time of listening prayer ask God to help you discern physical or spiritual hungers of people in your congregation, community, and global family. Invite the Spirit to move you to one hospitable act that "feeds" someone's hunger today.

Peace Covenant

Today, God, I will free my life from distractions that hinder a relationship to you.

18
Monday
February

I See!

By Donna Boyd of Independence, Missouri, USA

There are subtle, yet powerful, influences in the world, some even claiming to represent Christ, that seek to divide people and nations to accomplish their destructive aims. That which seeks to harden one human heart against another by constructing walls of fear and prejudice is not of God. Be especially alert to these influences, lest they divide you to divert you from the mission to which you are called.

—Doctrine and Covenants 163:3c

"It's not that I dislike her," I said to a dear friend, "but her personality irritates me. She has a talent for coming at the wrong times and staying too long. I want to love her, but she is harder to love than some others."

My friend's eyes twinkled, but then she turned a sympathetic ear. "Most of us face this problem as we grow in love for God and earnestly desire a positive affection for all our companions and colleagues," she explained.

"The first step, of course, is to see that no negative feelings remain for anyone. This should evolve with repentance. Obviously we cannot love *everyone* as long as we dislike *anyone*. When we seek a closer communion with the Divine, we feel a growing love for all God's people."

"I see! Love for God carries all of our personal relationships to a deeper level. Also, as we learn to love others, we draw closer to God."

Prayer for Peace

Gather us in your arms, God. Bring us together, leaving our negative selves behind. Help us tear down our dividing walls of fear and prejudice as we share the peace of Christ.

Spiritual Practice: Honoring the Worth of All Persons

Read Psalm 139:13–18. After each reading sit quietly and let the words sink deeply into your mind, heart, and body. Imagine God watching you grow in your mother's womb. What thoughts and feelings do you have about being "fearfully and wonderfully made" (Psalm 139:14)?

Sense the intimate knowledge God has of you and every child. Be aware of the sacred worth of each person. Weep with God over the soul-wounding forces and events that rob people of dignity and worth. How are you invited to notice, protect, heal, and affirm the spiritual identity of all God's beloved people today? Pray for God's compassion.

Peace Covenant

Today, God, I will not let negative influences sway me but will seek your peace.

19
Tuesday
February

A Tap on the Shoulder—a Life Changed

By Deb Crowley of Charlotte, Michigan, USA

"The Spirit of the Lord is upon me, because he has anointed me to bring good news to the poor. He has sent me to proclaim release to the captives and recovery of sight to the blind, to let the oppressed go free, to proclaim the year of the Lord's favor."

—Luke 4:18–19

For Moses, it was an ordinary day as he herded the grazing sheep. Then God called from a burning bush, and his life changed direction.

Matthew was at his booth, collecting taxes. He didn't much care for his job, but he lived comfortably (more than most) and was dedicated, though not popular. Then Jesus walked by, invited him to leave his booth and join him. Matthew's life was never the same.

Saul, later called Paul, was faithfully ridding society of the radical Christians who were upsetting religious and political norms. Just an average day of righteously justified persecution until the trip to Damascus, where he was struck blind and *saw* his life's mission dramatically turned around. Christ's mission became his mission.

Not all have extraordinary encounters with the Divine where God calls from a bush, a booth, or from the darkness. Few of us may ever face the choice to follow God in a direction that disrupts and changes the course of our lives, let alone the course of humanity! But God calls us just the same. God taps us on the shoulder, probes our conscience, or shakes us awake to be aware and to serve people in need.

Indeed, we are not Moses, Matthew, or Paul. Most likely our names will never be written in annals of history for generations to reflect on great deeds done.

A life heeding God's call, moment by moment, is no less radically changed. Our life's work becomes a culmination of simple acts of serving others, making a difference in the life of one person, relieving one burden at a time.

Prayer for Peace

Anoint us God. Tap us on the shoulder. Call us, and we will follow, we will serve. Spark change in our lives, God, and we will change others by sharing Christ's peace.

Spiritual Practice: Examining God's Call to Me and to All

Reflect on God's call in your life. Begin by prayerfully asking to recall particular moments when you have experienced God's presence and invitation. Write in your journal or quietly reflect on images and insights that come.

When has God seemed most real in your life? How and when has God called you to use your energies and gifts? When have you felt God's love in your life? When have you felt disconnected or resistant to God's call? How do your gifts and callings connect with the call of God you notice in your family, friends, congregation, or community?

Peace Covenant

Today, God, I will be awake and aware of those who need a vision of Christ's mission.

20
Wednesday
February

Global Village

By Lu Mountenay of Independence, Missouri, USA

> *Heed the urgent call to become a global family united in the name of Christ, committed in love to one another…*
>
> —Doctrine and Covenants161:6b

The local Foster Care and Adoption Association held its annual gala and auction fundraiser. It was a big event, with the theme, "Forever Families." I was puzzled why my husband and I were invited. Then I learned my sister, Pam, who had been a social worker for the state, was being honored posthumously with a Lifetime Achievement Award.

They used great words, which she deserved, to describe her work. Her son and daughter, Ben and Heidi, accepted the award for her. She would have been deeply touched. It was a bittersweet occasion.

The speakers impressed me. The master of ceremonies was Jason Holsman, a state legislator. He said, "The only completely renewable energy resource is love." He talked about the selfless generosity of foster and adoptive parents.

Kansas City's mayor, "Sly" James, shared a story from his childhood. He grew up in what he called *the ghetto*, but he stayed out of trouble. On his way home from school, James was stopped by a tough drug dealer, who tried to persuade him to sell drugs.

A small, elderly woman, sitting on her front porch, saw the encounter. She walked up to the drug dealer, James said, and poked him in the chest with a bony finger. "You leave this boy alone!"

The drug dealer said, "You ain't his mama." And the woman said, "TODAY I AM!" The young mayor-to-be went on his way and wasn't harassed again.

We also heard from a young man who was abused before he went into foster care and was adopted. Though he and his siblings were taken from life-threatening conditions (one of his brothers died from parental abuse), he still loved his mother.

Unconditional love…divine love. Some would say this is naïve love, all-he-had-ever-known love. But even as a fairly objective adult, he forgave and loved his imprisoned mother unconditionally. This is what we can learn from children. This is what we can learn from God.

And we can learn from little, elderly women, sitting on the front porch…keeping an eye on the sparrows of the neighborhood. We, too, can be community for any child, any day.

Prayer for Peace

God of wisdom, keep teaching us until we get it right. May we keep practicing until it is as natural as the love of a child.

Spiritual Practice: Offering Blessings of Community

Receive and share Blessings of Community. Begin with a prayer of gratitude for the relationships in your life. See and feel connections with family members, spiritual friends, people in your congregation, neighborhood, and the global village.

Peace Covenant

Today, God, I will keep an eye out for injustice.

21
Thursday
February

Working for Peace with Faith and Prayer

By R. Keith Lane of Pastor Valley Station, Kentucky, USA

Those of steadfast mind you keep in peace—in peace because they trust in you.

—Isaiah 26:3

One night in Ban Me Thuot, Viet Nam, I was in the Officers' Club, enjoying a game of bumper pool with another pilot. We heard the sound of mortars firing in the distance. Before we could leave the building for the safety of a bunker, the shells started landing. All we could do was take shelter inside the building.

As I lay in the corner, the man beside me began saying the Lord's Prayer. It reminded me of the assurance I had felt from God that I would be OK during the year I was to spend there. Nevertheless, something told me I needed to protect myself. I saw a chair with thick, removable rubber cushions.

I pulled them over us, and shortly the building took a direct hit to the roof. Two small pieces of shrapnel hit me, one on my right hand and one on my left knee. Later, I counted 28 holes in the cushions. Thankfully, the injuries weren't too bad, and I needed only a short visit to the infirmary.

A philosopher, Edmund Burke, said, "The only thing necessary for the triumph [of evil] is for good men to do nothing." There have been many times I sat back and said of a given situation, "It'll be OK, you'll see," and then did nothing to help. I since have learned that faith, prayer, and whatever we can do to back it up, with the blessing of God's grace, will bring us peace.

Prayer for Peace

We trust in you, steadfast God. We have faith in your grace. We will pray unceasingly for opportunities to share the peace of Christ.

Spiritual Practice: Pursue Peace on Earth

Read and reflect on Doctrine and Covenants 161:2a. Reflect on how you can "see violence but *proclaim* peace...*feel* conflict, yet *extend* the hand of reconciliation...*encounter* broken spirits and *find* pathways for healing." Prayerfully open yourself to God's yearning for peace and the divine vision of shalom. What act of justice or peacemaking does God invite you to pursue this day? Dwell on these words of pursuit: *see, proclaim, feel, extend, encounter, find.*

Peace Covenant

Today, I place my trust in you, God. I will determine my actions for pursuing peace.

22
Friday
February

Come to Me

By Robert Glenn of Evansville, Indiana, USA

"Come to me, all you that are weary and are carrying heavy burdens, and I will give you rest. Take my yoke upon you, and learn from me; for I am gentle and humble in heart, and you will find rest for your souls. For my yoke is easy, and my burden is light."

—Matthew 11:28–30

One Sunday our congregation was blessed to have a guest minister. The theme was the "Spirit of God." In his sermon the speaker shared how his business partner had taken three years of their tax money and misused it.

The speaker said he became depressed. He wanted to talk to someone about his burden. Then, unexpectedly, he got a phone call from a friend, a minister, who said he would fly to see him in a couple of hours.

They went to God and prayed. The speaker knew he had been blessed. He also knew when God blesses you in such a manner, God might ask you to be a blessing to someone else.

It wasn't long until one of his associates was in dire need of help. Our speaker felt prompted by the Spirit to visit her.

He was on his way to a conference, but he had enough time to visit this distressed woman, who had been praying for help. They talked and cried together. They shared her burden and went to God in prayer. This short, but timely, visit was a blessing.

When God leads and blesses us we should prepare to be a blessing to others. The congregation, as a source of witness, was a blessing to me and others seeking the way of Christ who said, "Come to me."

Prayer for Peace

Burden-sharing God, we are blessed to be a blessing. You have shared your peace with us that we might share it with others.

Spiritual Practice: Experience Congregations in Mission

Read and reflect on Doctrine and Covenants 164:9a–d. Reread the sentence, "If you truly would be Community of Christ, then embody and live the concerns and passion of Christ." Make a list of the issues you feel mattered most to Christ. Make another list of issues that matter to your congregation. Reflect on the similarities and differences. How can you help align the lists? Throughout the day, as issues arise, ask yourself, "Would this matter to Christ?"

Peace Covenant

As I have been blessed, God, so I will bless those who are burdened.

23
Saturday
February

Letting Go

By Barbara Howard of Independence, Missouri, USA

> *Jesus, looking at him, loved him and said, "You lack one thing; go, sell what you own, and give the money to the poor, and you will have treasure in heaven; then come, follow me." When he heard this, he was shocked and went away grieving, for he had many possessions.*
>
> —Mark 10:21–22

In Heinrich Hofmann's painting, "Christ and the Rich Young Ruler," the ruler is shown with his hand in a gesture of rejection of Jesus. His other hand is closed. Hands appear central to the painting. Jesus' face depicts sorrow, and the young man's face is sad, too.

His sadness seems connected to the position of his hand. He is moving away from Jesus, who has told him that to inherit the kingdom he must sell all his goods and give to the poor.

Sometimes when we confront difficulty, we express our pain and frustration bodily. The artist captured that moment on canvas. We can, without realizing it, make idols of our possessions. Jesus was not condemning the ruler's riches. He was, rather, asking him to put God at the center of his life.

Whatever is "opaque to God," wrote the German theologian, Paul Tillich, becomes our idol—what we worship. Riches mattered to the young ruler. He had interest in salvation, but he was unwilling to give up his riches to let God be the center of his life. He could not enter into genuine community with Jesus.

Many idols can keep us from enjoying genuine community with Christ: our opinions, hobbies, prejudices, and whatever we value more than a relationship with God. What do we need to release to participate fully in Community of Christ?

Prayer for Peace

Loosen our grip, God. Help us let go of that which does not make us whole. Help us bring the sharing of Christ's peace to the center of our lives.

Spiritual Practice: Open Hands

Stand or sit with your hands extended in front of you. Prayerfully ponder all the things you hold in your hands that make you feel too full, busy, drained, or tight. Spread your hands up and apart to release these things. Then hold your hands open and empty them again. Thank God for relationships that fill and feed your spirit. Pray for a generous heart and open hands that reach out to make room for all in the circle of Christ's community.

Peace Covenant

We are told, "You cannot shake hands with a clenched fist" (Indira Gandhi). Today I will extend an *open* hand for peace.

24
Sunday
February

Become a Covenant People

By Andrew Shields of Independence, Missouri, USA

> *But the word of the Lord came to [Abram]. "This man shall not be your heir; no one but your very own issue shall be your heir." He brought him outside and said, "Look toward heaven and count the stars, if you are able to count them." Then he said to him, "So shall your descendants be." And he believed the Lord; and the Lord reckoned it to him as righteousness. On that day the Lord made a covenant with Abram, saying, "To your descendants I give this land, from the river of Egypt to the great river, the river Euphrates…"*
>
> —Genesis 15:4–6, 18

How is God connected to what is most important to you?

Abram wanted to have a legacy through his children and their inheritance. God offered to be in relationship with him, to grant his deepest desires in an unexpected way. Abram agreed, even when circumstances were grim. It was impossible to see ahead to how God would fulfill the promises. Abram trusted in the relationship and the promise.

In the end, *we* want similar results. We want to feel connection with others. We want our lives to have meaning. We want to be successful. We may differ in our ways of thinking about those goals, but they are part of what it is to be human.

Today, God is offering us the same deal offered to Abram—be in covenant with God, and our desire for connection, meaning, and success will be met in an unexpected way. God offers security grounded in only one way—connection to God. Our connection to God is rooted in trust, even in the hard times.

The hard part of this deal is that it is not always possible to imagine how the future plays out—a way out of current difficulties into a more balanced life. Also, the Divine often calls us to take risks that do not make sense to people. They do not feel the pull of God's will toward a surprising decision.

The easy part of this deal is that no matter what others think of you, the world does not get to decide what you are. Your standing with God decides your value, and God sees you as beyond price. You are of great worth, part of the divine, in community with creation and Creator. If you can trust that, even with questions, you already have God's transforming grace.

Prayer for Peace

Covenant God, we would do our part to honor the covenant you offer to us. Root us in your grace. Open our hearts to your unexpected ways. Open our hearts to receive your grace and share Christ's peace.

Spiritual Practice: Deepening Roots

A tree with superficial roots will wither during drought or be uprooted by severe storms. A tree whose roots go deep is stable and draws from deep waters. Imagine yourself as a tree by a river or stream. Sense your roots extending deep into the Earth in search of God's Spirit. Reflect or pray about what you hope to find as your spirit searches for deeper identity in God.

Peace Covenant

Today, God, I will take a risk for a deeper identity with you.

25
Monday
February

A Lessson in Humility

By Greg Clark of Independence, Missouri, USA

As God's chosen ones, holy and beloved, clothe yourselves with compassion, kindness, humility, meekness, and patience. Bear with one another and, if anyone has a complaint against another, forgive each other; just as the Lord has forgiven you…

—Colossians 3:12–13

I sat in the hospital waiting room, focusing on my wife and her medical problems. Soon, a family of four entered, all middle-aged and older.

A glance determined their socioeconomic status. Their dress was slovenly. Their straggly hair was dirty, and so was their skin. One was missing several teeth.

They seemed oblivious and insensitive to others. They loudly and unabashedly discussed personal topics that were none of anybody else's business.

They were beyond annoying. And the longer they stayed, the more they annoyed.

Then one of them, a woman in her late 60s or early 70s, jolted me with a simple statement to a nearby pastor: "I want to become a minister someday."

My initial impression: "No how, no way."

Almost immediately, a wave of shame slammed into me. Who was I to judge her? Who was I, based on a few minutes of observation, to decide whether somebody was fit for ministry? Who was I to know what call she might have from God?

It struck me that she might be better qualified than I. After all, I knew about Colossians 3:12–13, which calls me to clothe myself "with compassion, kindness, humility, meekness, and patience" and to "bear with one another." Yet, here I was, a modern Pharisee, passing judgment—something I should never do.

God, I thank you for this humbling lesson. I pray you will forgive me and help me remember the Worth of All Persons. Help me to engage in compassionate ministries. And I pray you will bless the woman's need for a deeper relationship with you.

Prayer for Peace

Compassionate God, thank you for the lessons we learn from one another. Forgive us when we judge. Turn our hearts to sharing Christ's peace.

Spiritual Practice: Welcoming Unity in Diversity

Meditate on Unity in Diversity. Create a circle with your arms. See and feel the diverse people God invites inside the sanctuary of Christ's peace represented by this circle.

Who is easiest to welcome? Whom do you struggle to include? Confess the dividing walls between you and people too different or "dangerous" to invite into your spiritual home. Ask God to forgive and heal barriers that keep you and others from being one in Christ's peace.

Peace Covenant

I will remember, God, that when I accept others in their diversity, I strengthen my unity with them and you.

26
Tuesday
February

The Whole Tree!

By Shirley Phillips of Independence, Missouri, USA

"Humble yourselves, and continue in prayer to him; cry to him when you are in your fields, and over all your flocks; cry to him in your houses, and over all your household, morning, midday, and evening...But this is not all: you must pour out your souls in your closets, and your secret places, and in your wilderness. "And when you do not cry to the Lord, let your hearts be full, drawn out in prayer to him continually for your welfare, and also for the welfare of those who are around you."

—Alma 16:219, 221–222

We had several days of heavy rains and flash floods. Tree branches bent near the ground. Wind tore them apart. During one storm, about midnight, my daughter-in-law woke my son and told him their tree had blown down. Not concerned, he told her to go back to bed.

"No! It's the whole tree!"

He went out and found the huge tree that grew next to the house was on the ground, its roots fully exposed. The trunk sprawled across the yard and over the fence, just missing a busy street. What a blessing no one was hurt.

As I prayed that night, all I could say was thank you. Thank you, God, thank you. I often hold up my son and his family in my prayers, asking God to protect them and allow what is best for them and their souls. I feel close to God as I pray for my family.

Prayer for Peace

We cry to you, Lord, for protection and peace. We do what we can for the welfare of our families, and then we leave it with you. May we pray unceasingly with faith.

Spiritual Practice: Making Responsible Choices

Prayerfully seek God's guidance in your choices. Discernment invites us to orient our lives toward God and God's vision for us and creation. Begin by reviewing the responsibilities and opportunities in the day before you. Take these choices into prayer, asking God for wisdom and insight about what matters most.

Offer yourself to God with the prayer of Teresa of Avila: "God, what do you want of me today?" Sit prayerfully with this question as you review the day again. Be aware of images, thoughts, names, or actions that come to you. Ask for a blessing to live this day responsibly and compassionately in the spirit of Christ.

Peace Covenant

Today, God, I will pour out my soul to you.

27
Wednesday
February

Insert Your Name Here

By Julie Conway-Sword of Gainesville, Florida, USA

And I have a work for thee, Moses, my son…And worlds without number have I created, and I also created them for mine own purposes; and by the Son I created them, which is mine Only Begotten…and there is no end to my works, neither to my words; for this is my work and my glory, to bring to pass the immortality, and eternal life…

—Doctrine and Covenants 22:4a, 21c, 23b

It was a mid-February morning—cool, crisp air for our part of the world. We walked along a St. Augustine beach. Our eyes, except for viewing an unusual shell or two, were fixed on the horizon.

We rested our eyes just above the continuous waves. Suddenly, a pink crescent ray flooded our faces. Like the screeching and then suddenly silent sea gulls, we faced the water expectantly—waiting on God's next wonderful message.

I reflected on Moses' experience, when blessed by God's Spirit he talked with God, face to face.

And the Lord told him, "…worlds without number have I created…there is no end to my works, neither to my words…"

As we journey on life's beaches, we, too, can experience the giant, baptismal wave of God's wisdom, like a flood cleansing the eyes of our understanding, our commitments, our relationships, and our service in the mission of Christ.

Speaking to Moses, God said, "I have a work for thee, Moses, my son…" We can insert our own names, at any juncture of our lives and hear the Lord tell each of us, "I have a work for you, _________, my child."

Listening expectantly, we can respond to that call as we await God's next revelation, to be shared with the world.

Prayer for Peace

We are watching your miraculous creation, God, with thankfulness. We are listening, God, for your expectations of us. We await the words with which to share Christ's peace.

Spiritual Practice: Encountering Scripture as Continuing Revelation

Read and pray with Doctrine and Covenants as Continuing Revelation of God's vision for the church and creation. Choose a favorite section or focus on counsel in Sections 156—164. Read a few selected paragraphs slowly three or four times. Pause to pray for deep understanding after each reading.

Pray for the opening of your heart and emotions. Prayerfully ask to hear the phrase or word that speaks to you or touches your life. Stay with this word or phrase. What sense of divine presence or invitation comes? What is revealed?

Peace Covenant

Today, God, I will contemplate your many worlds and how I can fulfill my needed part in Christ's peace.

28
Thursday
February

Just a Phrase in the Bible

By Jim Cummings of Columbus, Ohio, USA

"Ask, and it will be given to you; search, and you will find; knock, and the door will be opened for you."

—Matthew 7:7

I think the most misunderstood phrase in the Bible comes from a saying of Jesus, "Ask, and it will be given to you; search, and you will find; knock, and the door will be opened for you."

God has a way of answering my prayers in ways that are not always what I directly ask or even hope for. I have found that God answers my requests for *material* possessions with *spiritual* blessings.

The poem, "Unanswered Prayer," by an unknown author, states, "We ask for things that we might enjoy life. God gives us life that we might enjoy all things." In a sermon I heard Sunday, the speaker told of almost unbearable challenges in her life. She told us she fell to her knees in prayer. Now, many years later, she can see where God answered her prayers in ways she never imagined at the time.

Keep in mind God does want us to keep the lines open. God wants us to be in relationship, even if we are not theologians, even if we don't have the purest motives for our prayers. Sometimes we are selfish, sometimes we are hurting.

God hears our prayers and wants us to keep communicating. We may not always recognize God's answer, but God is ready to bless us. When we ask in faith, we receive the ministry of the Holy Spirit. God blesses us with peace, hope, and joy. God blesses us with gentleness, love, and kindness. Who could ask or hope for more?

Prayer for Peace

Loving God, we know you hear our prayers. We know you are with us when we are searching for peace to share with others.

Spiritual Practice: Examining God's Call to Me and to All

Reflect on God's call in your life. Begin by prayerfully asking to recall particular moments when you have experienced God's presence and invitation. Write in your journal or quietly reflect on images and insights that come.

When has God seemed most real in your life? How and when has God called you to use your energies and gifts? When have you felt most deeply connected and responsive to God's movement in your life? When have you felt disconnected or resistant to God's call? How do your gifts and callings connect with the call of God you notice in your family, friends, congregation, or community?

Peace Covenant

Today, God, I will search with faith that I will be blessed.

1
Friday
March

Teach Me, God, to Wonder

By Mikal Shedd of Independence, Missouri, USA

He called a child, whom he put among them, and said, "Truly I tell you, unless you change and become like children, you will never enter the kingdom of heaven. Whoever becomes humble like this child is the greatest in the kingdom of heaven. Whoever welcomes one such child in my name welcomes me."

—Matthew 18:2–5

He's concentrating hard, trying to figure out how this works. Not yet 2 years old, my nephew is encountering his first crayon. He's familiar with pens and pencils and can spend a long time, for a toddler, spreading the spindly marks carefully across paper. However, this is clearly different. He turns the crayon repeatedly, looking at each end, touching the paper. He sniffs it, but doesn't taste it.

My sister takes the crayon from him and colors one of the pictures. He watches in amazement. She finishes the picture and moves the coloring book in front of him.

There is stunned silence.

He picks up a crayon and looks at it again. He colors a few scribbles, stops, and looks at it again. He looks up at my sister, eyes wide, startled, questioning.

Wonder.

The discussion over Jesus' command to become as a little child must include wonder. A lightning bug, a dust bunny, a new crayon—we miss the amazement. We forget to be awed by the spider, spinning its web, and we see only cobwebs and spider bites. No longer do we see the beauty of a dew-studded network. We no longer wonder, "How does it do that?"

In wonder, the Spirit awakens and takes over; the mind awakens, the curiosity quickens. We come alive. We encounter the kingdom anew.

How do you keep your life filled with wonder? Find one thing each day to truly wonder about: the color purple, a blue moon, a thousand cranes circling a marsh.

Wonder. It is the highest form of praise.

Prayer for Peace

Wonder-full God, awaken me to the wonder in the world around me.

Spiritual Practice: Listening to Children

Sit in your quiet place and center your heart and mind on God's presence. Spend several minutes asking God to bring into your awareness the names and images of children in your life. You may see their faces or hear their voices as you receive these impressions. Listen deeply to the unique gifts and needs of the children who come to mind. Offer a prayer of blessing for each child and the needs you perceive. You also may want to write a note or card and give a message of affirmation and love to each child.

Peace Covenant

Today, God, I will find wonder in a new particle of creation.

2
Saturday
March

"I Kept Encouraging Her"

By Josephine Kipampe of the Democratic Republic of Congo

> *…all shall give as they are able, according to the blessing…the Lord your God…has given you.*
>
> —Deuteronomy 16:17

This is the first of four stories from the Wasaidizi and Kafwa health workers in the Democratic Republic of Congo. These amazing women have been volunteers for nearly 20 years! Many times they have gone four or five years without any encouragement from me because civil war and other political issues prevented me from traveling to their country. These stories were first written in French or Swahili, translated into Bemba, and then into English. I think you'll enjoy reading them.

—Sherri Kirkpatrick,
HealthEd Connect executive director

This story is about an orphan named Kanyimbu Mpundu. She was 8 years old and in grade two at Alumashi School. Kanyimbu was cared for by her grandma. They made their house with homemade bricks. Kanyimbu's grandmother was a widow. Kanyimbu was very sick. She had a bad sore on her leg, and it was becoming worse.

One day we had a home visit program, and I met this girl. I found her grandma and asked if I could help with the sore. She said, "Yes, you are welcome."

Kanyimbu's grandmother had 12 in her family. Four of her children were prostitutes and were bringing problems to the widow. Problems grew, but I kept encouraging her.

I went to see the young girl and started washing her sore after applying the ointment, which we received from Sherri. I continued to wash the sore for Kanyimbu. And in almost a month, the sore was completely dry.

The girl who had been unable to walk and go to school started walking and going to school every day.

Her life in the past was very bad, but after the treatment, her life changed completely. Kanyimbu's grandmother appreciated the good work. Kanyimbu is walking well. Generosity is a blessing.

Prayer for Peace

We do what we can, God, and then with your help and the generous help of others, we do what we can't do by ourselves. Thank you for generous people.

Spiritual Practice: Healing for Broken Spirits

Begin with quiet prayer. Ask God to help you discern some "sore places" in the body of Christ and in God's creation. Become aware of people who feel separated, wounded, or left out. Ask God for words that will touch this person's broken spirit like healing ointment.

Peace Covenant

Today, God, I will act on any ideas I find to bring health and wholeness to others.

3
Sunday
March

Thirsting for God

By Scott Murphy, Council of Twelve Apostles

O God, you are my God, I seek you, my soul thirsts for you; my flesh faints for you, as in a dry and weary land where there is no water. So I have looked upon you in the sanctuary, beholding your power and glory. Because your steadfast love is better than life, my lips will praise you. My soul clings to you; your right hand upholds me.

—Psalm 63:1–3, 8

There was a time when I thirsted deeply for God. It came when I struggled through a conflict and experienced my own fear, anxiety, and questions. I thirsted for that human-Divine connection where I knew I could find the peace I needed.

In this psalm we find the beautiful expression of one who, amid his own fear and anxiety, came to fully recognize how precious life was when life was in God. In the desert the psalmist remembered what God had done for him and could not hold back the praise pouring from his heart. Life and love captured him, and he found peace.

Today, God invites us into the sacrament of the Lord's Supper to remember that same love and faithfulness of God felt by the psalmist now extended to our lives. We remember there is no life absent God's grace. There is no life absent God's gift. There is no life absent the life, death, and resurrection of Jesus Christ.

The psalmist found new life and peace in knowing that God's right hand upheld him. We find new life and peace as we become new creations in Christ.

But how does one live who thirsts deeply for God and finds new life in Christ? You live differently for the sake of others. Our yearning, our thirsting for God calls us to adopt a new way of being. Our choices and actions begin to speak louder about our need to abolish poverty and to end suffering. When we thirst that deeply for God, it is difficult to settle for the conditions of life boys and girls, women and men live in every day. Those who feel brokenness are thirsting for someone who thirsts for their welfare.

So, what are you thirsting for today?

Prayer for Peace

Steadfast and loving God, we thirst for you throughout our lives. We cannot hide from your grace. You are with us, even when we are not with you. We praise you for the joy you bring. We thank you for the gift of Christ's peace.

Spiritual Practice: Praying for Leadership of the Church

An important spiritual practice for disciples is praying for members of the body of Christ, particularly those who carry leadership responsibilities. Ask God to guide your awareness of persons who lead the community of faith in congregations, mission centers, and the World Church. Pray for God's outpouring of grace on each servant leader who comes to mind.

Peace Covenant

Today, God, I will name my blessings and praise you for them.

4
Monday
March

Let Go, Let God

By Ron Dawbarn of Manchester, Tennessee, USA

For those who want to save their life will lose it, and those who lose their life for my sake will find it. For what will it profit them if they gain the whole world but forfeit their life?

—Matthew 16:25–26

One weekend I took my family to the water-skiing area of a lake and joined with other families. They were more than willing to teach us to ski.

I tried it and decided I much preferred being in the boat, watching the skier, and letting the driver know what was happening.

My youngest daughter insisted she wanted to try. They suggested she might be a little young, but after much pleading on her part, they strapped her into a life jacket and sat her on the dock with her feet wedged into skis. The instructions were specific: If you fall, *let go of the rope* and we'll pick you up.

She sat on the edge, full of confidence. To my utter surprise, when the boat tugged her off the deck she came up on the skis like a pro.

We moved from the shore, hit a swell, and she went down. Instead of releasing the rope, she hung on. She disappeared from sight. I shouted for the driver to stop and jumped overboard. As soon as the boat lost speed she popped to the surface and almost into my arms.

When we got back in the boat I was relieved and angry. "I thought we told you to *let go of the rope* if you fell." Her only answer was, "I know, I know, but when I was under the water, I was afraid to let go."

I have often thought about her response and how it applies to many facets of life. The fear of the unknown is greater than the trauma of the moment, and so we back ourselves into impossible corners. We hang onto our ropes, afraid to let go and let God.

Prayer for Peace

God of our truest selves, we are vulnerable to your grace. Help us let go of what keeps us from sharing Christ's peace.

Spiritual Practice: Breathing with the Ocean

Sit or lie in a relaxed posture. Pay attention to your breathing. Let the rhythm become calm and even. Imagine sitting or lying on a warm, sandy beach with waves rolling in and out near your feet. Listen to the waves as they "exhale" and "inhale." Begin to breathe in time with the waves. Become aware of the ocean as the presence of God washing onto the shore to touch your body and spirit. With each breath receive what the ocean of God brings you. *Let go* of what is carried into the sea of God's presence.

Peace Covenant

Today, God, I will let go and let you.

5
Tuesday
March

Watching and Waiting

By Cara Clifford of Vienna, West Virginia, USA

Is not this the fast that I choose: to loose the bonds of injustice, to undo the thongs of the yoke, to let the oppressed go free, and to break every yoke?

—Isaiah 58:6

One spring I bought two dogwood trees for our yard. The years since have been dry and hot. I watered and fertilized the trees each year, thinking ahead to what their full potential would bring.

Last year the trees had some new growth, but there were signs that parts of the trees had not responded with new life. An unfriendly condition suppressed the trees in some way.

This spring I waited. Each day I looked out my window to catch the first signs of life and promise.

To my joy, traces of green emerged.

How God must watch every part of his creation. It is given to us to break the yoke which oppresses. We are free to grow and fulfill our potential to burst forth into our world. I sometimes wonder if God goes to some divine window and watches us, waiting for us to become that which God created us to be.

Prayer for Peace

For the gift of life we thank you, God. May we always respond to that gift with positive growth. Let your guiding Spirit help us in our formation as disciples, developing to our full potential. From your window, may you see new growth in us daily. May you watch us as we share the peace of Jesus Christ.

Spiritual Practice: Develop Disciples to Serve

Read and reflect on Psalm 42:1–2. As disciples of Jesus Christ, we are called to respond to people and their needs. The call to journey inward can restore us in times of physical or spiritual depletion.

Imagine you can feel a vessel at the center of your being (a clay jar, a crystal vase, a metal bucket, or other container). Imagine drawing something from the vessel to share with another person, but as you reach inside you find only a tiny pool of stagnant liquid. You are thirsty and dry; empty. Listen prayerfully again to the psalm, "As a deer longs for flowing streams, so my soul longs for you, O God. My soul thirsts for God, for the living God."

As you feel restored, thank God for the opportunity to be a responding, serving disciple while you move into the outward journey. Remember this exercise as you drink water throughout the day.

Peace Covenant

Today, God, I will cast off what keeps me from being your disciple.

6
Wednesday
March

What Am I Thinking?

By Sara Parkin of Midland, Michigan, USA

> *Then your light shall break forth like the dawn, and your healing shall spring up quickly; your vindicator shall go before you, the glory of the Lord shall be your rear guard. Then you shall call, and the Lord will answer; you shall cry for help, and he will say, Here I am.*
>
> —Isaiah 58:8–9

(Part 1 of My Journey with Alzheimer's Disease)

I was told I had Alzheimer's disease, and I knew what it meant. My goal is to tell my story as long as I can. Lu Mountenay invited me to share my experience in *Daily Bread,* with hopes that it might encourage others who have this disease or know someone who does. You are not alone.

My God, I need to use your words so others can know you. I can't do it alone. Lord I love you so much. You tell me what to do when I don't want to hear. Yet you give me a way to do what needs to be done. So Lord, I will keep entering in this journal, and it will get done with your help.

Yesterday I started on my knees—I prayed for God's will for this day. I prayed the words in my journal will make sense, and others will know God is with me in my walk with Alzheimer's disease. It will not go away, but it can be slowed down.

One day this past week, I met the doctor to find out the difference in my condition, comparing last year to now.

I am sure there were changes. I feel them, see them, hear them, laugh with them, cry with them. Yet I still have hope, joy, love, and peace on my journey with God and Alzheimer's disease. Well, I have been blessed—I am still in the early stage. I have lost some things, but I am still alive. Hooray! Thank you to all who were praying for and with me. I love you all.

Prayer for Peace

Bless you, God, for every day of life on this Earth. Help us form words to tell our story. Help us form lives that can share Christ's peace.

Spiritual Practice: Breathing God's Compassion

Light a candle and sit quietly, reflecting on the fire and light of God. Pay attention to your breathing and let it become calmer and deeper as you focus on God's presence. Ask God to breathe in you. Imagine each breath carrying the light of God into your lungs, bloodstream, and every cell in your body until you are filled with God's Spirit. Now envision breathing out God's compassion and grace each time you exhale. Pray to have the Spirit of Christ radiate from your life like the gentle flame of a candle.

Peace Covenant

Today, God, I will gain a new understanding of Alzheimer's disease and how I can help those afflicted.

7
Thursday
March

God's Eye

By Lu Mountenay of Independence, Missouri, USA

Are not five sparrows sold for two pennies? Yet not one of them is forgotten in God's sight. But even the hairs of your head are all counted. Do not be afraid; you are of more value than many sparrows.

—Luke 12:6–7

I spent a day in the garden with the birds. I cleaned and refilled the hummingbird bottles with sugar water (one part sugar, four parts water). Before I could stand back, there was a blizzard of impatient hovering. I refilled the cardinal feeder with sunflower seeds. The shy red birds held back until I was out of the way. I topped off the sparrow and goldfinch feeder with their favorite—black thistle. On they came. They were singing. I assumed they were happy. The birds were fed. My soul was fed.

That night it began to hail. Big heavy stones pelted the skylight on my bedroom roof. I looked out the window to make sure our car was in the garage. I was glad for my own roof. Then I thought about the birds. Where do the tiny creatures go when it hails? Are tree leaves big and strong enough to protect them? Do they hide under eaves? I imagined that if a hailstone pelted a sparrow on the head, it would be like me getting hit on the head with a bowling ball. I had to trust God to protect them.

Sometimes I feel vulnerable to pelting, stinging words. There is not a helmet built that will protect my feelings. I rely on God to watch me, with the sparrow, and send me the sanctuary of the Holy Spirit, which allows me to forgive. Forgiving takes away the sting.

After an hour or so of lying awake, worrying about the birds, God assured me they would be OK. I woke up in the morning to the sound of birds singing.

Prayer for Peace

"God of the sparrow, God of the whale" we stand in awe of you. "God of the earthquake, God of the hailstorm...how does the creature cry woe?" With gratitude and faith that you are watching.

—Jaroslav J. Vajda, adapted

Spiritual Practice: Forgiveness

Sit in silence for a few minutes, releasing all thoughts. At the end of the silence, say a silent prayer of gratitude. Now, think of something you have not forgiven, perhaps an action by a family member or a member of your congregation. As you hold that thought, breathe in deeply. With each breath, whisper "God, open my heart." Do this "breath prayer" seven times, remembering that Jesus asks us to forgive "seventy times seven." Throughout the day take time to practice the exercise, always asking, "God, open my heart."

Peace Covenant

Today, God, I will look to the creatures of the sky and feel your loving peace.

8
Friday
March

Spread the WORD

By Donna Boyd of Independence, Missouri, USA

> *Praise the Lord, all you nations! Extol him, all you peoples! For great is his steadfast love toward us, and the faithfulness of the Lord endures forever. Praise the Lord!*
>
> —Psalm 117

There are many accounts of people in the community who feel their prayers have been unanswered. Feasting on the word of God, however, we have examples of prayers of faith and can add them to our collective memory for strength on the path.

When our daughter, Viki, was an infant, she was very ill. It was a snowy night, and we decided to take her some 40 miles to prayer service with our congregation. When the elder (who lived 40 more miles up the mountain) called to say he was not coming because the Highway Patrol advised people to stay off the road, the host told him we had come for the sacrament of laying on of hands for the sick for Viki.

He then said he would come, but we told him not to. We firmly believed prayers from the safety of his home would be as effective.

Before we left for home, her fever was gone, and she was playing happily. Would I have had that faith without knowing the Bible account of the Centurion's servant and other stories of answered prayers?

Part of our mission is to invite people to Christ. We can do this by sharing stories from the life of Jesus. The wonderful stories of God's interaction with humans are ours to share. We share the words of the scriptures, we share our personal experiences, and thus we share the peace of Jesus of Christ.

Try to share with someone today a prayer to help strengthen faith.

Prayer for Peace

Attentive God, we know you hear our prayers and weep with us. What encouragement we have, knowing you rejoice with us, as well. Help us remember our experiences with you that give us faith and strength for the journey.

Spiritual Practice: Intercessory Reflection

Sit quietly with your eyes closed as you enter intercessory reflection and prayer. Ask God to bring persons to your mind and heart who need prayer. Be open to images of the persons or spiritual insight into their needs. Listen for signals from their lives and let the depth of God's love for them become powerful and real to you. Write, speak, or think a prayer of blessing and healing for these much-loved disciples and friends. Ask God to help you see ways to affirm and support them when you meet them in daily life.

Peace Covenant

Today, God, I will strengthen my faith with prayer.

9
Saturday
March

Wait...Together We Can Help Poor People

By Kali Kirkpatrick of Lee's Summit, Missouri, USA

He has told you, O mortal, what is good; and what does the Lord require of you but to do justice, and to love kindness, and to walk humbly with your God?

—Micah 6:8

My grandma and grandpa went to Africa and met boss Mirriam. When I write this, I am 8 years old, and she is 3. Boss Mirriam has HIV (human immunodeficiency virus). This is how my story starts. Wait, I forgot to tell you that boss Mirriam is not really a boss; they just call her "boss."

After my grandpa and grandma met boss Mirriam they started to raise money. They used the money to build schools for orphans and provide food. A school lunch costs 12 cents.

Wait, they also train moms to be health workers in Africa. My grandma and grandpa don't really do it all themselves. They have many friends who help them because they want everyone to be happy, healthy, and educated!

I learned that together we can help poor people.

Prayer for Peace

Creator God, to Abolish Poverty, End Suffering we need the help of many people. Soften our hearts, Lord. Educate us about faraway places. Help us be disciples who serve others and share Christ's peace.

Spiritual Practice: Generosity and Discipleship

Bring a basket or other container to your place of prayer. Meditate on the link between generosity and discipleship. Write a prayer of commitment in which you name specific acts of generosity and sharing to which you feel called. Fold the paper and place it in the offering container. Close by singing a hymn of gratitude or praise as you offer your gift to God.

Peace Covenant

Today, God, I will listen to the ideas of the young about how we can help those in need.

10
Sunday
March

Lost and Found

By Andrew Shields of Independence, Missouri, USA

> *…"Listen! For all these years I have been working like a slave for you, and I have never disobeyed your command; yet you have never given me even a young goat so that I might celebrate with my friends. But when this son of yours came back, who has devoured your property with prostitutes, you killed the fatted calf for him!" Then the father said to him, "Son, you are always with me, and all that is mine is yours. But we had to celebrate and rejoice, because this brother of yours was dead and has come to life; he was lost and has been found."*
>
> —Luke 15:29–32

Facing broken relationships is risky and difficult business.

The arrogant young man left his family and quickly spent all his money, ending in poverty and shame. It took courage (spurred by need) for him to return to his father to ask for a servant job. The elder brother dealt with the aftermath of his younger brother leaving, taking wealth and his father's pride with him. It took courage for the steadfast brother to push past his pride and indignation to accept his wayward brother.

The father was most badly hurt—his own son wanted wealth more than a father. He too faced barriers before he could accept his son back: his culture, his rights, his pride, his image as his son's teacher. All these barriers stood in the way of accepting the ungrateful wastrel back. As Jesus tells the story, all these barriers together could not restrain a father's joy at restoring a relationship with his lost son.

Part of being Christian means cultivating a relationship to God that lets us feel the joy God feels when even the most obnoxious of God's children are restored to right relationships. Part of our relationship to God is gratitude, which extends into right relationships with the force of God's love behind it. Restoring someone to right relationships means getting beyond the past and reflecting a fraction of God's love back to one who was lost and now is found.

There may be reasons you might not want to forgive those who have broken their relationships with you. None of them is good enough when a loved one repents and returns. God sets the example with us, and we live it out into the world. That's a big part of what it means to represent Christ.

Prayer for Peace

God of grace and reconciliation, may we respond as the good parent who welcomed a wayward child. May we, like the good parent, rejoice in finding a right relationship with an estranged one. May each relationship in our lives be formed with this Divine love. From this love, may we go out and share the peace of Christ.

Spiritual Practice: Healing and Reconciliation

Gather a small mound of stones. Meditate on the stones as symbols of differences and destructive acts that continue to separate and wound the human family. Name and anoint each "stone wound" with a drop of water or scented oil. Offer them to God in a prayer for healing and reconciliation.

Peace Covenant

Today, God, I will get past the past and get reconciled.

11
Monday
March

♫ Hymn of the Month: "God Whose Grace Redeems Our Story"

By Barbara Howard of Independence, Missouri, USA

For I am convinced that neither death, nor life, nor angels, nor rulers, nor things present, nor things to come, nor powers, nor height, nor depth, nor anything else in all creation, will be able to separate us from the love of God in Christ Jesus our Lord.

—Romans 8:38–39

One joy of my life was the privilege of working with the committee that developed the previous Community of Christ hymnal, *Hymns of the Saints.* During that time I also had the privilege of participating in several women's retreats throughout the church. I heard stories of women's lives that strengthened my faith and helped me see how God is always with us.

I believe God's love is luring us to goodness throughout our lives.

The testimonies I heard strengthened that conviction. Those two experiences came together as I worked on "God Whose Grace Redeems Our Story."

The hymn is my response to my favorite scripture, Romans 8:38.

God, whose grace redeems our story; God, whose love has held us fast,
in our times of joy or sorrow, your forgiveness frees our past.
Written in our history's pages are those times we've spent with you,
when we've found your Spirit working to transform our lives anew.

God, the author of this instant; God, whose voice is present tense,
help us love as you have loved us and forgive without defense.
For your mercy marks this moment, all abiding, boldly true,
plant your Spirit deep within us to transform our lives anew.

God, who calls us to the future and invites us from this place,
may the language of our witness use an alphabet of grace.
Weave your healing peace and justice through the vision we pursue.
Let your Spirit work within us to transform our lives anew.

Prayer for Peace

Source of the sacred story, we listen. May we go on to share *your* story and *our* story as we share the peace of Christ.

Spiritual Practice

Contemplate this hymn as a poem (or sing it with the BEACH SPRING tune).

12
Tuesday
March

A Moonless Night

By R. Keith Lane of Valley Station, Kentucky, USA

For in him all the fullness of God was pleased to dwell, and through him God was pleased to reconcile to himself all things, whether on earth or in heaven, by making peace…

—Colossians 1:19–20

Years ago, when my grandfather was a young man, he and my grandmother homesteaded on the plains of eastern Colorado. Life was hard. Cars were for rich city folks, and roads were a luxury. Walking was the primary way to get somewhere.

There were no sewers, electricity, or running water. People ate what they could grow or traded goods or a service for what they needed or wanted. If the roof leaked, you fixed it. If your wife or children got sick, you nursed them back to health, or they died.

Since theirs was the only house for miles, there was no light to be seen when it got dark. Grandpa used to say it was so dark sometimes that you couldn't see the hand in front of your face. When he was away from home preaching and teaching the gospel, he would be gone days, even weeks, at a time. Often when he got home, after walking miles and miles, it was long after the sun had gone down, and before the moon rose high enough to shed a little light.

Grandma always put a candle in the window to light the way.

Without Christ in our lives, it is like walking on a moonless night. We find ourselves going in circles, repeating the same mistakes over again. But with Christ, who is the light of the world, we know the path of the disciple. Christ sheds light that we may see the pitfalls of life and withstand its temptations. The light of Christ develops disciples who serve.

Prayer for Peace

Reconciling God, we praise you for sending the light of your Son to show us the way. He is our sun by day and our moon by night.

Spiritual Practice: Light

Close your eyes, and become centered with your breath. Reflect on the statement: "The light of God is in all things," as you breathe gently in and out. His light has a bright, soft beauty and radiates loving peace. The light of God reaches you and permeates you with a deep sense of peace. Rest in the light as it surrounds and fills you. Thank God that you live in God's light, and it lives in you.

Peace Covenant

Today, God, I will share the peace of Christ to brighten the world.

13
Wednesday
March

Beauty for Ashes

By Carolyn Brock of Redmond, Oregon, USA

To provide for those who mourn in Zion—to give them a garland instead of ashes, the oil of gladness instead of mourning, the mantle of praise instead of a faint spirit. They will be called oaks of righteousness, the planting of the Lord, to display his glory.

—Isaiah 61:3

I have an iridescent glass heart made from ash scattered by Mount St. Helens' violent eruption in 1980. Minerals in the ash create the heart's deep indigos and purples. Of course, when it rained down on gardens and housetops, cars and streets, the ash was powdery gray and not welcomed as attractive or useful.

The volcano's nearly symmetrical cone had graced the horizon of southwestern Washington and northwestern Oregon for hundreds of years. It became but a memory as tons of forested land exploded and eroded, burying plants, animals, and humans. The shape of the mountain and the view of the horizon changed forever.

Was it a loss? Yes, something to grieve about, certainly. Beauty and harmony appeared to have been overcome by violence and ugly debris. How interesting that human creativity looked for and found ways to redeem and reclaim the natural byproducts of the event. How remarkable that in just 20 years foliage and wildlife once again inhabited the decimated landscape.

God promises that what has turned to ash in our hands—the shape of life as we know it, the tears we cry for what we feel we have lost—can and will be redeemed.

Are we willing to exchange who we have been for who God calls us to become? Are we willing to embrace future joy by letting go of our fear and heaviness of heart? Are we willing to offer the ashes of our former selves to God, trusting that God will put us together again in a beautiful shape we ourselves may not even recognize?

Prayer for Peace

God of what was and what will be, mold us for our role in sharing Christ's peace.

Spiritual Practice: An Offering of Ashes

God promises healing for our wounds and losses. Hold (or imagine holding) a pinch of ashes in your hands as you become aware of situations in your life, family, congregation, and world that are broken, lost, or falling apart. Be honest with God about the fear, sadness, or burden you feel. Offer the ashes to God in prayer. Ask God to create beauty, peace, and healing in the places and people who now experience the ashes of despair and grief.

Peace Covenant

Today, God, I will look for joy in the tragic; beauty in the ashes.

14
Thursday
March

Practice and Prayer

By Julie Conway-Sword of Gainesville, Florida, USA

...let your light shine before others, so that they may see your good works and give glory to your Father in heaven.

—Matthew 5:16

In her light-blue, chiffon formal, with her violin tucked under her arm, Mom joyfully hurried out the door to play for a church friend's wedding. Earlier that day, Mom diligently had practiced her music and prayed for the Lord's presence.

As a parent of three active little girls, Mom often found her preparation time limited. She generously shared her musical talents at church services, weddings, and community events. I felt that whenever Mom played, the Spirit blessed her musical offerings; "ye receive the Spirit through prayer" (Doctrine and Covenants 63:16a).

So what did I learn from my mother's example? I learned that it's not only important to prepare to one's highest degree of musical proficiency, but to dedicate one's gifts to God's honor and glory.

When I was a Graceland University freshman I was invited to perform for the entire student body at the convocation. I practiced the piano, and I prayed. I felt a power not my own move my fingers easily over the keys. Later that day my experience led me to write:

"I walked with God today—
He sat beside me on the bench
and helped my fingers play.
I know—I know that somehow from above,
the music flowed through my full heart
expressing His great love."

Prayer for Peace

The glory is yours, heavenly Parent. Whatever we do to bless the world, we do in your name. In your name we share the peace of Christ.

Spiritual Practice: Examining God's Call to Me and to All

Reflect on God's call in your life. Begin by prayerfully asking to recall particular moments when you have experienced God's presence and invitation. Write in your journal or quietly reflect on images and insights that come.

When has God seemed most real in your life? How and when has God called you to use your energies and gifts? When have you felt most deeply connected and responsive to God's movement in your life? When have you felt disconnected or resistant to God's call? How do your gifts and callings connect with the call of God that you notice in your family, friends, congregation, or community?

Peace Covenant

The light I emanate today, God, will be to your glory.

15
Friday
March

Come out from the Dark

By Dorene Kilburn of Stratford, Ontario, Canada

> *We know that all things work together for good for those who love God, who are called according to his purpose.*
>
> —Romans 8:28

The wonders of the changing seasons are a joy to see.

We've all watched the early spring flowers push up through the cold earth and, in some places, through the snow. As the days get warmer, the bare branches of the trees begin to show signs of new growth and soon are clothed in green again.

Water lilies and water irises that have been sitting all winter in damp earth in a cold, dark basement begin to grow. No sunlight, no warmth, but they instinctively "know" what time of year it is and are eager to return to the pond to offer their colorful beauty.

Ladybugs and ants crawl out from under rocks. Frogs that have spent the winter deep in the pond now sit lazily on a log and call to a mate across the water. Soon a flicker picks a hole in a hollow evergreen tree and prepares a nest to raise a family.

Three hummingbirds return from the south on the same day as last year—the same hummingbirds with their distinctive personalities! Each creature has its purpose. Miracles in nature abound as the seasons change. What an awesome world God has created for us to enjoy!

Let us thank God for colorful expressions of love for us.

Prayer for Peace

God of the hopping frogs and darting birds, may we know our purpose, as do other creatures. May we hear your call to share peace.

Spiritual Practice: Spirit Centered Balance

As you walk or drive today, notice the unlikely places where you see growth, life, color, beauty. Review your daily schedule and habits. When and how do you attend to your spiritual center, and how does beauty "color" new life growing from that center? How do you balance intimacy with God's Spirit with active ministries of discipleship? Prayerfully reflect and journal on your need to learn "spirit-centered balance" that allows you to live as an oak of righteousness, a repairer of ruins in God's world.

Peace Covenant

Today, God, I will pray to discern my purpose—what Christ's mission means for me.

16
Saturday
March

At-one-ment

By John Bonney of Springfield, Oregon, USA

God, the Eternal Creator, weeps for the poor, displaced, mistreated, and diseased of the world because of their unnecessary suffering. Such conditions are not God's will. Open your ears to hear the pleading of mothers and fathers in all nations who desperately seek a future of hope for their children. Do not turn away from them. For in their welfare resides your welfare.

—Doctrine and Covenants163:4a

Why must we limit our understanding and idea of the Divine to narrow bands of possibility? The result is that we suffer from disconnectedness. Too often we and they separate us—create loneliness. Problems of this one small world and all that is on it, in it, and above it stem directly from this sense of disconnectedness.

If we would recognize how we connect with one another, we would not tolerate the conditions of hunger, war, disease, and other inequities. We wouldn't tolerate them because we would be one with everything. What hurts, limits, and degrades one also degrades all. A greater sense of awareness that we are part of an infinite whole, that we connect in all that matters, would bring a deep sense of atonement, at-one-ment.

Isn't that what unconditional love is about?

It is to recognize the Eternal in every life. It is to recognize the Presence that resides in each person with whom I agree or not, who I like or not.

Divine love causes me to be one with violent and destructive people. There is nothing outside the Divine. It is not possible.

That unconditional love is the love of the Creator for the created. It is a love that calls me not only to see, but to act with empathy and compassion.

This love brings me to the realization that someone—everyone, anyone—needs what I have to offer, my life if need be. There are no others. There is no one and nothing that is outside the unconditional love of God.

Prayer for Peace

Eternal Creator, author of unconditional love, may we offer this love to others. May we live with compassion. May we share the love and peace of Jesus Christ.

Spiritual Practice: Embodying God's Shalom

Find a way to express and embody God's shalom. Begin by prayerfully listening to your longing for peace. Become silent and imagine you can hear the groaning of the Earth's people, nations, and creatures. Prayerfully open yourself to God's yearning for peace and the divine vision of shalom.

What images, feelings, and words come to you? What prayer for peace comes to you from your time of listening? Speak or write this prayer. What small act of justice, kindness, healing, or peacemaking does God invite you to consider this day?

Peace Covenant

Today, God, it will not be *I* and *them*, but *us*, together as one.

17
Sunday
March

Accept the Gift

By Stassi Cramm, Council of Twelve Apostles

> *Mary took a pound of costly perfume made of pure nard, anointed Jesus' feet, and wiped them with her hair. The house was filled with the fragrance of the perfume.*
>
> —John 12:3

Jesus graciously accepted Mary's extravagant gift. Accepting gifts is not as easy as it sounds. Western culture teaches us, from an early age, to think beyond our own needs and to remember that it is "better to give than receive."

Many times when my husband and I go out to eat with my parents, the meal ends with a debate over who gets to pay for the meal. The *fight* over who pays has gotten so intense that my husband and dad once accidentally ripped the bill in two.

Few of us are good at receiving. We claim good reasons to think we should get to pay the bill, but part of the issue is our discomfort in being the on the receiving end of someone else's generous gift.

Recently we talked about our need to learn to better model Jesus in graciously accepting gifts. Receiving is an important skill for disciples. As disciples, first we receive, and then we give. "For God so loved the world that he gave his only Son…" (John 3:16).

We have to get past our sense of unworthiness and be willing to receive freely the grace that Christ offers. Only after we accept this generous gift given by God can we freely give by sharing the peace of Christ with others.

Today when my husband and I go out to dinner with my parents, each couple pays for its own meals. We're still working on our ability to accept the gift, but we are getting better. How's your ability to accept the gift?

Prayer for Peace

Your love, God, given so graciously, causes us to want to give to others. May we receive your grace, as well, that we might learn to accept the generosity of others. May we receive as well as share Christ's peace.

Spiritual Practice: Spiritual Learning

Meditate on a time when you learned about community from someone who took you in, fed you, taught you, shared stories and wisdom with you. What did you learn? Prayerfully create a list of qualities you need to learn from spiritual mentors and friends. Then write the names of people who serve as teachers, models, coaches, or encouragers in your life. Offer a prayer of gratitude and blessing for these spiritual "relatives" and friends.

Peace Covenant

Today, God, I will not deny anyone the opportunity to express generosity.

18
Monday
March

Waiting for the King

By Jeanne Hough of Clare, Michigan, USA

I wait for the Lord, my soul waits, and in his word I hope…

—Psalm 130:5

Silence—deliberate, yet without tedium
Serenity—stillness, without feelings of guilt
Solitude—just enough, without being lonely.
—Lu Mountenay

When I grow tired of my daily tasks, I often sit at my computer and play a mindless game of solitaire for a moment of serenity. As I put the available cards in order, I search for a king card. When one comes up, I must find an empty spot to build a column.

Most often there is no available spot, so I wait for the king until other cards get out of the way.

This is like my life. Looking for the king card is like my search for God. I know that I need God, but cannot put the Divine in the right place until I put other distractions out of the way. I must empty my life of what is not important and create a position of priority for what matters most—my relationship to God.

I cannot cheat on the computer by moving the cards just where I want them. There are rules of order. Is God placed in my set of rules for my life? Maybe I can take the opportunities I have to rest in solitude and use them to pray and meditate. I can then bring God back into the position of priority in my daily life.

Prayer for Peace

God, we pray for the peace of Christ in our world. We pray for peace in our lives. We pray for a few moments of silence and solitude that we may find and then share that peace with others.

Spiritual Practice: Connecting with God as Center

Connect with God through journal writing or contemplation. Open yourself to God's presence and share what flows from your heart and mind. Your "communication with God" might include thoughts, questions, feelings, needs, artwork, quotes, or scriptures. Or it might take the form of a prayer, psalm, or poem. Try to write or meditate at least five minutes each day.

What do you experience? Is this an effective way to connect with God? What surprises you? What new God images or questions emerge? What deepens or changes in your relationship with God, Christ, Spirit?

Peace Covenant

Today, God, I will put away the games and fold my hands in prayer.

19
Tuesday
March

The Extraordinary Occurs in the Ordinary

By Janné Grover of Lee's Summit, Missouri, USA

For as the earth brings forth its shoots, and as a garden causes what is sown in it to spring up, so the Lord God will cause righteousness and praise to spring up before all the nations.

—Isaiah 61:11

Long before children can understand ideas of God, Jesus Christ, and the Holy Spirit, they can recognize patterns of behavior and start to identify with happy and sad feelings. Children will develop an awareness of God in their own way and in their own time, but it may be surprising how this can happen at such a young age.

The earlier children learn habits of prayer and meditation, the earlier they can develop their own comfort with prayer and the importance of quiet moments that allow for reflection and simply being in the presence of God.

Spiritual practices are important for people of every age, and we easily can adapt them for children when they are new shoots, springing up. Spiritual practices help develop patterns of praise for the good in each day and ways we can learn from and seek God's guidance for the tasks that challenge us.

Our family shares in prayer together each night. At times it seems like we are just going through the motions. Sometimes when it's late and we are feeling grumpy, I wonder if it is effective. Then I realize it is significant when the kids set up prayer time and ask to share their highs and lows.

I was encouraged by something shared in a class: "It is in the ordinary that the extraordinary often occurs."

I have experienced this in the most original ways as my kids have shown me the extraordinary nature of God in the ordinary practice of family prayer time.

Prayer for Peace

We praise you, God, for the openness and learning nature of children. May we be steadfast in our guidance of spiritual practices and peaceful behavior.

Spiritual Practice: Making Responsible Choices

Prayerfully seek God's guidance in your choices. Discernment invites us to orient our lives toward God and God's vision for us and creation. Begin by reviewing the responsibilities and opportunities in the day before you. Take these choices into prayer, asking God for wisdom and insight about what matters most. If possible, practice this with children in your family or congregation community.

Peace Covenant

Today, God, I will try to represent faithful discipleship to a young one.

20
Wednesday
March

Spirit of Community

By Darren Goble of Humansville, Missouri, USA

However, timely resolution of pressing issues in various nations is necessary for the restoring work of the gospel to move forward with all of its potential. Therefore, let the proper World Church officers act in their callings—as already provided in church law—to create and interpret church policies to meet the needs of the church in different nations in harmony with the principles contained in this counsel.

Where possible and appropriate, convene national or field conferences to provide opportunities for broader dialogue, understanding, and consent. In those gatherings, let the spirit of love, justice, and truth prevail.

—Doctrine and Covenants 164:7c–d

My mission center had a session to prepare for a national conference. I was not sure what to expect, other than many people defending their ideas of what they thought was right. I was dreading what was about to take place.

God met me in my fear, and a spirit of community prevailed. Instead of heated debate, we shared stories. Instead of monopolizing the markets of rightness, people found a shared expression of vulnerability. Instead of crossed arms and eye rolling, there were open ears and open hearts.

It was a session of difficult topics, more-difficult questions, and the challenge of finding God's path for us. It was not what I expected, but it was what I needed.

We are not called to take the easy path. We sometimes are called to take the road less traveled. I am thankful God is with us on this journey.

Prayer for Peace

Just and gentle God, be with us on our journey of discernment. May your Spirit in us rise above opinions. May your love infuse all discussions. May Christ's peace be shared in all gatherings.

Spiritual Practice: Encountering Scripture as Continuing Revelation

Read and pray with Doctrine and Covenants as Continuing Revelation of God's vision for the church and creation. Choose a favorite section or focus on counsel in Sections 156—164. Read a few selected paragraphs slowly three or four times. Pause to pray for deep understanding after each reading.

Pray for the opening of your heart and emotions. Prayerfully ask to hear the phrase or word that speaks to you or touches your life. Stay with this word or phrase. Listen as fully and openly as you can. What sense of divine presence or invitation comes? What is revealed?

Peace Covenant

Today, God, I will listen more than I speak.

21
Thursday
March

All the Way to Brooklyn

By Jim Holloway of Murfreesboro, Tennessee, USA

> *Are any among you sick? They should call for the elders of the church and have them pray over them, anointing them with oil in the name of the Lord.*
>
> —James 5:14

It started as a simple request from a prayer partner in Ohio. She asked me and the other prayer circle members to pray for her friend, Brenda, who at age 40 had become pregnant. Brenda had lost a child a few years before in the first trimester. There were again the same possible dangers, and Brenda was asking for all the prayers she could recruit.

Several weeks later another e-mail asked the prayer partners to lift Brenda and the baby in prayer to our Lord even more. Because these prayer friends are not members of Community of Christ, I wondered how to approach them about the possibility of Brenda receiving the sacrament of laying on of hands for the sick.

I asked her to get out her Bible and read James 5:14. I told her our church believed strongly in this scripture. If Brenda and her husband were willing, I would arrange a visit with the pastor of a local congregation.

The pastor arranged for two ministers from the congregation to visit Brenda and her husband, to pray for and anoint her with consecrated oil. During the next several weeks there were more prayer requests and even some moments when we wondered if the baby would survive.

Brenda had faithfully placed her deep concerns in God's hands by asking many in the community to pray for her family.

At 28 weeks Brooklyn was born. She weighed less than three pounds and was 14 inches long. The doctors and nurses were pleasantly surprised at how she thrived. Except for the fact that Brooklyn was born several weeks early, there were no major complications!

We gave glory to God for what we felt was answered prayer. You just have to wonder if by some miracle, that small drop of oil placed on Brenda's head made it all the way to Brooklyn.

Prayer for Peace

Healing God, may we extend our faith outside our community so others may be blessed. May we search far and wide for ways to share Christ's peace.

Spiritual Practice: Offering Blessings of Community

Receive and share Blessings of Community. Begin with a prayer of gratitude for the relationships in your life. See and feel connections with family members, spiritual friends, people in your congregation and community, and people and creatures in God's sacred web of life. What blessings flow to you from these circles?

Reflect, pray, or write in your journal about the call to be "Community of Christ." Go deeper each day as you discern what act of blessing you are invited to complete.

Peace Covenant

Today, God, I will hold those in need up to your healing light.

22
Friday
March

Moving...Changing...Continuing

By Don Richardson of Nauvoo, Illinois, USA

Scripture is an indispensable witness to the Eternal Source of light and truth, which cannot be fully contained in any finite vessel or language. Scripture has been written and shaped by human authors through experiences of revelation and ongoing inspiration of the Holy Spirit in the midst of time and culture.

—Doctrine and Covenants 163:7a

My wife and I recently had moved to Illinois. We needed to get Illinois driver licenses, so we studied the State Driver's Manual. After we got our licenses, we were driving to a neighboring town. There was road construction, and we were the first car in line at a stop sign held by a worker. After a short wait, the worker began walking, moving the stop sign closer to the construction site and farther from us.

Should I follow him or stay put? I looked at my wife and said, "The manual did not tell us what to do when the stop sign moves."

We study good books, including the scriptures, and we listen to others we trust. We try to prepare for every possible event in life. But along comes a circumstance in which we have no experience or information.

It is at times like this we need to assess the problem, then, based on what we know from our past and our trust in the guidance of the Holy Spirit, try to make an intelligent decision.

Our divine Parent is always with us, even when the "road signs" of life appear to move and change on us. Trust in God.

Prayer for Peace

Never-changing God, we know it's more urgent than ever to keep communication with you open even when—especially when—our lives change. The Holy Spirit assures us of your care and love. It gives us the strength and faith to share the peace of Christ.

Spiritual Practice: Encountering Scripture as Continuing Revelation

Read and pray with Doctrine and Covenants as Continuing Revelation of God's vision for the church and creation. Choose a favorite section or focus on counsel in Sections 156—164. Read a few selected paragraphs slowly three or four times. Pause to pray for deep understanding after each reading.

Pray for the opening of your heart and emotions. Prayerfully ask to hear the phrase or word that speaks to you or touches your life. Stay with this word or phrase. Listen as fully and openly as you can. What sense of divine presence or invitation comes? What is revealed?

Peace Covenant

When I face new challenges today, God, I will call on you and your wisdom.

23
Saturday
March

The Needs of Another

By Cindy L. Korf of North Platte, Nebraska, USA

> *Faithful disciples respond to an increasing awareness of the abundant generosity of God by sharing according to the desires of their hearts; not by commandment or constraint. Break free of the shackles of conventional culture that mainly promote self-serving interests. Give generously according to your true capacity. Eternal joy and peace await those who grow in the grace of generosity that flows from compassionate hearts without thought of return. Could it be otherwise in the domain of God, who eternally gives all for the sake of creation?*
>
> —Doctrine and Covenants163:9

When our son moved from the college dorm into an apartment, my husband and I gave him a nice wooden computer desk.

A few months later when we visited him I noticed that the computer desk was missing, and his computer was spread over the kitchen table.

I asked him what happened to the computer desk. He replied that he had given it away.

A little perturbed, I asked, "Why? If you didn't want it, you could have sold it!" I could not understand why he would give away an expensive piece of furniture, especially when he could be using it.

His reply was, "My friend had a greater need for it than I."

My son's generosity humbled me into silence.

Prayer for Peace

Generous God, may we be cheerful givers. May we be mindful of what we have, not dwell on what we don't have. May we share from our overflowing cup *and* our half-empty plate. May we share the peace of Jesus Christ.

Spiritual Practice: Generous Offerings

Spend time meditating on the act of giving an offering. Begin by asking God for the spirit of generosity. Pray and reflect with these questions: How do I feel when I bring my offering to a worship setting and share it? What deep reasons motivate me to give? What is my best understanding of A Disciple's Generous Response? Considering my financial circumstances, do I feel I am giving to my true capacity? In other words, am I giving the amount I am capable of giving without jeopardizing the needs and well-being of my family? Is God asking me to be more generous? How will I respond?

Peace Covenant

Today, God, I will be grateful for what I have to share.

24
Sunday
March

From Fractured...

By David Brock, presiding evangelist

> *As he rode along, people kept spreading their cloaks on the road. As he was now approaching the path down from the Mount of Olives, the whole multitude of the disciples began to praise God joyfully with a loud voice for all the deeds of power that they had seen, saying, "Blessed is the king who comes in the name of the Lord! Peace in heaven, and glory in the highest heaven!"*
>
> —Luke 19:36–38

Today is Palm Sunday. It is the day of the first Christian parade! The grand marshal rides into the capital city along a crowd-lined street, and there is excitement! No majestic steed—just a donkey. The leader and his team are a ragtag bunch, but emotions are high. The adulation is overflowing. Tunics are laid before Jesus and the donkey, palm branches are waving in joy, and praise songs, chants, and shouts liberally pour over him as he passes.

The rabbi, the teacher, the healer, the forgiver, the preacher, the Lord, the one in whose presence people clamor to be. They know the authority in his voice, his touch, his eyes. He comes to their town and he just might be the savior they've been waiting for. Today is the day when our children parade down a pew-lined aisle in costumes, waving branches, shouting "Hosanna," and we celebrate them in their little ragtag production. It is festive and fun, and there is a hint of Easter hope in our jubilation. It is good!

Today is Palm Sunday. And though I can and do celebrate, I can't get away from...I can't put out of my thoughts...what happens at the end of the parade route. It is Passion Week. The most excruciatingly painful experiences and truths lie just ahead of Jesus, there in the capital city. And just ahead of us here, there is all the denial, betrayal, failure of nerve, scapegoating, and violence perpetrated by one human on another.

We cannot turn away from the physical suffering. We face the terrible fact of the ever-so-thin veneer of civility and conviction that quickly disappears when our own hopes disappear. We face a committed, "I'll stand by your side until death do us part" disciple, who denies he ever knew the one he once defended. The adulation quickly shifts to chants of "crucify him!" and causes me to feel fractured on Palm Sunday.

Prayer for Peace

Eternal Presence, be with us on our path from the mountain. May we understand the pain and suffering you endured, the love that made it so. May we share your love and Christ's peace with all who are burdened.

Spiritual Practice: Chalice Prayer

The chalice prayer is a form of intercession. Create a cup or chalice with your hands in front of your heart. Open your heart to God's concern for the Earth and human family as you hold them in your chalice. See beauty and suffering as you lift the chalice and release the creation (open hands) to be blessed and healed by God. Place yourself inside the chalice as you confess your deepest needs. Lift and release yourself to God for healing. "Thank you and amen."

Peace Covenant

Today, God, I will not deny your truth by my actions.

25
Monday
March

...Journeying...

By David Brock, presiding evangelist

> *Listen to the Voice that echoes across the eons of time and yet speaks anew in this moment. Listen to the Voice, for it cannot be stilled, and it calls you once again to the great and marvelous work of building the peaceable kingdom...*
>
> —Doctrine and Covenants 162:1b

During Passion Week, I still feel fractured. I often have that divided feeling. I'm torn between the awareness of my own unworthiness, my sinful self, and probably worse—my inattentive, remote, distracted repetition of prayers that could mean so much and yet often matters so little.

Yet, on occasion, the symbolic reenactment of the central person of my faith, the central event of our movement, and the encounter between the source of life and love, offers a moment of joy unspeakable. I often feel fractured and distracted...but sometimes I also am healed and whole!

Events that took place during Christ's Passion Week so many years ago shaped our community faith. But you know what? It is not just the truth and history that abide, the truth that undergirds, the truth that is most real. There is wideness in God's mercy. There is a balm in Gilead and Michigan and Missouri, in Siberia and Sudan, and to the ends of creation, that makes the wounded whole.

There is a love broad like beach and meadow.

There is a voice that echoes through the eons of time and down to our day...and beyond. A voice that call us by name, that calls us beloved son or daughter, that gives us our communal identity bearing a name that tells us who we are, what we are called to be, and what matters most.

Prayer for Peace

Center of life, we hear you calling us by name. We answer, recognizing Christ at the center of our faith. Source of life and love, we are yours. Use us as you will to share the peace of Christ.

Spiritual Practice: Time with God

Sit quietly and let your breathing become calm and deep. Ask God's Spirit to rest on you. See or sense the Spirit anointing you in the form of light, a dove, wind, color, or other images that might come. Ask to be made aware of God's love. Listen to the ways in which God wants to flow from your heart as living water. Give thanks that your name is "beloved," that our name is Community of Christ.

Peace Covenant

My prayer today, God, will not be distracted. I will *be* with you.

26
Tuesday
March

...to Wholeness

By David Brock, presiding evangelist

> *So then you are no longer strangers and aliens, but you are citizens with the saints and also members of the household of God, built upon the foundation of the apostles and prophets, with Christ Jesus himself as the cornerstone. In him the whole structure is joined together and grows into a holy temple in the Lord; in whom you also are built together spiritually into a dwelling-place for God.*
>
> —Ephesians 2:19–22

There is a bond beyond blood ties that binds us together with chords that we dare not break. We dare not break! All the agony and the ecstasy of Palm Sunday and Passion Week are taken up into God in Christ. God weaves them into a garment of beauty, like the bright *ti fai fai* the Tahitians wrap around their honored guests in Papeete on a praise-filled Sunday morning; like the shawls of India or Latin America that adorn the shoulders of hard-working wives and mothers and in which they wrap their children and grandchildren.

Just as in Christ's day, these are still the days of wonder and miracle—the miracle of a God who can take the disparate days and dimensions of our fractured lives and communities and make a circle. A God who shapes from the chaos the beauty of fractal patterns in what we perceive only as randomness.

In those rare moments when the eternal breaks through there is no *them* and *us*. There is no now and then, no worthy and unworthy, male or female, bond or free. There is only the Eternal Now, the One, the Whole. God saves us. God takes our fractured and divided selves, heals us, and makes us whole!

Prayer for Peace

We, the broken people, God, ask you to make us whole as only you can. Help us tear down walls that separate us, overcome prejudice that fractures us, open doors that shut others outside of us. Infuse us with Christ's peace that we may share it.

Spiritual Practice: Honoring the Worth of All Persons

Read Psalm 139:13–18. After each reading sit quietly and let the words sink deeply into your mind, heart, and body. Imagine God watching you grow in your mother's womb. What thoughts and feelings do you have about being "fearfully and wonderfully made" (Psalm 139:14)?

Sense the intimate knowledge God has of you and every child. Be aware of the sacred worth of each person. Weep with God over the soul-wounding forces and events that rob people of dignity and worth. How are you invited to notice, protect, heal, and affirm the spiritual identity of all God's beloved people today? Pray for God's compassion.

Peace Covenant

Today, God, I will reassemble the broken pieces of my relationships into a mosaic of wholeness.

27
Wednesday
March

Simple, Tangible Ministry

By Robert Glenn of Evansville, Indiana, USA

"Here is my servant, whom I have chosen, my beloved, with whom my soul is well pleased. I will put my Spirit upon him, and he will proclaim justice to the Gentiles. He will not wrangle or cry aloud, nor will anyone hear his voice in the streets. He will not break a bruised reed or quench a smoldering wick until he brings justice to victory. And in his name the Gentiles will hope."

—Matthew 12:18–21

A woman in our congregation holds the office of teacher. She understands what it means to be a servant to her brothers and sisters, and therefore to God. If one listed all that she does for friends, family members, and our congregation, it would be a long testimony. I will share some of it.

She takes food to those who have little or none and to those who are sick. She organized a vegetable soup detail with cooks who made and packaged several containers for the pantry. She invited a friend to have her granddaughter's baby shower at our church. All had a great time, and that grandmother, out of her thankfulness, made chicken noodle soup for our food bank. The teacher invited a woman whose washer and dryer had broken to bring laundry to her house to be washed.

This teacher counsels college girls and helps people find work. Her mind looks for ways to lighten the burden of others. She recently retired from nursing, but before she left she collected canes, grabbers, walkers, and other needed items for her workplace.

I admire her for her gracious spirit and humility in her ministry. This sister cares for others. She is a testimony to me of generosity. Her hands are God's hands.

Prayer for Peace

Let our hands be your hands, God. Let our eyes be your eyes—looking for ways to help others, looking for ways to share the peace of Christ.

Spiritual Practice: Hand Ministry

Place your hand on a piece of paper and trace around it to create an outline. Add details of fingernails, wrinkles, or skin color if desired. Look at your hand and meditate on what you do with your hands each day. Ask God to direct your thoughts to a person in need of blessing, kindness, or healing touch. Pray for wisdom about the specific act needed by this person and discern how and when you will use your hands to complete this ministry.

Peace Covenant

Today, God, my hands are your hands. Make me a servant.

28
Thursday
March

A Second "Last Supper"

By Tammy Lindle of Independence, Missouri, USA

Are any among you sick? They should call for the elders of the church and have them pray over them, anointing them with oil in the name of the Lord.

—James 5:14

Maundy Thursday is the Christian feast or holy day on the Thursday before Easter. It commemorates the Last Supper of Jesus with the apostles. Good Friday follows, and then eventually Easter, when the Christian church celebrates restored life!

I've shared in some remarkable "last supper" experiences. I had jaw surgery that required a splint for my mouth. My mouth was wired shut for six–eight weeks. This meant only blended foods through a syringe and absolutely no chewing. Doctors cautioned not to overeat before surgery, so I picked a wonderful meal at a favorite restaurant two nights before my surgery. Some good friends joined me.

The night before surgery my congregation's gardening group was at my house on gardening night. Following the evening's work the members gathered in my backyard and had a circle prayer for me. Their prayer and presence brought me peace, assuring me I was not alone on this journey. Following the prayer they took me out for ice cream "one last time." I count that last "meal" as one of the sacred events of my life.

Months later, I had to repeat the surgery. This time my mouth was "wired" shut for three months.

I had a second "last meal" to consider. Selecting the last solid food to eat for three months might seem easy for some.

I knew what was ahead of me following surgery. I enjoyed that dinner. I treasured the friends and family who would journey with me on this next trial. They brought peace and comfort to that "last supper." Being set free from the splint and wires was a new-life experience for me—something to look forward to! I can't help but wonder how Jesus felt about what lay ahead for him, following his last supper.

Prayer for Peace

Redeeming God, thank you for the gift of your Son. Thank you for those who pray for us and join us on our journeys. May we never leave anyone alone in their hour of need.

Spiritual Practice: Healing for Broken Spirits

Begin with quiet prayer. Ask God to help you discern some "sore places" in the body of Christ and in God's creation. Become aware of people who feel separated, wounded, or left out. Reflect on or write a short journal entry of healing words to at least one person who comes to mind. Ask God for words that will touch this person's broken spirit like healing ointment. Keep this person in your heart and prayers today and act on any ideas that come to bring blessing and wholeness.

Peace Covenant

Today, God, I will be awake and ready if anyone should need me.

29
Friday
March

Christ: Alone Then…Alone Now?

By Deb Crowley of Eaton Rapids, Michigan, USA

For with you is the fountain of life; in your light we see light. O continue your steadfast love to those who know you, and your salvation to the upright of heart!

—Psalm 36:9–10

Beneath the twisted olive tree
the Savior wept for you and me.
There he prayed throughout the night
waited for the morning light.
His friends just slept, they didn't care
he was alone in deep despair.
—Peggy Michael

In a 2010 survey, two-thirds of those polled knew that Easter is a religious holiday. But only 42 percent connected its meaning to Christ's resurrection. And only 2 percent of adults said they would describe Easter as the most important holiday of their faith.

Not everyone who connects Easter to religion has the facts straight. Two percent of those surveyed said Easter is about Jesus' birth. Another 2 percent said it's about Jesus' "rebirth." And 1 percent said it's a celebration of his *second* coming. Three percent described Easter as a celebration of spring or a pagan holiday.

In the same survey, 31 percent of active church-goers said they definitely would invite an unchurched friend to worship with them on Easter weekend. This Easter, share the truth and joy of the holiday with someone who doesn't know Jesus and the salvation he offers. Don't leave Christ alone in the garden. News of the resurrection is too good to keep to ourselves! Invite People to Christ!

Prayer for Peace

Ever-present God, we want to be present for you. May we not keep you waiting for our response. May we be present for those who are lonely. May we share with them the peace of Christ.

Spiritual Practice: Teacher-learner

The first disciples of Jesus followed to hear his words, to learn a new way of living, to practice what they learned in daily life. Prayerfully consider your role as a teacher-learner, disciple-apprentice; a people cultivator in Community of Christ.

Reflect on your response to the life of Jesus. Reflect on him as teacher, surrounded by people. Now think of him alone in the garden. Can you be present for him; present for others in his name? Write or think of people you feel called to nurture and encourage in specific ways. Ask God's blessing on you and your congregation as a community of teachers and learners.

Peace Covenant

Today, God, I will not leave anyone alone in the garden of despair.

30
Saturday
March

Empty Tombs

By Val Walker of Plainfield, Indiana, USA

Make a joyful noise to the Lord, all the earth; break forth into joyous song and sing praises. Sing praises to the Lord with the lyre, with the lyre and the sound of melody.

—Psalm 98:4–5

My family traveled to a Florida beach for a short vacation. It was close to Easter, and I was preparing a sermon. I prayed for a testimony to help focus my words in a fresh way.

I walked the beach daily in sugar-like sand, occasionally picking up shells. As names came to mind, I would toss a shell in the water and say a prayer for family and friends. As the waves broke on the shore, I could hear my congregation break forth in joyous song and praises on Easter morning. Could I break forth with a meaningful message?

I kept asking God to prompt me with ideas to share. One morning while walking the beach, the words "empty tombs" came to me. My thoughts were, "Obviously the tomb was empty. It's Easter! How is that different from any other Easter sermon?"

I kept on walking, challenging God again with the same question. After hearing "empty tombs" for the third time, I decided to listen closely. I reached down for a shell, and finally the answer came to me. This *shell* was an empty tomb—once home to a creature that outgrew it and found a new home, or died and became food for another. The shell itself was beautiful but no longer was needed by the creature that once lived in it.

Then came the words: "Are you an empty tomb? Have you shared Christ with others, letting him out of the tomb? Or do you keep him to yourself, not wanting to let anyone know what you have? Scared to share because you might not be accepted?"

I had my testimony.

That morning I gathered a whole bag of shells, many broken, some perfect, but all empty. They became mementos for everyone that Easter day, reminders that we need to empty the tomb, to share the Christ and create a spiritual home for someone else. We need to share as Christ would share.

Prayer for Peace

God of the breaking waves and the still, small voice, may we pause to listen for an answer when we call for you. May we hear your message in what is before us. May we find the sacred in the ordinary. May sharing Christ's peace be part of our everyday lives.

Spiritual Practice: Breathing with the Ocean

Sit or lie in a relaxed posture. Pay attention to your breathing. Let the rhythm become calm and even. Imagine sitting or lying on a warm, sandy beach with ocean waves rolling in and out. Listen to the waves as they "exhale" and "inhale." Begin to breathe with the waves. Become aware of the ocean as the presence of God washing onto the shore to touch your body and spirit. With each breath receive what the ocean of God brings you. Let go of what is carried into the sea of God's presence. Offer a prayer of thanksgiving. Ask how to share God's healing and peace today.

Peace Covenant

Today, God, when I call on you—I will pause to listen with expectation.

31
Sunday
March

Christ Is Risen

By Andrew Bolton, Council of Twelve Apostles

> *But Peter got up and ran to the tomb; stooping and looking in, he saw the linen cloths by themselves; then he went home, amazed at what had happened.*
>
> —Luke 24:12

Reading the entire text of today's scripture (Luke 24:1–12) has great value. Verse 12 is how the story *ends*. Peter, acting on the testimony of devoted women disciples, goes to see if the tomb is as empty as they say it is. He finds the tomb empty. All four gospels speak of an empty tomb. Where is Jesus? For some there are doubts about the resurrection experiences. Then in others there is joy and, for Peter in today's passage, amazement.

However, what do Jesus' crucifixion and resurrection mean? I have pondered this for years. This is what I now understand.

Because of the crucifixion of Jesus the Gospels describe human evil in its full, brutal, and cruel reality. The religious establishment accused an innocent man, and the oppressive Roman Empire executed him. It is another story of a human-rights violation, of an innocent victim who simply protested the rip-off of the poor in the temple system (Luke 19:45–48). The Gospels do not flinch in telling the truth about human evil. The Gospels take sinfulness seriously. Christianity, therefore, is not naïve about the human condition.

But that is not all. In the light of Easter morning, we witness the power of God to right a wrong, to bring healing for injustice, to turn the tables on evil. Jesus rises back to life. Good overcomes wickedness. Human history makes a decisive turn.

Of all people, Christians are the most realistic about human evil and at the same time the most hopeful about the kingdom where the worth of all people is celebrated and honored. That is the message of crucifixion Friday and resurrection Sunday for me.

And like Peter I am amazed.

Prayer for Peace

May we be amazed anew, God, at the healing power of the resurrection. May we be ever aware of the hope for the human condition because of Christ. May we share this hope and Christ's peace with all humanity.

Spiritual Practice: The Ashes of God's World

Hold an imaginary or real bowl of ashes in your hands. Let it represent the losses, sufferings, and injustices in the global community. Name things in the bowl that particularly grieve you. Pray a blessing on the Community of Christ as it responds to the ashes of God's world with healing words and reconciling actions.

Peace Covenant

Today, God, I will believe when I hear of the empty tomb.

1
Monday
April

Drinking from the Well

By Greg Clark of Independence, Missouri, USA

But the wisdom from above is first pure, then peaceable, gentle, willing to yield, full of mercy and good fruits, without a trace of partiality or hypocrisy.

—James 3:17

After spending a long Easter weekend away from the office, I returned Monday morning to see my plant in distress. Every stem, every leaf drooped. It looked beyond drab. It seemed worn out, tired, exhausted—much the way I felt.

The plant just needed water. Within a few hours of receiving a good drink, its leaves and stems perked up. It once again radiated freshness and health.

I thought of another drink of water—the one Jesus presented to the woman at the well. Jesus offered her *living* water. It changed her life, and she had to tell others.

I yearned to feel that way—energized, vibrant, and so excited that I couldn't keep joy to myself. But I didn't. I felt spiritually flat even though I'd been to three extraordinary worship services in the last few days.

What was wrong with me?

Finally, I recognized the problem. It's not enough to taste the living water. We must drink it *deeply*, letting it flow through our veins, soak into our cells, wash over our hearts.

We must let it change the way we respond, see, and feel.

I hadn't been doing that. Instead, I'd been dwelling on trust issues. As a result, I'd been going through the motions in my spiritual life without nurturing the passion, zeal, and joy of Christ within me. I was not taking part in of the fruits of the Spirit.

Unlike the plant, receiving a drink is not enough—not even at an inspiring Easter service. For this water to live in us, we must surrender to it completely. And after receiving it, we must offer it, in Christ's name, to others who thirst.

Prayer for Peace

Quench our thirst, God, with your good Spirit. We are willing to yield to your wisdom. We are open to receive Christ's peace, and share it.

Spiritual Practice: Vessel for Living Water

Visualize or feel a vessel at the center of your being (a clay jar, a crystal vase, a metal bucket, or other container). Imagine drawing something from the bucket to share with someone, but as you reach inside you find only a tiny pool of stagnant liquid. You are thirsty, dry, empty. Then something clear and cool begins to pour over you. It splashes and tumbles into the vessel, filling it to the brim. The living water of Christ pours on and through you. Your vessel fills and runs over, blessing your body and soul. Offer a prayer of thanksgiving and commitment to share living water with others.

Peace Covenant

I will surrender to you, God, and drink deeply of your living water.

2
Tuesday
April

The Fingerprints of Jesus

By Barbara Howard of Independence, Missouri, USA

> *"...let them seek peace and pursue it. For the eyes of the Lord are on the righteous, and his ears are open to their prayer..."*
>
> —1 Peter 3:11–12

The first successful hand transplant, completed in Kentucky in 1999, raised much discussion in our household. I wondered if the man who received the hand would carry the fingerprints of his donor or if his own DNA eventually would change the fingerprints. I called our friend who worked with the Genome Project in California.

"No," she said, "the fingerprints will always be the prints of the donor." Then she added a note that intrigued me: "But the blood of the recipient brings life to the hand and made those fingerprints continue after the death of the donor."

How like our life in Christ. The body and blood of Christ Jesus make us whole again. And it is that life in us that permits the power of the Holy Spirit to work through us. Even after the death of Christ, the resurrection makes possible the presence of Christ throughout history.

We are bearers of the "fingerprints" of Christ in our lives.

Whenever we respond to the Holy Spirit we leave the prints of Christ Jesus on those whose lives we touch. The ministry we offer always bears the "prints of the donor," our Lord Jesus Christ. The peace we share is the continuation of *his* peace.

Prayer for Peace

May our hands be kind hands, God, like the hands of Jesus. May we feel the Spirit of Christ in our veins. May we imprint his peace on the world.

Spiritual Practice: Hand Ministry

Place your hand on a piece of paper and trace around it to create an outline. Add details of fingernails, wrinkles, or skin color if desired. Look at your hand and meditate on what you do with your hands each day. Ask God to direct your thoughts to a person in need of blessing, kindness, or healing touch. Pray for wisdom about the specific act needed by this person and discern how and when you will use your hands to complete this ministry.

Peace Covenant

I will look for Christ's hands today, God, in all the lives that touch me.

3
Wednesday
April

Kirtland Temple Challenge

By Greg Savage of Lee's Summit, Missouri, USA

> *Then justice will dwell in the wilderness, and righteousness abide in the fruitful field. The effect of righteousness will be peace, and the result of righteousness, quietness and trust forever.*
>
> —Isaiah 32:16–17

The 175th anniversary of dedicating the Kirtland Temple was my third visit there. During the Sunday sermon, church President Stephen M. Veazey said:

> The Kirtland Temple story also challenges us to prepare better as disciples, priesthood, and leaders to share the gospel story with the world…The Kirtland Temple story also tells us that local and worldwide church mission walk hand-in-hand.

President Veazey went on to state that in this House of the Lord, Joseph Smith Jr. called Heber C. Kimball to go on the first overseas mission to England. At that point, my thoughts wandered back to the first time that I visited the Kirtland Temple.

I had just graduated from Graceland College. Two friends, Don Salyards and Les Blanchard, and I had decided to go to Europe for a couple of months. As we headed east to New York to catch our charter, we included a Kirtland Temple stop.

I recall going up the steps into the foyer behind our guide. The entire tour group got quiet. We followed the guide from room to room with reverence, respect, and awe, sensing the spiritual dedication and commitment of those early Saints.

After the tour, the guide took us aside and gave us permission to go back into the sanctuary to sit, meditate, and pray.

After that experience, we sat on a pier on Lake Erie to reflect and talk.

We decided we would look up the church's local congregations whenever we could during our summer travels. Little did I know that this was the beginning of a two-year journey of discipleship formation; of meeting and worshiping with Saints from the British Isles, Holland, and Germany; learning that God is universal and inclusive.

The sacred story of the Kirtland Temple touched my life in such a deep way that it continues to guide me on my life's journey.

Prayer for Peace

God of our history and future, may we abide in your presence. May the ministries of the temples form disciples of Christ and send them to share his peace.

Spiritual Practice: Praying for Leadership of the Church

An important spiritual practice for disciples is praying for members of the body of Christ, particularly those who carry leadership responsibilities. Ask God to guide your awareness to persons who lead the community of faith at congregational, mission center, and World Church levels. See or sense these persons and ask for insight into any particular physical, emotional, or spiritual needs they may have. Pray for God's outpouring of grace on each servant leader who comes to mind.

Peace Covenant

Today, God, I will share the gospel story.

4
Thursday
April

New Eyes

By Jim Cummings of Columbus, Ohio, USA

So the other disciples told him, "We have seen the Lord." But he said to them, "Unless I see the mark of the nails in his hands, and put my finger in the mark of the nails and my hand in his side, I will not believe." A week later his disciples were again in the house, and Thomas was with them. Although the doors were shut, Jesus came and stood among them and said, "Peace be with you." Then he said to Thomas, "Put your finger here and see my hands. Reach out your hand and put it in my side. Do not doubt but believe."

—John 20:25–27

Occasionally I see a person who is visually impaired on the street with a seeing-eye dog. Most seeing-eye dogs are German shepherds, but other breeds can be trained to do the same job. It takes about 24 months to train a seeing-eye dog. It takes about one month to train the new handler.

Handlers must learn to communicate with the dog and to place their full faith and trust in the dog. Only 10 percent of people can be trained successfully to use seeing-eye dogs. Once people are trained and disciplined, they can *see with new eyes.*

We, too, can learn to see with new eyes. We can learn to "walk by faith, not by sight" (2 Corinthians 5:7). It takes a desire to know God, a willing and open mind to learn about the Divine. We need to communicate by prayer, praise, and worship.

Accepting and returning God's love will set our new spiritual eyes aglow.

Healing and transformation begin with faith. Like Thomas, our challenge is to stop doubting and believe. Like the person led by the seeing-eye dog, we have to put our full faith and trust in God.

Prayer for Peace

Help us overcome our need for proof, God. Help us form a disciple's faith that is vulnerable to your grace and Spirit. We have peace, knowing Christ is alive in us, and we will share his peace.

Spiritual Practice: Light

Close your eyes, and become centered with your breath. Reflect on the statement: "The light of God is in all things," as you breathe gently in and out. Sense or see a point of light in the distance coming gradually toward you. With each breath it comes closer, growing in size and brightness. The light has a bright, soft beauty and radiates loving peace. The light of God reaches you and permeates you with a deep sense of peace. Rest in the light as it surrounds and fills you. Thank God that you live in God's light, and it lives in you.

Peace Covenant

Today, God, I will place my faith in you to lead when I can't see.

5
Friday
April

Perennial Savior

By Lu Mountenay of Independence, Missouri, USA

> *...the fruit of the Spirit is love, joy, peace, patience, kindness, generosity, faithfulness, gentleness, and self-control...*
>
> —Galatians 5:22–23

This scripture describes the spirit of my sister, Pam.

We were both avid gardeners. Besides going to flower markets, we would accept cuttings, seeds, and bulbs from friends and divide the plants however we could to spread them around—mostly in our own gardens.

We even put our lives in "peril" (smile) and dug up plants and small trees from condemned properties on which impatient bulldozers sat. We also gave plenty away. Most plants in Pam's yard, I have in my yard, too.

When my sister died, I had a few months before the foreclosure of her home. I couldn't stand to lose "our" flowers. I dug them up gently, left some for the bank, and brought them home to live in my garden for a while. Her flowers are part of Pam's legacy. Her children would soon have homes of their own, so I adopted the flowers until they have a place to plant them. We will divide them again to continue Pam's garden.

For now the bulbs, seeds, tubers, and roots are underground in their tomb of soil. We can't see them. Soon, being the perennials that they are, they will rise and bring with them joy and beautiful memories. In this, a part of Pam will always be with us.

Christ is our perennial Savior. Even though unseen, he is with us. Every year we celebrate his leaving the tomb and bringing joy and everlasting life into the light.

Prayer for Peace

Creator God, we would tend your garden gently. We praise you for your diverse and beautiful plant life. We praise you for the perennial cycle you have put in place.

Spiritual Practices: Fragrance

Remember or find a way to directly experience a fragrance you enjoy (fresh flowers, candle, fresh bread, pine trees, sea air, spices). Ask God to help you discern a situation to which you are called to bring reconciliation and healing. Pray that you might spread the peace of Christ as fragrantly and generously as the aroma you now experience.

Peace Covenant

Today, God, I will plant and nurture seeds of hope.

6
Saturday
April

Life Lessons and Strength from Emma Smith

By Cathy Loving of Independence, Missouri, USA

God is calling for a prophetic community to emerge...that is characterized by uncommon devotion to the compassion and peace of God revealed in Jesus Christ...

—Doctrine and Covenants163:11a

Most mentors are living people who guide and encourage us along life's journey. But because I am not like most people and have a passion for history, it is fitting my path is a bit different. My unexpected mentor is Emma Smith. Her accidental entrance into my life became a powerful and healing experience.

Leaders asked me to portray Emma Smith for the 2005 Bicentennial and Heritage Reunion in Nauvoo, Illinois. My first reaction was to say "no." I feared I might fail to present her the way she deserved. The "Elect Lady" intimidated me, both then and now.

I eventually agreed to the challenge, trusting God would guide me. At that reunion, Emma taught me more than I could imagine about myself and my faith. She continues to teach me about God's lasting love when I prepare and portray her at reunions, camps, or special events.

It is a delight when I have the opportunity at camps and reunions to share with the young children. Their imaginations are creative, and they easily pull me into Emma's stories. During those moments I catch myself strengthened by the acceptance she had for all, the satisfaction she found in daily life, and her constant trust in God to comfort her.

I never will understand the deep sorrow and struggles Emma experienced. But she continues to show me how to accept God's love graciously and to understand my own faith journey. My mustard seed of faith is slowly taking root and maturing, thanks to Emma's story. Through it I am guided when I doubt and am reminded to pray continuously for guidance. Because of her example, my fears drift away, and I'm overcome with peace.

Emma's lesson and steady trust in God help me take tiny steps of faith to become the person God calls me to be.

There have been moments of great doubt in my life, but God guides me—just as God guided Emma—one step at a time.

Prayer for Peace

May we be grateful for the church leaders of the past, God. May we be mindful of our present leaders and hold them up in our prayers.

Spiritual Practice: Praying for Leadership of the Church

An important spiritual practice for disciples is praying for members of the body of Christ, particularly those who carry leadership responsibilities. Ask God to guide your awareness to persons who lead the community of faith at congregational, mission center, and World Church levels. See or sense these people and ask for insight into any particular physical, emotional, or spiritual needs they may have. Pray for God's outpouring of grace on each servant leader who comes to mind.

Peace Covenant

Today, God, I will pray for the church's leaders around the world.

7
Sunday
April

We Are Witnesses

By Richard James, Council of Twelve Apostles

> *"We must obey God rather than any human authority. The God of our ancestors raised up Jesus...God exalted him at his right hand as Leader and Savior that he might give repentance to Israel and forgiveness of sins. And we are witnesses to these things, and so is the Holy Spirit whom God has given to those who obey him."*
>
> —Acts 5:29–32

I rejoice that Community of Christ has many members throughout the world. The diversity of language, culture, and witness is a powerful expression that God is with us, and all people are of worth to God and us.

As I travel in Eastern Europe and North Asia, I am conscious that many people make a significant decision to become members of Community of Christ. They choose to live their discipleship outside established orthodox churches, which play important roles in their communities.

They choose a life of faith in which they are not always able to talk openly about their faith. Sometimes their personal lives would be in danger if authorities knew they belonged to our church.

They make a bold decision, one they are happy to make, but there is a price. Some cannot even tell their own family they are members, and others have to be careful who they speak to, in fear of retribution or even permanent damage to the continuing ministry of the church in their country.

Their willingness to be witnesses of Jesus Christ is inspiring. They testify of a living Christ who calls us to make this world a better place to live in. They are determined to follow Jesus and to be a part of Community of Christ. What a witness they are of the resurrected Jesus. They are alive in Christ.

The early disciples must have faced similar problems and experiences. Because of their faith, they stood and made a difference. As we engage in Christ's mission we, too, can stand and offer our witness. The Holy Spirit is with us as we proclaim Jesus Christ and promote communities of joy, hope, love, and peace.

Prayer for Peace

Give us courage, God, to witness of you and your Son. Help us stand firm in the Enduring Principles we claim. Make our voices loud and our actions clear as we proclaim and share the peace of Christ.

Spiritual Practice: The International Community

Find (or imagine) a globe or map of the world. Look at all the nations and find a country other than your own. Notice the geographic distance between your homeland and this one. Picture a person living there. Pray for this person. Sense God's love connecting you just as the oceans connect the continents. Thank God for the spiritual connection you have with all of God's people around the globe. Ask a blessing on the church as a community sharing Christ's peace, drawing all into the family of God.

Peace Covenant

Today, God, I will "send the sound, the Earth around," the message of Christ's mission.

8
Monday
April

Go Now!

By Donna Boyd of Independence, Missouri, USA

And there came a voice to them, a pleasant voice, as if it were a whisper, saying, "Peace, peace be to you because of your faith in my well beloved, who was from the foundation of the world."

—Helaman 2:112

Sometimes we put tasks off until later; but we learn that blessings come from timely obedience. We learn to trust that "still, small voice," the Spirit that leads us to do good…now!

Our friend had just had surgery. She had three small boys and could not work. Not only was she too proud to ask for help, she would avoid accepting help whenever possible.

My husband was preparing to do a monologue presentation of Joseph Smith III. I suggested we drop off some food staples for our friend on the way. He mildly protested that we were short of time. He suggested we could go the next day and stay longer to visit.

I told him I was sure we should go now—that our friend needed us. He agreed to stop. Perhaps that is one of the greatest strengths of our marriage; we each value and respect the other's spiritual insights.

We drove to her house, and I jumped out to leave the food, barely greeting her. She thanked me, admitting the cupboards were bare.

We continued to church and arrived just in time. It was an outstanding service. My husband captivated me by his portrayal of the historical figure.

I was unaware of the unpredictable April weather outside. When we left the church, we saw the ground was covered by a sheet of ice. We made our way to the car and said, almost at the same time, that we were glad we had taken the food before the service.

Why? Our friend lived on a steep hill, and we did not have snow tires. We felt blessed that we made the choice to go when we did.

Prayer for Peace

Whispering God, we hear you. You lead by your peaceful, loving voice. Let us not hesitate to follow you when you call.

Spiritual Practice: Making Responsible Choices

Prayerfully seek God's guidance in your choices. Discernment invites us to orient our lives toward God and God's vision for us and creation. Begin by reviewing the responsibilities and opportunities in the day before you. Take these choices into prayer, asking God for wisdom and insight about what matters most.

Peace Covenant

Today, God, I will listen and respond by sharing Christ's peace where it's needed.

9
Tuesday
April

Fear Not!

By Gwen Simpson of Lamoni, Iowa, USA

> *. . . do not fear, for I am with you, do not be afraid, for I am your God; I will strengthen you, I will help you. . .*
>
> —Isaiah 41:10

"Fear not!" The message of assurance given throughout the Christmas story speaks often to my life, not just at Christmas, but throughout the year.

Our oldest granddaughter turned 13 last week. As we celebrated with her I recalled when she was 2. We lived in another state and went to visit Tori and her new baby sister, Addy. Tori was at an age of exploration, but also at an age when new experiences and new people could seem a bit scary. She invited me to go outside and see her new swing set.

We climbed down the back stairs and were about to step into the yard when I hesitated. I was looking with delight at the new signs of spring. Tori, not knowing why I stopped, thought I might be afraid because I wasn't on my home turf. "It's OK Grandma Gwennie, take my hand," she assured me as she reached up and took my hand in her small one.

In the voice of this small child, God spoke to me. Tori couldn't know of our coming move from the big city to a small town in Iowa or the multitude of transitions and uncertainties facing my life—but God did.

"Fear not, Gwen." This scripture passage became personal for me. Fill in the blank for yourself: "Fear not, ________________."

Prayer for Peace

Gentle Shepherd, we feel you with us in our times of fear. We learn from children the meaning of trust. May we learn to trust as they do. May we learn to trust in and share the peace of Christ.

Spiritual Practice: Listening to Children

Sit in your quiet place and center your heart and mind on God's presence. Spend several minutes asking God to bring into your awareness the names and images of children in your life. You may see their faces or hear their voices as you receive these impressions. Listen deeply to the unique gifts and needs of the children who come to mind. Offer a prayer of blessing for each child and the needs you perceive. If you feel led, you also may want to write a note or card and give a message of affirmation and love to each child.

Peace Covenant

Today, God, I will put my name into your scriptures, that they will be personal to me.

10
Wednesday
April

Disciples Grow in Love

By Robert Glenn of Evansville, Indiana, USA

How precious is your steadfast love, O God! All people may take refuge in the shadow of your wings. They feast on the abundance of your house, and you give them drink from the river of your delights. For with you is the fountain of life; in your light we see light.

—Psalm 36:7–9

When a baby is born into a family, we can see a change in the dynamics of that family from the viewpoints of parents, siblings, grandparents, and extended family. Babies are a blessing from God; they embody divine love and grace. God creates us so we might have joy.

This joy expresses itself in many ways over time. We see it when we witness the growth of the child through adolescence, young adulthood, and continuing formation as an adult. When we reach our older years, we may have witnessed this many times, often with new eyes.

The love shared between family members and God is beautiful. I have witnessed the effect children have and the blessing they are to many families. I also have found that people become bruised and broken when families do not grow with one another.

How sad it is when we do not fully embrace and share the love of God.

The examples of Jesus and the way he lived his life help us connect and understand God's love. We can rejoice in God's love when relationships are reestablished.

Prayer for Peace

Steadfast and loving God, we take refuge in your love and the love of our families. Where families are broken, may we bring healing and reconciliation. Where there are rifts, may we build bridges. Where there is loneliness, may we share God's love. Where there is anger, let us share the peace of Jesus Christ.

Spiritual Practice: Develop Disciples to Serve

Read and reflect on Psalm 42:1–2. As disciples of Jesus Christ, we are called to respond to people and their needs. The call to journey inward can restore us in times of physical or spiritual depletion. Imagine you can feel a vessel at the center of your being (a clay jar, a crystal vase, a metal bucket, or other container). Imagine drawing something from the vessel to share with another person, but as you reach inside you find only a tiny pool of stagnant liquid. You are thirsty and dry; empty. Listen prayerfully again to the psalm, "As a deer longs for flowing streams, so my soul longs for you, O God. My soul thirsts for God, for the living God." As you feel restored, thank God for the opportunity to be a responding, serving disciple while you move into the outward journey. Remember this exercise as you drink water throughout the day.

Peace Covenant

Today, God, I will look for ways to build bridges with your love.

11
Thursday
April

Invasion of Love: Transformation Journey (Part 1)

By Nancy Hylton of Seattle, Washington, USA

Be merciful, just as your Father is merciful.

—Luke 6:36

I made an unexpected journey early one morning on our island campgrounds.

My heart was heavy for a friend who felt she could never claim salvation because of the life she once lived. I wanted so much for her to understand the depth of divine grace, forgiveness, and love so she might live in hope, rather than despair.

As I stood on the shore, the first rays of sunrise shimmered across the waves. I took in the beauty and listened to the water lapping against the rocks.

Slowly, at first, a transformation began to take place around me. I sensed the light of the sunrise engulfing me, taking weight from my body. I am sure I was still standing, but I did not feel connected to the beach.

The experience continued ever deeper into the light, until I lost sight of everything else around me. I felt completely safe, loved beyond imagination, at peace with creation and myself.

As the journey continued around me and through me, a sense of well-being permeated my soul. I had never felt this before (or in the same way since). I soon became aware I was in a vast ocean of love, which simultaneously touched every fiber, molecule, and atom of who I was.

Quietly, I returned to the shore, listening to the water rush over the stones, watching the sun make the water sparkle. How does one respond to such an invasion of love?

I said, "Thank you," which was inadequate, yet necessary! Next, I questioned, "What do you want me to do with this experience, Lord? Why was I blessed with such a gift? Why here? Why now?" I knew I needed to share this with my heavy-hearted friend. Could this be her hope?

Prayer for Peace

God who touches Earth with beauty, may our hearts be open to your grace. May we never doubt your love and understanding. May we never doubt we have Christ's peace to share with those who are burdened.

Spiritual Practice: Flowing Water

If possible, sit where you can hear the sound of water—a fountain, stream, the sea, (perhaps a CD of water sounds). Listen to the sound as you thank God for the life-giving, life-shaping power of water. Pray for God's blessing on all the parched places of the Earth where there is injustice, oppression, violence, and disregard for life. Pray for God's justice to be released and imagine it flowing over the Earth, restoring righteousness and wholeness. Now, get up and drink a glass of clear, cold water as you pray, "God, let your justice flow through me as a disciple of Christ Jesus."

Peace Covenant

Today, God, I will watch and listen to your creation.

12
Friday
April

Surrender to Love: Transformation Journey (Part 2)

By Nancy Hylton of Seattle, Washington, USA

I lift up my eyes to the hills—from where will my help come? My help comes from the Lord, who made heaven and earth.

—Psalm 121:1–2

As I walked quietly toward the main campground, I heard the forest awakening around me. A family of bald eagles was out for a morning ride on thermal streams above the camp. At first they were close enough that I could see their powerful wings, holding weight against the air—I could see them lift with subtle but powerful precision.

Higher and higher they circled into the clouds, until they disappeared. Yet, I knew those eagle eyes could easily see me! Another gift—gifts upon gifts. My heart overflowed like the psalmist's.

I was there for a women's retreat, which was coming to a close. It was time for the final meal. A good friend walked up to me and directed my attention toward the woman whose burdens I carried on my heart. "You need to talk with her," my friend said gently. "I know…thank you," I replied, praying, "Lord, I know you have this handled, just show me what to do."

I smiled and asked permission to sit down across from my burdened friend. Neither of us ate much, but our presence continued with little awareness of what was happening around us. I was prompted to tell her how troubled I was about her sense that she could not ask for or expect forgiveness from God.

Finally, almost in desperation, I knew the transformation experience on the beach that morning was meant to be shared with *her*. I told her what happened; that I felt as if in an *ocean of love* with every fiber of my being! I told her, "A God that loves like that, does not condemn anyone who turns to and seeks the Divine with a broken heart."

We embraced as the retreat closed. I hoped I could help open a small pathway toward healing. I hoped I was an instrument of God's love and acceptance. For my part, the experience on the beach that morning changed my life forever. I continue to feel God's infinite love washing over me. I know my Redeemer lives, and I am called to struggle with others who seek his love.

Prayer for Peace

God who permeates the world with love, grow love in us that we might share. Grow healing and peace in us that we may change lives.

Spiritual Practice: Chalice Prayer

The chalice prayer is a form of intercession. Create a cup or chalice with your hands in front of your heart. Open your heart to God's concern for the human family as you hold them in your chalice. See beauty and suffering as you lift the chalice and release hurting persons (open hands) to be blessed and healed by God.

Peace Covenant

Today, God, I will wash in your ocean of healing love.

13
Saturday
April

He Is with Us!

By Michelle Booth of Grain Valley, Missouri, USA

While they were talking and discussing, Jesus himself came near and went with them, but their eyes were kept from recognizing him…When he was at the table with them, he took bread, blessed and broke it, and gave it to them. Then their eyes were opened, and they recognized him; and he vanished from their sight.

—Luke 24:15–16, 30–31

One morning driving to the office, I felt our team's meeting weighing on my mind. I was bringing our lectionary reflection that morning and was stepping a little out of my comfort zone.

The scripture passage that morning was from Luke 24:15–16, 30–31, the story of two disciples walking the road to Emmaus. Jesus joins them along their journey and they begin to talk with him but do not recognize him. As they near the village they invite him to stay and eat with them. As Jesus breaks the bread and gives it to them they suddenly recognize him. Just as quickly as they recognize him, Jesus disappears.

This scripture reminds me of another drive to work. My car radio, tuned to my favorite Christian station, connected the Emmaus story to the modern day.

A woman working at a pharmacy counter got a phone call from her husband. He was in the military and called to tell her they were sending him to Iraq. He gave her a long list of supplies he would need. She started to cry, telling him they had only US$20 in their bank account.

Another woman was at the counter, waiting to pick up her prescription. When the pharmacy clerk hung up the customer said, "I'll be right back." She returned about 30 minutes later with all the supplies the woman's husband needed, plus more. She told the woman other soldiers would need these. She then handed the woman some cash for postage. The clerk knew that customer was the hands and feet of Jesus that day!

Christ is ALIVE! I know he walks with me on my journey. Sometimes I see him, sometimes I don't. However, I know he's always with me.

Prayer for Peace

Ever-present God, may we be the hands of Christ. May we share from our bounty, and even from our shallow bowl. May we share the peace of Jesus Christ.

Spiritual Practice: Generosity and Discipleship

Bring a basket or other container to your place of prayer. Meditate on the link between generosity and discipleship. Write a prayer of commitment in which you name specific acts of generosity and sharing to which you feel called. Fold the paper and place the prayer in the offering container. Close by singing a hymn of gratitude or praise as you offer your gift to God.

Peace Covenant

I will keep my eyes open, God, and recognize Jesus in the stranger.

14
Sunday
April

Be God's Instrument

By Richard James, Council of Twelve Apostles

> *But the Lord said to him, "Go, for he [Paul] is an instrument whom I have chosen to bring my name before Gentiles and kings and before the people of Israel; I myself will show him how much he must suffer for the sake of my name."*
>
> —Acts 9:15–16

I remember as a 14-year-old boy wanting to learn to play the guitar. It was difficult because our family budget did not allow for any private tutoring. It was hard even to know how to tune the guitar. However, I wished to play in church, so I found a basic guitar book. Through a slow, often-painful struggle I played a few chords.

Then someone asked me to play in Sunday school. I was not competent, but with encouragement and much practice, I agreed to play. I had the urge to use my giftedness to help in God's work. I said, "Here I am, Lord," and in that prayer I found a confidence that God would use me, and God did!

In my life as a disciple of the risen Christ I have found that responding in similar ways with "Here I am, Lord" opens doors that did not seem possible. I make myself available for God to use me, not dictating time and place, but just being available. It is in those moments that God uses me as an instrument, and the witness of the risen Christ becomes real. I know the presence of God transforms lives. God touches people in that moment, and in that moment, they reflect on the experience of God's grace.

I recall this past summer, when I preached at a reunion. I had prepared, and knew what I wanted to say. Before the service, those words were taken from my mind, and I sensed the invitation of the Spirit to wrestle with what God wanted me to say. The result was a powerful witness of Christ calling and challenging the people to a renewed understanding of discipleship in Community of Christ.

People reconciled with one another; others accepted the challenge to reengage with the church. People committed themselves to Christ.

When we open ourselves to God and witness of the risen Christ, the power and presence of the Holy Spirit is evident. God opens doors. Christ is risen. He is risen indeed!

Prayer for Peace

Great Composer, gather your disciples, with their countless gifts. May our eyes focus on Christ for our direction. May our hearts listen to your Spirit for the movement of life. May we tune our instruments to play in harmony and peace with one another.

Spiritual Practice: Examining God's Call to Me and All

Reflect on God's call in your life. Begin by prayerfully asking to recall particular moments when you have experienced God's presence and invitation. When has God seemed most real in your life? How and when has God called you to use your energies and gifts? When have you felt most deeply connected and responsive to God's movement in your life? When have you felt disconnected or resistant to God's call? How do your gifts and callings connect with the call of God you notice in your family, friends, congregation, or community?

Peace Covenant

Today, God, I will have my gifts tuned and ready for your call.

15
Monday
April

♫ Hymn of the Month: "Can Steel and Stone and Swirling Spire"

By Danny Belrose of Independence, Missouri, USA

> *The Temple is an instrument of ongoing revelation...Let the Temple continue to come to life...the Temple calls the entire church to become a sanctuary of Christ's peace, where people from all nations, ethnicities, and life circumstances can be gathered into a spiritual home without dividing walls, as a fulfillment of the vision for which Jesus Christ sacrificed his life.*
>
> —Doctrine and Covenants163:8a–c

I composed "Can Steel and Stone and Swirling Spire" in response to two phrases in Doctrine and Covenants, Section 163:8a–b: "The Temple is an instrument of ongoing revelation" and "Let the Temple continue to come to life."

Winston Churchill said that we shape our buildings, and ever after they shape us. In other words, the test for every church sanctuary, every sacred space, every worship and educational activity is praxis! (Praxis is a recurring process of transformative action and reflection.)

The Temple is more than an architectural marvel of swirling stone, steel, and glass; its ministries flow outward, extending far beyond its fixed physical footprint. The Temple serves to bless *not* simply those who gather within its walls but also (and, perhaps primarily) those who may never enter its doors.

The hymn text reminds us the Temple "*comes alive in us*" whenever the dining room table, the office desk, and the workbench become extensions of the Communion table.

Can steel and stone and swirling spire
Though planted in some distant place
Become God's blessing to all nations—
The lost, the labeled, and displaced?

Can they who never see its form
Find solace in such sacred space?
Can ministries of living water
Flow far beyond its resting place?

God's temple comes alive in us—
In every nation, tribe, and home
It lives and breathes in every soul
That seeks the peace of God's shalom.

Prayer for Peace

Outreaching God, may we carry the ministries of the Temple far and wide. May our journey outward come from a place of inner strength. May we share the peace of Jesus Christ in our homes, our congregations, our communities, and the Temple—out to the world.

Spiritual Practice

Contemplate this hymn as a poem (or sing with the ST. CLEMENT tune).

16
Tuesday
April

God-centered

By John Bonney of Springfield, Oregon, USA

When your willingness to live in sacred community as Christ's new creation exceeds your natural fear of spiritual and relational transformation, you will become who you are called to be.

—Doctrine and Covenants164:9b

My wife had laparoscopic surgery. The nerve involved was highly displeased. Injured nerves are said to be "hot." A hot nerve does not simply settle down after the trauma is over. It takes nerves a long time to cool, perhaps months.

When my wife came home from the hospital, I told her how difficult it was for me to see a loved one suffer and not be able to do anything about it. Suffering from pain, she was a bit prickly. She said, in no uncertain terms, "It's always about *you*!"

I thought about that, and realized that, of course, it's about me. How else can I relate to what goes on around me? Everything in my life is about me. I look out at the world from me, the center. For good or ill, we each are the center of our own universe. We can demur all we want, and make an effort not to focus on ourselves or from ourselves, but it's a lost cause.

We are trapped within our mind and body, and we relate to the world from our perspectives. Yes, we are vain, and we are self-centered or centered on and from ourselves.

We *can* reach a useful balance. Selflessness is fine and should be practiced and understood. But when we are selfless, we are still in relation with ourselves—that's who we are.

The moments when I have not focused on myself have been few. When I move away from self-centeredness, I find I am in contact with the Eternal. I am no longer an individual noodle, but find myself realizing I am part of a pot full of noodles.

The result is a disappearance of rigidity—psychological, emotional, physical, mental rigidity. In my experience there is a blending from one with all, and all with the One. At these times I find I am not the center, and it's not about me.

It's about what matters most. It's about God, Jesus Christ, the Holy Spirit—the eternal community—and how I can share this with others.

Prayer for Peace

Ever-creating God, give us courage to let go of ourselves so we may grow closer to you. May we be at peace with who we are.

Spiritual Practice: Honoring the Worth of All Persons

Read Psalm 139:13–18. After each reading sit quietly and let the words sink deeply into your mind, heart, and body. Imagine God watching you grow in your mother's womb. What thoughts and feelings do you have about being "fearfully and wonderfully made" (Psalm 139:14)?

Sense God's intimate knowledge of you and every child. Be aware of the sacred worth of each person. Weep with God over the soul-wounding forces that rob people of dignity and worth. How are you invited to notice, protect, heal, and affirm the spiritual identity of all God's beloved people today? Pray for God's compassion.

Peace Covenant

Today, God, I will not fear my spiritual, God-centered self.

17
Wednesday
April

...Yet Another Journey

By Sue Holloway of Murfreesboro, Tennessee, USA

The salvation of the righteous is from the Lord; he is their refuge in the time of trouble. The Lord helps them and rescues them...and saves them, because they take refuge in him.

—Psalm 37:39–40

The doctor said if I had to have cancer, breast cancer was the best type to have. It was operable, and I would not need a full mastectomy. Still I was devastated. What if the lumpectomy and recommended "targeted radiation" did not work and I needed a full mastectomy? I had too many "what ifs..."

I knew God would help me with whatever was on my plate, but still I feared. Prayer requests were going to be the order of the day. My husband, Jim, and many of his co-workers through their prayer network were helpful with this, as were my former co-workers and members of our church family.

My doctor scheduled the surgery, and three days later the pathology reports showed no other cancer present. The next day I went and had a scan to be sure the balloon was in place and the targeted radiation would work. Bad news struck again. There was a problem with the balloon, and the doctor would have to remove it.

The radiologist said to me, "We can wait a few weeks and try again, or we can schedule the regular six to seven weeks of radiation." I said, "Let's try again." Again we sent out prayer requests across the country. The doctor installed the second balloon and did a scan, which showed no problems. I completed my last radiation treatment and was declared *cancer free.*

All I could do was fall on my knees and praise God. I know our prayers are not always answered the way we want. But this is an answer I wanted to share. God has seen me through yet another journey.

Prayer for Peace

Healing God, we are aware of your presence on the journeys of our lives. We travel knowing you are with us in the high places and in the low. We call on you when we need your rescuing love. Thank you, God, for our place in your refuge, for our place in your ever-expanding arms of grace, and for your strength so freely shared. May we respond by freely sharing the peace of Christ.

Spiritual Practice: Time with God

Sit quietly and let your breathing become calm and deep. Ask God's Spirit to rest on you. See or sense the Spirit anointing you in the form of light, a dove, wind, color, or other images that might come. Ask to be made aware of God's love. Listen to the ways in which God wants to flow from your heart as living water. Give thanks that your name is "beloved," that our name is Community of Christ.

Peace Covenant

Today, God, I will travel with one who is in a low place, sharing your comfort along the way.

18
Thursday
April

Beyond the Clouds

By Dorene Kilburn of Stratford, Ontario, Canada

Now the eleven disciples went to Galilee, to the mountain to which Jesus had directed them. When they saw him, they worshiped him; but some doubted. And Jesus came and said to them, "All authority in heaven and on earth has been given to me. Go therefore and make disciples of all nations, baptizing them in the name of the Father and of the Son and of the Holy Spirit, and teaching them to obey everything that I have commanded you. And remember, I am with you always, to the end of the age."

—Matthew 28:16–20

Two companions and I planned to attend World Conference in 1950. It was a long way from Ontario, Canada, so we decided to fly. It was our first time in an airplane, and we were a little apprehensive.

On the day of the flight the sky was overcast, and it was bitter cold. When we got to the airport, ominous clouds covered the sky. It looked as if we could soon be in the middle of a snowstorm...and then we were! We boarded the plane, settled in our seats, and waited nervously. The weather couldn't be much worse.

After a long time, the pilot announced we were about to take off. We soared through the clouds, and to our amazement, the plane burst through into a blue sky! The clouds were a billowy blanket below us, and the sun was shining.

If we allow ourselves to be enveloped by God's Spirit, we will find that beyond the "dark and cloudy" days we experience from time to time, there is a brighter day waiting. God will guide us through discouragement and loneliness and will place in our path someone who is sensitive to our needs. Someone who will bring us the love and support Jesus showed will be there to lift us above the dark clouds. Each day, may we look hopefully to the promise that God is with us always.

Prayer for Peace

Creator God, lift us to where we can feel the warmth of your light. We know you are there, but sometimes we can't see you. To the end of the age, may we share the peace of Jesus Christ.

Spiritual Practice: Light

Close your eyes, and become centered with your breath. Reflect on the statement: "The light of God is in all things," as you breathe gently in and out. Sense or see a point of light in the distance, coming gradually toward you. With each breath it comes closer, growing in size and brightness. The light has a bright, soft beauty and radiates loving peace. The light of God reaches you and permeates you with a deep sense of peace. Rest in the light as it surrounds and fills you. Thank God that you live in God's light, and it lives in you.

Peace Covenant

Today, God, I will not doubt you are with me.

19
Friday
April

I'm Going Down

By Sara Parkin of Midland, Michigan, USA

> *Collectively and individually, you are loved with an everlasting love that delights in each faithful step taken. God yearns to draw you close so that wounds may be healed, emptiness filled, and hope strengthened...*
>
> —Doctrine and Covenants163:10

(Part 2 of My Journey with Alzheimer's Disease)

When my doctor told me I had Alzheimer's disease, I thought, "I'm going down. My life will be over." I am a retired nurse who started as a nurse's aide in a nursing home. After getting my degree, I became a registered nurse at a hospital. Last, I was a caregiver in people's homes.

As a nurse, there were times I would sit with my patients to listen to their fears and joys, crying or laughing with them. Sometimes I would hold a hand as they left this life.

I am scared because I have cared for many patients who had different forms of dementia. (Alzheimer's is one form.) I always knew I would die someday, but not so soon. I am 67 years old; but my Mom is 90. It's too early for me! I will not be able to do the things I have put off, because I'm going down.

I remember my patients had goals, thoughts, and emotions just like me. I know what it is going to do to me and my family. I am the patient now, and I don't like it. My thinking was, "I'm going down. I don't have a choice. I can't do anything. I'm going down."

Then one day, something happened. Words came into my mind. "Sara, you are alive, and still able to do some things. So go get up and do them! You are not alone."

There *are* many things I can do—alone or with others. Even those days when I'm feeling down, I can remember I am alive. I can cry. I can yell. I can laugh, or dance, or sing aloud. I can still connect with my family, friends, and others I meet. We can talk and share our stories. I know the Divine will be with me, even when the time comes when I no longer remember it.

Maybe you are like me. I have gifts I can continue to use for now. I have a chance to do some things I want to do but had been putting off. It is amazing how God walks with us and never leaves us alone.

Prayer for Peace

Healing God, draw us close. Fill our emptiness. Strengthen our hope. We thank you for walking with us. We thank you for friends who help us share Christ's peace.

Spiritual Practice: An Offering of Ashes

God promises healing for our wounds and losses. Hold (or imagine holding) a pinch of ashes in your hands as you become aware of situations in your life, family, congregation, and world that are broken, lost, or falling apart. Be honest with God about the fear, sadness, or burden you feel. Offer the ashes to God in prayer. Ask God to create beauty, peace, and healing in the places and people who now experience the ashes of despair and grief.

Peace Covenant

Today, God, I will get out of my chair and do what matters most.

20
Saturday
April

Reduce→Reuse→Recycle

By Candy Brayton of Independence, Missouri, USA

The earth is full, and there is enough and to spare; yea, I prepared all things, and have given unto the children of the earth to be agents unto themselves.

—Doctrine and Covenants 101:2f, adapted

"Reduce-Reuse-Recycle" was the caption on a thermal mug I brought home from college. Mom loved it, and I ended up buying one for her. In the years after, she would joke about how she was "green" before it became trendy.

Mom devoted herself to teaching children about Jesus. Her chosen medium was handicrafts, using repurposed materials—one person's trash was Mom's treasure. I remember washing hundreds of plastic Communion cups and then burning holes in the bottoms with a hot roofing nail.

Colored with permanent markers and strung on scrap yarn, they became unique wind chimes in children's hands. The repurposed cups became a reminder of the story of the Last Supper and the sacrament of Communion.

Mom would use scrap felt and fabric to create flannel-graph stories and worship centers. Partly burnt wooden matches became crosses to hang on a wall. Coffee cans, cigar boxes, potato chip cans, rolled oats box cylinders, concentrated juice cans, egg cartons, and more—were all fair game.

In truth, Mom was "green" by necessity. Church school, vacation Bible school, and camp budgets were always tight. She would search for ideas and supplies while contributing modest dollars from her own funds. Her passionate prayers for ministry to the children always led her to needed supplies.

Mom learned through trial and error, without the benefit of "how to" books. Many congregations today have multiple resources available that Mom didn't have. Take the time and care to utilize "garbage gems."

Recycling and repurposing materials is a fun way to teach children of all ages the stories of Jesus' love. Recycling connects us to two Enduring Principles: Sacredness of Creation and Responsible Choices. God bless you in your generous ministry.

Prayer for Peace

Creator God, we know a shortage of resources often causes disputes. May we be good stewards of all we use as our discipleship reflects the peace and justice of Christ.

Spiritual Practice: Making Responsible Choices

Prayerfully seek God's guidance in your choices. Discernment invites us to orient our lives toward God and God's vision for us and creation. Begin by reviewing the responsibilities and opportunities in the day before you. Take these choices into prayer, asking God for wisdom and insight about what matters most. Be aware of images, thoughts, names, or actions that come to you. Ask for a blessing to live this day responsibly and compassionately in the spirit of Christ.

Peace Covenant

Today, God, I will leave a small footprint on the Earth, which will have a large, positive impact on the environment.

21
Sunday
April

Alive in the Lord

By Ron Harmon, Council of Twelve Apostles

> *Now in Joppa there was a disciple whose name was Tabitha, which in Greek is Dorcas. She was devoted to good works and acts of charity. At that time she became ill and died…They laid her in a room upstairs…Peter…knelt down and prayed. He turned to the body and said, "Tabitha, get up." Then she opened her eyes…*
>
> —Acts 9:36–37, 40–41

The sun set as we gathered around the fire after a full day at camp. I was thinking ahead to the soft pillow and bed that awaited me in the lodge.

I was not prepared for what I was about to experience.

John was a new member of the church I had met earlier in the day in my class. When I asked the class members to share something we might not know about them, John shared his life journey and experience with Christ through a small Community of Christ congregation.

John's story was raw, difficult to hear at times, yet powerful. He experienced God's love through a genuine and caring community. His life was different as a result. He shared his story with intensity and delight as he described the radical change in his life. Images of John's story flashed through my mind as he began to play an old, worn guitar before the beginning of campfire.

At first I was taken aback by the harsh sound of strange chords and off-key, impromptu singing. He was making the words up as he went. I could not recognize the words, but the joy in his voice moved me. As people gathered for the campfire he continued to sing. It was as if no one noticed he was singing out of tune.

Here was a man who was alive in Christ and at home with his surroundings. The community that welcomed him continued to affirm his place among them. Like Tabitha in Acts 9, John often had found himself on the margins of society. This was his experience in a world that often does not recognize the possibilities of new life. I smiled inside the next day when I heard John playing and singing a new song of joy and hope.

Prayer for Peace

Ever-present God, we are alive in Christ. We become new through your Spirit. We are fulfilled in doing Christ's mission and sharing his peace.

Spiritual Practice: Music for Meditation

Identify a form of music for meditation. Choose music that carries a soulful, spiritual, or healing quality for you. Sit quietly and soak in the intent of the composer. Allow healing waves of sound to lift your spirit.

Peace Covenant

Today, God, I will listen to the heart of the singer and not-so-much the song.

22
Monday
April

"Turn Off the Water, Mom!"

By Janné Grover of Lee's Summit, Missouri, USA

> *The earth, lovingly created as an environment for life to flourish, shudders in distress because creation's natural and living systems are becoming exhausted from carrying the burden of human greed and conflict. Humankind must awaken from its illusion of independence and unrestrained consumption without lasting consequences.*
>
> —Doctrine and Covenants 163:4b

On a walk through the nearby park on a sunny day, I was struck by the awesomeness of God's creation. I stopped and took a 360-degree view. I saw sunlight streaming through the colors of changing foliage. Squirrels were running and jumping between trees. I saw a fuzzy caterpillar crossing the path, birds in flight, and clusters of delicate, white wildflowers. I was filled with a sense of God's presence. I paused for a few moments to soak it in and praise God for the gift of life and the fullness of creation.

As I continued on my walk, my thoughts of praise turned to disappointment as I saw trash lying on the path. I wondered why some people are so irresponsible. I shook my head with a sense of satisfaction, knowing I would not litter.

How self-righteous of me! I began to realize I have the luxury of deciding how I care for and use the natural resources at my disposal. Sure, I do what I can to recycle and practice environmental friendliness. However, everything I do still allows me certain conveniences, and nothing I do moves me beyond what is easy and comfortable. I know when I turn on the faucet that I will have clean water. And if I choose, I can spend as much time as I want in a hot shower—carelessly wasting water.

One Community of Christ Enduring Principle is Sacredness of Creation. I am thankful we live in a time when there is increasing awareness of pollution. Local and global efforts are made to become better stewards of our natural resources. I am pleased my kids are learning good practices at school and at church and are holding me accountable for letting the water run too long.

I now pick up trash on my walk instead of shaking my head in frustration and judgment of the carelessness of others. It may not make a huge difference in the global picture, but planting small seeds of change can lead to good effects for all creation.

Prayer for Peace

Creator of Earth, may we show gratitude for this life-giving planet by how we care for it. Help us end conflict and greed that destroy habitats. Lead us in the way to share Christ's peace.

Spiritual Practice: Caring for God's Sacred Creation

Choose a way to notice, give thanks, and care for God's sacred creation. Prayerfully consider one of the following practices or create your own. Walk in nature with a spirit of gratitude while looking and listening for God in all things. Write or pray a psalm of praise for the Earth's beauty or a prayer of healing and blessing for its wounds. Give thanks.

Peace Covenant

Today, God, I will turn off the water and leave more to share.

23
Tuesday
April

A Handful of Earth

By Peggy Michael of Cantonment, Florida, USA

For in him all the fullness of God was pleased to dwell, and through him God was pleased to reconcile to himself all things, whether on earth or in heaven, by making peace through the blood of his cross.

—Colossians 1:19–20

How briefly gates and fences
measure the plot of land
where I toil and pray.
Who tilled this ground before I came?
Will we meet someday and
discuss our stewardship over it?
Sometimes I talk to God
about the tenants
who have worked this soil,
coaxing their daily bread from it.
As I kneel among the peas and cabbages,
I thank God for lending
this scrap of good earth to me
for a few seasons.
I dig and plant and
ask God to bless it for me
and for future generations
that will toil, plant, and pray
where I now stand.

Yes, this is the promised land.
Promised to a people
willing to toil and trust,
plow and pray,
and subdue the nurturing earth.
Teach us that we
must harness the passions that
threaten to consume all nations.
How long will pride and greed
rule the helpless
and rob generations
of their rightful heritage?
O, God of mercy,
starting with this land—
subdue us, refine us,
and mold us into a people
willing to give themselves
to the greatest cause of the ages—
the right of a future.

Prayer for Peace

Creator God, bless us with a determination to be stewards of your Earth— keepers of the soil and protectors of the plants and trees. Curb our consumerism and greed. Enable us to live lives that honor the sacredness of your creation.

Spiritual Practice: Weeding the Garden

Inner transformation can take place amid daily activities and work. Try cultivating the spiritual discipline of grace and acceptance while weeding the garden. As you pull each weed, offer a short prayer. Tug. (*God remove from my heart all prejudice and fear.*) Tug again. (*God, keep me from making unjust judgments.*) As you remove the weeds, continue praying. (*Plant in my heart the seeds of your love.*) If you don't have a garden, try this kind of prayer while engaging in repetitive activities or work today (cleaning out a closet, washing dishes, cleaning the floors, mowing the lawn).

Peace Covenant

Today God, I will remember that if I can't reuse it or recycle it, I might not need it in the first place.

24
Wednesday
April

Rooted in God

By Carolyn Brock of Redmond, Oregon, USA

> *Blessed are those who trust in the Lord, whose trust is the Lord. They shall be like a tree planted by water, sending out its roots by the stream. It shall not fear when heat comes, and its leaves shall stay green; in the year of drought it is not anxious, and it does not cease to bear fruit.*
>
> —Jeremiah 17:7–8

Once in an African desert we came upon a woman digging for water.

Her thin, muscular body was dripping with sweat as she used a large tin can to scoop up soil along a dry riverbed. After hours of hot, strenuous work, she finally found the water.

Tilting her head back, she poured the full can over her head and face, then laughed. The work of going deep into the earth in search of life-giving liquid was forgotten as the water caressed her skin, and she took a long, cool drink.

A deep underground river of Spirit is our source of life and joy. But it is not found merely by tapping into the surface waters. The transformation of the whole self requires digging through layers of ego and fear, illusions and false centers of meaning.

Finding God at our center and choosing Spirit as our integrating identity is work that demands trust and perseverance. It is also the way we discover our thirst for God's touch, God's revitalizing presence.

As a people we have struggled long and hard, digging away at superficial issues—differences in language, names, words, interpretations of doctrines.

Perhaps the real question must become: "Is God's life flowing through us?" Have we dug down to what is essential, the presence of God in our bodies, minds, and spirits? Is that when we shall learn who God would have us become as Community of Christ?

Prayer for Peace

Faithful God, we trust in you. We seek your living water. We will share Christ's peace.

Spiritual Practice: Deepening Roots

A tree with superficial roots will wither during drought or be uprooted by severe storms. A tree whose roots go deep is stable and draws from deep waters. Imagine yourself as a tree by a river or stream. Sense your roots extending deep into the earth in search of God's Spirit. Reflect or pray about what you hope to find as your spirit searches for deeper identity in God.

Peace Covenant

Today, God, I will dig deep to find the disciple you would have me be.

25
Thursday
April

Heads Up!

By Art Smith of Independence, Missouri, USA

> *Peace I leave with you; my peace I give to you. I do not give to you as the world gives. Do not let your hearts be troubled, and do not let them be afraid.*
>
> —John 14:27

On my first scuba dive in Cartagena, Colombia, with my friend, Erv, a new portion of God's creation opened before my eyes. But a big part of scuba for me was about overcoming fear. You have to calm down, keep your wits about you, manage the pressure in your ears and your lungs, watch your gauges, and remember to breathe slowly and steadily.

After I'd gotten familiar with the gear in just a few feet of water, Erv led us out a little deeper. I was following her closely, not so much watching sea life as the ends of Erv's flippers. I started to feel a little more comfortable. There came a moment when I watched Erv double back behind me, apparently checking on another diver. I'd become comfortable enough that I actually let her out of my sight.

A moment later I glanced over my shoulder. Erv wasn't there. Nobody was there! I looked over my other shoulder. No Erv! Nobody! I felt my heart start to race and my breathing increase. I maneuvered my flippers, legs, and arms to spin my body around, doing a full 360-degree turn. Still no Erv! I started to panic.

In the world where I normally walk, if someone I'm following ducks away for a moment, a quick check over the left or right shoulder or turning completely around is sure to bring them back into sight. But the underwater world is different.

It *finally* dawned on me to look up. In a startling moment I discovered Erv and the others hovering right above my head. I couldn't help but think about how this experience is like my walk with God. How easy it is to become frightened and feel abandoned when all the while God is so close that—if I'm not careful—we could bump heads.

Prayer for Peace

Ever-present God, when we feel we have lost sight of you, help us remember you are in every dimension of our lives. Just because we don't find you where we think you should be, may we be aware of your permeating presence over, under, around, and within us. May Christ's Spirit permeate us as we share his peace.

Spiritual Practice: Flowing Water

If possible, sit where you can hear the sound of water—a fountain, stream, the sea, (perhaps a CD of water sounds). Listen to the sound as you thank God for the life-giving, life-shaping power of water. Pray for God's blessing on all the parched places of the Earth where there is injustice, oppression, violence, and disregard for life. Pray for those who cannot find God. Now, get up and drink a glass of clear, cold water as you pray, "God, let your presence flow through me as a disciple of Christ Jesus."

Peace Covenant

Today, God, I will see your creation with new, all-encompassing eyes.

26
Friday
April

Missing Pieces, Missing Peace

By Jeanne Hough of Claire, Michigan, USA

Heed the urgent call to become a global family united in the name of the Christ, committed in love to one another, seeking the kingdom for which you yearn and to which you have always been summoned. That kingdom shall be a peaceable one and it shall be known as Zion.

—Doctrine and Covenants 161:6b

One of my greatest pleasures is to volunteer at our senior center.

My recent project was to sort out donations of myriad jigsaw puzzles. After working a long time, it is frustrating to find pieces are missing, and the project cannot be completed. We search for the missing pieces to no avail. We have to discard that puzzle so others will not repeat that frustration.

Our search for God and the peaceable kingdom also can be puzzling. Our patience wears thin while we search for an answer to prayer. If our closeness and awareness of God's presence is missing, we lack the peace that God's love and assurance can give us, and it is easy to give up the search.

The scriptures assure us that God is with us always. We must patiently and continuously search for assurance to live a life of peace and comfort in connecting with the Divine, in connecting with other kingdom builders, and in continuing to Pursue Peace on Earth.

Prayer for Peace

Mysterious God, we accept that we need to seek your kingdom and to ask questions along the way. May we not grow weary or impatient, but take time to learn what you would have us do; to take time to share the peace of Christ.

Spiritual Practice: Pursue Peace on Earth

Read and reflect on Doctrine and Covenants 161:2a. Reflect on how you can "see violence but *proclaim* peace...*feel* conflict, yet *extend* the hand of reconciliation...*encounter* broken spirits and *find* pathways for healing."

What does the peace of Christ mean to you? Begin by prayerfully listening to your longing for peace. Prayerfully open yourself to God's yearning for peace and the divine vision of shalom. What act of justice or peacemaking does God invite you to pursue this day? Dwell on these words of pursuit: *see, proclaim, feel, extend, encounter, find.*

Peace Covenant

Today, God, I will search for all the pieces for putting together peace.

27
Saturday
April

Cast Your Nets...Mosquito Nets

By Sherri Kirkpatrick of Lee's Summit, Missouri, USA

"When you are in the service of your fellow beings you are only in the service of your God."

—Mosiah 1:49

We were back in Zambia after having the always unpredictable Congo experience. As we crossed the border today, the immigration officials spent an hour poring over our passports and—aha!—they found my passport had not been stamped out when I went into Congo.

What to do? They finally decided the clerk who failed to do the stamping, needed to come fix it. But he was off today. Finally they decided to call him in from home. He ultimately arrived, and after hemming and hawing for another hour we were released!

However, the Wasaidizi health workers were amazing as usual. The doctor from Kaboka came to Lubumbashi to meet with us. He said one of the biggest problems right now is malaria. It is especially deadly for the pregnant women who become anemic and hemorrhage during childbirth. Children under 5, who have no immunity, also suffer. For the cost of US$3, we can buy a mosquito net, and the whole family can sleep under it. I think we have a new project to pursue!

We will visit the Kasompe school tomorrow. They have finished putting new floors in the classrooms and painting the walls inside and out. We understand the parts for the new desks are made but not assembled. Things are moving, albeit slowly. We're eager to meet with the teachers and get an update. Christ's mission, our mission—to Abolish Poverty, End Suffering—continues.

Prayer for Peace

God of grace, keep in front of our eyes the needs of the Earth's people. Keep us ever aware of how we can help. Help us remember this is part of sharing the peace of Christ.

Spiritual Practice: Generous Offerings

Spend time meditating on the act of giving an offering. Begin by asking God for the spirit of generosity. Pray and reflect with these questions: How do I feel when I bring my offering to a worship setting and share it? What deep reasons motivate me to give? What is my best understanding of A Disciple's Generous Response? Considering my financial circumstances, do I feel I am giving to my true capacity? In other words, am I giving the amount I am capable of giving without jeopardizing the needs and well-being of my family? Is God asking me to be more generous? How will I respond?

Peace Covenant

Today, God, I will research where my generosity might do the most good.

28
Sunday
April

Make No Distinction

By Peter Judd of Kansas City, Missouri, USA

The Spirit told me to go with them and not to make a distinction between them and us.

—Acts 11:12

I often have said it would be easier for me if everyone in the church thought and acted like I do and had the same priorities. Although I say this jokingly, I must admit there is much truth in it. I confess that I am much more at ease with like-minded people than with those who are different.

So when my wife, Kris, and I decided to start attending Norton Heights Congregation in northeast Kansas City, Missouri, I quickly realized I was leaving my comfort zone. We started going there because Kris felt a strong call to minister with disadvantaged children. I went along to support her.

Norton Heights was then and still is a diverse congregation. Many people there are different from me in various ways. Educationally and socioeconomically, there are notable differences among the members. They cover a wide range: Some are new Christians, while others have been disciples for decades. Theologically, some are traditional, while others are progressive. In a small congregation, these differences make life interesting.

It has been easy for me to judge the ways and ideas of some to be inferior to mine. Yet whenever this happens I discover ways I am blessed and enriched by those who are different. The "me versus them" gives way to "us," and I am humbled and judged by my thoughts that separate.

Over the years since I started attending Norton Heights I have come a long way in learning not to make distinctions. I have come to love the people of my congregation—not just those who are like me, but every one, no matter how different. We are family. We rejoice together as we become one in Christ.

Prayer for Peace

God of differences, God of common ground, may we bless others as we are blessed by them. May we be aware of the diverse gifts that are brought into your sanctuaries and embrace them for your purpose. May we welcome them and employ them to share Christ's peace.

Spiritual Practice: Welcoming Unity in Diversity

Meditate on Unity in Diversity. Create a large circle with your arms. See and feel the diverse people God invites inside the sanctuary of Christ's peace represented by this circle.

Who is easiest to welcome? Whom do you struggle to include? Confess the dividing walls between you and people too different or "dangerous" to invite into your spiritual home. Ask God to forgive and heal barriers that keep us from loving one another.

Peace Covenant

Today, God, I will be part of the "us" team, working for Christ's mission.

29
Monday
April

Silly Prayer?

By Eustacia Judd of Norwalk, Connecticut, USA

The wilderness and the dry land shall be glad, the desert shall rejoice and blossom; like the crocus it shall blossom abundantly, and rejoice with joy and singing...then the lame shall leap like a deer, and the tongue of the speechless sing for joy.

—Isaiah 35:1–2, 6

"Please God, I know this isn't world peace or anything important, but could I please have a deer in the backyard?"

Even as I prayed I thought it sounded silly. Most people want deer to stay *out* of their yard. But this desperate grandma wanted a deer *in* the yard.

The request stemmed from a promise I had made weeks before. Our 4-year-old granddaughter was coming from Texas to stay with us in Connecticut for three weeks. Her parents were moving into a new home.

When we talked about her visit she was concerned about leaving her parents. To give her something to look forward to I said, "Deer come to our backyard." Later my husband said he hadn't seen a deer in the yard in a while, and I realized I hadn't either. Hopefully our granddaughter would forget my promise.

They flew to Connecticut a few days later. On the way home we stopped at a farm to watch horses and hopefully take her mind off grandma's promise. However, as we pulled into the driveway our excited granddaughter asked, "Are the deer here now?"

There were no deer, nor were there any for the next few days. So, off I went to the feed store to buy deer food. A week passed, and still no deer. I had done everything I could think of, except one. Pray. So I took my request "upstairs."

How blessed and thankful I was when the next morning a doe was eating the food. I woke our granddaughter early, and she went outside and slowly walked toward the deer. She got a lot closer than I ever did. She was thrilled! Every day for the rest of her visit, at least one deer visited our yard for something to eat.

How thankful I am that God hears the silly prayers of grandmas.

Prayer for Peace

We know, listening God, that no prayer is insignificant. Whether for world peace or for a butterfly to land on a flower in our garden, we pray with faith that you will hear. We know prayers are answered in unexpected ways, but our prayers always cause us to grow in understanding of all our blessing. They cause us to grow in our understanding of how to share Christ's peace.

Spiritual Practice: Joy of Gratitude

Stand, if possible, with arms outstretched. Imagine God filling your arms with all that you have: family, friends, and possessions. Hold out your arms until they feel tired. Now, bring your arms across your body. Place your hand over your heart and thank God for the abundance that fills your life. Sit for a time aware of that abundance. Then ask God to help you open your heart in gratitude and share freely with others.

Peace Covenant

Today, God, I will not cast aside a prayer thought, thinking it unworthy.

30
Tuesday
April

A Swarm of Help

By Cindy L. Korf of North Platte, Nebraska, USA

Do not be discouraged. You have not been promised an easy path, but you have been assured that the Spirit that calls you will also accompany you. That Spirit is even now touching alive the souls of those who feel the passion of discipleship burning deeply within. Many others will respond if you are persistent in your witness and diligent in your mission to the world.

—Doctrine and Covenants 162:3a–b

This past spring had been unusually wet, resulting in an unusual mass of mosquitoes and gnats.

One evening when a friend and I were outside, we decided it was unbearable to continue our walk because of the insects swarming over and around us and into any open orifice.

Suddenly, a blue dragonfly zoomed into the swarm of black gnats, scattering them. Another dragonfly joined the first one. And then, a large group of dragonflies was zooming overhead and around us, keeping the black gnats and mosquitoes at bay. My friend and I were able to continue with our walk and visit.

How often problems come swarming around us to a point where we lack the will to continue. We feel defeated. Yet God has not left us alone to face obstacles or difficulties. God's Spirit is present and nearby, ready to help overcome struggles on life's journey.

Prayer for Peace

Ever-present God, your Spirit may come as a rushing wind, tongues of flame, silence, or a swarm of dragonflies. May we be aware of the help that comes from you. Help us accept the mystery of your creation. May we be at peace, knowing you are with us in many ways.

Spiritual Practice: Caring for God's Sacred Creation

Choose a way to notice, give thanks, and care for God's sacred creation. Prayerfully consider one of the following practices or create your own. Walk in nature with a spirit of gratitude while looking and listening for God in all things. Write or pray a psalm of praise for the Earth's beauty or a prayer of healing and blessing for its wounds.

Learn about and engage in an act of Earth-keeping such as recycling, simple living, or fasting from over-consumption of resources. Notice the diversity of the planet's creatures and be gentle to plants, animals, trees, and people! Fall in love with the vast, intricate wonder of God's creation and give thanks.

Peace Covenant

Today, God, I will accept the mystery that you are.

1
Wednesday
May

Looking at Four Elements of Love

By John Bonney of Springfield, Oregon, USA

> *We know that we have passed from death to life because we love one another... We know love by this, that he laid down his life for us—and we ought to lay down our lives for one another.*
>
> —1 John 3:14, 16

For me *love* is the foundation of everything. I gradually recognized that love, however defined, is a noun requiring other words. It is a catalyst to loving action. Love is causal. Love is the flame that ignites the fire. It is the hidden yeast that allows the dough to rise. Love is not just a warm fuzzy feeling toward a limited number of people or a dog; at least not the understanding of love that I pursue.

In the joy and mystery of the journey, I came to know love had to be *unconditional.* If it were not, then it could not fill the role I believe love plays in creation. Unconditional love, divine love, carries only one requisite—there *are* no requirements. We often talk about unconditional love, and then go on to suffocate it by loading it with conditions. There is no place for conditions in God's love.

Each step on my journey to discover love caused me to look closely at the life and ministry of Jesus. I see in Jesus an unusual depth of commitment. He displayed a tremendous depth of love and the highest form of humanity. He gave of himself out of love for others. He put his life on the line for those in need, for those who are vulnerable, in other words—everyone. He embodied *sacrificial* love.

Unconditional, sacrificial, and now *radical.* Again looking at the life of Jesus, I see a love that was radical. Radical in the first century and radical today. It steps over, passes through, and moves beyond all the human-erected barriers. It scares the power structures of society: governments, religious leaders, politicians, the wealthy. Radical love is not the status quo.

The burden carried by *unconditional, sacrificial, radical* love is not yet fitted in place without the catalyst of *vulnerability.* Practicing this love, we become aware of humans in need, troubled, at risk. We see how love can heal as we open our hearts to others. We see compromised ecosystems, the failing Earth. We are prompted into the action of love. Amid this action, we, too, become vulnerable to God's grace-full love.

Prayer for Peace

Your love, God, is hard to put into words. We pray that your love will be the catalyst for us to share the love and peace of Jesus Christ.

Spiritual Practice: Connecting with God as Center

Open yourself to God's presence and share what flows from your heart and mind. Your "communication with God" might include thoughts, questions, feelings, needs, artwork, quotes, or scriptures. Or it might take the form of a prayer, psalm, or poem. What surprises you? How do you feel God's love? What deepens or changes in your relationship with God, Christ, Spirit?

Peace Covenant

"When the power of love overcomes love of power, the world will know peace."

—Jimi Hendrix

2
Thursday
May

Salt and Light

By Peggy Michael of Cantonment, Florida, USA

"You are the salt of the earth; but if salt has lost its taste, how can its saltiness be restored? It is no longer good for anything, but is thrown out and trampled under foot. You are the light of the world. A city built on a hill cannot be hidden. No one after lighting a lamp puts it under the bushel basket, but on the lampstand, and it gives light to all in the house. In the same way, let your light shine before others, so that they may see your good works and give glory to your Father in heaven."

—Matthew 5:13–16

O people of the kingdom,
why do you scatter the congregation
and diminish her strength
in the day of her deliverance?
The world is weary and confused,
consumed by petty hurts and shallow mantras.
Multitudes cry for a righteous plan
and a people who will embody it.
Who will build that city on a hill
that will illuminate
the darkening world?
...Those engaged in Christ's mission.

Prayer for Peace

God, though I am but a tiny wick, I can light a darkened room. So touch the eternal flame to me, O God, and I will ignite another, until all the world is aglow. Until Christ's peace is here for all—because we have shared our light.

—Peggy Michael, adapted

Spiritual Practice: Light

Close your eyes, and become centered with your breath. Reflect on the statement: "The light of God is in all things," as you breathe gently in and out. Sense or see a point of light in the distance coming gradually toward you. With each breath it comes closer, growing in size and brightness. The light has a bright, soft beauty and radiates loving peace. The light of God reaches you and permeates you with a deep sense of peace. Rest in the light as it surrounds and fills you. Thank God that you live in God's light, and it lives in you.

Peace Covenant

Today, God, I will give you the glory for any light I may shine.

3
Friday
May

Nouwen: A Humble Servant

By Dorene Kilburn of Stratford, Ontario, Canada

For the kingdom of God is... righteousness and peace and joy in the Holy Spirit. The one who thus serves Christ is acceptable to God and has human approval.

—Romans 14:17–18

We are changed by every person with whom we interact. Henri Nouwen was such a person in my life.

Henri was a Catholic priest who was more comfortable in a crewneck sweater than a clerical robe. He was born in Holland and then became a professor of theology at Notre Dame, Yale, and Harvard.

He held a passion to proclaim the good news. I "met" him almost 20 years ago through the many books he has written. He spoke of his own struggle and growth in the spiritual life, a struggle with which I could identify.

Henri's simple message of God's love touched people of all faiths. I am one of those people. Through his books he started me on a new path. In the mid-1980s, God called Henri from Harvard University to a very different life among adults who are intellectually impaired in a L'Arche community in Toronto, Ontario, Canada. He became pastor to those people, saw their inner beauty, and soon realized they had much to teach him about love and acceptance.

Because my husband and I are friends of a L'Arche community near us, we had the opportunity to be with this humble servant of God and got to know Henri before his untimely death in 1997 at age 63.

I was grateful to be in his presence and sometimes found myself thinking, "This must be close to being in the presence of Jesus." To experience his total focus on our conversations reminded me that all too often I have not been totally present to someone else when I should have been.

Henri's example of a life lived close to God continues to inspire me, as do these words from his book, *A Cry for Mercy.* "I pray that this will be my ministry: to join people on their journey and to open their eyes to see you." As disciples of Jesus Christ, this could be the prayer of each of us. Invite People to Christ.

Prayer for Peace

God of mercy, inspire us to invite people to Christ's peace.

Spiritual Practice: Embodying God's Shalom

Find a way to express and embody God's shalom. Begin by prayerfully listening to your longing for peace. Become silent and imagine you can hear the groaning of the Earth's people, nations, and creatures. Prayerfully open yourself to God's yearning for peace and the divine vision of shalom. What images, feelings, and words come to you? What prayer for peace comes to you from your time of listening? What small act of justice, kindness, healing, or peacemaking does God invite you to consider this day?

Peace Covenant

Today, God, I will share your love and your peace with another.

4
Saturday
May

Their Own Story

By Jeanne Marie Bwalya Chola
of Lubumbashi, Democratic Republic of Congo

And the king will answer them, "Truly I tell you, just as you did it to one of the least of these who are members of my family, you did it to me."

—Matthew 25:40

In the community of Kampemba, there was a woman named Mwelwa, aged 70 years. Her husband was long retired. After a few years, life was bad for Mwelwa. To find food for the family when the husband is not working is very difficult in Africa.

As the family suffered, several died. Four children died, and then a daughter died after giving birth. This old mama was desolate after losing five children in three years.

Now life has changed. People in the community know her, and she has been supported by them. Also a non-governmental organization, HealthEd Connect, has supported this family. HealthEd Connect has helped by equipping the Kafwa (community health workers) to be ready when need arises. The Kafwa are community problem solvers!

This mama says thank you so much for the assistance and support you have given. You have made her life better. Life for this mama has changed. She has a lot of friends in the community and outside the community to look after her family.

Editor's note: World Hunger/Tangible Love funds, provided through the Mission Initiative of Abolish Poverty, End Suffering, have helped support the work of HealthEd Connect.

Prayer for Peace

We know you weep with us, compassionate God, when we weep for the loss of our loved ones. At these times we receive blessings of care from the community. May we share those blessings and the peace of Christ with strangers and our families.

Spiritual Practice: Abolish Poverty, End Suffering

Read and reflect on John 21:15–17 as a meditation. Let your mind be drawn to places where people have no homes. Think of refugees whose homes were destroyed by war or natural disaster. Be aware of the hungry and homeless, who wander the streets or live in shelters. Let the images fill your mind. Offer a prayer for those who are suffering. Imagine Christ tending those sheep. Think of ways you might end their suffering as part of your mission. Throughout the day, carry in your mind the voice of Christ saying: "Feed my lambs…tend my sheep…feed my sheep."

Peace Covenant

Today, God, I will pray to perceive needs and work to end suffering.

5
Sunday
May

Proclaim the Good News

By John Wight, senior president of seventy

> *. . . we immediately tried to cross over to Macedonia, being convinced that God had called us to proclaim the good news to them.*
>
> —Acts 16:10

"There's a big waterfall right over there!" a boy, perhaps 6 or 7 years old, shouted to me on a hiking trail in the Colorado Rockies. Several minutes later, as I was hiking down, three women excitedly pointed and, though subdued, called to me, "Look! There are some deer over there!"

I had seen many beautiful waterfalls and majestic deer in my life. But in these cases I was touched by the excitement and joy of these folks, able to share their experience with someone else. The little boy probably broke every rule his parents had taught him about not talking to strangers. The women violated conventional wisdom by talking with a man they did not know on a mountain trail in the middle of nowhere. But they could not contain themselves. They had to proclaim the good news about a waterfall and some deer.

This experience brought to mind several stories in the scriptures of people who couldn't keep from sharing the good news of Jesus Christ. One example is the story of the woman at the well. She was so excited about her meeting with Jesus that she forgot her water pot and ran back into town to share her good news.

As disciples of Jesus Christ, we have the best news anyone could hear. Perhaps it is time for us to throw caution to the wind, boldly "proclaim the good news," and invite people to Christ!

Prayer for Peace

Send us, O God, to proclaim your holy Word. As we are inspired by the good news of Christ and his mission, may we share our joy with others. May we share the peace of Christ.

Spiritual Practice: Examining God's Call to Me and All

Reflect on God's call in your life. Begin by prayerfully asking to recall particular moments when you have experienced God's presence and invitation. Write in your journal or quietly reflect on images and insights that come.

When has God seemed most real in your life? How and when has God called you to use your energies and gifts? When have you felt most deeply connected and responsive to God's movement in your life? When have you felt disconnected or resistant to God's call? How do your gifts and callings connect with the call of God you notice in your family, friends, congregation, or community?

Peace Covenant

Today, God, when I see your sunrise, your waterfall, your deer in the woods, I will tell all who might hear of your generosity.

6
Monday
May

♫ Hymn of the Month: "O Living God, Whose Presence Now Surrounds Us"

By Harry Fielding of Bellara, Queensland, Australia

> *The importance of evaluating and aligning ministerial roles and relationships to reach individuals and nations most effectively with the liberating truths of the gospel is always incumbent on the church.*
>
> —Doctrine and Covenants 164:8a

I have been blessed to visit and minister in almost 30 countries. I have experienced cultural diversity and polar extremes of poverty and wealth. But through all the diversity (and sometimes tragedy), I have found a common theme of love and faith. I have come to understand the psalmist's idea that no matter how we try, we can never escape the presence of God.

This hymn expresses my firm conviction that we are grounded in divine presence.

If we each live in that power and realize it in our everyday lives, a world of harmony and peace is possible.

I am grateful for the thousands of lives that have intersected with my own and have helped me form this view.

O living God, whose presence now
surrounds us
and fills our hearts with joy and hope and peace,
help us to see that in your world around us
your Spirit breathes, your love will
never cease.
But weary souls, that love not comprehending,
still need to know that your love brings release.

Creation groans for freedom, liberating,
grant us, O God, ears well-attuned to hear,
for in this moment, God, we are creating
the future that may bring your Kingdom here.
Help us, O God, live daily in compassion; make
choices that will show your reign is near.

O God of love help us, your love indwelling
break down dividing walls of hate and war.
Help us to be disciples who are willing
to walk the path where love reigns evermore.
O use us God, and in your service free us
for lives of love, with your love at our core.

The peace of Christ be in us and shown
through us
and fill our world with harmony and peace.
The peace of Christ will fill us and renew us
and bring us new directions and release.
Help us to be responsive, God, work
through us;
Your spirit breathes, your love will never cease!

Prayer for Peace

God of wisdom, may we be the vessels from which your liberating truths are shared. May we also invite people to the love and peace of Christ.

Spiritual Practice

Contemplate this hymn as a poem (or sing it to the INCARNATION tune).

7
Tuesday
May

Faith in the Mission

By Don Richardson of Nauvoo, Illinois, USA

> *"...For truly I tell you, if you have faith the size of a mustard seed, you will say to this mountain, 'Move from here to there,' and it will move; and nothing will be impossible for you."*
>
> —Matthew 17:20

My wife decided to repaint the walls in our living room.

We picked up color strips at the paint store. After much deliberation, she narrowed the choices to six or seven colors. Together we chose the color we would use.

My wife started painting the room. After doing part of the room, we were unhappy with the color. We had hoped it would look darker, although it did seem to darken a *little* after it dried.

We already had the paint, so we finished the room despite the color. We weren't sure we had made a good decision but were still enthusiastic about the project.

Then we hung new curtains. What a difference those made! With the new curtains and the new paint, the room looked much better than we had thought. We were happy with the "finished" results. Our faith in our work waned for a while, but then it was revived.

Sometimes when we are trying to serve God, we are not completely happy with how things are going. We get impatient and discouraged. We don't seem to have the faith to carry us through. We may wish we had done things differently, but because we have started the way we have, we make adjustments and try to complete our ministry. It ends up being much better than we thought it would because God was directing us all along, in spite of our hesitancy.

When God is in charge, the results will be positive in the end. As we minister to others, may we remember who leads the way and let Christ be our constant companion as we make our choices. May Christ's mission be our mission.

Prayer for Peace

Creator God, we have faith that when we make Christ's mission our mission, your purposes will be fulfilled—Christ's peace will be shared.

Spiritual Practice: Making Responsible Choices

Prayerfully seek God's guidance in your choices. Discernment invites us to orient our lives toward God and God's vision for us and creation. Begin by reviewing the responsibilities and opportunities in the day before you. Take these choices into prayer, asking God for wisdom and insight about what matters most.

Offer yourself to God with the prayer of Teresa of Avila: "God, what do you want of me today?" Sit prayerfully with this question as you review the day again. Be aware of images, thoughts, names, or actions that come to you. Ask for a blessing to live this day responsibly and compassionately in the Spirit of Christ.

Peace Covenant

Today, God, I will choose a Mission Initiative and ask your direction to act on it.

8
Wednesday
May

God's Shaping Breath

By Carolyn Brock of Redmond, Oregon, USA

When he had said this, he breathed on them and said to them, "Receive the Holy Spirit."

—John 20:22

Like many of you, I have watched a glassblower gather hot liquid onto a pipe and blow air inside to shape it into a vase, an ornament, or a bowl.

The glass artist works with the piece, dips it, using tools to mold, twist, and refine the substance into elegant, functional forms. But the initial shape, the body of the piece, comes from those first expanding breaths. We wait in expectation to see what the glassblower will create with the power of his breath, the tools in her hands.

God breathes on us and in us. What shape does God intend as we are formed by divine breath? Jesus breathed on his disciples so they might share his presence and proclaim the gospel. God breathed into us so we might become living beings, expressions of God's life, love, and purpose. Just as the glassblower creates beauty and functionality, we are to express God's beauty and functions.

God's justice shapes things into forms that bring peace, joy, and life to the global family. Is God working with us, forming us, breathing into us a new identity, a new beauty and functionality, new expressions of divine justice and mercy? Will we choose to become a new creation?

Prayer for Peace

Breathe on us, O God. Continually reshape us into Christ's disciples. May we be vessels filled with your presence. May we share this fullness with our global family as we share the peace of Christ.

Spiritual Practice: Breathing God's Compassion

Light a candle and sit quietly, reflecting on the fire and light of God. Pay attention to your breathing and let it become calmer and deeper as you focus on God's presence. Ask God to breathe in you. Visualize each breath carrying the light of God into your lungs, bloodstream, and every cell in your body until you are filled with God's Spirit. Now envision breathing out God's compassion and grace each time you exhale. Pray to have the Spirit of Christ radiate from your life like the gentle flame of a candle.

Peace Covenant

Today, God, I will accept the shaping of your breath and become an expression of your love.

9
Thursday
May

Being Met by the Community

By Darren Goble of Humansville, Missouri, USA

> *...who made heaven and earth, the sea, and all that is in them; who keeps faith forever; who executes justice for the oppressed; who gives food to the hungry. The Lord sets the prisoners free; the Lord opens the eyes of the blind. The Lord lifts up those who are bowed down; the Lord loves the righteous. The Lord watches over the strangers; he upholds the orphan and the widow...*
>
> —Psalm 146:6–9

I moved to Independence, Missouri, to work at the bookstore in the Temple. It was a difficult start. I moved from California to Missouri with nothing but a suitcase of clothes. If it had not been for volunteers in the bookstore and museum, I wonder how I would have survived that first year.

From their generosity, I received several bags of groceries, my first set of plates and tableware, clothes, the use of their laundry facilities, and friendship. They always seemed to know what I needed and helped me at just the right time.

I would walk around the Temple's rooftop garden, touching the granite walls, thinking how blessed I was to be there. It was not until years later I realized the blessing was not in the place; the gift was in the people.

I am thankful for God's gift of those who helped a young man's first steps into the world. I have received Blessings of Community.

Prayer for Peace

Lead us at just the right moment, God, to know when and where our help is needed. Help us watch over strangers and make them friends. May we share what we can, especially the peace of Christ.

Spiritual Practice: Generosity and Discipleship

Bring a basket or other container to your place of prayer. Meditate on the link between generosity and discipleship. Write a prayer of commitment in which you name specific acts of generosity and sharing to which you feel called. Fold the paper and place the prayer in the offering container. Close by singing a hymn of gratitude or praise as you offer your gift to God.

Peace Covenant

Today, God, I will lift the spirits of someone who is feeling down.

10
Friday
May

She Left with a Smile

By Julie Conway-Sword of Gainesville, Florida, USA

The spirit of the One you follow is the spirit of love and peace. That Spirit seeks to abide in the hearts of those who would embrace its call and live its message. The path will not always be easy, the choices will not always be clear, but the cause is sure and the Spirit will bear witness to the truth and those who live the truth will know the hope and the joy of discipleship in the community of Christ. Amen.

—Doctrine and Covenants161:7

Bev was eating alone at the motel breakfast bar when my husband, Marion, entered to get a cup of coffee.

He noticed her despondent look and kindly joined her in conversation. The night before we had celebrated our 60-year high school reunion at a banquet, and now it was over. Bev was alone again. It had been only a few weeks since her husband, Bill, had passed away after many years of her caregiving.

Marion and I were on a schedule to attend the special service at the Temple, memorializing the tragedy of 9/11. We estimated that if we left by 7:00 a.m. and drove straight through, we could arrive in time. But here sat Bev, desperately needing to talk, and it seemed right to give her our full attention. Nothing else seemed important.

We listened as she unraveled the story of her husband's illness, surgeries, recoveries, uncertain future, and the way he finally slipped away to peace in his heavenly home. We listened until she was talked out. Then we exchanged phone numbers, prayed together, and hugged.

Because we had spent time with her, she told us, she felt that coming to the reunion had been helpful after all. She left with a smile.

We arrived at the Temple a half hour early and realized we had been blessed by being a blessing. God is compassionate.

Prayer for Peace

Companion God, we praise you for your faithful presence. When hurting souls don't feel you near, may we be your presence for them. When others don't feel at peace, may we share Christ's peace with them.

Spiritual Practice: Healing for Broken Spirits

Begin with quiet prayer. Ask God to help you discern some "sore places" in the body of Christ and in God's creation. Become aware of people who feel separated, wounded, or left out. Reflect on or write a short journal entry of healing words to at least one person who comes to mind. Ask God for words that will touch this person's broken spirit like healing ointment. Keep this person in your heart and prayers today and act on any ideas that come to bring blessing and wholeness.

Peace Covenant

Today, God, I will make myself aware of the lonely, and respond with compassion.

11
Saturday
May

Gently Used

By Sandi Ecker of Boyne City, Michigan, USA

...all shall give as they are able, according to the blessing of the Lord your God that he has given you.

—Deuteronomy 16:17

Anyone who knows Ruthie will tell you that she's a take-charge person. So no one in the Boyne City Congregation was surprised when Ruthie took charge of the new God's Work Children's Clothing Pantry. Inspired and named by the children of the congregation, the pantry welcomes all as volunteers distribute new and gently used clothing to children.

On the second Saturday of each month, children scamper through the pantry's organized aisles, searching for just the right outfit. Thanks to a mission grant, as well as congregational funding, the clothing is free. Families come and exchange gently used outgrown clothes for larger sizes. It's working!

Your contributions to world mission tithes help congregations such as Boyne City provide life-changing ministry to children and families. Thank you for your faithful and generous response.

Prayer for Peace

Loving Parent, may the abundance of our pantries be shared with all who have need. May hospitality and love accompany goods shared. May hope be shared along with Christ's peace.

Spiritual Practice: Experience Congregations in Mission

Read and reflect on Doctrine and Covenants 164:9a–d. Re-read the sentence, "If you truly would be Community of Christ, then embody and live the concerns and passion of Christ." Make a list of the issues you feel mattered most to Christ. Make another list of issues that matter to your congregation. Reflect on the similarities and differences. How can you help align the lists? Throughout the day, as issues arise, ask yourself, "Would this matter to Christ?"

Peace Covenant

Today, God, I will look to the children for inspiration on ways to be generous.

12
Sunday
May

Believe in God

By Barbara Borkowski of Lee's Summit, Missouri, USA

About midnight Paul and Silas were praying and singing hymns to God, and the prisoners were listening to them. Suddenly there was an earthquake, so violent that the foundations of the prison were shaken; and immediately all the doors were opened and everyone's chains were unfastened. When the jailer woke up and saw the prison doors wide open, he drew his sword and was about to kill himself, since he supposed that the prisoners had escaped. But Paul shouted in a loud voice, "Do not harm yourself, for we are all here." The jailer...fell down trembling before Paul and Silas. Then he brought them outside and said, "Sirs, what must I do to be saved?" They answered, "Believe on the Lord Jesus, and you will be saved, you and your household."

—Acts 16:25–31

We have become a skeptical, critical people. We must be. Our culture and media impress on us claims of riches, beauty, weight loss, and popularity. We need to sort through all of those questionable claims to discover what is real and what is believable. Advertising surrounds our lives, and to survive we develop filters to sift through the variety of images created to capture our attention and imagination.

In today's scripture passage we read an amazing story that contains claims of healing, release, and freedom. Those are big claims—much bigger than riches, beauty, weight loss, and popularity. Healing, release, and freedom are spectacular claims that change who we are and who we will become.

Ironically, it is the jailer in this story who receives healing, release, and freedom. Jailers imprison and secure others. This jailer understands that his world has just turned upside down, and he asks the pivotal question, "What must I do to be saved?" The answer was to believe on the Lord Jesus.

As modern skeptics and critics, does it take turning our world upside down for us to believe? Can healing, release, and freedom be that simple? Perhaps that's why this ancient story still captures our attention and imagination. It is a fantastic story, and yet it is a mirror of our own experience. It is through our connection with the Lord Jesus that we find freedom, release, and healing. It really is that simple.

Prayer for Peace

Help us realize, God, that life doesn't have to be complicated to be full. Help us let go of the obstacles to our connection with you and what matters most.

Spiritual Practice: Invite People to Christ

Read and reflect on Doctrine and Covenants 162:3b and 163:2b. Pray to be aware of people who might be receptive, and therefore blessed, by your sharing of the message of the living Christ. Imagine being in relationship with them and inviting them to Christ. In preparation, discover your personal testimony of Christ. "Be persistent in your witness and diligent in your mission to the world." Repeat this mantra throughout the day: "Christ's mission, our mission, my mission."

Peace Covenant

Today, God, I will share the simplicity of following Christ with another.

13
Monday
May

Blue Monday

By Donna Boyd of Independence, Missouri, USA

Who is wise and understanding among you? Show by your good life that your works are done with gentleness born of wisdom. ... But the wisdom from above is first pure, then peaceable, gentle, willing to yield, full of mercy and good fruits, without a trace of partiality or hypocrisy. And a harvest of righteousness is sown in peace for those who make peace.

—James 3:13, 17–18

The expression "blue Monday" has many stories—some hundreds of years old—about its possible origin. A more recent story hangs the expression on a custom many women once had of doing their laundry on Monday, using "bluing" instead of bleach to help the clothes look and feel clean. For some it meant hauling water, heating it on the stove (or fire), and doing back-breaking labor to wash, rinse, wring, and hang the clothes to dry.

Today, though laundry remains inconvenient for some men and women, it is not the onerous burden it once was.

Instead, for younger people, Monday may mean returning to work and school after a weekend of late hours, neglected homework, overeating, and perhaps suffering sunburn or insect bites. We are not at our best, but most Mondays we are required to present ourselves front and center, behaving optimally.

I resolved years ago that because one-seventh of my God-given life would be on Mondays, I would not fall victim to an attitude that sabotaged my work week. God blessed me with the ability to work as long as necessary. My vulnerability to divine grace will enhance my service and discipleship. I praise God for all the "rosy Mondays" in my life.

Prayer for Peace

Daily God, we praise you for our days of working and the restful Sabbath. May we live every day as disciples of Christ, sharing his peace.

Spiritual Practice: Making Responsible Choices

Prayerfully seek God's guidance in your choices. Discernment invites us to orient our lives toward God and God's vision for us and creation. Begin by reviewing the responsibilities and opportunities in the day before you. Take these choices into prayer, asking God for wisdom and insight about what matters most.

Offer yourself to God with the prayer of Teresa of Avila: "God, what do you want of me today?" Sit prayerfully with this question as you review the day again. Be aware of images, thoughts, names, or actions that come to you. Ask for a blessing to live this day responsibly and compassionately in the Spirit of Christ.

Peace Covenant

Today, God, I will pray while I work.

14
Tuesday
May

Are We Alone?

By Sara Parkin of Midland, Michigan, USA

The Lord is my shepherd, I shall not want. He makes me lie down in green pastures; he leads me beside still waters; he restores my soul. He leads me in right paths for his name's sake. Even though I walk through the darkest valley, I fear no evil; for you are with me; your rod and your staff—they comfort me. You prepare a table before me in the presence of my enemies; you anoint my head with oil; my cup overflows. Surely goodness and mercy shall follow me all the days of my life, and I shall dwell in the house of the Lord my whole life long.

—Psalm 23

(Part 3 of My Journey with Alzheimer's Disease)

The other day I was having a pity party for myself. No one else was in the house. Crying out loud, wiping eyes, nose running. No one loved me. No one really knows what it feels like to be an Alzheimer's person. Then I stopped and cleaned my face, becoming aware I *am* loved and not alone, that other people *do* know what it feels like.

God is here. God is unconditional love. God loves me. God is my higher power. I looked back through my journal to read the blessings I can remember God gave me. I wanted to share part of my journal entry with you…

Alzheimer's sucks.

Sorry. It hit me again, and I was mad, sad, and I did not want to write anything that day. Then, I remembered that God has blessed me a lot. I started to write about blessings I could remember that day. I believe the Holy Spirit had a part in my writing.

I was never alone! We are never alone! There are ways we can be comforted in our homes or elsewhere. Snuggle up with a pet or soft quilt. Read, watch TV, talk to friends on the phone. For me, two sources of comfort are prayer and the 23rd Psalm.

Try any one or all of these along with the Holy Comforter.

Prayer for Peace

Tender Shepherd, thank you for always being near. Thank you for being the light in our darkest nights. Thank you for your healing Communion table of grace.

Spiritual Practice: Honoring the Worth of All Persons

Read Psalm 139:13–18. After each reading sit quietly and let the words sink deeply into your mind, heart, and body. Imagine God watching you grow in your mother's womb. What thoughts and feelings do you have about being "fearfully and wonderfully made" (Psalm 139:14)?

Sense the intimate knowledge and love God has of you and every child. Be aware of the sacred worth of each person. Weep with God over the soul-wounding forces and events that rob people of dignity and worth. How are you invited to notice, protect, heal, and affirm the spiritual identity of all God's beloved people today? Pray for God's compassion.

Peace Covenant

Today, God, I will visit someone who sits in the dark.

15
Wednesday
May

Love Your Neighbor

By Eleanor St. Clair of Oak Harbor, Ohio, USA

"Which commandment is the first of all?" Jesus answered, "The first is, 'Hear, O Israel: the Lord our God, the Lord is one; you shall love the Lord your God with all your heart, and with all your soul, and with all your mind, and with all your strength.' The second is this, 'You shall love your neighbor as yourself.' There is no other commandment greater than these."

—Mark 12:28–31

My daughter's family was to arrive early that evening. They were coming from out of state and would stay for the weekend. It had been months since they had been here, and I was excited! I planned to clean house and prepare food so I wouldn't have to spend too much time in the kitchen after they arrived. An exciting and busy time!

Then a young mother called, asking me to take her husband to the welfare office. Having done this before, I knew how long the wait could be. I hated to say "no," but I told her that I couldn't. Frustration exploded within. "Why me, God? Why does everybody call me? I have a life, too!" Then I asked myself the question, "Do I love my neighbor as myself?"

The Holy Spirit would not let me forget the sound of despair in her voice. She had made other calls for help, and they had refused her, as well. I called her back and said I would take him. With a big sigh of relief, she said, "I knew you would. Thank you *so* much." I met their needs and raced for home.

When my daughter arrived, I had finished all my work. I was in a state of dazed disbelief. There is no way I could have done it alone. Even though my response initially was of begrudging obedience, God still was generous to me. I can only believe that God strengthened me so I might do what mattered most. You can't outdo God's generosity. It was a lesson I've never forgotten.

Prayer for Peace

Generous God, help us respond to our global neighbors without hesitation. May we be present for them as you are present for us. As you are generous with us, may we be generous as we share the peace of Christ.

Spiritual Practice: Offering Blessings of Community

Receive and share Blessings of Community. Begin with a prayer of gratitude for the relationships in your life. See and feel connections with family members, spiritual friends, people in your congregation, and neighborhood communities. What blessings flow to you from these circles? Reflect, pray, or write in your journal about the call to be "Community of Christ." Go deeper each day as you discern what act of blessing you are invited to complete.

Peace Covenant

Today, God, I will step away from my agenda to respond to the call from a neighbor in need.

16
Thursday
May

The Day Caden Visited the Temple

By Geoff Henshaw of Independence, Missouri, USA

> *Then little children were being brought to him in order that he might lay his hands on them and pray. The disciples spoke sternly to those who brought them; but Jesus said, "Let the little children come to me, and do not stop them; for it is to such as these that the kingdom of heaven belongs." And he laid his hands on them and went on his way.*
>
> —Matthew 19:13–15

I serve on weekends as a tour guide at the Temple in Independence, Missouri. People from many faith communities and of different age groups visit the Temple, wishing to have a tour.

One October, a family visited. The group was comprised of the parents, grandparents, a great-grandfather, and 2-year-old Caden.

The tour follows the Worshiper's Path to the Temple Sanctuary. As the group approached the top of the path, Caden's interest had waned in this adult-oriented tour.

I was aware of his restlessness and reminded the adults of how Jesus welcomed the children into his arms and stated, "of such is the kingdom." Kneeling down, I gently placed my hands on Caden's face and said to him, "You are the kingdom of God."

Caden giggled and smiled, and we continued the tour.

Such moments have deep meaning for me. Sometimes God's light surprises, and we are all blessed as I was the day Caden visited the Temple with his family.

Prayer for Peace

Loving God, make us aware of the attributes of children that we might emulate for the cause of your kingdom. May we never take for granted their "insights." If, at first, we smile at the silliness of what they say, may we revisit, reflect, and discover the unguarded truth they tell. May we adopt their innocence and nonjudgmental nature. May we learn from them ways to share Christ's peace.

Spiritual Practice: Listening to Children

Sit in your quiet place and center your heart and mind on God's presence. Spend several minutes, asking God to bring into your awareness the names and images of children in your life. You may see their faces or hear their voices as you receive these impressions. Listen deeply to the unique gifts and needs of the children who come to mind. Offer a prayer of blessing for each child and the needs you perceive. If you feel led, you also may want to write a note or card and give a message of affirmation and love to each child.

Peace Covenant

Today, God, I will spend time with a child and consider it time well spent.

17
Friday
May

Beloved Son

By Vivian Betts of Sutton, United Kingdom

> *Jesus Christ, the embodiment of God's shalom, invites all people to come and receive divine peace in the midst of the difficult questions and struggles of life. Follow Christ in the way that he leads to God's peace and discover the blessings of all of the dimensions of salvation.*
>
> —Doctrine and Covenants163:2a

When our first son was 6 years old, he died of leukemia. He was a much-wanted and loved son, and for a time our lives were empty and sad. A few years later, on a Sunday morning, I was at church, sitting near the back, trying to keep my little ones quiet. I heard a commotion from the porch. It was the sound of excited and happy children.

I looked out the door, and I saw our son among these children. He was holding someone's hand. He looked at me and recognized me, but then he looked into the face of whoever was holding his hand, and he wanted to stay. He could not come to me.

I thank God for this experience of assurance that one day we will be together again. Until then, I know my son is in a peaceful and happy place with his Creator.

Prayer for Peace

We accept the invitation from your Son, God, to receive divine peace. We will follow him as the embodiment of your shalom and share his peace.

Spiritual Practice: Embodying God's Shalom

Find a way to express and embody God's shalom. Begin by prayerfully listening to your longing for peace. Become silent and imagine you can hear the groaning of the Earth's people, nations, and creatures. Prayerfully open yourself to God's yearning for peace and the divine vision of shalom.

What images, feelings, and words come to you? What prayer for peace comes to you from your time of listening? Speak or write this prayer. What small act of justice, kindness, healing, or peacemaking does God invite you to consider this day?

Peace Covenant

Today, God, I will remember the loved ones who have passed on and know they are at peace with you.

18
Saturday
May

From the Philippines: Planting Global Ministry

By Andrew Bolton, Council of Twelve Apostles

> *...the earth is full, and there is enough and to spare; yea, I prepared all things, and have given unto the children of the earth to be agents unto themselves.*
>
> —Doctrine and Covenants 101:2f, adapted

Most people don't realize how a simple task such as planting a tree can become a global ministry. But sowing good seed makes a positive impact. Trees reforest stripped hillsides that suffer from soil erosion. Trees provide firewood and fruit. And, most importantly, they lessen carbon dioxide, slowing global warming.

This process is so important to the Philippines that the Southeast Asia Mission Center Conference passed a resolution calling on church members to be more environmentally conscious. The resolution began a tree-planting project led by Chito Magabilin, a full-time Community of Christ minister.

In what is now a communal effort that includes churches, parents, school, and neighbors, Chito teaches how to grow the trees, including mahogany and mango, in small outdoor pots. The Philippine Department of Natural Resources recently provided land for the project. Chito's group planted almost 7,000 trees.

It is powerful to witness participants' enthusiasm! Your world mission tithes sow good seeds. Thank you for responding so generously.

Prayer for Peace

Creator God, thank you for the miracle of tiny seeds. Bless the planting we do and let it multiply throughout the Earth. May the soil provide nutrients to the trees and the trees provide support to the soil. May we know we are blessed to be a blessing.

Spiritual Practice: Trees

Watch the trees outside your window for a few moments. Close your eyes and meditate on Alma's words about seeds and trees. If you were to plant and grow the Word of God in your heart, what kind of tree might symbolically represent this process? Envision a *seed* as it grows into a tree of life and blessing. Ask God to show you how to begin (see Alma 16:152–173).

Peace Covenant

Today, God, I will participate gently in your great circle of life, leaving a small footprint on your Earth.

19
Sunday
May

Come, Holy Spirit

By Linda Booth, Council of Twelve Apostles

> *"In the last days it will be, God declares, that I will pour out my Spirit upon all flesh, and your sons and your daughters shall prophesy, and your young men shall see visions, and your old men shall dream dreams. Even upon my slaves, both men and women, in those days I will pour out my Spirit; and they shall prophesy."*
>
> —Acts 2:17–18

When the Spirit comes, ministry and mission go into motion.

While driving through Clarksville, Tennessee, Paula Williams experienced the Spirit guiding her to plant a new congregation there. The Spirit was so persistent that Paula and her husband began to plan for their household move. Paula asked for a list of church members in the area and discovered there were several.

In faith, Paula and her husband moved to Clarksville. As they unloaded their rented truck, a neighbor boy, Malick, came to check them out. Before they settled into their home, Paula contacted church members and began to get to know Malick's family and her other neighbors.

Before long, a dozen people began to meet in her home for companionship and eventually pray and study the Bible together. Soon many neighbors, friends, and families were coming to learn about Jesus. People didn't want to leave because they enjoyed being together. The Holy Spirit was transforming lives and preparing these new disciples to witness of Jesus Christ and provide compassionate ministry to others.

Today, the Clarksville congregation meets in a rented building on a busy street. Many neighbors and new friends have been baptized and confirmed. Some were called to serve in the priesthood. The congregation is developing them as Jesus' disciples and sending them in his mission.

I doubt if any of these folks has heard a mighty wind or seen tongues of fire resting above the congregation. However, the Holy Spirit has come in power. A new community forms in Christ's name. The church emerges and lives in a new place!

Prayer for Peace

Holy Spirit, rest on us when you would have us act. Rest on us and call us to love and to share the peace of Christ.

Spiritual Practice: Experience Congregations in Mission

Read and reflect on Doctrine and Covenants 164:9a–d. Reread the sentence, "If you truly would be Community of Christ, then embody and live the concerns and passion of Christ." Make a list of the issues that you feel mattered most to Christ. Make another list of issues that matter to your congregation. Reflect on the similarities and differences between the lists. How can you help align the lists? Throughout the day, as issues arise, ask yourself, "Would this matter to Christ?"

Peace Covenant

Today, God, I will respond as your Spirit leads.

20
Monday
May

One in the Spirit

By Greg Savage of Lee's Summit, Missouri, USA

> *When the day of Pentecost had come, they were all together in one place. And suddenly from heaven there came a sound like the rush of a violent wind, and it filled the entire house where they were sitting. Divided tongues, as of fire, appeared among them, and a tongue rested on each of them. All of them were filled with the Holy Spirit and began to speak in other languages, as the Spirit gave them ability.*
>
> —Acts 2:1–4

Pentecost is the dramatic event in which God enters with spiritual power the house of gathered disciples, who came from many parts of the world. This gift was promised by Jesus earlier and by the prophet Joel, quoted in Peter's sermon.

Amid diversity, the Pentecostal gift of the Holy Spirit empowered the disciples to proclaim the peace of Jesus Christ. Peter delivered his sermon with such great spiritual influence that 3,000 believed. This suggests the outpouring of the Spirit is meant for all people.

In 1972 my brother, some American and German friends, and I traveled from Germany to the campgrounds of Dunfield House in the British Isles for the annual International Youth Camp. At this camp seven nations were represented. All the classes and worships were translated into English, Dutch, and German. We were of different genders and cultures, spoke different languages, and had various skin tones and body types, ranging from huge to small. We were all together "in the same box."

During that week, none of the differences mattered because we were experiencing the Holy Spirit. It was the glue that bound us as we sang "We Are One in the Spirit."

Pentecost for us today testifies of the continuing gift of the Holy Spirit calling us to live in Christ's promise. This is not an annual event. God enters humanity daily with the gift of the Holy Spirit for the inspiration of all.

Prayer for Peace

Holy Spirit, we answer your call. May we be open to you daily. May we be ready and willing to share the peace of Jesus Christ.

Spiritual Practice: Welcoming Unity in Diversity

Meditate on Unity in Diversity. Create a large circle with your arms. See and feel the diverse people God invites inside the sanctuary of Christ's peace represented by this circle.

Who is easiest to welcome? Whom do you struggle to include? Confess the dividing walls between you and people too different or "dangerous" to invite into your spiritual home. Ask God to forgive and heal barriers that keep us from loving one another.

Peace Covenant

Today I will look to you, God, for wisdom and knowledge.

21
Tuesday
May

Sacred Verbs

By Lu Mountenay of Independence, Missouri, USA

Keep on doing the things that you have learned and received and heard and seen in me, and the God of peace will be with you.

—Philippians 4:9

I work many crossword puzzles, always looking for the elusive word, the mysterious phrase. One catch that often trips me up is assuming a word in the clue is a noun, when it is intended as a verb. It makes all the difference.

Examples: Cross = a religious symbol *or* movement from one side to another. Fly = an insect with wings *or* soaring above the Earth. Rise = a low hill *or* the act of moving upward. Share = part of a financial stock *or* the act of giving or telling. The following poem is all about action, all about what we *do* on the journey, all about fulfilling Christ's mission. (Is *mission* a verb?) I call these my *sacred verbs*:

cross the Red Sea
wander in the wilderness
covenant with God.
follow the star
kneel at the manger
sing
rejoice.

fly to Egypt
teach in the temple
welcome children
love enemies
tell the story
speak truth
pray in the garden
journey to the cross
follow...reflect...repent...cry...

rise from the dark
bask in Christ's light
heal in the Spirit
embrace the call
lift your eyes
hear the cries
respond

invite people
abolish poverty
end suffering
pursue peace
develop disciples
congregate
be still
know God
discern...pray...anoint...bless...

Prayer for Peace

Creator God, as we see your creative actions in the universe, may we take action to co-create with you—making Christ's mission our mission; making Christ's peace our peace.

Spiritual Practice: Praying for Leadership of the Church

An important spiritual practice is praying for those who carry leadership responsibilities. See or sense persons who lead the community of faith at congregational, mission center, and World Church levels. Pray for grace on each servant leader.

Peace Covenant

Today, God, I will turn my passive words into active verbs.

22
Wednesday
May

Example of Love

By Evelyn Richardson of Nauvoo, Illinois, USA

> *The wolf shall live with the lamb, the leopard shall lie down with the kid, the calf and the lion and the fatling together, and a little child shall lead them.*
>
> —Isaiah 11:6

I can't say I am always a shining example of love. Children learn by copying what they see others do or what they hear others say. I was reminded of this one Sunday as I sat on the piano bench at church to play for A Disciple's Generous Response.

Four young ushers stood ready to go forward for the prayer of blessing when a 2- or 3-year-old boy went up to one of them. He couldn't wait for the basket to come to him. He dropped his offering into the plate with enthusiasm and returned to his grandmother.

If the rest of the congregation could have seen his face, members would have recognized what it means to be a cheerful giver. Are we cheerful in all our giving? Do we let our love shine from our faces? Are we examples of love and generosity for our children?

Surely that morning a little child was doing what he had seen some big folks do, and adding his example of how we can do it better. Are we sharing generously and according to our true capacity that others may know our hearts as we respond? What examples are we setting, not only in word and action, but in our attitudes and expression of how we feel about our action?

Yes, a little child shall lead us. May we follow the example of children as we follow Christ. Children are the church *now and in the future.* May we work together to develop communities of joy, hope, love, and peace for all of God's children, big and small.

Prayer for Peace

Creator God, by witness of our heart, soul, mind, and strength, may we show our love for you and our neighbors. By example of our way of living, may we share Christ's love and peace.

Spiritual Practice: Teacher-learner

The first disciples of Jesus followed to hear his words, to be taught, to learn a new way of living, to practice what they learned in daily life. Prayerfully consider your role as a teacher-learner, disciple-apprentice; a people cultivator in Community of Christ. In your journal write the names of several persons you discern as teachers or mentors and several you feel called to nurture and encourage in specific ways. Ask God's blessing on you and your congregation as a community of learners.

Peace Covenant

Today, God, I will show love in a way children can understand.

23
Thursday
May

A Very Present Help

By Karen Anne Smith of Ludington, Michigan, USA

> *God is our refuge and strength, a very present help in trouble. Therefore we will not fear, though the earth should change, though the mountains shake in the heart of the sea; though its waters roar and foam, though the mountains tremble with its tumult. Selah*
>
> —Psalm 46:1–3

My son, Alex, and I had just arrived at the Scottville Riverside Park. Alex ran gleefully ahead to see the river.

I quickened my pace to catch up. It was a cold and cloudy autumn day, so no one else was around.

I stepped on something wrong and went down, twisting my already-arthritic knee. Oh, the pain! All I could do was lie in the grass and mud, crying out, "Help me God."

I was alone with my severely autistic son, with a busy street not far away. I called Alex to come to me, hoping he would respond and not run into traffic. He did come, and he knew how to help me up gently, without excessive tugging. He kept his cool and helped me! I am so proud of him.

When you meet someone who is severely disabled and mute, never doubt someone is in there—a person, a brain, a soul. Never doubt how close God is when you need help. You can bet God was helping Alex help me.

Prayer for Peace

God whose help comes in unexpected ways, may we never doubt the source. May we always see the worth of persons that you see. May we be aware that everyone can share Christ's peace.

Spiritual Practice: Opening to God's Presence

Today's practice is a prayer of blessing for our bodies as we open them to God's presence and purposes. Place your hands over your face and eyes, asking God for compassionate vision and insight (30 seconds of silence). Place your hands on your head and ask to be blessed with the mind of Christ (silence). Put your hands over your ears and pray for deep listening to the sounds, words, and needs around you (silence). Place your hands over your throat and ask God to grant you wise, healing speech (silence). Put both hands over your heart and ask to receive and generously share God's compassion and peace (silence). Say "thank you and amen."

Peace Covenant

Today, God, I will be aware of potential, even when it is hidden behind a disability.

24
Friday
May

Gabi's Story: The Power of Prayer

By R. Keith Lane of Valley Station, Kentucky, USA

> *First of all, then, I urge that supplications, prayers, intercessions, and thanksgivings should be made for everyone…so that we may lead a quiet and peaceable life in all godliness and dignity.*
>
> —1 Timothy 2:1–2

The triplets were born seven weeks early. "Gabi" was first, weighing three pounds, five ounces, only one minute before her sister, and two minutes before her brother.

Gabi was a little fighter and slowly began to gain weight.

But a week after her birth the nurse noticed symptoms that led to a diagnosis of necrotizing enterocolitis (NEC). Her intestines were breaking down. NEC is the leading cause of death in premature infants and almost always leaves some permanent damage to survivors.

The doctor immediately took her off oral feeding because her intestinal tract had not developed fully. Nurses added hefty doses of antibiotics to her IV bottles.

We feared for her life. We asked our prayer group—friends and family from Australia, Oregon, Illinois, Kentucky, Virginia, and Georgia—to pray for Gabi. We held her up to God's healing light.

A week went by, and we prayed for Gabi every day. The doctor said she thought Gabi might be able to begin normal feeding again. From then on, she has thrived and had no permanent damage. We are grateful for the Blessings of Community, which supported our family through prayer.

Prayer for Peace

Compassionate God, we hold the children of the world up to your healing light. Where there is sadness, let there be joy. Where there is illness, let wholeness thrive. Where there is violence, let us share the peace of Christ.

Spiritual Practice: The Chalice Prayer

The chalice prayer is a form of intercession. Create a cup or chalice with your hands in front of your heart. Open your heart to God's concern for the Earth and human family as you hold them in your chalice. See beauty and suffering as you lift the chalice and release the creation (open hands) to be blessed and healed by God. Form the chalice again and hold persons who have particular needs—friends, loved ones, even enemies. Lift them and release them for God's blessing. Place yourself inside the chalice as you confess your deepest needs. Lift and release yourself to God for healing. "Thank you and amen."

Peace Covenant

Today, God, I will pray without hesitation, as I become aware of needs.

25
Saturday
May

Family Camp

By Karen Porter of Liberty, Missouri, USA

> *So we, who are many, are one body in Christ, and individually we are members one of another. We have gifts that differ according to the grace given to us: prophecy, in proportion to faith; ministry, in ministering; the teacher, in teaching; the exhorter, in exhortation; the giver, in generosity; the leader, in diligence; the compassionate, in cheerfulness.*
>
> —Romans 12:5–8

Jaeden was 13 and had been going to family camp since he was 3. That year the junior high youth had three teachers. Anytime during the day you might see the kids talking with them. The teachers had great rapport with the kids and had late-night sessions in the dining hall after "lights out."

There was a thunderstorm late on our last night there. Our cabin was about as far from the dining hall as one could get. When it was time for the kids to start heading to their camp lodging, I got a text message from Jaeden. "Grandma, everyone is staying a little while longer, can I stay too?" My reply was, "Sure, the weather is too bad to walk back to the cabin, so stay." About 2:00 a.m. I woke up as he came in.

It's usually a chore to get him go to the worship services, but that year he was going on his own. I'd find him sitting with his friends and a teacher. When we were loading the van to head for home I heard him ask his little sister, "Do you love Jesus?"

Thanks to donations for campgrounds and campership funds, we have camps and provide our youth with awesome experiences they can't get in other ways.

Prayer for Peace

Creator God, we're on the upward trail, singing your praises as we go. Camping, worshiping, working together, sharing the peace of Jesus Christ.

Spiritual Practice: Joy of Gratitude

Stand, if possible, with arms outstretched. Imagine God filling your arms with all that you have: family, friends, and possessions. Hold out your arms until they feel tired. Now, bring your arms across your body. Place your hand over your heart and thank God for the abundance that fills your life. Sit for a time aware of that abundance. Then ask God to help you open your heart in gratitude and share freely with others.

Peace Covenant

Today, God, I will remember our church campgrounds and the spiritual experiences shared there.

26
Sunday
May

God Cares

By Steve Jones, presiding bishop

Oh Lord, our Sovereign, how majestic is your name in all of the earth.

—Psalm 8:1

Many times while working for the church, I have experienced God's ever-attending care for the whole church. Let me share three of those moments.

After the 2000 World Conference I attended a meeting of the Church Name Change Committee. Our consultant said, "Stop, don't you know what this name change is all about? Sure, you have to change signs, letterhead, business cards, and make other changes. But this is about a God who loves you enough to call you by a new name."

From that experience, the committee refocused its efforts on the mission impact of our name change and developed the 40-day, spiritual-journey practices for families. God cared about spiritual and missional formation.

Two years later, at the 2002 World Conference, the Presiding Bishopric presented to the church a new understanding of tithing. This understanding moved us from a formula-based method of tithing to one based on generosity principles. Our journey as a Presiding Bishopric was notable. We experienced and understood that our (yours and mine) sharing of tithing could not be a calculation. It must be a response to God's generosity and our willingness to receive and then share it.

Finally, in 2010 and 2011, we again embarked on what leadership believed was a critical issue of how the church was funded. We challenged priesthood members to respond beyond the US$5 each week that a little more than 60 percent of priesthood members were contributing. Again God surprised us, because what we thought was a funding issue turned into a discovery.

We discovered the mission of Community of Christ and how *Christ's mission is our mission.* The Holy Spirit guided church leaders to look beyond funding and to discover our mission. What emerged were five Mission Initiatives that call us to respond as disciples to Christ's mission.

There have been many other examples of how God cares for the church and its members. These three discoveries, for me, point to how majestic is the name of the Lord.

Prayer for Peace

Generous God, we are thankful for you continually revealing Christ's mission to us. We are awed by the surprising ways we can make Christ's mission our mission; new ways we can respond to your generosity and share the peace of Christ.

Spiritual Practice: Ongoing Revelation

One Enduring Principle of Community of Christ is Continuing Revelation. We are a people always in process, becoming shaped by God's interaction with us. In prayer, listen deeply to the name, "Community of Christ." Write or say a prayer asking God to continue to form us through our name. Listen deeply to what it would mean to live in community, following and sharing the way of Christ.

Peace Covenant

Today, God, I will be open and expectant of your constant and surprising nature.

27
Monday
May

A Time and Place for Spiritual Practice

By Candy Brayton of Independence, Missouri, USA

For as the earth brings forth its shoots, and as a garden causes what is sown in it to spring up, so the Lord God will cause righteousness and praise to spring up before all the nations.

—Isaiah 61:11

In this fast-paced era, it can be difficult to set aside time for thoughtful, deliberate prayer. We settle for quick prayers for safe travel, hurried blessings for our fast-food, and only a minute spent on our e-mailed prayer lists. Nothing is wrong with that, but God sometimes desires a deep conversation with us that is longer than 140 characters with spaces.

It shames me to admit, but I just recently, *finally*, put forth the effort to have a regular time for prayer. I'm the person for whom the saying "out of sight, out of mind" is true. To correct that, I have set aside a small area in my home to use as sacred space.

Occupying this space is a decorative cloth, a candle, rocks placed to form a cross, a journal, and a book of daily devotionals. I see this first in the morning and last at night. Each morning I begin by lighting the candle and thanking God for another day. I read the daily devotional and follow the spiritual practice.

In the evening, I write in my journal blessings for which I am most grateful and what I'd like to change in my life. If I have specific concerns, I then speak to God about them. I finish by thanking God again for another day. I snuff out the candle, taking its light with me throughout the day. This prayer time takes about fifteen minutes.

Be creative with your sacred space. Customize it to fit you. Add a chime or flowers. Decide if it's to be for personal use or for the whole family. You could even set up space for family worship and personal space for each family member. Plant the seeds now and reap the results for a lifetime.

Prayer for Peace

When we pray to you, God, we are in sacred space. Help us discipline our prayer life with regularity. Help us sow seeds of spiritual practices that we may draw on when we are low. May our prayer-life make us strong in our faith and in our sharing of Christ's peace.

Spiritual Practice: Connecting with God as Center

Connect with God through journal writing or contemplation. Open yourself to God's presence and share what flows from your heart and mind. Your "communication with God" might include thoughts, questions, feelings, needs, artwork, quotes, or scriptures. Or it might take the form of a prayer, psalm, or poem. Try to write or meditate at least five minutes each day.

What do you experience? Is this an effective way to connect with God? What surprises you? What new God images or questions emerge? What deepens or changes in your relationship with God, Christ, Spirit?

Peace Covenant

Today, God, I will set aside time to pray and return there every day.

28
Tuesday
May

The Family We Choose

By Barbara Howard of Independence, Missouri, USA

As God's chosen ones, holy and beloved, clothe yourselves with compassion, kindness, humility, meekness, and patience. Bear with one another and, if anyone has a complaint against another, forgive each other; just as the Lord has forgiven you, so you also must forgive. Above all, clothe yourselves with love, which binds everything together in perfect harmony. And let the peace of Christ rule in your hearts, to which indeed you were called in the one body. And be thankful. Let the word of Christ dwell in you richly; teach and admonish one another in all wisdom; and with gratitude in your hearts sing psalms, hymns, and spiritual songs to God. And whatever you do, in word or deed, do everything in the name of the Lord Jesus, giving thanks to God the Father through him.

—Colossians 3:12–17

My granddaughter, Grace, recently finished three years of preparation for confirmation in the Episcopal Church.

On the way to the sacramental service, she asked her mother, "Why church? I mean, why is it important to join; to belong? I belong to my family. I am a member of a soccer club, an ice hockey team, and stuff at school. Why church?"

Her mother wisely responded, "Why do *you* think church is important?"

Grace, quiet for a time, responded with conviction. "I think church is the family I choose. The family that members choose to be their family. It's a lot like our family. I know the people at church will be there for me for the rest of my life. I know I belong, and they care about me, no matter what. Yep, church is the family ***I*** choose."

Perhaps one way we can offer ministry is to cultivate those preparing for baptism, enrich their understanding of scripture, offer support for service projects, deepen their testimony of a living, loving God. Develop Disciples to Serve. Provide opportunities for them to sense they are *choosing* a family of unconditional love.

Prayer for Peace

Loving God, we choose to be in your presence. Thank you for being there, always. We choose to be with your community. May we always invite others to join us as we share Christ's peace.

Spiritual Practice: Develop Disciples to Serve

Read and reflect on Psalm 42:1–2. As disciples of Jesus Christ, we are called to respond to people and their needs. The call to inward journey can restore us in times of physical or spiritual depletion. Imagine you can feel a vessel at the center of your being (a clay jar, a crystal vase, a metal bucket, or other container). Imagine drawing something from the vessel to share, but inside you find only a tiny pool of stagnant liquid. You are thirsty and dry. Listen prayerfully again to the psalm. As you feel restored, thank God for the opportunity to be a serving disciple while you move into the outward journey. Remember this exercise as you drink water throughout the day.

Peace Covenant

Today, God, I will try to be the person others choose to be with.

29
Wednesday
May

Drippin' and Droopin'

By Suzanne McMillan of East Sandwich, Massachusetts, USA

> *He said, "My presence will go with you, and I will give you rest."*
>
> —Exodus 33:14

Summer temperatures in the coastal town where we live rarely surpass 90 degrees. One spring we had three consecutive days with temperatures in the 90s.

It was only May. It was suffocating, and I worried.

Adults were ill-prepared, school kids were drippin' and droopin', animals were panting heavily, and pregnant women were uncomfortable. The Public Health Department issued heat advisories, warning about poor air quality and urging us to stay indoors.

Except for air-conditioner salespeople, there was near universal welcome of the cool breeze accompanying a weather front arriving after 72 hours. Calming, soothing relief gently refreshed us, freeing us to stand outside and drink it in while taking deep, cleansing breaths, filling us with life anew.

God's presence, the breath of the Spirit, often feels that way, too. Welcomed as healer of sagging spirits, balm of wounds, cool rest for weary travelers, it frees us from the heavy weight on our hearts and spirits.

Prayer for Peace

Healing God, surround us with your calming breath. Lift our spirits. May we be open to you that we may find rest and peace. May we share that peace with other weary travelers.

Spiritual Practice: Breathing with the Ocean

Sit or lie in a relaxed posture. Pay attention to your breathing. Let the rhythm become calm and even. Imagine sitting or lying on a warm, sandy beach with ocean waves rolling in and out near your feet. Listen to the waves as they "exhale" and "inhale." Begin to breathe in time with the waves. Become aware of the ocean as the presence of God washing onto the shore to touch your body and spirit. With each breath receive what the ocean of God brings you. Let go of what is carried into the sea of God's presence. Offer a prayer of thanksgiving. Ask how you can share God's healing and peace today.

Peace Covenant

I will freely breathe in your presence, God, and rest in your Spirit.

30
Thursday
May

A Joyful Day at Chemotherapy

By Nancy Hylton of Seattle, Washington, USA

How beautiful upon the mountains are the feet of the messenger who announces peace, who brings good news, who announces salvation, who says to Zion, "Your God reigns." Listen! Your sentinels lift up their voices, together they sing for joy...

—Isaiah 52:7–8

My mother remarried many years after my father passed away. We recently learned her new husband's stage-four cancer, which had been in remission, had begun to metastasize. He has an exceptional oncologist, and yesterday he had his first day of treatment, not to cure, but to try to give mom and "dad" more precious time together.

I prayed, "Lord, help me find practical ways to hold them up in this uncertain future." I joined my sister and them at the chemo session. I have no doubt that God answers prayer and, in this case, in most remarkable ways!

Yesterday, in what I can describe only as a desperate medical treatment, we shared together in one of the most joyous family companionship days I can remember since mom and dad's blessed wedding day.

We laughed frequently and felt warmth in that tiny clinical room despite complex machines and multiple bags of poison dripping into his body. He was teasing, playing with words, and joking. When the nurses figured him out, they caught the joke "infection" and joined in the fun. He set aside his suffering and lifted his voice in joy.

He is a remarkable man with a positive witness. We looked at family pictures, talked of our many blessings, prayed together, and experienced overflowing cups of God's joy and love throughout the eight-hour treatment. God blessed us beyond measure!

As I was driving home, I realized I was privileged to be part of a remarkable experience. I thought of the many people I saw alone that day in the same condition. What an opportunity for ministry. Are you aware of someone who is going through a similar experience? Will those who suffer be left alone?

As a people with a mission to end suffering, we need to intentionally focus our listening skills and become the hands of Jesus.

Prayer for Peace

God who suffers with us, help us be present for others. Help us develop listening skills, a comforting witness, and a sense of peace to share with those who suffer.

Spiritual Practice: Offering Blessings of Community

Receive and share Blessings of Community. Begin with a prayer of gratitude for the relationships in your life. See and feel connections with family members, spiritual friends, people in your congregation and community, and people and creatures in God's sacred web of life. Reflect on the call to be "Community of Christ." Discern what act of blessing you are invited to complete and how you can reach out to those who are alone.

Peace Covenant

Today, God, I will respond to those who suffer, one lonely person at a time.

31
Friday
May

Evidence of God's Care

By Colleen LeRoy of Layton, Utah, USA

> *Peace I leave with you; my peace I give to you. I do not give to you as the world gives. Do not let your hearts be troubled, and do not let them be afraid.*
>
> —John 14:27

One morning while I was walking to catch my bus, the Creator caught my breath as I stopped to watch a hawk fly from one tree to another.

She had food for her little ones.

As I watched her preside over her nest, I became aware of God's constant presence and care for us. God sees our needs and provides food for our nourishment. God knows our concerns—we need not fear. We need only be vulnerable to God's grace.We are blessed with divine generosity and love.

God's arms gather me in—
reaching far as hawk can fly
tenderly hold me safe
as we sweep across the sky
from dawn to fading light
companions through the night

God's love sends me out—
to gather and embrace
to soar with every hawk in flight,
a fledgling falters, needing grace
draw me safe within the nest,
then send me out to feed the rest.

—*Lu Mountenay*

Prayer for Peace

We open ourselves to you, our ever-present Companion. We open ourselves and pause in the middle of our busy day. We are mindful from where the wind beneath our wings comes, and to where that wind blows us. We are mindful of where you send us and with whom we will share. We pray this journey leads us in pursuit of Christ's peace.

Spiritual Practice: All Living Things

Take a walk and find a tree where you can sit (or imagine walking and sitting beneath a tree). Lean against the tree and feel the texture of the bark. Listen to the wind move through the leaves. Sit quietly and sense God's presence flowing through the tree and all creation. Offer a prayer of gratitude for your connection to all living things. Ask for grace to discern and carry out one small act of justice or healing that creates greater wholeness for the plants, animals, trees, waters, air, and land that are part of the community of creation.

Peace Covenant

Today, God, I will look for those near the risky edge of the nest and bring them to the center of the community.

1

Saturday
June

MMMs with BFFs at Camp

By Sarah Humphrey, Mary Humphrey, and Ciara LaRoque
of Independence, Missouri, USA

And the king will answer them, "Truly I tell you, just as you did it to one of the least of these who are members of my family, you did it to me."

—Matthew 25:40

At camp we did lots of activities. We helped direct campfire, and our cabin groups made up funny skits. My favorite thing about camp was the trail where we walked alone and thought about God. Where the trail led, nobody knew until the end.

The path was lit by candles and had beads at different stations. You would pick up the beads and put them on a string like a necklace. As the trail ended we found the old tabernacle.

As we sat there we talked about things in our lives and how we wanted to help others. We stayed there for hours, talking and thinking. I would like to thank my church for sending me to middle school camp.

—*Sarah*

For two years I've gone to middle school camp. I LOVE IT THERE.

My MMM (most memorable moment) was on the "walk of faith." On that walk we were blindfolded and sent into the dark to follow an obstacle course. We had to trust that people would be there for us, and that God would protect us from running into tables or smacking into a tree!

That night I learned a lot about my life, and I want to thank my congregation for sending me to camp.

—*Mary*

My experience at junior camp was awesome! I really grew closer to God. The adults did dramas, and I think that helped me understand the stories in the Bible. Luckily I got in the cabin with Sarah and Grace. At first I thought it was going to be a bunch of strangers. But it wasn't like that. We all got to know each other right from the start. Now we are BFFs (best friends forever). As we worshiped in the tabernacle, I could feel God's Spirit with all of us.

So thank you to my congregation for helping me pay for junior camp.

—*Ciara*

Prayer for Peace

Thank you, God, for a community of caring and generous people. With your Spirit, God, we are molded by them. We have memories and friendships that will last a lifetime. We are taught skills and principles to shape our lives and share the peace of Christ.

Spiritual Practice: Generosity and Discipleship

Bring a basket or other container to your place of prayer. Meditate on the link between generosity and discipleship. Write a prayer of commitment in which you name specific acts of generosity and sharing to which you feel called. Fold the paper and place the prayer in the offering container. Close by singing a hymn of gratitude or praise as you offer your gift to God.

Peace Covenant

Today, God, I will consider making an offering to campership programs as a response to your generosity.

2
Sunday
June

Glorify God

By Ron Harmon, Council of Twelve Apostles

> *O sing to the Lord a new song; sing to the Lord, all the earth. Let the heavens be glad, and let the earth rejoice; let the sea roar, and all that fills it; let the field exult, and everything in it. Then shall all the trees of the forest sing for joy*
>
> —Psalm 96:1, 11–12

I recently moved because of a new assignment for the church. One feature I like most about our new home is a room with large windows.

I can see across a beautiful landscape of sky and trees. As I write, a north wind is blowing, and the last colorful leaves are letting go of the trees.

I have taken in this scene many times before, yet each autumn it seems strangely new. The rhythms and patterns of the season bear witness to the enduring and trustworthy nature of God's love. They are like a familiar song that warms our soul and leads us into a deeper appreciation of the glory of God.

Seasons change. We experience life's challenges and joys, and they shape us over time. This year I heard the north wind rustling through the leaves with renewed intensity. Although familiar, it took on added depth because I am not the same person I was a year ago. Encounters of joy and pain carved deeper places within to recognize the beauty of creation in all its diversity.

The songs of praise expressed in the winds transitioning between seasons are the same. But our ability to sense them changes as we grow. We grow in our appreciation for all that makes life full and rich in God's presence.

The song God calls us to sing is one of hope. It sees the world not as it is but as it might be. We see beauty in the ordinary and possibility in places others view as hopeless. We reveal God's glory when we invite others to live with us in the deeper possibilities of what we and our world might become.

Prayer for Peace

God whose Spirit blows in the trees, may we hear the melody of hope for a new and peaceful world.

Spiritual Practice: Time with God

Sit quietly and let your breathing become calm and deep. Ask God's Spirit to rest on you. See or sense the Spirit anointing you in the form of wind. Ask to be made aware of God's love. Listen to the ways in which God wants to flow from your heart as living water. Give thanks that your name is "beloved," that our name is Community of Christ.

Peace Covenant

Today, God, I will listen anew to the patterns of nature.

3
Monday
June

♫ Hymn of the Month: "God Within, God Around"

By Randall E. Pratt of Lee's Summit, Missouri, USA

> *"Be still, and know that I am God!"*
>
> —Psalm 46:10

I was impressed by this simple song or chant while hiking (and gasping for breath!) on a mountain trail in a national park in Colorado. The day was sunny, the alpine flowers beautiful, and the view of the snow-capped peaks magnificent! When I am away from all the distractions of my "normal" busy life and responsibilities, it is easier for me to sense the presence of God. I feel God within me and around me when I'm not surrounded by walls.

Celtic spirituality for centuries has spoken of the "thin veil" that separates heaven from Earth. God is not distant or apart from us, even if our ability to sense or experience God is sometimes limited. And, sometimes I make that "veil" much thicker with all the busyness that claims my time, attention, and identity. I simply forget that God is present, close, real.

When I feel far from God, it is not because God is far from me. If I stop looking, stop listening, stop sensing, and stop seeking, God seems distant.

This simple song is a reminder for me of God's close, intimate, pervasive reality in my life. This is a reality I can find, touch, and inhale when I seek it. The chant refrain can be sung many times (three to 10 during a worship service), so this reality deepens within and around us as we linger in the presence of God. (Only the refrain chant will be in the new hymnal.)

Refrain Chant

God within, God around, in all creation God is found.
Holy Presence, near us, with us.

Stanzas

Mountain and plain, desert and sea; all places praise your majesty!

Maker of all, your gift this world. You touch us by Spirit and Word.

How do we know? How can we see? We sense by faith your mystery!

Author of time, all time you see. Our souls alive eternally.

Now in this time, here in this place, we find your joy, we share your grace!

Prayer for Peace

Eternal and ever-present God, we sense your creative spirit everywhere. Our souls come alive in your grace. We are still. We know.

Spiritual Practice

Contemplate this hymn as a poem. Use the refrain chant as a mantra, several times over.

4
Tuesday
June

Interrupt Yourself

By Lu Mountenay of Independence, Missouri, USA

What do people gain from all the toil at which they toil under the sun? A generation goes, and a generation comes, but the earth remains forever. The sun rises and the sun goes down, and hurries to the place where it rises. The wind blows to the south, and goes around to the north; round and round goes the wind, and on its circuits the wind returns. All streams run to the sea, but the sea is not full; to the place where the streams flow, there they continue to flow…

—Ecclesiastes 1:3–7

Ladies and gentlemen—we interrupt this scripture passage to bring you the following story:

I have a niece named Carmen. She talks nonstop. She often stops mid-sentence and asks, "Oh, and can *I* say something?" She actually interrupts herself!

It reminds me of a Spiritual Formation Team meeting with about 12 others in Florida. After dinner we settled into serious work. However, I realized it was time for the sun to set. I felt it was time for us to see the sun set, even though our big window did not face west.

I took a chance. I rudely interrupted our team leader, Carolyn Brock, and said, "Let's go out on the deck and watch the sun set." Looks of surprise and then hesitation flashed around the table. But everyone stood and said, "Let's do it." Then doubts went through my mind—I hope it's a good one.

It was! (How could a sunset *not* be good?) It was colorful and stunning. After a while, one by one, we reluctantly returned to the table. The team thanked me for the interruption.

Yes, the sun sets every day. Ho-hum. But do we look at it every day with appreciation? Look and see anew the gift of the Creator? Do we interrupt our daily, hourly, and by-the-minute agenda to be aware of the creative Spirit in all elements? I am comforted by the cycle of life, which day after awesome day brings me back full circle to my God, and I offer gratitude.

Prayer for Peace

Creator God, we aren't always aware of the rising or the setting of the sun and the moon, and yet you faithfully send them to greet us each day and night. We take comfort in this routine, which sometimes can take us by surprise.

Spiritual Practice: Light

Close your eyes, and become centered with your breath. Reflect on the statement: "The light of God is in all things," as you breathe gently in and out. Sense or see a point of light in the distance coming gradually toward you. With each breath it comes closer, growing in size and brightness. The light of God reaches you and permeates you with a deep sense of peace. Rest in the light as it surrounds and fills you. Thank God for the divine light in you.

Peace Covenant

Today, God, I will proclaim the glory of your work. I will "send the sound the Earth around, from the rising to the setting of the sun."

5
Wednesday
June

What We Have Here…Is a Failure to Communicate!

By John Bonney of Springfield, Oregon, USA

> *Scripture is an indispensable witness to the Eternal Source of light and truth, which cannot be fully contained in any finite vessel or language. Scripture has been written and shaped by human authors through experiences of revelation and ongoing inspiration of the Holy Spirit in the midst of time and culture. …Scripture, prophetic guidance, knowledge, and discernment in the faith community must walk hand in hand to reveal the true will of God. Follow this pathway, which is the way of the Living Christ, and you will discover more than sufficient light for the journey ahead.*
>
> —Doctrine and Covenants 163:7a, d

I love words and language, including nonverbal communication. It astonishes me how much we assume and translate according to our own understanding. Sometimes, I'm amazed we communicate at all. Words are notoriously slippery and ambiguous. Using them is like trying to pick up gelatin with chopsticks.

At church we may offer our thoughts in the form of a sermon or perhaps a morning message. We assume the meanings of the words we use are clear to the listener. Perhaps they are, but only with the qualification of the listener's language, culture, experience, and agenda.

I remember speaking in a nearby congregation. An elderly man was there—a sweet, enjoyable person. *He was hard of hearing.* We spoke after the service. He was all smiles and full of excitement. He told me how much he appreciated my sermon, and he discussed what he thought I'd said.

What this dear man heard was entirely different from what I thought I'd said. So I just smiled and thanked him, and we went our way—each of us thinking we knew what the other was saying. We also can be *hard of understanding.*

How do we know we are hearing what God is communicating? How do we not reshape God's meaning into what we want to hear? I think through prayer, study, and discernment we can find God's light for the journey. We let the words and Spirit form as well as inform us, not try to form the words and meanings ourselves. Have faith that as long as we don't use God's words to diminish others, they will bring us light and truth.

Prayer for Peace

Eternal Source of light and truth, give us faith to discern your words. Give us light to follow Christ's path to peace.

Spiritual Practice: Encountering Scripture as Continuing Revelation

Read and pray with Doctrine and Covenants as Continuing Revelation of God's vision for the church and creation. Choose a favorite section or focus on Sections 156—164. Read a few paragraphs and pause to pray for deep understanding.

Pray for the opening of your heart and emotions. Prayerfully ask to hear the phrase or word that speaks to you or touches your life. Stay with this word or phrase. Listen as fully openly as you can. What sense of divine presence or invitation comes?

Peace Covenant

Today, God, I will set aside my agenda and will listen and better understand.

6
Thursday
June

The Mystery of Prayer

By Dorene Kilburn of Stratford, Ontario, Canada

Then Jesus told them a parable about their need to pray always and not to lose heart. ...And will not God grant justice to his chosen ones who cry to him day and night? Will he delay long in helping them? I tell you, he will quickly grant justice to them. And yet, when the Son of Man comes, will he find faith on earth?

—Luke 18:1, 7–8

Those who believe in God know the value of prayer. Most believers have had experiences with prayer. Yet, we often find prayer a mystery. When we ask God for guidance, sometimes we get clear and immediate answers. Sometimes we don't. There are times when we wait days, weeks, months, even years.

Perhaps an answer to our prayer question is "no." Perhaps divine wisdom has chosen not to grant our "wish" because God knows, better than we do ourselves, what is best for us. It may take a long time for us to realize the wisdom of God's "no." Sometimes, when we think God is not answering our prayer, the answer may be, "Not yet...later."

Perhaps while we wait for that answer, we are learning a valuable lesson in patience. We can be sure that God does hear our prayers. God rejoices with us, and understands our uncertainties. God weeps with us. God will guide us in our spiritual journey, every step of the way.

Prayer for Peace

Faithful God, we know you are listening to our prayers. We know you weep with us when our hearts break. We know you rejoice in our faithfulness and in our sharing of Christ's peace.

Spiritual Practice: Chalice Prayer

The chalice prayer is a form of intercession. Create a cup or chalice with your hands in front of your heart. Open your heart to God's concern for the Earth and human family as you hold them in your chalice. See beauty and suffering as you lift the chalice and release the creation (open hands) to be blessed and healed by God. Form the chalice again and hold persons who have particular needs—friends, loved ones, even enemies. Lift them and release them for God's blessing. Place yourself inside the chalice as you confess your deepest needs. Lift and release yourself to God for healing. "Thank you and amen."

Peace Covenant

Faithful God, I will pray always. I will not lose heart.

7
Friday
June

P.S. "I Love You."

By Dianna Vanderkarr of Flint, Michigan, USA

> *"You have heard that it was said, 'You shall love your neighbor and hate your enemy.' But I say to you, Love your enemies and pray for those who persecute you, so that you may be children of your Father in heaven; for he makes his sun rise on the evil and on the good, and sends rain on the righteous and on the unrighteous."*
>
> —Matthew 5:43–45

During our son's recovery after intruders shot him in his home, I have had time to share precious time with him. During one moment, he shared about the grace God has given him in allowing him to forgive.

He related that if one of the young intruders were caught and able to turn his life around, then that is what my son would want. He did not want vengeance or "an eye for an eye," but grace. We learn from our children, no matter their age or ours. I'm reminded how vulnerable we are to God's grace, which freely was given to my family, expressed through my son's words. I'm reminded that we also can extend grace.

P.S. I always end a phone conversation with family by saying, "I love you." I never know when it will be the last time to say those words to them. It's important to me.

Prayer for Peace

God of grace, we would open ourselves to the forgiveness with which you bless us. Help us soften our hearts that we may forgive others. May we follow your guidance to love our enemies, even when it's a challenge. Take from us all indifference to pain and suffering. Help us feel compassion and weep with your tears. May all our actions be peaceful.

Spiritual Practice: Forgiveness

Sit in silence for a few minutes releasing all thoughts. At the end of the silence, say a silent prayer of gratitude. Now, think of something you have not forgiven, perhaps an action by a family member or a person from your congregation. As you hold that thought, breathe in deeply. With each breath, whisper, "God, open my heart." Do this "breath prayer" seven times, remembering that Jesus asks us to forgive "seventy times seven." Throughout the day take time to practice the exercise, always asking, "God, open my heart."

Peace Covenant

Today, God, I will forgive as I have been forgiven.

8
Saturday
June

Linked by Grace

By Kenneth McLaughlin of Independence, Missouri, USA

How does God's love abide in anyone who has the world's goods and sees a brother or sister in need and yet refuses help?

—1 John 3:17

Not long ago I felt privileged to visit several villages in Malawi, a country in Africa. I was a part of an Outreach International site-visit group, and I loved seeing Outreach International's impact for good.

On a beautiful, sunny, warm afternoon we left the bus and walked across a dusty plateau to share a few moments of village life. Two adults and children greeted us and walked with us to our destination. There was singing, laughter, and a sense of mutual gratitude.

After touring some homes, agricultural fields, and barns, it was time to head back. And then it happened. Three little boys walked up beside me and held my hands. It was unexpected. It was a moment of grace.

They traded off so all three had a chance to be linked to me. Mostly we walked in silence, but there was occasional laughter and pointing to scenery. We reached the bus and said farewell.

I do not doubt that we all are linked as one family with God as the divine Parent. We need and depend on one another. We cannot succeed until all of God's children have an opportunity to succeed. And we can do so much to make life better for all. Do you have the means to enable moments of grace?

Prayer for Peace

God of grace, may our moments with you be frequent. May our awareness of injustice be keen. May we share moments of grace and peace with one another.

Spiritual Practice: Abolish Poverty, End Suffering

Read and reflect on John 21:15–17 as a meditation. Let your mind be drawn to places where people have no homes. Think of refugees whose homes were destroyed by war or natural disaster. Be aware of the hungry and homeless, who wander the streets or live in shelters. Let the images fill your mind. Offer a prayer for those who are suffering. Imagine Christ tending those sheep. Think of ways you might end their suffering as part of your mission. Throughout the day, carry in your mind the voice of Christ saying: "Feed my lambs…tend my sheep…feed my sheep."

Peace Covenant

Today, God, I will examine how I might help another.

9
Sunday
June

Respond in Faith

By Wim van Klinken, director of International Headquarters

> *But she said, "As the Lord your God lives, I have nothing baked, only a handful of meal in a jar, and a little oil in a jug; I am now gathering a couple of sticks, so that I may go home and prepare it for myself and my son, that we may eat it, and die." Elijah said to her, "Do not be afraid; go and do as you have said; but first make me a little cake of it and bring it to me, and afterwards make something for yourself and your son."*
>
> —1 Kings 17:12–13

We can view the story of Elijah's meeting with the widow of Zarephath as a miracle story in which God provides food. But a closer look at the two verses above and the widow's response that follows shows us the miracle is a response in faith.

To the widow, Elijah is a foreigner who has faith in a different God. Her faith governs her certainty that the future is dire for her and her son, and they are about to die of starvation. But Elijah shares this unbelievable message of hope and says, "Do not be afraid," followed by the bold request to give him some food first!

The story does not tell us, but there must have been something about Elijah, the way he approached her, the way he talked to her, or the look on his face. He brought faith, he brought hope. But most of all, she responded in faith. She trusted the man of God who asked her to believe in the future and even to risk the welfare of her family. "She went and did as Elijah said, so she as well as he and her household ate for many days."

This story makes me wonder how much faith I have in the stranger, in the foreigner. Am I willing to listen to someone else, not of my tradition, who brings a message of hope? Or am I led by voices of fear for the existence of myself and those I love—voices that make me selfish and not willing to generously share the resources I have? I also wonder if I have enough faith to help the stranger, like Elijah did, and share a message of hope for the future, even when the future looks dire.

Prayer for Peace

Faithful God, let us take this message of faith to heart. May we be like Elijah, who had faith to share with a stranger. May we be like the widow, who responded in faith to one who was strange to her. May we share the message of hunger satisfied, hope in the future, and in the peace of Christ.

Spiritual Practice: Welcoming Unity in Diversity

Meditate on Unity in Diversity. Create a large circle with your arms. See and feel the diverse people God invites inside the sanctuary of Christ's peace represented by this circle.

Who is easiest to welcome? Whom do you struggle to include? Confess the dividing walls between you and people too different or "dangerous" to invite into your spiritual home. Ask God to forgive and heal barriers that keep us from sharing with one another.

Peace Covenant

Today, God, I will not hesitate to share my witness with a stranger.

10
Monday
June

The Real World

By Janné Grover of Lee's Summit, Missouri, USA

Listen to its teachings and discover anew its principles. Do not yearn for times that are past, but recognize that you have been given a foundation of faithful service, even as you build a foundation for what is yet to be.

—Doctrine and Covenants162:2b

I have had several experiences that remind me of the joy and blessings of being in community. The makeup of the community may vary, and the blessings may come in various ways, but all are important. These blessings reinforce Community of Christ's mission to promote communities of joy, hope, love, and peace.

Our family attended a reunion where we spent the week with family and friends from our congregation and mission center. It was wonderful to draw apart and experience being in a community centered on Christ and focused on renewal and forming discipleship.

After spending time at reunion, it is difficult for me to face going back into the "real world." I want to be back in that peaceful place, away from the distractions and responsibilities of everyday life.

I am reminded, however, that I am completely missing the point of service and outreach. I can't be part of the outward journey if I just want to cling to the safety of that unique and sacred community. I am called to take those experiences, gain strength from them, and participate in creating that sense of sacred community wherever I am.

Prayer for Peace

Thank you, God, for meeting us in our sacred places. May we take your Spirit with us to share wherever we go. Help us share the peace of Christ in our everyday lives.

Spiritual Practice: Offering Blessings of Community

Receive and share Blessings of Community. Begin with a prayer of gratitude for the relationships in your life. See and feel connections with family members, spiritual friends, people in your congregation and community, and people and creatures in God's sacred web of life. What blessings flow to you from these circles? How have you felt the love of the community?

Reflect, pray, or write in your journal about the call to be "Community of Christ." Go deeper each day as you discern what act of blessing you are invited to complete.

Peace Covenant

Today, God, as I share in my community, I will invite people to Christ.

11

Tuesday
June

It's Peaches Tonight

By Greg Savage of Lee's Summit, Missouri, USA

For the kingdom of God is not food and drink but righteousness and peace and joy in the Holy Spirit. The one who thus serves Christ is acceptable to God and has human approval.

—Romans 14:17–18

What do peaches have to do with stewardship? Technically, nothing! But, every time I see a can of peaches, I think of my friend, Walter, a good steward.

As a graduation present, some friends and I went to Europe. We met Walter on our first full day in London. We hit it off with him—joking and kidding one another as if we had been friends for years.

The first meal we had with him and his sister, Jenny, we learned about peaches. "When we have company and there is a spoon at the head of the plate," he explained, "Jenny will probably serve my favorite dessert, peaches." We had peaches that night.

Walter shared his testimony of how their family had lived in the slums of London and had come to know the gospel through contact with Community of Christ. He spoke of having "water soup" as a child. The soup was made from cast-off bones from the butcher shop and maybe some onion and bits of potato. His mother would pray over the meal, but often would not have a bowl herself. He testified that the principles of A Disciple's Generous Response helped lift his family from its impoverished condition.

Walter loved the Lord and served in any way he could. He was a printer by trade and used one week of his vacation to travel, at his own expense, with one of the missionaries to share the gospel. He and Jenny lived in a three-bedroom house close to the church. Over the years, they hosted many visitors who came to the Enfield Congregation.

Their ministry of hospitality was a comfort and a blessing to all.

When I see peaches, I think of Walter—a testimony of one who responded to God's abundance with Mission Initiatives at heart.

Prayer for Peace

God of righteousness and peace, we take joy in your Holy Spirit. May our service be acceptable to you. May it be a blessing to others.

Spiritual Practice: Reflection on Hunger

Bring a piece of bread to your worship space and hold it in your hands. Reflect on all the people and processes that made this bread possible. See and remember the farmers growing and harvesting the grain; the millers, bakers, transportation workers, and grocers. Offer a prayer of gratitude and blessing for all who have worked to create this bread. Take a bite. Chew slowly, and let it become part of your body. Ask for compassion and courage to offer bread to all who hunger.

Peace Covenant

As I look on the blessings of life, God, I will be reminded of ways to bless others.

12
Wednesday
June

A Spiritual Fit

By Donna Boyd of Independence, Missouri, USA

> *But the wisdom from above is first pure, then peaceable, gentle, willing to yield, full of mercy and good fruits, without a trace of partiality or hypocrisy.*
>
> —James 3:17

I worked in a small branch library where I was the only employee. A card catalog file and table were delivered in two pieces. The table had no top, but had ridges to fit the card file.

I tried several ways to put them together with no success. Finally, I decided the wrong table had been sent, so I set the file on another table.

When a librarian came from the county, she was surprised to see the file on a different table. She told me the two pieces had been together in another library and were sent directly to me. So I decided to try again. With my husband's help, I finally fit them together.

I find spiritual concerns to be similar. People read promises in the scriptures and want to claim the blessings that are theirs. They want everything magically to fit together. The results often disappoint when they do not understand the connection between doing the work of the kingdom and receiving the fruits.

Sometimes our testimonies can renew the faith of those around us. As we Invite People to Christ, together we can share the fruits.

Prayer for Peace

God of wisdom, without partiality we will follow your guidance. Being vulnerable to your grace, we will extend mercy to one another. Being willing to yield, we will share of the fruits of the spirit. We will share Christ's peace.

Spiritual Practice: Teacher-learner

The first disciples of Jesus followed to hear his words, to be taught, to learn a new way of living, to practice what they learned in daily life. Prayerfully consider your role as a teacher-learner, disciple-apprentice; a people cultivator in Community of Christ. In your journal write the names of several persons you discern as teachers or mentors and several you feel called to nurture and encourage in specific ways. Ask God's blessing on you and your congregation as a community of learners.

Peace Covenant

Today, God, I will gently invite people to Christ.

13
Thursday
June

Riding Tandem with God

By Jena Wight of Blue Springs, Missouri, USA

> *. . . but those who wait for the Lord shall renew their strength, they shall mount up with wings like eagles, they shall run and not be weary, they shall walk and not faint.*
>
> —Isaiah 40:31

I was riding on the back of a broken bicycle, holding on for dear life—literally and figuratively. My World Service Corps partner, Tara, and I had been in Africa for over a month. We were starting to feel the physical and emotional strains of our living conditions.

As I rocked and bumped along the road on the way to preach at the Milenje Congregation in Malawi, I wondered how I could stand before the people and say anything significant when I felt frustrated and tired.

So I prayed—almost the whole bike ride to the church. I prayed for everything from strength for Tara, to forgiveness for my attitude, to asking that my heart be softened.

We arrived at the church, and Tara and I looked at each other and knew we'd both been doing the same thing on the ride.

We started morning Bible study in the little church, with the sun peeking through the small holes that served as windows.

Babies, teenagers, adults, the pastor, and our host father sat on clay benches. The eager eyes of the people were trained on us. They were full of willingness and openness.

I shared the story of "Footprints in the Sand."

As I got to the last line, my voice caught as I realized—God is carrying me. Here. Now.

Like the promise in Isaiah, God took away my weariness and gave me strength. I knew as I sat there I would be OK.

No matter what happened the rest of the summer, or the rest of my life, I had a new peace—a new strength and dependence on God, who carries me still.

Prayer for Peace

We depend on you, God, for leadership and spiritual strength. You are the brace when our knees would buckle; our penetrating light when our eyes would fall wearily shut. You give us faith when we doubt ourselves. Your arms carry us when we fall short of our mission. You are our words when we forget how to share the peace of Christ.

Spiritual Practice: The International Community

Find (or imagine) a globe or map of the world. Look at all the nations and find a country other than your own. Notice the geographic distance between your homeland and this one. Picture a person living there. Pray for this person. Sense God's love connecting you just as the oceans connect the continents. Thank God for the spiritual connection you have with all of God's people around the globe. Ask a blessing on the church as a community sharing Christ's peace, drawing all into the family of God.

Peace Covenant

Today, God, I will remember Christ's mission is my mission.

14
Friday
June

Ministries of Blessing in Nepal

By Terry Connell of Silver Spring, Maryland, USA

> *...who made heaven and earth, the sea, and all that is in them; who keeps faith forever; who executes justice for the oppressed; who gives food to the hungry.*
>
> —Psalm 146:6–7

My wife, Charlene, and I spent a month in India, and four days in neighboring Nepal. In India we visited relatives of Charlene's father, who was Indian. We also presented a check from the sale of Charlene's parents' property to the Damien Welfare Society, which her father helped found. The society set up many leper colonies in the 1960s and still treats patients with Hansen's disease.

We visited the Kathmandu Congregation in Nepal. The service was joyful, with energetic participation and great singing. The 200 attendees paid close attention as the service continued for two hours. The prayers were long, as customary. The children's choir and two young soloists delighted us.

Charlene spoke in Hindi about her great-grandfather's conversion to Christianity from being a Hindu priest. She closed by teaching a praise hymn in Hindi. For the message of the day, I drew from my experiences in ministry, and another minister translated for me. I expressed encouragement and assurance of support through the Holy Spirit. I shared how others around the world were praying for the people of Nepal.

As a concrete example of this, I had asked evangelists from the Chesapeake Bay USA Mission Center to write letters of greeting and support to give encouragement to one sister in Nepal who was a newly ordained evangelist. This sister played a significant role in starting the Nepal church. Also, the past president of the mission center wrote a letter. The evangelist also wrote to the pastor of the Kathmandu Congregation.

I gave these letters to the leaders as I spoke of their responsibilities and their years in the service of Christ. They expressed their appreciation for the kind thoughts and assurances of support through prayers for them. They were deeply touched, knowing many others are concerned for them and wish them well. This is one of the Blessings of Community.

Prayer for Peace

God whose children span the Earth, may we reach out and share Christ's peace with people of all lands. May we always keep them in our prayers.

Spiritual Practice: Embodying God's Shalom

Begin by prayerfully listening to your longing for peace. Become silent and imagine you can hear the groaning of the Earth's people, nations, and creatures. Prayerfully open yourself to God's yearning for peace and the divine vision of shalom. What images, feelings, and prayers for peace come to you from your time of listening? What act of justice, kindness, healing, or peacemaking does God invite you to consider?

Peace Covenant

Today, God, I will check the Daily Prayer for Peace country in the front of this book and pray for the people of that nation.

15
Saturday
June

Continue in Their Footsteps

By Carole Heathers of Stratford, Ontario, Canada

"...give, and it will be given to you. A good measure, pressed down, shaken together, running over, will be put into your lap; for the measure you give will be the measure you get back."

—Luke 6:38

As I sit by the river at our church campgrounds, Ziontario, I feel peace through the beauty God has created here. I listen as the water flows over the rocks, and I feel tension fall away from my body. I smell the sweet fragrance of the cedars, and I slow my breathing. I hear the sounds of birds, and I quiet my mind. The wind blows gently through the trees, and I know God is here.

My bench was placed in this special spot by our family. It is in memory of my mother- and father-in–law. I remember how much they loved this place and how willingly they worked to maintain the campgrounds. Not only them, but a large group of friends.

They worked, ate, played, laughed, and cried together. This group of dedicated people gave their labor and financial support to these grounds because they wanted future generations to experience the blessings of our church camping program.

Most of them are gone now, but they instilled in us an appreciation and love for these grounds and a wish to continue in their footsteps.

So I listen to the river, I smell the cedar, I hear the birds, I sit in peace because of the faithfulness of those who loved and cared for this place.

May I be so faithful and generous.

Prayer for Peace

Generous God, we would be generous, too. You fill our senses with your creation. Our hearts are filled with the peace of Christ, and we are ready to share.

Spiritual Practice: Spiritual Hunger

Jesus discerned hungers of body and spirit, and he fed them through a physical, verbal, spiritual ministry of presence. In a time of listening prayer, ask God to help you discern physical or spiritual hungers of people in your congregation, community, and global family. Invite the Spirit to move you to one hospitable act that "feeds" someone's hunger today.

Peace Covenant

Today, God, as I prepare my mission tithes, I will ponder the places and programs that develop disciples to serve.

16
Sunday
June

Make Responsible Choices

By Dave Schaal of Independence, Missouri, USA

"I spoke to Naboth the Jezreelite and said to him, 'Give me your vineyard for money; or else, if you prefer, I will give you another vineyard for it'; but he answered, 'I will not give you my vineyard.'" His wife Jezebel said to him, "Do you now govern Israel?...I will give you the vineyard of Naboth..." Two scoundrels came in and...brought a charge against Naboth, in the presence of the people, saying, "Naboth cursed God and the king." So they took him outside the city, and stoned him to death. As soon as Ahab heard that Naboth was dead, Ahab set out to go down to the vineyard...to take possession of it. Ahab said to Elijah, "Have you found me, O my enemy?" He answered, "I have found you. Because you have sold yourself to do what is evil in the sight of the Lord, I will bring disaster on you..."

—1 Kings 21:6–7, 13, 16, 20–21

I am writing this in December. Where I live, December is cold, and the voices on the radio remind me of children in my city who go without the warmth of a good coat.

Last week, I stood in a store looking at a coat that I wanted. I stood a long time, wondering what a "responsible choice" would be. There would be nothing inherently wrong with me buying it. At the same time, my mind went to those kids. I could use the money to help them.

So, I stood motionless in front of the coat, greed and guilt arguing with each other. What does it mean to make a responsible choice? To neglect the poor is unchristian. To neglect my own needs is unwise. The gospel is easy in principle. It's more challenging in the specific.

I share this struggle with you today because I am thankful for it. I am thankful because it is the fruit of my involvement in Community of Christ. Were it not for my faith community, it would be easy to surrender to the demands of consumer culture that declare "it's all about me...my happiness...and my capacity to buy."

In my faith community, though, I am reminded that caring for the poor is at the heart of our call as disciples of Jesus Christ. I remember the scriptures that shape our church, in the welfare of those children resides my welfare.

My struggle in front of the coat was real, and I still struggle at times to know what the responsible choice is. I praise God, though, that I belong to a church that invokes that struggle in me, because of its faithful demands that we love and care for people in need.

Prayer for Peace

Merciful God, may we always pause and evaluate our decisions in light of justice.

Spiritual Practice: Abolish Poverty, End Suffering

Read and reflect on John 21:15–17 as a meditation. Let your mind be drawn to places in the world where people have no homes. Think of those who are refugees from their homeland. Be aware of those who are hungry and homeless, who wander the streets or live in shelters. Let the images fill your mind.

Offer a prayer for those who are suffering. Imagine Christ tending those sheep. Think of ways you might end their suffering, as part of your mission. Throughout the day, carry in your mind the voice of Christ saying: "Feed my lambs...tend my sheep."

Peace Covenant

Today, God, it will not be "all about me."

17
Monday
June

Who's Your Coach?

By Evelyn Richardson of Nauvoo, Illinois, USA

Whoever serves me must follow me, and where I am, there will my servant be also. Whoever serves me, the Father will honor.

—John 12:26

It was our day off from the Joseph Smith Historic Site in Nauvoo, Illinois. We had our list of tasks to accomplish—pick up groceries, gas up the car, get the mail, and so on. We drove across the river into Iowa for our groceries.

My husband, Don, and I were commenting on the surroundings when a church sign caught our attention. It read, "Life without God is like trying to dribble a football."

Now you can add your own interpretation to that message. I quickly recalled playing basketball in high school and the occasional times I hit my foot with the ball. It went flying in a direction I hadn't planned.

Life can be like that, too. Without having God's direction and with wrongly shaped principles we might as well be trying to dribble an American-style football. Our direction will be driven by the winds, and we may be tossed to and fro.

We each must seek to discover what God would have us be and do in service to others. One Enduring Principle is Continuing Revelation. It states, "In humility, individually and in community, we prayerfully listen to understand God's will for our lives, the church, and creation more completely."

Don't try to dribble a football. God is our head coach, and we need divine guidance in our lives. Follow Christ.

Prayer for Peace

Creator God, may we use the gifts you have given us in the way you intended. May we develop as disciples who make responsible choices to use our tools and talents to share the peace of Christ.

Spiritual Practice: Hand Ministry

Place your hand on a piece of paper and trace around it to create an outline. Add details of fingernails, wrinkles, or skin color if desired. Look at your hand and meditate on what you do with your hands each day. Ask God to direct your thoughts to a person in need of blessing, kindness, or healing touch. Pray for wisdom about the specific act needed by this person and discern how and when you will use your hands to complete this ministry.

Peace Covenant

Today, God, I will not dribble footballs or kick basketballs, but I will use my hands and feet according to your purposes.

18
Tuesday
June

Lamenting Tears, Cleansing Tears

By Peggy Michael of Cantonment, Florida, USA

> *Save me, O God, for the waters have come up to my neck. I sink in deep mire, where there is no foothold; I have come into deep waters, and the flood sweeps over me. I am weary with my crying; my throat is parched. My eyes grow dim with waiting for my God.*
>
> —Psalm 69:1–3

O hard and rigid heart, why do you withhold yourself from those burdened with sorrow? Are you afraid to touch soiled hands and dusty feet? How much does a smile cost? Withholding smiles costs more.

Repent your stubborn ways. Feel the comforting warmth of bodies near you. Remember those far away—those whom only a prayer can reach. O hard and rigid heart, beware, lest your own tears mingle with the forgotten.

Despair mingles with hope as tears fall upon the ground.

Tears recall moments of tenderness and regret. The unchecked flood sweeps away my pride and harsh thought.

My head, now bowed low, is no longer cast about in haughty nods.

When my tears stop flowing I can see more clearly, for they have washed clean the windows of my soul.

Prayer for Peace

Creator God, your living water blesses us. It does not overcome us with deep, turbulent floods. We have not had to wait as long for you as have those who suffer. Is it we, God, who have caused suffering by our apathy and greed? Prompt us to swift action so Christ's justice and peace will not delay.

Spiritual Practice: Flowing Water

If possible, sit where you can hear the sound of water—a fountain, stream, the sea, (perhaps a recording of water sounds). Listen to the sound as you thank God for the life-giving, life-shaping power of water. Pray for God's blessing on all the parched places of the Earth where there is injustice, oppression, violence, and disregard for life. Pray for God's justice to be released and imagine it flowing over the Earth, restoring righteousness and wholeness. Now, get up and drink a glass of clear, cold water as you pray, "God, let your justice flow through me as a disciple of the Lord Jesus."

Peace Covenant

Today, God, I will respond immediately to tears. I will not make the suffering wait.

19
Wednesday
June

Well of Transformation

By Darrell Belrose of Calgary, Alberta, Canada

> *. . . and above all things, clothe yourselves with the bonds of charity, as with a mantle, which is the bond of perfectness and peace; pray always, that you may not faint until I come; behold, and lo, I will come quickly, and receive you unto myself. Amen.*
>
> —Doctrine and Covenants 85:38c

From the birth of an idea to the fruit of its life, time and frustration levels swung from one extreme to the other. But in the end the journey was overwhelmingly sweet and satisfying. The expected ending was ironically just the beginning!

This was the case when I planned an "Invitational Retreat" for the missionary-minded folks in the Canada West Mission Centre.

Two guest ministers shared equally their leadership in "mindfulness" practices and "tangible kingdom" opportunities. Not only did we learn to look at doing church differently, we sensed God's call for us to respond affirmatively. We also discovered we were going much deeper within—to our God-center—where God wanted to love us. We rested within God's presence, and the "well of transformation" refreshed us.

Our collective journey brought many opportunities to build connections with our group. God challenged us with a call for each of us to go beyond our horizons, to sense a personal call. Today, God reassures us of blessing as we continue to trust the divine promises for our futures.

I praise God for ideas birthed, for guest ministers who willingly gave of themselves.

I am most thankful for those who are willing to respond to the call and walk in partnership down unknown roads on pathways of mission.

Prayer for Peace

Transforming God, we are open to your calling. We are willing to respond. Inspire us with ideas to continue Christ's mission, with ways to share his peace.

Spiritual Practice: Invite People to Christ

Read and reflect on Doctrine and Covenants 162:3b and 163:2b. Pray to be aware of people who might be receptive, and therefore blessed, by your sharing the message of the Living Christ. Imagine being in relationship with them and inviting them to Christ. In preparation, discover your personal testimony of Christ. "Be persistent in your witness and diligent in your mission to the world." Repeat this mantra throughout the day: Christ's mission, our mission, my mission.

Peace Covenant

Today, God, I will live as an open invitation to Christ.

20
Thursday
June

A Small Price to Pay

By Jeanne Hough of Clare, Michigan, USA

Let us then pursue what makes for peace and for mutual upbuilding.

—Romans 14:19

I sat in my recliner, suffering in great pain after a serious fall. I broke my arm and bruised my whole body. Why did this have to happen? My favorite ministry project is to serve at Clare's Senior Center. I was indispensable. I took charge of all the little tasks that needed to be done—calling bingo, buying prizes, baking cakes for birthday and anniversary celebrations. I decorated for holidays. And coming up next week, the silent auction flea market, of which I was in charge, needed to be set up for bidding.

Now what do we do? As chair of the Senior Advisory Board I often found myself complaining that I had to do everything, and no one else helped. The truth is I needed to feel needed. Now I had to find others who would see the project through. Their response amazed me.

They set up the silent auction with 10 big tables of donated, saleable items. The auction went off without a hitch and was a huge success. It was then that I realized others also need to feel needed. This turn of events made their blossoming possible.

I found an interesting way to look at indispensable people like me. My mishap put me out of commission, and others in the community stepped up. They had the opportunity and joy of being needed. Thank you, God, for helping me find a positive at the cost of my discomfort. It was a small price to pay.

And to those who lead: Don't hesitate to share with those who usually follow. Let them experience the opportunities and joys of accomplishment while serving in their own way.

Prayer for Peace

God of grace, when we feel needed, we feel we are addressing what matters most. Help us remember to share that feeling with others. May we build up others to have the confidence to share the peace of Christ.

Spiritual Practice: Offering Blessings of Community

Receive and share Blessings of Community. Begin with a prayer of gratitude for the relationships in your life. See and feel connections with family members, spiritual friends, people in your congregation and community, and people and creatures in God's sacred web of life. What blessings flow to you from these circles?

Reflect, pray, or write in your journal about the call to be "Community of Christ." Go deeper each day as you discern what act of blessing you are invited to complete.

Peace Covenant

Today, God, I will take a break from being indispensable, and allow others to feel needed.

21
Friday
June

God: Hidden below the Surface

By Peggy Young of Blue Springs, Missouri, USA

For you shall go out in joy, and be led back in peace; the mountains and the hills before you shall burst into song, and all the trees of the field shall clap their hands.

—Isaiah 55:12

It's June 20, the summer solstice in the northern hemisphere, the transition of spring into summer. The riotous blooming of spring is over. Farmers planted their fields. Seedlings are starting to grow. Of all the seasonal shifts, this one, to me, is the least noticeable.

The arrival of spring is dramatic. Warmth returns. Lush greens replace tired browns. Blossoms and flowers of all colors cheer the landscape. Birdsong fills the air. Almost as spectacular is the arrival of fall with the turn of color in the leaves and a decided chill in the evening air. And who can miss the advent of icy winds and shimmering snow in winter?

A rise in temperature, however, is usually the only sign summer has arrived. We tend not to notice the tiny buds left behind after warm breezes blow away the flowers. Crops grow in the fields with subtle change. Unless you walk among the rows, you are unaware of the produce taking shape and getting larger. Yet, it is happening.

We often become impatient during times in our lives when we don't see any productivity. But though we may be unaware, something is happening. God is always working within us, behind the scenes, and hidden below the surface. Previously planted seeds may be ripening unseen in our hearts and souls. When the harvest of our hearts is ready, will we be ready to reap?

Perhaps a fresh chance will arise to forgive someone who wronged us long ago. Perhaps a new idea will burst into our awareness, ready for us to write about, speak about, or just accept. Perhaps an opportunity to show love, long in preparation, will come about.

Let us rejoice during times of unseen growth and preparation and pray that we recognize the harvest when it arrives.

Prayer for Peace

We are joyful, Creator, for we know the harvest lies just below the surface. We hear the birds sing and know the soil is ready to burst with new life. A fresh chance lies just ahead to forgive and to share Christ's peace.

Spiritual Practice: Caring for God's Sacred Creation

Choose a way to notice, give thanks, and care for God's sacred creation. Prayerfully consider one of the following practices or create your own. Walk in nature with a spirit of gratitude while looking and listening for God in all things. Write or pray a psalm of praise for the Earth's beauty or a prayer of healing and blessing for its wounds.

Learn about and engage in an act of Earth-keeping such as recycling, simple living, or fasting from over-consumption of resources. Notice the diversity of the planet's creatures and be gentle to plants, animals, trees, and people! Fall in love with the vast, intricate wonder of God's creation and give thanks.

Peace Covenant

Today, God, I will nurture the seeds growing in my soul.

22
Saturday
June

Children of Courage and Compassion

By Sherri Kirkpatrick of Lee's Summit, Missouri, USA

The earth is full, and there is enough and to spare; yea, I prepared all things, and have given unto the children of the earth to be agents unto themselves.

—Doctrine and Covenants 101:2f, adapted

Children from Escondido, California, want the children in Zambia, a country in Africa, to know they have friends in the USA.

The Escondido children drew pictures and words depicting courage and compassion. They also sent photos of themselves. They are eager to develop a continuing connection with the children in Chipulukusu and Kasompe in Zambia.

One person with passion is often the catalyst for moving an entire group. A fourth-grade class in West Des Moines, Iowa, is no exception. Braedon Kirkpatrick made an impassioned plea to his class for the kids in Africa. As a result the class partnered with HealthEd Connect on a character-development project.

One class posed for a photo while holding the posters made for children of the schools in Kasompe and Chipulukusu, showing in pictures and words the characteristics of respect and responsibility.

The children learned about the kids in Africa through a class presentation by Braedon. The pictures accompanied the HealthEd Connect team and were presented to the children in the Zambian schools. Pictures will be taken of the children in Zambia and sent back to the fourth-grade classes in West Des Moines. Friendship, caring, and new awareness now stretch around the world. What fun!

Kendra, Maya, and Georgia Seagraves from California were so touched by the needs of the children in Zambia that they decided to make their connection a long-term project. They put a jar on the kitchen table where they placed donated money they earned or were given, and they graciously accepted other donations from family. When Kendra received US$10 in a birthday card, she immediately ran to the jar and donated the entire amount.

They have donated enough to provide 1,500 school lunches! What an awesome response by awesome kids.

Prayer for Peace

God of all nations, help us send our compassion around the world. May we learn from the generous response of the children how to share your peace.

Spiritual Practice: Honoring the Worth of All Persons

Sense the intimate knowledge God has of you and every child. Be aware of the sacred worth of each person. Weep with God over the soul-wounding forces and events that rob people of dignity and worth. How are you invited to notice, protect, heal, and affirm the spiritual identity of all God's beloved people today? Pray for God's compassion.

Peace Covenant

Today, God, I will make generous choices for what matters most.

23
Sunday
June

Where Do We Encounter God?

By David Brock, presiding evangelist

> *Now there was a great wind...but the Lord was not in the wind; and after the wind an earthquake, but the Lord was not in the earthquake; and after the earthquake a fire, but the Lord was not in the fire; and after the fire a sound of sheer silence... Then there came a voice to him that said, "What are you doing here, Elijah?" He answered...the Israelites have... killed your prophets with the sword. I alone am left, and they are seeking my life... Then the Lord said to him, "Go...you shall anoint Hazael as king over Aram."*
>
> —1 Kings 19:11–15

Being a prophet is difficult!

Elijah risks his life to stand up for God before the prophets of Baal. And what is his reward? A pledge by Queen Jezebel to kill him within 24 hours! Afraid and feeling sorry for himself Elijah flees into the wilderness, lies down under a lonely tree, and pleads with God for death.

But, God is not done with Elijah. God does not abandon him, but provides warm baked cake and fresh water...*twice*! Later, there is a cave to shelter him and the presence of the Holy in the unforgettable "sound of sheer silence." God does *not* let Elijah have the desire of his discouraged heart to go to sleep and never wake up.

Being a prophet is difficult!

God nurtures and cares for Elijah but does not stop there.

God demands, "What are you doing here, Elijah?" And God gives a directive: "Get up and eat!...Go out!...Stand on the mountain!" And, again, later: "Go, return on your way!...Go, anoint the king!"

If Elijah's life is a guide for our own, we can assume God meets us anywhere God wants, but often not where *we* expect. Many proclaim God's presence in earthquake, wind, and fire, but sheer silence may more often be the place of encounter. It may be in notable and public ways—walls come down; there is a sea change in political and economic arenas; societies free captives and restore justice.

But is God less present in our fears, in our lonely, wilderness places, in our want-to-give-up-and-die times? Sometimes God encounters by nurturing and protecting and comforting. Sometimes God says, "Get up...Go out... Stand...Return...Go!"

Being a *disciple* is difficult!

Encounters with God can be difficult. However, they also restore, refresh, and renew. We cannot go anywhere where God will not or cannot meet us. Thanks be to God!

Prayer for Peace

Covenant God, you are there, in the silence, to comfort us when we are afraid, to feed us when we are hungry, to give us strength for Christ's mission.

Spiritual Practice: Reflection on Hunger

Hold a piece of bread in your hands. Reflect on the people and work that made this bread possible: the farmers, millers, bakers, transportation workers, and grocers. Offer a prayer of gratitude and blessing for all who worked to create this bread. Ask for compassion and courage to offer bread to all who hunger.

Peace Covenant

Today, God, I will *get up* and *go out* to engage in Christ's mission.

24
Monday
June

Under the Bed

By Ward Serig of Pensacola, Florida, USA

> *A poor widow came and put in two small copper coins, which are worth a penny. Then he called his disciples and said to them, "Truly I tell you, this poor widow has put in more than all those who are contributing to the treasury. For all of them have contributed out of their abundance; but she out of her poverty has put in everything she had, all she had to live on."*
>
> —Mark 12:42–44

Several children in our congregation were preparing for the time when they would enter the waters of baptism. Their teacher asked, "What are some ways you help your parents at home?" One boy responded, "I push everything in my room under the bed so it will look like I cleaned the room."

I have often thought about the youngster's reply. I find myself wondering if, and when, I have pushed things "under the bed" and out of sight to impress others. Jesus came down hard on those in his time who behaved in this manner. He didn't think much of those who prayed in public to remind their hearers how righteous they were.

He affirmed the widow who gave her last, small bit rather than those whose large coins made a loud noise when tossed into the offering bowl. He rebuked those who tithed meticulously but were dishonest in their private dealings, not caring about helping those in need.

Perhaps when I am tempted to push debris "under the bed" I should ask myself, "When will it pile up and be pushed out on the other side for all to see?" A better question might be, "What would Jesus do?"

Prayer for Peace

All-seeing and all-knowing God, may we be sincere in our generosity and give with sacrificial love. May we never separate ourselves from you by trying to hide that for which we are ashamed. May we come repentant and freely receive your grace. May we be transparent and genuine so we may freely share Christ's peace.

Spiritual Practice: Making Responsible Choices

Prayerfully seek God's guidance in your choices. Discernment invites us to orient our lives toward God and God's vision for us and creation. Begin by reviewing the responsibilities and opportunities in the day before you. Take these choices into prayer, asking God for wisdom and insight about what matters most.

Offer yourself to God with the prayer of Teresa of Avila: "God, what do you want of me today?" Sit prayerfully with this question as you review the day again. Be aware of images, thoughts, names, or actions that come to you. Ask for a blessing to live this day responsibly and compassionately in the Spirit of Christ.

Peace Covenant

Today, God, I will repent and rejoice in your grace.

25
Tuesday
June

A New Life in Christ

By Cindy L. Korf of North Platte, Nebraska, USA

I will make a covenant of peace with them; it shall be an everlasting covenant with them; and I will bless them and multiply them, and will set my sanctuary among them forevermore. My dwelling place shall be with them; and I will be their God, and they shall be my people.

—Ezekiel 37:26–27

I live in a part of the USA once called the "Great American Desert." It is land that was considered unfit for cultivation and inhabitation by people, mainly because of the lack of water. Yet, as the early pioneers traversed this land, the sight of lone windmills soon sprinkled the terrain. Those windmills—the source of water and life—changed this land into a place of value and new life.

We, too, are sparse in an inhospitable world. We who would be sanctuaries and signal communities for those on a spiritual journey can point to a God whose dwelling place is among us. Through Christ, each of us becomes a new person, a landmark offering hope and life in a barren world. We can be windmills for the wearied voyager by directing them to the living water of Christ. Here they will find a new and blessed life. What once was considered worthless is now rich and valuable.

Prayer for Peace

God who sends us Living Water, we need not thirst again. God who sets sanctuary among us, we are not afraid. God who calls us to be sanctuary for others, may we share the peace of Christ.

Spiritual Practice: Invite People to Christ

Read and reflect on Doctrine and Covenants 162:3b and 163:2b. Pray to be aware of people who might be receptive, and therefore blessed, by your sharing of the message of the Living Christ. Imagine being in relationship with them and inviting them to Christ. In preparation, discover your personal testimony of Christ. "Be persistent in your witness and diligent in your mission to the world." Repeat this mantra throughout the day: "Christ's mission, our mission, my mission."

Peace Covenant

Today, God, I will be a beacon for the lost, a well for the thirsty.

26
Wednesday
June

Hospitality

By Carolyn Brock of Redmond, Oregon, USA

> *Be patient with one another, for creating sacred community is arduous and even painful. But it is to loving community such as this that each is called. Be courageous and visionary, believing in the power of just a few vibrant witnesses to transform the world…*
>
> —Doctrine and Covenants 161:3c

Fish in coconut sauce, fried crickets, warm Coke, and spiced chai (tea) were among the delicacies we enjoyed in the homes of African church friends. We soon learned the hospitable sharing of food is a central theme of African community life.

We never entered a home, no matter how small, in which hosts did not offer food or drink. This was not preferential treatment for white missionaries. Everyone who enters an African home is offered food. To fail to give or accept hospitality is an offense, a sign that community and trust do not exist.

Feeding one another, sharing our basic substance, is the way we support each other's being. To be in community means to live together in life-sustaining, soul-nurturing ways. Survival in tribal terms hinges on being in community.

What can we do about the survival of our tribe? How does our survival depend on being in community? How can we live up to the name "Community of Christ" without also taking on the hospitable, inclusive behaviors of Jesus, who shared physical and spiritual food? Jesus' actions define community as life-supporting, wholeness-promoting relationships with all God's people.

How does "creating sacred community" imply a deeper, more complex, diverse journey of becoming than we have previously imagined for ourselves? We begin by opening our hearts in hospitable ways to all who need to be "fed."

Prayer for Peace

God of all tribes, kindred, and tongues, we need to be fed by your Spirit and by one another. May we feel welcome at your table of grace.

Spiritual Practice: Welcoming Unity in Diversity

Meditate on Unity in Diversity. Create a large circle with your arms. See and feel the diverse people God invites inside the sanctuary of Christ's peace represented by this circle.

Who is easiest to welcome? Whom do you struggle to include? Confess the dividing walls between you and people too different or "dangerous" to invite into your spiritual home. Ask God to forgive and heal barriers that keep us from loving one another.

Peace Covenant

Today, God, I will go deeper and work on my becoming.

27
Thursday
June

Creative Suffering

By Barbara Howard of Independence, Missouri, USA

By the tender mercy of our God, the dawn from on high will break upon us, to give light to those who sit in darkness and in the shadow of death, to guide our feet into the way of peace.

—Luke 1:78–79

Listen to the story of the plagues of locusts that devastate the countryside of South Africa. Hordes of insects come in cycles. They cover the land, devouring every plant in sight. Landowners run out and try to drive the locusts away. It is useless. Like a tidal wave, they sweep over the countryside. The land lies stripped and bare from their destruction. Then the insects, gorged from all they have eaten, die. They cover the ground in piles of corpses.

Now the heartbroken farmer must act. He rakes them together and plows the predators underground. From the plowing, and from the remains of these despicable creatures will come the greatest crop he has ever grown.

We can accept human suffering and tragedy in this way. Beethoven finished what some consider his greatest work after he became deaf. Milton wrote some of his finest poetry after he was blind. Some people have been able to take pain and affliction and use it as strength.

Viktor Frankl describes this powerful use of suffering in his book, *Man's Search for Meaning.* Living in the death camps of Nazi Germany, he came to believe and live the principle that regardless of the circumstances, life held great meaning. He used his suffering creatively. He affirmed there is a dimension of life that we experience only through pain.

The life of Jesus is the lived-out principle of creative suffering. May we develop the courage to use our suffering creatively.

Prayer for Peace

In the despair of our illnesses, God, give us strength to survive. In our survival, give us hope that we might focus our minds on life. In our living may we creatively engage in community with others. God, help us recognize blessings in trials. Help us creatively share the peace of Christ.

Spiritual Practice: Connecting with God as Center

Connect with God through journal writing or contemplation. Open yourself to God's presence and share what flows from your heart and mind. It might take the form of a prayer, psalm, or poem. Try to write or meditate at least five minutes each day.

What do you experience? Is this an effective way to connect with God? What surprises you? What new God images or questions emerge? What deepens or changes in your relationship with God, Christ, Spirit?

Peace Covenant

Today, God, I will not dwell on my darkness, but I will center myself on Christ.

28
Friday
June

Make a Difference

By Sara Parkin of Midland, Michigan, USA

"You are the light of the world. A city built on a hill cannot be hid. No one after lighting a lamp puts it under the bushel basket, but on the lampstand, and it gives light to all in the house. In the same way, let your light shine before others, so that they may see your good works and give glory to your Father in heaven."

—Matthew 5:14–16

(Part 4 of My Journey with Alzheimer's Disease)

Alzheimer's patients can make a difference in the world. When we see someone who looks burned-out, fatigued, tired, or tapped out, we can make a change in their lives. We can pray, listen, place our hands on their shoulder, ask if we can help, or let them know we care. We will make a difference.

To do this, we need to take care of ourselves. We need to keep our brains working and play games. We can risk doing something that is challenging to us—try it. If it doesn't work, it is not a failure because we will have learned something new. We will have learned it is something we can't do at this time. So, we can try something else.

We can exercise, walk, move in our chair while watching TV, or move our arms, neck, and fingers. We can laugh, dance, or do dishes. We can just move at our own rate and rest when we need to.

Eat fresh fruit, fresh veggies, lean meat, fish, rice, potatoes. Pray for others. Pray for self. Write in a journal. Have quiet time with God, who journeys with you.

Prayer for Peace

Thank you, God of light, for shining in our darkness. May we shine, too, for others. Use us in Christ's mission. May we use our gifts and our light to share Christ's peace.

Spiritual Practice: Examining God's Call to Me and to All

Reflect on God's call in your life. Begin by prayerfully asking to recall particular moments when you have experienced God's presence and invitation. Write in your journal or quietly reflect on images and insights that come.

When has God seemed most real in your life? How and when has God called you to use your energies and gifts? When have you felt God's love in your life? When have you felt disconnected or resistant to God's call? How do your gifts and callings connect with the call of God you notice in your family, friends, congregation, or community?

Peace Covenant

Today, God, I will ponder how I can make a difference.

29
Saturday
June

Soften My Heart, Lord

By Deb Crowley of Charlotte, Michigan, USA

"And the king will answer them, 'Truly I tell you, just as you did it to one of the least of these who are members of my family, you did it to me.'"

—Matthew 25:40

How can we work hand-in-hand with God to change lives? Perhaps it's in response to a phone call to rush to the hospital. There we pray for a friend who received a life-threatening diagnosis. Perhaps we answer a midnight call that summons us to the bedside of one leaving this world. Maybe it's in response to a stranger who seeks help paying a utility bill. There are no strangers among us.

A family in emotional, spiritual, or financial crisis needs someone to invest time. We can do that. Spend time. Be present. A co-worker needs a listening ear. We listen. A frenzied parent, stressed to the limit, needs help with childcare. Let them come.

God softens our hearts to respond to the plight of children sold into slavery in Africa, Asia, and other places. Are we aware, are we angered to action?

We can travel from our comfortable homes to aid families in crisis after a natural disaster, nearby or far way. God nudges our conscience to dig deeper into worldwide issues and possible remedies. God calls us to do something about them.

Perhaps our actions rely on world mission tithes.

"Abolish Poverty, End Suffering." These are easy words to say. Acting on them can bring stunning results. Lives are changed.

Prayer for Peace

Generous God, humble us for your service. Soften our hearts in alignment with Christ's mission. May we work together to share Christ's peace.

Spiritual Practice: Embodying God's Shalom

Find a way to express and embody God's shalom. Begin by prayerfully listening to your longing for peace. Become silent and imagine you can hear the groaning of the Earth's people, nations, and creatures. Prayerfully open yourself to God's yearning for peace and the divine vision of shalom.

What images, feelings, and words come to you? What prayer for peace comes to you from your time of listening? Speak or write this prayer. What small act of justice, kindness, healing, or peacemaking does God invite you to consider this day?

Peace Covenant

Today, God, I will do my part to Abolish Poverty, End Suffering.

30
Sunday
June

Accept God's Mission

By Dale Luffman, Council of Twelve Apostles

> *Now when the Lord was about to take Elijah up to heaven...Elijah said to Elisha, "Stay here... But Elisha said, "As the Lord lives, and as you yourself live, I will not leave you." As they continued walking and talking...Elijah ascended in a whirlwind into heaven. Elisha kept watching and crying out, "Father, father! ...But when he could no longer see him...he picked up the mantle of Elijah...*
>
> —2 Kings 2:1–2, 11–13

We can learn many of the skills for ministry. This is my experience. We often seek a minister of high competence, one who has gained the community's confidence of faith. We look to people who embark on the vocation of ministry. This is the case for Elisha as he looks to Elijah, who sought him out to cloak him with his prophetic mantle. God called Elisha to be a minister to promote God's purposes for Israel.

Elisha serves Elijah and receives on-the-job training. Developing the skills of ministry is not easy. It is based on more than desire or personality. Formation of disciples is hard work! That is why Community of Christ tries to aid developing ministry by offering seminary and Ministerial Education and Discipleship Studies courses. Elisha comes to understand that preparing for ministry is not only hard, but costly, sometimes confusing, and exhausting. Elisha stretches as he is tested.

Often, ministry does test us. A competent, learned mentor like Elijah is significant to the Elishas of this world. They help those who embark on developing the gifts of ministry that honor God and serve the needs of people of faith.

But it is hard to let go of those who wisely lead and teach us. We find it easier to follow than lead. Elisha discovers this. Grieving, Elisha nonetheless takes up the mantle of Elijah and extends the prophetic witness. He does not give up! Elijah had called Elisha to vigilance and to faithful witness so Yahweh's mission might be evident in Israel's life. Elisha receives the testimony that he needs in Elijah's departure.

He now picks up his mantle and is confirmed in his new role of ministry.

Prayer for Peace

We are listening for your call, God. We await our part in Christ's mission. We will prepare ourselves as disciples to share Christ's peace.

Spiritual Practice: Develop Disciples to Serve

Read and reflect on Psalm 42:1–2. As disciples of Jesus Christ, we are called to respond to people and their needs. The call to journey inward can restore us in times of physical or spiritual depletion.

When you are thirsty, dry, and empty, listen prayerfully again to the psalm: "As a deer longs for flowing streams, so my soul longs for you, O God. My soul thirsts for God, for the living God." As you feel restored, thank God for the opportunity to be a responding, serving disciple. Remember this exercise as you drink water throughout the day.

Peace Covenant

Today, God, I will pick up my mantle and accept a new role.

1
Monday
July

A Good Fit

By Lu Mountenay of Independence, Missouri, USA

> *Listen to the Voice that echoes across the eons of time and yet speaks anew in this moment... Listen carefully to the many testimonies of those around the world who have been led into the companionship of the Community of Christ. The richness of cultures, the poetry of language, and the breadth of human experience permit the gospel to be seen with new eyes...*
>
> —Doctrine and Covenants 162:1b, 4a

We are now halfway through the year. I hope you find *Daily Bread* a valuable part of your spiritual journey. As the editor, I'm the fortunate person who gets to read these stories first. I want to share some thoughts about how each page comes together. The ideas and words of many people draw together to form these daily devotionals. Care is taken so each devotional creates a cohesive flow from one moment to the next. I have found some surprising collaboration.

If you submitted reflections or stories, you may notice a bit of "editing." Some are shortened; others have minor grammatical edits. I try hard to keep the intended message. Also, I may insert, as summary, some "language" of Community of Christ—like an Enduring Principle or Mission Initiative, as they are implied by the story.

If your story tells how members of the church have been there for you, to pray for you, help you, comfort you, I try to point out that these are Blessings of Community. **It fits.**

If a story tells how a congregation has set up a pantry for those who are hungry and homeless, I might note this as an example of Experience Congregations in Mission or Abolish Poverty, End Suffering. **It fits.**

The stories also fit with the scripture passages. This is not a hard match to make. To have scriptures reflected in our life stories, we must be doing something right. The pool of spiritual practices comes from members of the Spiritual Formation Team. Almost as soon as I read a story, I can match it with a practice that fits. I draw on all these features to write the short Prayer for Peace and Peace Covenant sections. At times it seems they almost write themselves (but don't tell my employer).

I shouldn't be surprised that almost every story, testimony, scripture reflection, and poem includes language inspired by the leadership of the church and our books of scripture. It's amazing how that happens! I guess Christ's mission must be our mission!

Please keep writing. And thank you.

Prayer for Peace

Your Continuing Revelation, God, causes us to see with new eyes. It gives us new voice to share our reflections. It gives us creative ways to share Christ's peace.

Spiritual Practice: Connecting with God as Center

Connect with God through journal writing or contemplation. Open yourself to God's presence and share what flows from your heart and mind. Your "communication with God" might include thoughts, feelings, or scriptures. It might take the form of a prayer or poem.

Peace Covenant

Today, God, I will write in my journal or reflect on the spiritual writings of another.

2
Tuesday
July

Take the Spirit with You

By Betty Bennett of Independence, Missouri, USA

> *You who are my disciples must be found continuing in the forefront of those organizations and movements which are recognizing the worth of persons and are committed to bringing the ministry of my Son to bear on their lives.*
>
> —Doctrine and Covenants 151:9

After working weekends in a hospital for two years, I missed the joy of teaching children at Sunday school. I felt that I was unable to serve God to my capacity. When I attended family camp that summer, this concern was on my mind. I needed encouragement and enthusiasm to continue in my career.

The guest minister was asked how long he had been working for God (referring to the time he had served in church employment). His immediate reply was "All my life!" The truth pierced me like an arrow. All of us have opportunity to serve God every day of our lives, wherever we are—at work or in Sunday school.

I go to work more eagerly now, knowing I go with Christ. There is joy in loving the tiny infants in my care and in sharing with their parents.

As you live this day, you can choose to serve God. Wherever you go today—to school, to work, or to a neighbor's house—take the Spirit of God with you. Experience the joy of service. Share the peace of Jesus Christ, outside as well as inside the walls of the church.

Prayer for Peace

Ever-present God, help us realize your love always encompasses all people, in all places. *Our* love must do the same. May our hands be your hands, our smile your smile. May our voice speak your words. May our sharing be the peace of Jesus Christ.

Spiritual Practice: Develop Disciples to Serve

Read and reflect on Psalm 42:1–2. As disciples of Jesus Christ, God calls us to respond to people and their needs. The call to journey inward can restore us in times of physical or spiritual depletion. Imagine you can feel a vessel at the center of your being (a clay jar, a crystal vase, a metal bucket, or other container). Imagine drawing something from the vessel to share with another person, but as you reach inside you find only a tiny pool of stagnant liquid. You are thirsty and dry; empty.

Listen prayerfully again to the psalm, "As a deer longs for flowing streams, so my soul longs for you, O God. My soul thirsts for God, for the living God." As you feel restored, thank God for the opportunity to be a responding, serving disciple while you move into the outward journey. Remember this exercise as you drink water throughout the day.

Peace Covenant

Today, God, I will bring the peace of Christ to the forefront.

3

Wednesday

July

Beginning (Part 1)

By Charles Curry of Apple Valley, Minnesota, USA

The beginning of the good news of Jesus Christ, the Son of God. As it is written in the prophet Isaiah, "See, I am sending my messenger ahead of you, who will prepare your way; the voice of one crying out in the wilderness: 'Prepare the way of the Lord, make his paths straight,'"

—Mark 1:1–3

It is the beginning of the good news.

In the middle of the day, walking wherever I need to go, I see a wild man dressed roughly. He is demanding a response—he offers a strange washing to make me clean.

Across the centuries and cultures, I imagine responding with a "yes"; but this is a "head trip." There is a comfortable distance between John and me. I can't smell the camel hair or hear the creak of his leather belt as he moves. It is easy to say "yes" when I know the next part of the story. Or do I?

This is the beginning of the good news: the fire in John's voice, the wild look in his eye, the offer to make me clean.

It is the beginning of *my* good news if I can answer your question, "Who do you say I am?" Jesus, un-ask this—this unfair question.

After 60-some years I barely know myself. How can I possibly know you—you who stills the sea, who heals in seen and unseen ways, who walks where I will not or cannot walk? Still you call me to walk with you.

Let me live in that shadowy house beside the road, being a shallow friend. It is so much easier than actually following you. I know so little about the pain you willingly undertook. Even those much closer to the events disagree on why you did what you did.

I want to stay quietly on the sidelines. A well-studied answer keeps my heart secure. But here you are in front of me with your rude question. Were you ever hesitant or polite?

There has always been a subversive tone in your voice. A tendency toward what sounds like anarchy. Even though it isn't exactly—depending on how you look at it.

Your question frightens me; the answer more.

Will you accept my joining you on the road as an answer for now?

Can I think about it as we go?

Prayer for Peace

Thank you, God, for questions asked by Christ that compel us to listen and impel us to action. Thank you for his parables that help us imagine his message. And, thank you for the invitation to learn who Jesus is and to follow.

Spiritual Practice: Examining God's Call to Me and to All

Reflect on God's call in your life. Begin by prayerfully asking to recall particular moments when you have experienced God's presence and invitation. Write in your journal or quietly reflect on images and insights that come for your part in Christ's mission.

Peace Covenant

Today, God, I will think about it as I go…I will open myself to your guidance.

4
Thursday
July

The Question Remains (Part 2)

By Charles Curry of Apple Valley, Minnesota, USA

"...who do you say that I am?"

—Mark 8:29

Since we're just talking, Jesus, is it fair to ask *you* the same question? Who do *you* say *I* am? I mean, under the show, behind the script of my own making, in the shadows that fall behind my hopes, who do you say I am?

I mean, among the small accomplishments, great disappointments, terrible realizations—who do you say I am now? When I say I am serving you and sacrifice my children in your name while I serve, who do you say I am?

I mean, when I choose the comfort of reason over the distress of crowds, who do you say I am? When I abandon you in the name of righteous anger or justice—even in your name—Jesus, who do you say I am?

Who do you say I am now? Since we are just talking, Jesus, is it fair to ask?

Let's say I answer like Peter did (the rock that crumbled even when he knew the answer), "You are the Son of God." After 2,000 years how can I answer this on my own? Can I invoke the Wesleyan Quadrilateral for Theological Thinking? Can I examine this answer using scripture, reason, tradition, and experience?

This is a test, isn't it? Here I am—at this study, at this exercise, at this computer right now—wrestling with this question. I wrestle as your ancestor, Jacob, did with his God. (I even have the sore bones to prove it.)

So how do I approach this, Jesus, Son of God, Son of Man? I suppose I could examine my deeds and compare them to yours. If this is a test, I hope you grade on a generous curve. I will depend on your grace and the touch of your Spirit. With your grace, your touch, your Spirit, *I* can go with that if *you* can.

Prayer for Peace

God of wisdom, thank you for the ability to explore what scripture means to us and to examine how it engages our own experience and how it applies to Christ's mission to share his peace.

Spiritual Practice: Making Responsible Choices

Prayerfully seek God's guidance in your choices. Discernment invites us to orient our lives toward God and God's vision for us and creation. Begin by reviewing the responsibilities and opportunities in the day before you. Take these choices into prayer, asking God for wisdom and insight about what matters most. Ask for a blessing to live this day responsibly and compassionately in the Spirit of Christ.

Peace Covenant

Today, God, I will pray for wisdom as I look to scripture.

5
Friday
July

I Cannot Hold You (Part 3)

By Charles Curry of Apple Valley, Minnesota, USA

> *...and he took the seven loaves, and after giving thanks he broke them and gave them to his disciples to distribute; and they distributed them to the crowd... They ate and were filled; and they took up the broken pieces left over, seven baskets full... Jesus went on with his disciples to the villages of Caesarea Philippi; and on the way he asked his disciples, "Who do people say that I am?" And they answered him, "John the Baptist; and others, Elijah; and still others, one of the prophets." He asked them, "But who do you say that I am?" Peter answered him, "You are the Messiah."*
>
> —Mark 8:6, 8, 27–29

"Who do *you* say that I am?" I have found more answers—but these cannot hold me.

I say you are a poem—of which school is impossible to say. If I look to old psalms, you are there. But psalms cannot hold you.

If I look to the stories about you, you are there. But stories cannot hold you.

If I look to my own life, you are there. But I cannot hold you.

Who can write the poem that you are? Who dares attempt such a task? Even the simple act of breaking bread is never the same for you. There is no generic loaf: *this* flour, *this* yeast, *this* water—all are particular and various. Your hands tear *this* loaf at *this* place on its crust—each time different for you. And for us. Every day new?

Is that who you are?

"But you, my child, reach for the loaf. Always. It represents me. Always. And those who were or will be. Always. Is *that* who I am to you?"

Each time I read you, there is a shift. Another layer added. Another meaning—hidden or exposed. Is that who you are?

Invite me. Engage me. Pull me into your poem. Help me write my own. Help me write you still and again into the question.

Prayer for Peace

Mystery God, you sent your miracle Son. We celebrate by breaking his body, reading his words, praying his prayer, writing his poem—so we might know him more deeply. Who are we? We are disciples of the Messiah. We are those who will share grace and peace with the world.

Spiritual Practice: Many Names of God

In many languages, God's name contains the sound "Ahhh," a sound we make when we are breathing out or sighing. Our prayer will use the Ahh names for God. Breathe out each name for God. You may speak the name of God or find a single musical note to hold or chant as you sing God's name. Pray or sing each name several times as you call on the God of many names: Yaweh, Adonai, Jehovah, Yeshua, Sophia, Allah, Alpha, Omega. Say or sing "amen" to close.

Peace Covenant

Today, Jehovah, I will reflect on what you are in my heart, knowing you are beyond mere words.

6
Saturday
July

My Bell...My Mission Initiative

By Louita Clothier of Lamoni, Iowa, USA

> *For where your treasure is, there your heart will be also.*
>
> —Luke 12:34

When our church bell rings on Sunday mornings, I feel I own a part of that bell. During the two decades after the old brick church burned in Lamoni, the children in our congregation gave money to buy a bell for the new church.

As a child, I routinely brought a nickel and a penny to church, temporarily held at the Coliseum movie theater. The nickel was my offering, and the penny went into a little white wooden church with a slot in it, for the bell. So at a penny a week, from the time my family moved to Lamoni until we built the church, I figure I own about $3 worth of that bell, which 60 years ago cost about $200.

That feeling of ownership is one of the rich blessings of supporting our congregation budget. New parents do not decide whether to buy necessities for their baby. Rather, out of love, they provide food, clothing, and shelter. It is what they *want* to do.

Because I love our congregation's home, made sacred by the experiences we have there, I own part of our new heating system; I own some of the paper used to print our bulletins; I *own* the youth ministries.

It is more difficult to sense ownership when supporting the more-distant needs of the World Church. The new offering envelopes allow us to earmark our offerings for one or more of the five Mission Initiatives. This enables us to claim ownership in a more direct way.

It is true that where our treasure is, there will our hearts be also. But I have found the reverse also is true: "Where our hearts are, there will our treasure be." Because my heart is in Community of Christ, I now own part of the new church in Novosibirsk, Russia.

Prayer for Peace

Ever-present God, just as we experience our own congregation in mission, may we support these experiences in congregations throughout the world. We send our prayer everywhere, so no one will be denied the sanctuary and companionship of a congregational home.

Spiritual Practice: Experience Congregations in Mission

Read and reflect on Doctrine and Covenants 164:9a–d. Reread the sentence, "If you truly would be Community of Christ, then embody and live the concerns and passion of Christ." Make a list of the issues you feel mattered most to Christ. Make another list of issues that matter to your congregation. Reflect on the similarities and differences. How can you help align the lists? Throughout the day, as issues arise, ask yourself, "Would this matter to Christ?"

Peace Covenant

Today, God, I will reflect on part of the worldwide church I claim as my own, and I will support it.

7
Sunday
July

Humble Yourself

By Lu Mountenay of Independence, Missouri, USA

> *. . . "Father, if the prophet had commanded you to do something difficult, would you not have done it? How much more, when all he said to you was, 'Wash, and be clean'?" So he went down and immersed himself seven times in the Jordan, according to the word of the man of God; his flesh was restored like the flesh of a young boy, and he was clean.*
>
> —2 Kings 5:13–14

"Wash, and be clean." How easy that is! I have a button from an office-supply store. When you press it, a recorded voice says, "That was easy." I've used it often to ease tensions at awkward times. When we humble ourselves and laugh at our own expense, it's easier to forgive ourselves and accept the gifts of others.

When I finally admit I *might* be wrong, I can repair relationships. When I finally admit that, even if I'm right, it doesn't matter what others think. What matters are the feelings of other people in my life. I need to get past having to be *right* all the time and accept a serving of humility. It doesn't taste so bad if it means reconciliation with one who was once estranged.

Got it?

Get it?

Get over it!

Did I catch that someone else's opinion matters more than mine? (I got it.) Do I take the time to listen and understand their view? (I get it.) Can I get over it? (Get over what? It doesn't matter anymore.) I move on.

The Spirituality of Imperfection (Ernest Kurtz and Katherine Ketcham) holds an interesting sentiment: "I'm *not* all-right, and you're *not* all-right, but *that's* Okay—THAT's all-right."

Nobody's perfect. But, things would be perfect if everyone were humble, like Christ, who said, "Take my yoke upon you, and learn from me; for I am gentle and humble in heart, and you will find rest for your souls" (Matthew 11:29). Perhaps being humble is one way to "Wash, and be clean."

Prayer for Peace

Creator God, help us accept each other and self as you accept us—with all our flaws. May we pause and be humbled by the mote in our own eye when we begin to judge others. May we share the peace of Christ with a gentle and humble heart.

Spiritual Practice: Weeding the Garden

Inner transformation can take place during daily activities and work. Try cultivating the spiritual discipline of grace and acceptance while weeding your spiritual garden. As you pull each "weed," offer a short prayer. Tug. (*God remove from my heart all prejudice and fear.*) Tug again. (*God, keep me from making unjust judgments.*) As you remove the weed, continue praying. (*Plant in my heart the seeds of your love.*) If you don't have a garden, try this kind of transforming prayer while engaging in repetitive activities or work today.

Peace Covenant

Today, God, I will find rest for my soul, because—even though not perfect, I am loved.

8
Monday
July

♫ Hymn of the Month: "Clothe Us in Your Spirit"

By Sandra Webb-Johnsen of Milton, Washington, USA

> *...holy and beloved, clothe yourselves with compassion, kindness, humility, meekness, and patience. Bear with one another and, if anyone has a complaint against another, forgive each other; just as the Lord has forgiven you, so you also must forgive. Above all, clothe yourselves with love, which binds everything together in perfect harmony.*
>
> —Colossians 3:12–14

Music has always touched a deep place in my soul.

I hear music as I walk in the forest and as I drive down the road. "Clothe Us in Your Spirit" came to me on the breezes in the woods as they blew through the trees and played with the leaves and branches. The wind whispered that the love of God surrounded me

As I wrote down the melody I'd heard and worked out the harmony, I found the song was about the Holy Spirit. Just like the breezes, the Holy Spirit had wrapped itself around me, comforted me, inspired my understanding, and renewed my soul.

The parallel of clothing expressed some feelings and functions of the Spirit, and so the lyrics came to be. The hymn "Clothe Us in Your Spirit" stands as a testimony of my experience with the Holy Spirit and its empowering momentum on my faith journey in this lifetime.

Clothe us in your Spirit.
Robe us in your light.
Enfold us in your vision
and your wisdom's might.
Weave in us forgiveness.
Wrap us in your gracious care.
Clothed to build your kingdom,
blessed with love we share.

Clothe us with your presence.
Robe us in your light.
In daily strands of healing,
mending lives to grow.
As we choose your bidding
and through you compassion find,
we'll weave peace and justice
clothing all human-kind.

Prayer for Peace

Holy Presence, surround us with your Spirit. Weave the gifts of the Spirit into our souls. Strengthen the fabric of our being so we may share the peace of Christ.

Spiritual Practice

Contemplate this hymn as a poem.

9
Tuesday
July

In God's Own Time

By Carol Norris Vincent of Independence, Missouri, USA

Trust in the Lord with all your heart, and do not rely on your own insight. In all your ways acknowledge him, and he will make straight your paths.

—Proverbs 3:5–6

Ministers in the Methodist Church called me to be a Stephen Minister (caring ministry). At the same time, my husband was undergoing the first of several cancer surgeries. The timing was terrible, I thought, because my husband would need much care, and my time might be limited. I also felt I might be the one in need of ministry. However, I felt that this was something I needed to do, and with God's help, I could do it.

In the next two years, I ministered to two dying women. I felt God was preparing me for what was to come. Indeed that ministry prepared me for the spiritual journey with my husband as he was dying.

I returned to my roots in Missouri after my husband's death and joined Community of Christ. A few years later, I was called to be an elder. I am disabled with post-polio issues. I am in the waning years of my life. I was concerned about being able to fulfill the ministry to which I considered committing myself. I again was concerned about the timing. After much prayer and reading my dad's priesthood manual, I decided to accept the call.

In the journal I kept during my husband's illness, I again turned to a scripture that came to me when I decided to accept the call to be a Stephen Minister. Proverbs 3:5–6 says, "Trust in the Lord with all your heart, and do not rely on your own insight. In all your ways acknowledge him, and he will make straight your paths." That scripture has guided me in the past and will in the future. No matter when God calls me, or what is already on my plate, I will trust God and answer the call.

Prayer for Peace

God, may we not be receptive to your call *only* when we feel ready. We know you ask us to do only what we can do. And with your strength and grace, we can do what matters most, *when* it matters most. Right now, God, we will answer the call of Christ's mission to share his peace.

Spiritual Practice: Examining God's Call to Me and to All

Reflect on God's call in your life. Begin by prayerfully asking to recall particular moments when you have experienced God's presence and invitation. Write in your journal or quietly reflect on images and insights that come.

When has God seemed most real in your life? How and when has God called you to use your energies and gifts? When have you felt most deeply connected and responsive to God's movement in your life?

Peace Covenant

Today, God, I will drop whatever I'm doing to answer your call.

10
Wednesday
July

Ratta-tat-tat!

By Cindy L. Korf of North Platte, Nebraska, USA

Jesus said to him, "Have you believed because you have seen me? Blessed are those who have not seen and yet have come to believe."

—John 20:29

I thought I heard a woodpecker in the trees. After a moment of silence, the tapping sounded again. Not believing there could be a woodpecker here, I scanned every tree nearby, trying to spot the bird. Silence. Then, the drumming echoed again.

I left the path, following the sound to try to find its source. I felt the need to see for myself, to know if it truly was a woodpecker. I looked into the trees the few times the rhythmic drumming filtered through the air. But, soon the drumming stopped. I never did find him, being left only with my self-doubt.

There are times when I "hear" God but I refuse to believe. I find myself wanting to prove it with backup senses, thinking I have to "see" to believe, and to know what I hear is real. This doubt has prevented me from believing and responding, and as a result, has kept me from the blessings that faith brings.

Prayer for Peace

When we doubt, God, "show" us your presence as we look at your creation, "touch" our hearts with your love, help us "savor" your grace as we are forgiven. May we inhale Earth's perfume and trust you are with us.

Spiritual Practice: Connecting with God as Center

Connect with God through journal writing or contemplation. Open yourself to God's presence and share what flows from your heart and mind. Your "communication with God" might include thoughts, questions, feelings, needs, artwork, quotes, or scriptures. Or it might take the form of a prayer, psalm, or poem. Try to write or meditate at least five minutes each day.

What do you experience? Is this an effective way to connect with God? What surprises you? What new God images or questions emerge? What deepens or changes in your relationship with God, Christ, Spirit?

Peace Covenant

Today, God, I will know you are with me in the silence. I will know you are here in the dark.

11
Thursday
July

Our Faith, God's Outcome

By Michalina Bartlett of Gainesville, Florida, USA

May the God of hope fill you with all joy and peace in believing, so that you may abound in hope by the power of the Holy Spirit.

—Romans 15:13

Facing a new experience or difficulty can create stress even though you know God is with you. Not knowing the future raises fear. However, the unknown also challenges our faith in God.

As we face unknown outcomes, of this I am sure: God will use our presence and loving spirit to bring ministry. The words won't matter as much as our willingness to serve. God has given us the gift of a kind and loving spirit to use as we choose. Although the venue may be different, the situation might be the same—hurting people need God's blessing and our presence. We step into the blessing by our willingness to serve. God waits for us in this place. If we rely on the Divine, the outcome will be God's outcome.

We may already know all this, but in moments of challenge, it helps to hear assurances of love and God's presence from someone else.

When facing unknown experiences, God works with our willingness and through the power of the Holy Spirit to bring ministry. Our words won't matter as much as our willingness to serve. Prayerfully walk by faith, not by sight, and do not let the outcome be a concern. Give up control.

The outcome belongs to God.

Prayer for Peace

Compass God, point us toward our ministry and give us faith to follow. Lead us to places where we can share the peace of Christ.

Spiritual Practice: Making Responsible Choices

Prayerfully seek God's guidance in your choices. Discernment invites us to orient our lives toward God and God's vision for us and creation. Begin by reviewing the responsibilities and opportunities in the day before you. Take these choices into prayer, asking God for wisdom and insight about what matters most.

Offer yourself to God with the prayer of Teresa of Avila: "God, what do you want of me today?" Sit prayerfully with this question as you review the day again. Be aware of images, thoughts, names, or actions that come to you. Ask for a blessing to live this day responsibly and compassionately in the spirit of Christ.

Peace Covenant

Today, God, I will let go of expected outcomes and accept what comes with faith.

12
Friday
July

Who?

By John Bonney of Springfield, Oregon, USA

> *"...I would that you should remember to retain the name written always in your hearts, that you are not found on the left hand of God, but that you hear and know the voice by which you shall be called, and also the name by which he shall call you."*
>
> —Mosiah 3:16

Olivia has a lovely voice, and I enjoy hearing her speak. She has a wonderfully rich, caressing contralto. I cannot quite characterize her vocalizations as singing, in the way many other birds "sing." You see, Olivia is an owl. I named her when I discovered her in the undeveloped area south of my home.

Hers is a lovely, muted, almost-sensuous call in the dark, early morning hours.

Our sensitivities, culture, and experiences influence what we hear. And I suppose each owl sounds different to other owls. For me, I do not hear the proverbial "hoot" that we English-speaking people generally spell as "whoo." But I get "hooo, hoo-hoo." It's a single and a double sound. It's subtle, primitive, spectral, and mysterious. "Hooo, hoo-hoo." I don't know who Olivia calls, I just know I like the call and feel like answering.

I have long appreciated other animal sounds, as well—frogs and coyotes. I love the sounds of the birds in the spring and early summer. I am especially drawn to the liquid warble of the redwing blackbird. The song of the robin tells many stories. There is something, also, wild and lonely in the sounds of the seagull and the goose.

But the sound of the owl, or at least this particular owl, speaks to me on a whole new level. It puts me in mind, once again, of the presence of the One who creates and the love borne us by that Creating One. Who? Who-who? It's the Eternal Creative Presence, that's who. And is it really a mystery *who* the Creator calls?

Prayer for Peace

Creator of the calling birds, may we listen with new understanding. May we hear our name when we are called to share Christ's peace.

Spiritual Practice: Voices of God

What is the voice of God saying to us? Do we hear the whispers of God's longing for shalom, God's dream of beauty and wholeness for all creation? Do we hear the "voice" of God calling to us in faces and eyes, in the sounds of suffering and joy, in scripture and sacred word, in tears and laughter, in silence and noise? Spend a few moments reflecting on when and how God's voice has spoken to you. When did you first feel called to join God in the pursuit of peace and justice? How does that call to shalom continue to come to you through the many "voices" of God?

Peace Covenant

I will respond, God, when I hear you call.

13
Saturday
July

The Gifts of the "Other"

By Donna Boyd of Independence, Missouri, USA

> *May the God of steadfastness and encouragement grant you to live in harmony with one another, in accordance with Christ Jesus, so that together you may with one voice glorify the God and Father of our Lord Jesus Christ.*
>
> —Romans 15:5–6

God's gifts are all around us. Some we recognize the first time we see them. Others we grow into recognition.

Some are complete for us to enjoy and share. Some are tools and talent with which we build and create. What we do with them, how we share them is our gift to God.

Communication is one way we share. Listening is more than half of that gift. Take a moment to think of one of God's gifts to you. Plan how to share it today.

Reflect on someone with whom you share your life.

How can you help that person see and foster God-given giftedness?

Sincere compliments open our eyes to gifts we may not have seen. When you compliment someone, you also are praising God, who created the person. We can be generous as God is generous with us. When you feel led to share Blessings of Community, tell someone "Good-onya, mate."

Prayer for Peace

Steadfast Creator, we praise you for gifts and talents we have received. We give thanks for the encouragement we receive to develop and share these gifts. May we employ them in sharing Christ's peace.

Spiritual Practice: Offering Blessings of Community

Receive and share Blessings of Community. Begin with a prayer of gratitude for the relationships in your life. See and feel connections with family members, spiritual friends, people in your congregation and community, and people and creatures in God's sacred web of life. What blessings flow to you from these circles? How have you felt the love of the community?

Reflect, pray, or write in your journal about the call to be "Community of Christ." Go deeper each day as you discern what act of blessing you are invited to complete.

Peace Covenant

Today, God, I will be aware of the gifts of others and share with them what a blessing they are.

14
Sunday
July

Who Is Your Neighbor?

By Dave Brown, Presiding Bishopric

"Which of these three, do you think, was a neighbor to the man who fell into the hands of the robbers?" He said, "The one who showed him mercy." Jesus said to him, "Go and do likewise."

—Luke 10:36–37

I always thought if I ever lived the Good Samaritan story I would play the role of the Samaritan. Then, in 1977, I lived the role of the man left beside the road in need. I had not fallen into the hands of robbers but was caught in a flash flood in midtown Kansas City.

The flood submerged my car and left me and five others stranded. It was 9:30 at night, and none of us knew how we would get to our homes as we stood in a dark parking lot in front of an abandoned building.

Then, all at the same time, five Samaritan cars pulled into the parking lot. Each driver, after learning we were stranded, agreed to take one of us for help. Because I was the youngest, I agreed to stay in the parking lot until the others got safely away. I waited 10 minutes, wondering what I was going to do. Then another Samaritan car pulled in.

The driver saw me alone. As he came closer, I noticed he was of a different ethnic background, just as in the scripture. As I stood there, wondering whether he would show mercy, he stopped and asked if I needed a ride. As I got in his car, I saw a clue as to why he did not hesitate to help. On the front seat was a well-used Bible.

James "did likewise" and took me to his home and cared for me until a friend could pick me up at 3:00 the next morning.

Through this experience I realized that ending the suffering of others is a natural way of sharing in the mission we have been given by Christ.

Prayer for Peace

Compassionate God, when faced with another's suffering, may we take on the role of the Good Samaritan. When we face trouble ourselves, may we show our gratitude and praise you for those who show us mercy.

Spiritual Practice: Abolish Poverty, End Suffering

Read and reflect on John 21:15–17 as a meditation. Let your mind be drawn to places where people have no homes. Think of refugees, whose homes were destroyed by war or natural disaster. Be aware of the hungry and homeless, who wander the streets or live in shelters. Let the images fill your mind.

Offer a prayer for those who are suffering. Imagine Christ tending those sheep. Think of ways you might end their suffering as part of your mission. Throughout the day, carry in your mind the voice of Christ saying: "Feed my lambs…tend my sheep…feed my sheep."

Peace Covenant

Today, God, I will "Go and do likewise."

15
Monday
July

I Forgot to Nap

By Sara Parkin of Midland, Michigan, USA

> *"Come to me, all you that are weary and are carrying heavy burdens, and I will give you rest. Take my yoke upon you, and learn from me; for I am gentle and humble in heart, and you will find rest for your souls. For my yoke is easy, and my burden is light."*
>
> —Matthew 11:28–30

(Part 5 of My Journey with Alzheimer's Disease)

Today, for me, Alzheimer's clouds of weariness are forming where they are not wanted. One minute I feel great, and the next I am exhausted. I'm thankful it does not happen all the time.

I know there are times when I can't understand why I don't want to go places I usually like to go. It might be I worked too hard or did not take my nap. How can I forget to take my nap when I'm so tired?

I do know that I can make it better: I can pray for strength, for endurance or for freshness. I can dance with God as I sit in my chair, listening to music. This picks me right up! I can pick up a phone and call a sister who makes me laugh, or I can ask my husband for a hug.

I prayed, wrote in my journal, ate healthy food, and walked around the block.

I also know Christ is with me whether I am down or up. When we think we are getting weary, bushed, jaded, or wiped out, we know we are not alone, and we have ways to stop the weariness. Thank You, God! I will rest in you.

Prayer for Peace

Burden-lifting God, may we be willing to let go and give our weariness over to you to carry when we're not able. Help us be willing to be vulnerable to your grace. May we draw on your strength to help us share Christ's peace.

Spiritual Practice: Healing for Broken Spirits

Begin with quiet prayer. Ask God to help you discern some "sore places" in the body of Christ and in God's creation. Become aware of people who feel separated, wounded, or left out. Reflect on or write a short journal entry of healing words to at least one person who comes to mind. Ask God for words that will touch this person's broken spirit like healing ointment. Keep this person in your heart and prayers today and act on any ideas that come to bring blessing and wholeness.

Peace Covenant

Today, God, I will save my strength for that which matters most.

16
Tuesday
July

Developing Disciples

By Evelyn Spence of Council Bluffs, Iowa, USA

> *Finally, brothers and sisters, farewell. Put things in order, listen to my appeal, agree with one another, live in peace; and the God of love and peace will be with you.*
> —2 Corinthians 13:11

Our congregation has several programs to reach out to neighborhood youth. For the last three months "Adam" (not his real name) has been coming to Sunday school and worshiping with us. His enthusiasm is infectious, and he loves music. He has found a home in our congregation.

He is equally congenial with young people and adults. If a family arrives and is unfamiliar with our congregation, he leads the children to the proper classroom. If we have a dinner following the worship service, he clears the plates.

We do not yet know his mother or grandmother, with whom he lives, but it seems they have raised an intelligent, mannerly young man. We hope his enthusiasm continues. We hope those of us who are acquainted with him will be supportive enough to help him grow in his discipleship. We hope we can reach out and include his family.

We need to have opening, welcoming arms for those who seek to join our worship and fellowship. Please bless us, God, with hearts that love and nurture. We wish to embrace others with your love and peace and to continue Christ's mission.

Prayer for Peace

Generous God, thank you for our congregations and the community of love they provide. Thank you for this place of peace, sanctuary, learning, worship, and mission. May we find Christ's peace as we share it with others.

Spiritual Practice: Develop Disciples to Serve

Read and reflect on Psalm 42:1–2. As disciples of Jesus Christ, we are called to respond to people and their needs. The call to inward journey can restore us in times of physical or spiritual depletion. Imagine you can feel a vessel at the center of your being (a clay jar, a crystal vase, a metal bucket, or other container). Imagine drawing something from the vessel to share with another person, but as you reach inside you find only a tiny pool of stagnant liquid. You are thirsty and dry; empty. Listen prayerfully again to the psalm, "As a deer longs for flowing streams, so my soul longs for you, O God. My soul thirsts for God, for the living God." As you feel restored, thank God for the opportunity to be a responding, serving disciple while you move into the outward journey. Remember this exercise as you drink water throughout the day.

Peace Covenant

Today, God, I will teach and learn with my congregation.

17
Wednesday
July

Shaped by a Name

By Carolyn Brock of Redmond, Oregon, USA

> *But now thus says the Lord, he who created you, O Jacob, he who formed you, O Israel: Do not fear, for I have redeemed you; I have called you by name, you are mine... because you are precious in my sight, and honored, and I love you.*
>
> —Isaiah 43:1, 4

My mother named me after a 1940s movie star named Carolyn Jones. Like most kids I went through a phase of hating my name and imagining all kinds of creative choices. Over time Hispanic friends have shaped my name by calling me Carolina. British-French-African inflections of church friends addressed me as "Sister Carolyn." Other voices hold my name up in prayer—smiling people who greet me by name as we pass by one another.

Yet in my deepest moments of awareness, the name "Carolyn" is not nearly as important as sensing that I am known. I am known by the One who created me, the One still forming me, the One who knows, names, and loves every person and all people.

A multitude of names and labels forms each of us: Caucasian, African American, Hispanic, Asian, Christian, Hindu, Muslim, male, female, mother, father, grandparent, and many more. Sometimes amid the names, we wonder if others truly understand us for who we are. That is, if we can remember who we are underneath the names. Whatever names we are called, they do not define our essence as only God can see and know.

Our names are always less than the reality of who we are, though they reveal important truths. As we reflect on our identity, let us consider carefully and prayerfully the names by which we have been called. Let us remember that God knows our identity and holds us precious, no matter what words are used to name us as a people.

Prayer for Peace

Creator, tender Shepherd, Holy Spirit, Lord, God and the many other names to which you answer our prayers, we can never know or imagine them all. To us they all mean love and grace.

Spiritual Practice: Many Names of God

In many languages, God's name contains the sound "Ahhh," a sound we make when we are breathing out or sighing. Our prayer will use the Ahh names for God with a gentle arm movement that opens us to God's presence. Begin with hands in front of you at chest level and move them up and in a large arc or circle as you breathe out each name for God. You may either speak the name of God or find a single musical note to hold or chant as you sing God's name. Pray or sing each name several times as you call on the God of many names: Yaweh, Adonai, Jehovah, Yeshua, Sophia, Allah, Alpha, Omega. Say or sing "amen" to close.

Peace Covenant

Today, God, when you call my name through others in need, I will answer through deed.

18
Thursday
July

In the Image of Christ

By Dorene Kilburn of Stratford, Ontario, Canada

> *As revealed in Christ, God, the Creator of all, ultimately is concerned about behaviors and relationships that uphold the worth and giftedness of all people and that protect the most vulnerable…It requires whole-life stewardship dedicated to expanding the church's restoring ministries, especially those devoted to asserting the worth of persons…*
>
> —Doctrine and Covenants 164:6a, 9c

Moments when we gain new insight about *who* and *whose* we are often happen when we least expect them. They happen when we are not even looking for them.

My husband and I recently attended a funeral in an Anglican church. We have been to that church several times. The beautiful stained-glass windows speak to my soul. But I was not deeply moved by the liturgy until I noticed a thought in the readings that jumped at me: "May you see the face of Jesus in everyone you meet, and may everyone you meet see the face of Jesus in you."

It occurred to me that those few words encapsulated what is required of a disciple of Jesus Christ. To see the face of Jesus in everyone we meet means we must see with Jesus' eyes. He saw the worth and potential of each person. Often, not-so-lovable exteriors masked those souls, and lives changed because of Christ's unconditional love.

It is sometimes hard for us to see with Jesus' eyes. It's hard put aside our biases and see the spark of divinity that's there, even in those with whom we may not feel comfortable. It is a humbling challenge to live so other people can see the face of Jesus in us. With the help of Jesus—our friend, mentor, and perfect example of goodness and mercy—we can be what he calls us to be, his presence in our world today.

Prayer for Peace

God of the diverse creation, help us see Christ in everyone we meet. May our behavior make us worthy reflections of Christ. May we share your shalom as embodied in Christ's peace.

Spiritual Practice: Honoring the Worth of All Persons

Sense the intimate knowledge God has of you and every child. Be aware of the sacred worth of each person. Weep with God over the soul-wounding forces and events that rob people of dignity and worth. How are you invited to notice, protect, heal, and affirm the spiritual identity of all God's beloved people today? Pray for God's compassion.

Peace Covenant

Today, God, I will devote myself to asserting the Worth of All Persons.

19
Friday
July

What Can I Give?

By Ward Serig of Pensacola, Florida, USA

> *...the fruit of the Spirit is love, joy, peace, patience, kindness, generosity, faithfulness, gentleness, and self-control. There is no law against such things.*
>
> —Galatians 5:22–23

During our church's family camp, J.J. prepared the congregation for the offertory celebration at the evening worship service. J.J. and his family had limited finances, but J.J. was proud of his hair, which draped down his back almost to his waist. It hadn't been cut for at least a year and was always neatly groomed.

For the evening he had worked it into a single, tightly woven braid. He encouraged us to consider how we might show the Enduring Principle of Grace and generosity. He had the mission center president walk up behind him with a large pair of scissors and sever his braided hair just above his neckline.

J.J. explained that although he didn't have much in the way of worldly goods to place in the offering tray, his hair was something he could give. He would give it to Locks of Love, an organization that makes wigs for cancer patients who lose their hair while undergoing chemotherapy.

By this selfless and sacrificial act of love, J.J. reminded us there are many ways to share the bountiful gifts God blesses us with.

Prayer for Peace

Generous God, we often think we cannot give as you have given. Help us find ways of showing love that might require sacrifice. Help us set aside our shallow agendas and act to meet the needs of another. Help us grow in our ways of giving and sharing the peace of Christ.

Spiritual Practice: Experience Congregations in Mission

Read and reflect on Doctrine and Covenants 164:9a–d. Reread the sentence, "If you truly would be Community of Christ, then embody and live the concerns and passion of Christ." Make a list of the issues you feel mattered most to Christ. Make another list of issues that matter to your congregation. Reflect on the similarities and differences. How can you help align the lists? Throughout the day, as issues arise, ask yourself, "Would this matter to Christ?"

Peace Covenant

Today, God, I will explore how I might meet the needs of another, beyond financial gifts.

20
Saturday
July

Made in the Image of God

By Sue Phipps of Independence, Missouri, USA

> *There are many lives waiting to hear the redeeming words of the gospel, or to be lifted from hopelessness by the hands of loving servants. But they will be lost to you without the generous response of disciples who share from their own bounty that others may know the joys of the kingdom…You have been given the principles of generosity, rightly interpreted for a new time. These principles call every disciple to tithe faithfully in accordance with means and capacity…The call to respond is urgent. Look to the needs of your own congregations, but look also beyond your walls…*
>
> —Doctrine and Covenants 162:7a, c—d

Camp MITIOG (Made in the Image of God) is a summer camp sponsored by the Midland Mission Center. The sponsors devote the camp to creating high-quality life experiences and lasting memories for children born with spina bifida. Participation is without regard to gender, race, religion, economic condition, or educational status.

The campers enjoy a resident outdoor environment, staffed by professional and community volunteers who provide for their special medical, physical, and emotional needs. Your contributions to the Mission Initiative of Abolish Poverty, End Suffering help provide Tangible Love grants such as those that support Camp MITIOG. This fund makes mission real in ways that bring hope and healing to families, congregations, and the greater community.

Thank you for responding generously to this need.

Prayer for Peace

Creator God, many times the physical limitations of our bodies frustrate us. When we see those who suffer more, we have compassion. Lead us to follow our hearts and be led to share the joys of the kingdom—to share the hope and peace of Jesus Christ.

Spiritual Practice: Abolish Poverty, End Suffering

Read and reflect on John 21:15–17 as a meditation. Let your mind be drawn to places where people have no homes. Think of refugees whose homes were destroyed by war or natural disaster. Be aware of the hungry and homeless, who wander the streets or live in shelters. Let the images fill your mind. Offer a prayer for those who suffer. Imagine Christ tending those sheep. Think of ways you might end their suffering as part of your mission. Throughout the day, carry in your mind the voice of Christ saying: "Feed my lambs…tend my sheep…feed my sheep."

Peace Covenant

Today, God, I will put on a heart filled with compassion and follow where it leads.

21
Sunday
July

What Matters Most

By Scott Murphy, Council of Twelve Apostles

Now as they went on their way, he entered a certain village, where a woman named Martha welcomed him into her home. She had a sister named Mary, who sat at the Lord's feet and listened to what he was saying. But Martha was distracted by her many tasks..."Martha, Martha, you are worried and distracted by many things; there is need of only one thing. Mary has chosen the better part, which will not be taken away from her."

—Luke 10:38–42

Recently I had the privilege of attending a congregation I had shared with five years earlier. My first visit was to help with the Co-Missioned Pastor Initiative. Afterward, I knew the young new pastor had a big job ahead of her in casting a vision and setting goals.

When I entered the church five years later, I was in awe of what I saw. It was not the small, struggling congregation I had seen before. The church was filled with people of broken lives who were on a journey toward healing. And these lives were experiencing joy. A congregation that I thought was ready to die was now alive with a vibrant ministry that was changing lives.

How did this happen? The pastor and members of the congregation did not lose focus on what mattered most.

At the heart of our scripture reading today is the question "What matters most? In this story, both Martha and Mary are doing important tasks. However, as Jesus challenges Martha about her worry and distractions, we recognize that Martha had lost focus on what was important in her ministry of hospitality and neglected to give attention to Jesus' words.

Hearing this scripture confronts each of us to consider the times when we are doing church work absent the attention and focus on Christ's mission. If we look closely enough, we may find that too many times we engage in acts of mission based on what we want rather than listening for how and where the Holy Spirit is calling us into mission.

In the end, our distractions and worries wear us down and rob us of the joyful blessing of the mission that calls us. Let us listen so we can do what matters most.

Prayer for Peace

May we sit at your feet, Lord, and listen to your words.

Spiritual Practice: Making Responsible Choices

Prayerfully seek God's guidance in your choices. Discernment invites us to orient our lives toward God and God's vision for us and creation. Begin by reviewing the responsibilities and opportunities in the day before you. Take these choices into prayer, asking God for wisdom and insight about what matters most.

Peace Covenant

Today, God, I will set aside the mundane of every day and find every day sacred.

22
Monday
July

Gather Us In

By Peggy Michael of Cantonment, Florida, USA

When your willingness to live in sacred community as Christ's new creation exceeds your natural fear of spiritual and relational transformation, you will become who you are called to be. The rise of Zion the beautiful, the peaceful reign of Christ, awaits your wholehearted response to the call to make and steadfastly hold to God's covenant of peace in Jesus Christ.

—Doctrine and Covenants 164:9b

These thoughts came to me as I was ministering in a congregation that was considering closing its doors. Since then, the congregation has grown and is now thriving.

People are gathering. They wave hello, stop to chat, and invite one another in. People are coming—world travelers and the homebound.

Men and women, put down your tools of labor; children, put down your toys; cast aside idle pastimes to answer Christ's call.

People come who have considered building community; others come who have never heard of it. They sit together to talk of Christ and ponder his mission. Christ stirs their hearts with hope as they sing praises, pray, and listen for the Divine.

They consider God's bright promises of what is yet to be, what is beyond the horizon. The crowd is gathering. People are coming. Don't close the doors. People are coming!

Prayer for Peace

O God, I would give my heart to you, but it is encased in a wall of stone. It is sealed with the mortar of doubt and pride, hardened by time spent alone. I am troubled by this and cry out to you, "Cast this barrier down. I can't, for I put all my strength into building it." Why does this spinning sphere continue to fling us beyond your reach, O God? Gather us in so the sea of loneliness will not swallow us—so we will not be too far from people to share Christ's peace.

—Peggy Michael

Spiritual Practices: Blessings of Community

Receive and share Blessings of Community. Begin with a prayer of gratitude for the relationships in your life. See and feel connections with family members, spiritual friends, people in your congregation and community, and people and creatures in God's sacred web of life. What blessings flow to you from these circles?

Reflect, pray, or write in your journal about the call to be Community of Christ. Go deeper each day as you discern how you can invite people to Christ.

Peace Covenant

Today, God, I will seek the company of a stranger to make a friend.

23
Tuesday
July

Another Garden to Plant

By Gary Beebe of Orange, California, USA

I planted, Apollos watered, but God gave the growth.

—1 Corinthians 3:6

Recently, I had a marvelous experience of sharing and witnessing of my faith while hospitalized.

I had symptoms of a heart attack. My daughter insisted I go the emergency room. I lived through four days of tests, adjustments to the miserable hospital bed, not-so-wonderful gowns, and interrupted sleep for the staff to check vitals and draw blood.

After all this and living on a (bland!) diet, the test results showed my heart was in excellent shape. My lungs were clear, and my blood was flowing as it should. I prayed my health and ministry would continue!

Despite the inconvenience and time off work, the four days in the hospital provided an outstanding opportunity to share my life's story and hear the life stories of the hospital staff. The nurses and assistants were the greatest. And, what an array of international talent and skill—two nurses were from the Philippines, one from Vietnam, one from San Salvador, and one born in the United States.

Once we began to share our stories, the conversations flowed to family, children, and concern for an autistic son. This opened a door for me to introduce a nurse, who is the mother of an autistic boy, to church friends. They told their story of helping raise their autistic granddaughter, giving support and encouragement.

Jamie, my nurse from San Salvador, bonded strongly with me. Before going off shift, he came into my room and asked if I would offer a prayer for his mother, who recently had suffered a stroke, and for his 9-year-old son, whom he loves deeply.

I gave him a copy of the *Herald*, on which I wrote our address and phone number and invited him to call any time. From this experience another opportunity to witness was given to me—another garden to plant. Thank you, God.

Prayer for Peace

Nurturing Gardener, may we plant seeds for you to tend. May we help weed out obstacles that impede growth. May we be the living water and peace of Christ.

Spiritual Practice: Invite People to Christ

Read and reflect on Doctrine and Covenants 162:3b and 163:2b. Pray to be aware of people who might be receptive, and therefore blessed, by your sharing of the message of the Living Christ. Imagine being in relationship with them and inviting them to Christ. In preparation, discover your personal testimony of Christ. "Be persistent in your witness and diligent in your mission to the world." Repeat this mantra throughout the day: "Christ's mission, our mission, my mission."

Peace Covenant

Today, God, I will follow through when I find opportunities to witness of Christ's peace.

24
Wednesday
July

Listen and Trust

By Suzanne McMillan of East Sandwich, Massachusetts, USA

> *... Test my words. Trust in my promises for they have been given for your assurance and will bear you up in times of doubt...*
>
> —Doctrine and Covenants 155:7

My parents claim I learned to swim before I learned to walk. Many people who grow up near water learn to swim at an early age, so part of me thought everyone learned to swim before they grow up.

When my sister-in-law came from the Southwest United States for a visit, I knew she had never seen the ocean. But it took me a while to realize she had never learned to swim. After pacing up and down the beach, she finally accepted my invitation to take her swimming.

On a beach with a rocky slope, choppy surf, and slight undertow, conditions were less than ideal. I explained in detail what she probably would experience and should do. I would let go of her completely, and she would hold onto my back while I swam to a shallow, flat, submerged sandbar. There, she would be able to stand, jump, and start to feel her body float.

Parenting and working in the medical field, I've experienced my share of asking people to trust. But those 30 minutes with Mindy held some of the most remarkable moments of trust I ever have experienced.

Until she finally was able to grit her teeth and venture out, holding my hand, trust didn't mean a lot to her.

She slowly gained confidence, the white knuckles of two hands giving way to only one hand hanging on. She went from trusting in her ability to float to having my hand move a few inches from hers as she paddled. Her new courage held as much joy and wonder for me as for her.

The Creator has gifted us with a vast world and new experiences that hold wonder. God is there, keeping us in safe arms if we but listen and trust.

Prayer for Peace

Creator, how wonderful is your diverse world. Thank you for the joy we feel when we overcome our fears. We reach out to embrace the world with two hands. You are always there waiting for us, and for that we feel humbled and encouraged to share the peace of Jesus Christ.

Spiritual Practice: Flowing Water

If possible, sit where you can hear the sound of water—a fountain, stream, the sea, (perhaps a CD of water sounds). Listen to the sound as you thank God for the life-giving, life-shaping power of water. Pray for God's blessing on all the parched places of the Earth where there is injustice, oppression, violence, and disregard for life. Now, get up and drink a glass of clear, cold water as you pray, "God, let your justice flow through me as a disciple of Christ Jesus."

Peace Covenant

When I begin to feel doubt, God, I will put my trust in you to bear me up.

25
Thursday
July

Make Me a Blessing

By Evelyn Richardson of Nauvoo, Illinois, USA

Do not be conformed to this world, but be transformed by the renewing of your minds, so that you may discern what is the will of God—what is good and acceptable and perfect.

—Romans 12:2

The young man in a wheelchair played his guitar and sang beautifully. I asked if he would provide music for A Disciple's Generous Response at an upcoming service. I was to preside, and my husband was to give the morning message.

He asked what he should sing. I told him I had faith in him and would leave it up to him. His quick response was, "I guess I'll sing, "Skip to My Lou." I just smiled and said, "Whatever you say!" I did not see him until the following Sunday's service.

The theme was "Nothing Can Separate Us from God's Love." The young man wheeled himself to the front of the church and began.

"Lou, Lou, Skip to my Lou" as he looked out the corner of his eye at me. I smiled as he continued…"Lou, Lou, Skip to my Lou. Lou, Lou, Skip to my Lou. Skip to my Lou, God's children."

His sweet voice continued, and my heart melted. "Bring your offerings to the Lord. Bring your offerings to the Lord. Bring your offerings to the Lord, and God will surely bless you."

Yes, we were blessed as that ministry of music added to God's loving presence in our worship that morning. I find when we make our offerings to God, we are blessed. Who knows how many others also will receive blessings because of that offering?

From our Enduring Principles we learn, "We offer all we are and have to God's purposes as revealed in Jesus Christ. We generously share our witness, resources, ministries, and sacraments according to our true capacity."

May we allow God to use us as ministers, blessing all we contact on life's journey.

Prayer for Peace

God of love, accept our outpouring of praise as we sing from our heart. Assure us our simple offerings are worthy and serve as a blessing for you. May we invite all to join in our song.

Spiritual Practice: Growing a Gracious, Generous Heart

Open your heart to God's grace and generosity with a "breath prayer." Let your breathing slow and deepen. Be aware of God's breath moving in and out of your heart. Spend several minutes focusing on breathing in God's generosity. With each breath, silently name one gift for which you are thankful. Let your heart expand to contain God's gracious outpouring of love. With each breath out, name one gift you want to share from the overflow of your heart.

Peace Covenant

Today, God, I will be aware of blessings from new places.

26
Friday
July

On the Way Back: A New Perspective

By Becky Willis Shantz of Lamoni, Iowa, USA

Lift up your eyes and fix them on the place beyond the horizon to which you are sent. Journey in trust, assured that the great and marvelous work is for this time and for all time.

—Doctrine and Covenants 161:1a

In the home of my sister, Kathy, sit some tiny sand dollars. She displays these small treasures among unique shells collected from her strolls along the beaches of the Gulf of Mexico. One inch or less in diameter, these tiny sand dollars are rare.

Kathy and her husband were already late for departure. But Kathy could not leave without one last walk along the shore, so off to the island they went. They walked north, along seawalls and rocky points. Between the rocks were small areas of sandy beach.

After a short while, they turned and headed back. About 50 yards from the end, Kathy spotted a tiny sand dollar near some rocks. Excitedly, she directed all her attention to the area. Her excitement grew as she spotted another, then another, and yet another. She searched every sandy nook.

We have scoured the same shore several times since with no success. We marveled that Kathy found the sand dollars. But how had she not spotted them the first time she passed?

She missed them while walking one way with many barriers blocking them from sight. The walk back gave a different perspective. With this new perspective, Kathy's vigilant eye made the discovery.

How often do we miss God's treasures when we look from only one perspective? What discoveries lie ahead when we are willing to look from another point of view? Perhaps from someone else's perspective? The message seems to say, "Keep walking, keep looking, and be open and observant." When the pressures of life control our journey, God may be close. What strength, wisdom, and knowledge reveal themselves to us as we lift our eyes and draw close to God?

Prayer for Peace

Thank you, God, for your creation, which surrounds us. Your creation that is ours to discover, cherish, and appreciate. Ours to share in story. Ours to share with Christ's peace.

Spiritual Practice: Encountering Scripture as Continuing Revelation

Read and pray with Doctrine and Covenants as Continuing Revelation of God's vision for the church and creation. Choose a favorite section or focus on counsel in Sections 156—164. Read a few selected paragraphs slowly three or four times. Pause to pray for deep understanding after each reading.

Peace Covenant

Today, God, I will look beyond the horizon, I will look down around my toes. Then I will walk back and discover what I may have missed.

27
Saturday
July

Young Adults in the Ukraine

By Igor Karpachov of Donetsk, Ukraine

"Blessed are the peacemakers, for they will be called children of God."
—Matthew 5:4–14

Community of Christ is sharing Christ's peace with young adults in Donetsk, Ukraine. We come together, pray to handle every day, and try to realize the commitment we made through baptism.

Young people in Ukraine are beginning to see one another as unique and beloved children of God and members of a sacred community. When we gather each Sunday morning, we open our hearts to everyone. We reach out to others during the week, cheerfully sharing compassion. Young adults realize God will be with them always. Through this we are spiritually enriched.

Your contributions to world mission tithes make mission real to young adults in places such as Donetsk. Here we are developing disciples to serve. Thank you for responding generously and giving a sense of mission to these young people.

Prayer for Peace

God of all nations, gather us with gifts given to us by your grace. Gather us and help us send our gifts the world around, in proportion to our faith, responding with compassion and generosity. Help us share the peace of Christ with diligence.

Spiritual Practice: The International Community

Find (or imagine) a globe or map of the world. Look at all the nations and find a country other than your own where you know someone. Notice the geographic distance between your homeland and theirs. Pray for this person. Sense God's love connecting you just as the oceans connect the continents. Thank God for the connection you have with this person and with all of God's people around the globe. Ask a blessing on the church as a community sharing Christ's peace, drawing all into the family of God.

Peace Covenant

Today, God, I will reflect on my gifts and the ministry I can offer. I will explore ways I can use them to serve you.

28
Sunday
July

Teach Us to Pray

By Andrew Bolton, Council of Twelve Apostles

"So I say to you, Ask, and it will be given you; search, and you will find; knock, and the door will be opened for you. For everyone who asks receives, and everyone who searches finds, and for everyone who knocks, the door will be opened."

—Luke 11:9–10

I was 8 years old when I started to pray to God to make Dad better. We had lost the farm because our debts were too great. For the first time I heard my parents arguing. It puzzled me at first. Later I was afraid and sick to my stomach.

Worst of all, Dad drank, especially Tuesdays and Fridays, when he went shopping in a neighboring town. He would stop at the pub on the way home. He was always horrible after drinking. Always bad-tempered, often sarcastic. Sometimes he would hit my brothers. I prayed for five or six years.

Then one Tuesday, a cold, wet English day, Dad was late coming home. This usually meant he had been drinking longer and would be even worse when he returned. I hurried to complete my jobs for the night—feeding the hens, getting logs for the greenhouse boiler, and more. I then decided to go to my bedroom and be out of the way when Dad came home.

I got to the kitchen, and to my surprise Dad was already home. He was sober and speaking gently to my mother. Relieved, I went to bed.

On Friday Dad came home sober, again. The next Tuesday, Dad was sober. This continued. I began to do better in school. Dad became the gentle father I remembered from when I was younger. Our family began to do better financially. The tension in my mother eased. We were all happier.

How was my prayer answered? My mother later told me she met with Dad's doctor, who then confronted Dad. At the right moment, God opened the door to sobriety for my father and brought hope and healing to my family. God answered my prayers.

I am still grateful.

Prayer for Peace

Open-door God, we praise you for being present for us. Let us never be the cause of the door closing. May we knock and ask continually. May we seek you and never stop sharing the peace of Christ we find with you.

Spiritual Practice: Healing for Broken Spirits

Begin with quiet prayer. Ask God to help you discern some "sore places" in the body of Christ and in God's creation. Become aware of people who feel separated, wounded, or left out.

Reflect on or write a short journal entry of healing words to at least one person who comes to mind. Ask God for words that will touch this person's broken spirit like healing ointment. Keep this person in your heart and prayers today and act on any ideas that come to bring blessing and wholeness.

Peace Covenant

Today, God, I will not hesitate to knock and ask through prayer.

29
Monday
July

Who Knows?

By Terry West of Clay Cross, Derbyshire, England

> *Be fervent in your witness, passionate in your discipleship, and vigorous in your labor on behalf of peace and justice. Where two or three such disciples form community, there will the Spirit be. Many will come to see.*
>
> —Doctrine and Covenants162:8b

Let me share a few facts:

I would like to point out that I do not have a religion. My wife, Jackie, works for Community of Christ as a bookkeeper at the Clay Cross, United Kingdom, offices. She attends church every week with our children, Brandon and Tyler. We're bringing them up with strong Community of Christ principles. I do attend church on occasion to support my family.

A couple of years ago we went to reunion (family camp) at Dunfield House for three days. This was the first time I had met with a large gathering of church members outside the Clay Cross Congregation.

The next year we attended reunion for the whole week—what a joy!

The camp was full of great spirit. The singing was wonderful. Conversation was a pleasure. I was asked to say a few words about what I gained from my reunion experience, which I gladly did. What came across most was the unconditional love from everyone.

The passion and commitment of the young adults was high—they are the church's future. It was a shame the week had to end.

On returning home, I was sitting at the dining table, just pondering. I noticed my wife's *Daily Bread* on the table. I picked it up and started to read. I got involved with the stories inside, which led me to send you this story.

The point I'm trying to make is the people, each and every one, of Community of Christ have something special. This experience will stay with me forever, and I hope one day to say I am a member. For now, it's just one step at a time. Who knows?

I needed to let someone know my thoughts. Thanks for listening.

Prayer for Peace

God, keep us ever mindful that we always witness of you. May we always have an inclusive and sharing spirit. May we always share Christ's peace.

Spiritual Practice: Invite People to Christ

Read and reflect on Doctrine and Covenants 162:3b and 163:2b. Pray to be aware of people who might be receptive, and therefore blessed, by your sharing of the message of the Living Christ. Imagine being in relationship with them and inviting them to Christ. In preparation, discover your personal testimony of Christ. "Be persistent in your witness and diligent in your mission to the world." Repeat this mantra throughout the day: "Christ's mission, our mission, my mission."

Peace Covenant

Today, God, I will extend to a stranger an invitation to "come and see."

30
Tuesday
July

Sawing off the Branch behind Me

By Nancy Hylton of Seattle, Washington, USA

> *How blessed are they! For they published peace; they published good tidings of good; and they declared to the people that the Lord reigns.*
>
> —Mosiah 11:207

My older brother, Jim, was always more of a seeker than I. But, my sister remembers well that we would endlessly discuss religious questions. She called us deluded nerds. My brother's search for a "New Testament church" took him to the Woodland Park Congregation of Community of Christ.

A short while later he received confirmation through the Holy Spirit that this was where God had been prompting him for years. I refused to attend his rebaptism when he invited me, thinking he had gone off the deep end.

He was so excited about what he discovered in the Book of Mormon, he made me the recipient of his persistent nagging. He interrupted me to read me this or that passage while I was trying to study.

One day I remember consciously giving in to his nagging. I stopped and paid attention as he read aloud passage after passage. It was enlightening and confusing! For all of my life I had been taught the Book of Mormon was not "scripture."

I felt an urgency to respond that would not go away. I felt myself mentally climbing onto a shaky limb, needing to saw it off to separate me from previous misconceptions. I trusted God to catch me. I asked myself, "How could a book that testifies so powerfully of the love, divinity, and peace of Christ be wrong?"

I went to church with Jim. As I walked into the sanctuary, a clear voice inside my head said, "This is where I want you to be." I asked Jim, "How do I get baptized?" Jim said, "You have to do something called cottage meetings (what we used to call discipleship-preparation lessons)."

Today, my brother and I live on opposite coasts of the USA. We both serve as priesthood members. I am excited about the growing responsiveness and courage as our congregation steps forward in faith where God is calling us. It's a privilege to take part in Christ's mission, which develops disciples to serve.

I have never regretted the difficult decision to saw off that branch behind me so many years ago.

Prayer for Peace

Revealing God, may we be the prophetic people you call us to be. May we be the ones who share Christ's peace with neighbors.

Spiritual Practice: Making Responsible Choices

Prayerfully seek God's guidance in your choices. Discern God's vision for us and our mission. Begin by reviewing the responsibilities and opportunities in the day before you. Ask God for wisdom and insight about what matters most.

Peace Covenant

Today, God, I will separate myself from negative misconceptions.

31
Wednesday
July

The Village Between

By Elizabeth Else of St. Thomas, Ontario, Canada

If it is possible, so far as it depends on you, live peaceably with all.

—Romans 12:18

Music and literature can deeply affect our discipleship. I have found their worth as we include them in worship and community experience. As a child, I huddled by the radio, listening to classical symphonies and inspiring choirs.

I also loved stories. I immersed myself in children's books and the church's former publications, *Zion's Hope* and *Stepping Stones.* I waited expectantly each month for my bundle of papers to arrive from International Headquarters in Independence, Missouri, to my small town in faraway Canada.

A few years ago, I shared in a community production of *Fiddler on the Roof.* As a village character I sang from the outer edges of the stage. But during the wedding scene, I was near the center, surrounded by others. As the men began to dance, I was caught up in something bigger than simple community theater.

I felt as if I were in a real village with real people, with dust rising from the dancers' feet. Here danced a people, struggling to preserve their traditions and faith despite holocausts, alienation, and economic difficulty. I suddenly felt connected to many "villages" throughout the world. I thought of my own "village" within Community of Christ.

Sometimes we feel alienated as we struggle in a difficult economy. We try to be faithful, caught between traditions and new understandings. We despair at the world's troubles. But let us take strength from the divine spark placed within each of us.

May we celebrate joys among sorrows. May we move forward despite our doubts. May we forge community when fear and negativity would drive us apart. May we choose life. In our communities of joy, hope, love, and peace, may we shout "*L'chaim*!"—"To life!"

Prayer for Peace

Creator of time and space, may we embrace traditions from the past as we move peaceably forward. May we embrace traditions of other cultures and welcome them into our worship experience. May we live peaceably with all people.

Spiritual Practice: Music for Meditation

Identify a form of music for meditation. If hearing music is not an option, choose a song you can sing or play on a musical instrument. Choose music that carries a soulful, spiritual, or healing quality for you. Sit quietly and soak in the melody and resonance. Allow healing waves of sound to pierce body, spirit, and emotions. What do you feel or see as you listen? Does the music have colors? What spiritual message comes? How are you being restored, nurtured, healed, or moved to compassionate response?

Peace Covenant

Knowing it depends on me, God, I will bridge gaps for peace.

1
Thursday
August

The Spiritual Being

By Dorene Kilburn of Stratford, Ontario, Canada

> *When your willingness to live in sacred community as Christ's new creation exceeds your natural fear of spiritual and relational transformation, you will become who you are called to be.*
>
> —Doctrine and Covenants 164:9b

My husband picked up a book on Native American spirituality. A statement jumped out at him: "We are not human beings having a spiritual experience. We are spiritual beings having a human experience." This quote from French priest, philosopher, and mystic, Teilhard de Chardin, piqued our interest, so we bought the book.

I don't think either of us fully understands, even now, what that statement means, though we continue to gain insights as we study and pray.

Humans often search for happiness in the wrong places and in the wrong ways. Getting to the top of the corporate ladder and amassing an impressive investment portfolio does not ensure happiness or even security.

If we see ourselves as spiritual beings on a human journey, then our priorities are different. We long for communion with God. We want our spirit to be in tune with the Spirit. We strive for transforming friendship with Jesus Christ. That spiritual connection makes our human experience significant. It also comforts and bears us up in the dark places.

As spiritual beings, God gives us new insight and perhaps a glimpse beyond the horizon. We see new possibilities for service as Christ shows us his mission for us. Each new day is an adventure with him.

Prayer for Peace

Holy Spirit, transform us so we may recognize ourselves as spiritual beings. Keep us aware of our role in the sacred community. Keep us steadfastly sharing the peace of Jesus Christ.

Spiritual Practice: Spiritual Hunger

Jesus discerned hungers of body and spirit, and he fed them through a physical, verbal, spiritual ministry of presence. In a time of listening prayer, ask God to help you discern physical or spiritual hungers of people in your congregation, community, and global family. Invite the Spirit to move you to one hospitable act that "feeds" someone's hunger today.

Peace Covenant

Today, God, I will share my spiritual being with another.

2
Friday
August

The Man in the Hoodie

By Cindy L. Korf of North Platte, Nebraska, USA

O Lord, you have searched me and known me. You know when I sit down and when I rise up; you discern my thoughts from far away. You search out my path and my lying down, and are acquainted with all my ways. Even before a word is on my tongue, O Lord, you know it completely. You hem me in, behind and before, and lay your hand upon me.

—Psalm 139:1–5

I was struggling with personal issues and wondered where God was. After a night of worry, I woke early and decided to go for a walk on my favorite trail beside the river. I knew the walk among the trees, birds, and rising sun would give me a quiet sanctuary to pray and find God.

As I turned onto the trail, a man in hooded sweatshirt turned onto the trail ahead of me, carrying a container. He started walking down "my" trail. I was irritated—I wanted the trail for myself. I needed to be alone on the trail to enjoy the beauty and morning solitude.

Yet, this man was walking in front of me. I thought if I walked slowly, he would get far enough ahead of me that I could have the trail to myself. But much to my surprise, the man walked at my pace, and occasionally stopped to pick up trash to put into his container. All along the trail the man stayed a few feet ahead of me and picked up litter. He left the path clean and beautiful for me to walk.

It dawned on me, Jesus goes before us, preparing the way for us. Yet, in our self-absorption we fail to realize or have the faith that he is there and has already gone before us.

Prayer for Peace

God before us, God behind us, God who walks quietly beside us—may our awareness of you dawn on us as we walk our path of life. May we realize when our life is clean and beautiful it is because we are open to your gentle hand on us. Walk with us as we share Christ's peace.

Spiritual Practice: Welcoming Unity in Diversity

Meditate on Unity in Diversity. Create a large circle with your arms. See and feel the diverse people God invites inside the sanctuary of Christ's peace represented by this circle.

Who is easiest to welcome? Whom do you struggle to include? Confess the dividing walls between you and people too different or "dangerous" to invite into your spiritual home. Ask God to forgive and heal barriers that keep us from loving one another.

Peace Covenant

Today, God, I will see Christ in people different from myself.

3
Saturday
August

The Blessing of Giving

By Art Emerson of Addison, Maine, USA

> *...for during a severe ordeal of affliction, their abundant joy and their extreme poverty have overflowed in a wealth of generosity on their part. For, as I can testify, they voluntarily gave according to their means, and even beyond their means, begging us earnestly for the privilege of sharing in this ministry to the saints—and this, not merely as we expected; they gave themselves first to the Lord and, by the will of God, to us...*
>
> —2 Corinthians 8:2–5

When I think of A Disciple's Generous Response, I usually think of helping those who have less or helping in the aftermath of disaster. Recently, however, I learned that we can help Develop Disciples to Serve by *empowering others* to become disciples who respond generously.

I discovered that an offertory was not part of the worship services among migrant and immigrant Hispanics in our area. Those responsible for the services *assumed* the worshipers had no money to give. However, I believe everyone should have the opportunity to take part in the offering.

When Community of Christ decided to organize a Hispanic congregation, we decided to include an offertory as part of every worship service. That way everyone could give from God's blessing in their lives—whatever their gifts might be.

The response has been heart-warming! Not only do the adults eagerly take part in the offering, they help their children give. As we receive the offering each week, I also am reminded to give from my blessings.

When we take the time to recognize God's generous presence, love, and blessing in our lives, we will respond generously. Your contributions to the Develop Disciples to Serve Mission Initiative help equip men, women, and children to be true and living expressions of the life, ministry, and continuing presence of Christ. Thank you for responding generously.

Prayer for Peace

Generous God, for those who wish to give, may we provide the opportunity to offer a blessing in this way. May we accept with grace and gratitude any gift offered.

Spiritual Practice: Generosity and Discipleship

Bring a basket or other container to your place of prayer. Meditate on the link between generosity and discipleship. Write a prayer of commitment, naming specific acts of generosity and sharing to which you feel called. Fold the paper and place the prayer in the offering container. Close by singing a hymn of gratitude or praise as you offer your gift to God.

Peace Covenant

Today, God, I will recognize and give thanks for the sincerity of the giver.

4
Sunday
August

Share Generously

By Lu Mountenay of Independence, Missouri, USA

> *"Take care! Be on your guard against all kinds of greed; for one's life does not consist in the abundance of possessions. So it is with those who store up treasures for themselves..."*
>
> —Luke 12:15, 21

I feel challenged by the Mission Initiative, Abolish Poverty, End Suffering. Not just discuss it. Not just relieve it. Not just reduce it. ABOLISH it. Big job! Help wanted!

It's hard for me to write from an impoverished point of view, because I've never known poverty. I can only imagine. I just left a Shalom Place encounter at the Temple entitled "Voices for Racial Justice." Brad Martell, Peace and Justice Ministries, guided us through a discussion about poverty, why it exists, and what we can do about it.

I guess I'm all fired up. This thought comes to me: I need to raise my *voice*, as well as my eyebrows, when I see injustice!

Charitable giving is great as a stopgap, duct-tape measure. It's necessary to relieve suffering, for now. It's good for the material "haves" to give to the "have-nots." But in tandem with sharing, I need to understand.

I need to explore *why* the "have-nots" have naught, why I am a "have" and *they* are "have-nots." Why I write "I" and "they," when it should be "we" together, in community.

In London, getting on and off the "Tube," I heard, "Mind the gap." Just so you step far enough to safety. I could do more than just *mind* the growing gap between the very rich and the very poor (not that I'm very rich...well... maybe I am). I need to find ways to *bridge* the gap and take giant steps for peace and justice. I need to promote *justice* that doesn't try to *justify* the existing canyon of a gap.

This wide difference in wealth divides, denies, separates, segregates, isolates, marginalizes, endangers, and excludes. It causes humans to suffer.

Christ is the bridge that invites, welcomes, reaches, teaches, embodies, embraces, serves, and shares. Generously. Can I do any less?

Prayer for Peace

God of justice, we come with heavy hearts, knowing we haven't yet done all we can to end suffering. Help us make Christ's mission our mission. Help us share the peace and justice of Jesus Christ.

Spiritual Practice: Abolish Poverty, End Suffering

Reflect on John 21:15–17 as a meditation. Let your mind be drawn to places where the hungry wander the streets or live in shelters. Let their images fill your mind. Offer a prayer for those who are suffering. Imagine Christ tending those sheep. Think of ways you might end their suffering as part of your mission. Throughout the day, carry in your mind the voice of Christ saying: "Feed my lambs...tend my sheep..."

Peace Covenant

Yes, God, I will shed tears of compassion, but then I will break a good sweat working for justice.

5
Monday
August

♫ Hymn of the Month: "Dear God, We Come This Hour to Ask"

By Dennis Aldridge of Eardisley, England

> *...look to the sacraments to enrich the spiritual life of the body. It is not the form of the sacrament that dispenses grace but it is the divine presence that gives life. Be respectful of tradition and sensitive to one another...*
>
> —Doctrine and Covenants 162:2d

I have written many hymns and songs, and most have found use in the British Isles. A young couple was planning a wedding in the Sutton-in-Ashfield church. The mother of the bride, herself a minister, had been moved by some of my hymns, and she asked me to write one for the wedding.

That is how I came to write "Dear God, We Come."

I like hymns that tie the present-day church to what has gone before. We are the same church and have brothers and sisters who walked with Jesus Christ in the flesh. I looked for what the scriptures tell us about Jesus at Bethany, Cana, and the Sermon on the Mount. Then I thought of my own happy marriage. Married couples need the friendship of Jesus Christ, and they need joy and hope—therefore the hymn.

Dear God, we come this hour to ask your blessing from above
on these who join their lives today in sacrament of love.
The gifts we ask are joy and hope to help them on life's way,
and friendship of your only son for this and every day.

Just as in Cana, Christ was there so here may Christ be guest,
and as he came to Bethany so may their home be blest,
and as he spoke on mountainside so may they hear his voice,
and as they sense his smile for them so may their hearts rejoice.

Help them, dear God, to live in love, each for the other pure,
not counting cost. So may their joy through all their lives endure.
Enfold them now with loving grace, accept the vows they make.
Preserve their days, fulfill their hopes, we pray, for Jesus' sake. Amen

Prayer for Peace

Sacramental God, bless us on our journeys of life. Surround us with a loving and supporting community. May we bring Christ into our everyday lives and share his peace.

Spiritual Practice

Contemplate this hymn as a poem (or sing to NORSE AIRE tune).

6
Tuesday
August

Pray Anywhere, Anytime

By Sara Parkin of Midland, Michigan, USA

Then Jesus told them a parable about their need to pray always and not to lose heart. He said, "In a certain city there was a judge who neither feared God nor had respect for people. In that city there was a widow who kept coming to him and saying, 'Grant me justice against my opponent.' For a while he refused; but later he said to himself, 'Though I have no fear of God and no respect for anyone, yet because this widow keeps bothering me, I will grant her justice, so that she may not wear me out by continually coming.'" And the Lord said, "Listen to what the unjust judge says. And will not God grant justice to his chosen ones who cry to him day and night? Will he delay long in helping them? I tell you, he will quickly grant justice to them. And yet, when the Son of Man comes, will he find faith on earth?"

—Luke 18:1–8

(Part 6 of My Journey with Alzheimer's Disease)

Where do I pray? Anywhere!

I remember one time in the grocery store when a friend needed a prayer for a family member. We hugged and prayed in the aisle. Then one time in Brazil, in the church, the pastor started the prayer. My head was down, eyes closed, I listened quietly and realized people were talking at the same time.

How rude!

But then I started really listening. I heard one person praying for the pastor, another praying for family, another praying for the person who would be sharing the sermon. All were praying different prayers. I was the only one not praying aloud. Now I can pray anywhere, any time.

Today, I woke up, at 5:20 a.m. I prayed with God, talking about the sun coming up, thanking God for looking over me through the night (sometimes I have nightmares). Then I sat up in bed with arms open and let God do the talking.

When I listen I might just get what I am to do with today. Do I always listen? I try, but I lose my focus, looking at my laptop, which waits for me to press its keys. I look at my book, sitting unread in the chair, and the dog, waiting for me to take it outside.

These things can wait. I don't have to wait long for God, who does not delay.

Prayer for Peace

Faithful God, we know you are always with us and are just waiting for us to call on you. May our faith be strong, our spirits close to you, and our love for one another overflowing. May we faithfully share the peace of Christ.

Spiritual Practice: Intercessory Reflection

Sit quietly with your eyes closed as you enter intercessory reflection and prayer. Ask God to bring persons to your mind and heart who need prayer. Be open to images of the persons or spiritual insight into their needs. Listen for signals from their lives and let the depth of God's love for them become powerful and real to you. Write, speak, or think a prayer of blessing and healing for these much-loved disciples and friends. Ask God to help you see ways to affirm and support them when you meet them in daily life.

Peace Covenant

Today, God, I will not hesitate to call on you for strength.

7
Wednesday
August

From the Diversity Team: Everyday Diversity

By Peter Smith of Odessa, Florida, USA

> *Hear, O my people of the church, I am Jesus Christ of whom you have sung and testified and in whose name you pray. I am the spirit of love and peace which is in the world and yet not known by the world.*
>
> —Doctrine and Covenants 157:11

The incredible diversity we encounter every day in the world constantly amazes me. God created each of us uniquely, gifting us with talents and abilities, filling us with hopes and dreams and blessing us with opportunities to live to our potential.

We live in a worldwide community of more than 7 billion people, and Community of Christ's Enduring Principles challenge members. Unity in Diversity celebrates the traits and characteristics that make each person unique. Yet, we also find many common threads that connect us as God's children. Our Creator "views all people precious." God calls us to accept this challenge wholeheartedly and without reservation.

As a pastor, I have been blessed to experience moments of Unity in Diversity. During a baptismal service, three people chose to enter the waters of baptism.

Max recently had turned 8, and he was excited to begin his journey as a disciple. Bob, a retiree, had been a part of the congregation for years. One day he recognized a sincere need within his heart to take his commitment to the next level. A friend had introduced Sherry to the congregation. She had found herself loved and accepted in a way she never had felt before.

Each chose baptism for a different reason, but this day we celebrated as a united body—the body of Christ.

The congregation had an opportunity to share statements of support for each baptismal candidate. As members shared, I looked in awe around the room at these disciples of Jesus Christ. Each came to this place because of a unique story. They united in one common goal: to grasp the mission of Christ as their own. We celebrate our diversity, united by our faith in Jesus Christ!

Prayer for Peace

Creator God, having chosen to follow Christ, we pray we will be the reason the world will come to know him. May we share his peace with all nationalities, races, ethnicities, age groups, genders, sexual orientations, and abilities. And may we find we are more alike than different.

Spiritual Practice: Welcoming Unity in Diversity

Meditate on Unity in Diversity. Create a large circle with your arms. See and feel the diverse people God invites inside the sanctuary of Christ's peace represented by this circle.

Who is easiest to welcome? Whom do you struggle to include? Confess the dividing walls between you and people too different or "dangerous" to invite into your spiritual home. Ask God to forgive and heal barriers that keep us from loving one another.

Peace Covenant

Today, God, I will sing and testify of Christ so this diverse world will know him.

8
Thursday
August

Structured to Work Together

Becky Willis Shantz of Lamoni, Iowa, USA

"Everyone then who hears these words of mine and acts on them will be like a wise man who built his house on rock. The rain fell, the floods came, and the winds blew and beat on that house, but it did not fall...And everyone who hears these words of mine and does not act on them will be like a foolish man who built his house on sand. The rain fell, and the floods came, and the winds blew and beat against that house, and it fell..."

—Matthew 7:24–27

Contrary to the teachings of Jesus Christ, people often build homes on the vast sandy beaches of the world. True to his warning, building on sand destroys lives and homes, because such foundations cannot withstand storms. What does it take to build buildings that withstand the fiercest storms? While writing on this theme for a series of children's lessons a couple of years ago, I consulted with my brother, Dan, a builder.

The state of Florida requires buildings in coastal areas to be on pilings. These cement columns must go down through the ground at least 10 feet below sea level. Typically, each piling must support 25–40 tons! The pilings also must go above ground one floor, like stilts. Each piling has to be able to carry its share of the load. One can't do it alone. They all have to work together. The builder *must* follow the engineer's plans or risk the collapse of the building.

Besides pilings, breakaway walls help protect the building. These walls cover the lower part of the building so the pilings don't show. In a storm surge, these walls break away, so the force of the water can go through the lower part of the building and not knock it off the pilings. The walls and the water compromise so as not to destroy the building.

Compare these pilings to Jesus' advice. He tells his disciples to follow his words to build lives that can withstand problems. Just as the pilings work together in strengthening and supporting the building, so we are strengthened and supported by one another through the Blessings of Community.

Prayer for Peace

Foundation of Being, may we always choose to follow your wisdom.

Spiritual Practice: Making Responsible Choices

Prayerfully seek God's guidance in your choices. Discernment invites us to orient our lives toward God and God's vision for us and creation. Begin by reviewing the responsibilities and opportunities in the day before you. Take these choices into prayer, asking God for wisdom and insight about what matters most.

Peace Covenant

Today, God, I will hear your words and act on them.

9
Friday
August

Ministry of a Bulldogger

By Carl Mesle of Independence, Missouri, USA

He said also to the one who had invited him, "When you give a luncheon or a dinner, do not invite your friends or your brothers or your relatives or rich neighbors, in case they may invite you in return, and you would be repaid. But when you give a banquet, invite the poor, the crippled, the lame, and the blind."

—Luke 14:12–13

Irby was from Denver, Colorado. He was a world champion bulldogger.

A what? A bulldogger works in rodeos, lassoing steers. While riding his horse and with record speed, Irby would bring the steer down and have it completely tied up so it couldn't move. Hands in the air—stop the clock!

Irby attended a Community of Christ World Conference. Being far from home, other members would extend their hospitality to this interesting man and invite him to their home. Before accepting, he would ask, "How are things in your home?"

If the answer was, "fine" or "good," Irby would say, "Thanks, but I need to visit the homes where there is a need for ministry."

Prayer for Peace

Compassionate God, help us to go beyond our circle of friends, and search for those in need. When we invite guests to our home, may we offer hospitality to those we have yet to befriend. Give us the awareness to sense loneliness in others and show interest in their need for peace.

Spiritual Practice: Invite People to Christ

Read and reflect on Doctrine and Covenants 162:3b and 163:2b. Pray to be aware of people who might be receptive, and therefore blessed, by your sharing of the message of the Living Christ. Imagine being in relationship with them and inviting them to Christ. In preparation, discover your personal testimony of Christ. Be "persistent in your witness and diligent in your mission to the world." Repeat this mantra throughout the day: "Christ's mission, our mission, my mission."

Peace Covenant

Today, God, I will go where I am needed.

10
Saturday
August

New Congregation Engages in Mission Initiative

By Debbie Hogan of New Port Richey, Florida, USA,
and Brenda Cummins of North Fort Myers, Florida, USA

> *Like good stewards of the manifold grace of God, serve one another with whatever gift each of you has received.*
>
> —1 Peter 4:10

Excitement rose in 2011 as 31 people attended the first worship service in the New Port Richey Congregation in Florida.

Each week, all who attend share hot meals. Services typically last about three hours, including the meal and community-building activities.

As the members provide a witness of Jesus Christ, relation-building skills, and ministry, the congregation partners with community projects that relate to the Abolish Poverty, End Suffering Mission Initiative. This congregation remains a place where people can share meals, ministry, and mission.

Your generous contributions make it possible for congregations such as New Port Richey to make mission real. Thank you for responding generously to move forward.

Prayer for Peace

Creator God, may we be aware of needs in our communities and around the world. May we always be ready to address those needs by witnessing for Christ and sharing his peace.

Spiritual Practice: Experience Congregations in Mission

Read and reflect on Doctrine and Covenants 164:9a–d. Reread the sentence, "If you truly would be Community of Christ, then embody and live the concerns and passion of Christ." Make a list of the issues you feel mattered most to Christ. Make another list of issues that matter to your congregation. Reflect on the similarities and differences. How can you help align the lists? Throughout the day, as issues arise, ask yourself, "Would this matter to Christ?"

Peace Covenant

Today, God, I will expand the breadth of my sharing.

11
Sunday
August

Live in Faith

By Steve Jones, presiding bishop

> *Now faith is the assurance of things hoped for, the conviction of things not seen.*
>
> —Hebrews 11:1

"You have stage-four lung cancer," the doctor told Merilee, my 61-year-old sister. Her choices were clear. Seek treatment with little hope for a positive result because of its progression, or turn in faith and walk hand-in-hand with Christ to her heavenly Parent.

For Merilee, the decision was easy because seven years ago she had made another life-changing choice. She had decided to take Christ's hand and be baptized. This changed everything. Her life became one of peace, purpose, and hope.

All the doctors could promise was six months to a couple of years. Her faith in Christ was the promise of eternal life. Her decision was easy. She chose the hope of eternal life.

And so Merilee stepped forward in faith. She gave up her business of cleaning houses. She sold her mobile home and two-thirds of her earthly possessions. She packed her car, left good friends, and came to our home.

Merilee's life choices reflected a living faith so she could have the hoped-for assurance of eternal life. Her life inspired all who knew her. Might our life choices reflect our living faith. May we choose what matters most.

Prayer for Peace

Faithful God, how good it is to live with the assurance of your presence. How good it is to pray, knowing you listen. May we choose to leave our burdens with Christ. May we choose to share Christ's peace.

Spiritual Practice: Making Responsible Choices

Prayerfully seek God's guidance in your choices. Discernment invites us to orient our lives toward God and God's vision for us and creation. Begin by reviewing the responsibilities and opportunities in the day before you. Take these choices into prayer, asking God for wisdom and insight about what matters most.

Offer yourself to God with the prayer of Teresa of Avila: "God, what do you want of me today?" Sit prayerfully with this question as you review the day again. Be aware of images, thoughts, names, or actions that come to you. Ask for a blessing to live this day responsibly and compassionately in the spirit of Christ.

Peace Covenant

Today, God, I will call on you to guide my choices. I will follow your guidance with faith.

12
Monday
August

The Light of Christ's Mission

By Donna Boyd of Independence, Missouri, USA

> *There was a man sent from God, whose name was John. He came as a witness to testify to the light, so that all might believe through him. He himself was not the light, but he came to testify to the light. The true light, which enlightens everyone, was coming into the world.*
> —John 1:6–9

Before we begin to understand the light that shines in the darkness of our lives, we sometimes try to hide from it. Have you ever lifted a large rock and watched little creatures scurry for a new, dark place to hide? This is the way a troubled soul might react to the light of the gospel of Jesus Christ at first. After we choose baptism into new life in Christ, his mission draws us in. We timidly, then earnestly, seek the light.

As we grow in faith and wisdom, our response to the light of Christ changes. We seek to continue in the light and to draw others into it. Because we have new life in Christ, we can shine into the darkness of others' lives. When we separate ourselves from the Divine, without seeking forgiveness, our light dims. We may begin to hide ourselves from the light of the gospel.

To continue in the light of God's grace, we must become vulnerable to it.

Sometimes we glimpse more light than we can understand. As we stretch toward this light, we understand our need to engage in Christ's mission. Only as we reveal the light of Christ in our daily lives can we lead others to him.

Prayer for Peace

Light, we linger in your brightness. We see you shining in Christ. We see Christ reflected in one another. May we not hide from your light, but seek it. May we seek to do Christ's mission by inviting others to share in his peace.

Spiritual Practice: God's Healing Light

Today's intercessory prayer is adapted from the Quaker tradition. Become still and turn your attention to God. Prayerfully identify a person who is in need of healing, blessing, or guidance. Close your eyes and imagine God's presence surrounding the person. See or sense the person being held in God's light. Continue holding the person in the light and release the person into whatever blessing God knows is needed. Words are not necessary. Trust the Spirit to see and penetrate more deeply than human awareness. Thank God and close with "amen."

Peace Covenant

Today, God, I will invite another to share in Christ's peace.

13
Tuesday
August

Lying Dormant

By Peggy Michael of Cantonment, Florida, USA

We know that all things work together for good for those who love God, who are called according to his purpose.

—Romans 8:28

A seed lodged in the crevice of a stone wall. The sun and rain soon quickened it with life. It sent tender roots downward and unfolded chartreuse leaves. As I studied the unlikely home, I marveled at the seed's determination to find invisible nourishment in such an inhospitable place. On seeing this miracle I vowed to let God quicken me also with growth, no matter the conditions around me.

I once saw myself as a wrinkled seed. The Spirit thrust me into the earth. I marveled that, though dormant, I would swell and fill Earth's garden when God touched me with living water. I join the community from tiny diverse packets, producing golden corn, glistening green peas, and squash of many shapes. Petunias and sunflowers would soon nod to me from once-barren corners of the plot.

If such plenty can come from dry, wrinkled seeds, I wondered, what can God's quickening touch do to me? For what purpose am I called forth?

Prayer for Peace

Like the unplowed field, Creator, our potential lies beneath a resistant crust. May we let the planter soften our hearts and prepare us for new growth. May we grow toward our purpose of sharing Christ's peace.

Spiritual Practice: Trees

Watch the trees outside your window for a few moments. Close your eyes and meditate on Alma's words about seeds and trees. If you were to plant and grow the Word of God in your heart, what kind of tree might symbolically represent this process? Envision a seed as it grows into a tree of life and blessing. Ask God to show you how to begin (see Alma 16:152–173).

Peace Covenant

Today, God, I will push through hard places and grow into my purpose.

14
Wednesday
August

Live as Healing Leaves

By Carolyn Brock of Redmond, Oregon, USA

On either side of the river, is the tree of life with its twelve kinds of fruit, producing its fruit each month; and the leaves of the tree are for the healing of the nations.
—Revelation 22:2

In the desert of northeastern Kenya live the Turkana people, nomads who follow their camels and goats over the parched earth. There are few trees in the desert. Occasionally along a dry riverbed a few hardy palms survive. Scrubby thorn trees or scattered acacias dot the landscape.

It is not difficult to understand how the Turkana use trees as places of coolness and healing. The concept of healing relates to being made "cool," and the people often carry those who are sick to rest in the shade of a tree.

On the other side of the continent in Gabon, another tribal people hold one particular tree in special favor. They often use branches and leaves of the sore tree for healing, for reconciliation rituals, as symbols of life and health in the village (Thomas G. Christensen, *An African Tree of Life*).

We follow Jesus Christ, the one who brought healing and cooling relief to all God's people. As we seek to become like him, we will need to learn the skills of healing, the tools of reconciliation, the languages of life and community. God calls us to be leaves on the tree that bring healing to all nations. May the Spirit flow through us and teach us to live as a healing Community of Christ.

Prayer for Peace

God of the trees and rice fields, God of the deserts and seas, we gather at these resting places to be community, to heal.

Spiritual Practice: Healing Leaves

Spend some time meditating on leaves. Take a walk and look at leaves on trees; watch leaves bud, sway in the wind, fall to the ground. Hear them crunch under your feet. Gather a small supply to place in a basket or vase. Use sight, smell, touch, and hearing to explore the qualities of leaves. Consider how leaves bring healing, life, and beauty to our lives. Close with prayer about your desire to offer healing as generously as a leaf on a tree.

Peace Covenant

Today, God, I will not look at "healing of the nations" as a daunting task. I will take one step at a time. We will take many steps as community.

15
Thursday
August

The Spirit Leads to Peace

By Shirley Remmenga of Fort Collins, Colorado, USA

May the God of steadfastness and encouragement grant you to live in harmony with one another, in accordance with Christ Jesus, so that together you may with one voice glorify the God and Father of our Lord Jesus Christ.

—Romans 15:5–7

Silently, sweetly, and warmly it resided in my being. I did not recognize its presence in the beginning. I had a sense, but not a *knowing.* I was an obedient child, taught carefully and lovingly about God. I learned to pray when I was tiny. I could feel and see God's presence in nature—the crops, the weeds, the garden, the storms, the sunshine, and the rain. It was in the animals—tame and wild—the soil, the flowers, the bees, and much more.

Gradually I began learning about the Holy Spirit—about the soft voice within that helped me, comforted me, taught me, and inspired me. I began to *know.* I remember clearly the voice within that told me not to let my brothers' teasing bother me. Rather, it told me that I should not react at all to the teasing. So I followed the gentle lead, and sure enough…peace. It took only a couple weeks before they stopped teasing me.

This is just one example of how I grew to recognize and follow the Holy Spirit's guidance. Year by year we became better acquainted, and I began to *know*, deep inside me. Of course, I still don't know all, but I do know the Holy Spirit is real for me.

The Spirit is always present, guiding my life, and making it possible to live joyfully with a positive, optimistic outlook. The Holy Spirit silently, sweetly, warmly, and continuously lives in my deepest being. How beautiful is the Spirit's presence.

Prayer for Peace

Steadfast God of encouragement, reside in us. Help us always be aware of your warm presence. Help us be open to your shalom. Help us share your presence and Christ's peace with all.

Spiritual Practice: Voices of God

What is the voice of God saying to us? Do we hear the whispers of God's longing for shalom; God's dream of beauty and wholeness for all creation? Do we hear the "voice" of God calling to us in faces and eyes, in the sounds of suffering and joy, in scripture and sacred word, in tears and laughter, in silence and noise? Spend a few moments reflecting on when and how God's voice has spoken to you. When did you first feel called to join God in the pursuit of justice and peace? How does that call to shalom continue to come to you through the many "voices" of God?

Peace Covenant

Today, God, with your presence, I will be open to your shalom.

16
Friday
August

In Good Hands

By Barbara Howard of Independence, Missouri, USA

> ...*I will not forget you. See, I have inscribed you on the palms of my hands.*
> —Isaiah 49:15–16

> If you look deeply into the palm of your hand, you will see your parents and all generations of your ancestors. All of them are alive in this moment. Each is present in your body. You are the continuation of each of these people.
>
> —*Thich Nhat Hanh*
> Present Moment, Wonderful Moment

As our daughter, Joy, visited with my sister, Beverly, she suddenly exclaimed, "Aunt Bev, your hands are exactly like Mom's." It's true, and both of us have hands identical to our mother's. But she left us a legacy far greater than the shape of our hands. Her faith in Christ Jesus was sure and strong. Memories of the communion of Community of Christ since early childhood and our mother's church family nurtured her faith.

I am thankful for my mother's hands and even more grateful for her legacy of faith. It was with great delight that I received a card written by our son, Jim, who writes for a greeting-card company. The verse began:

> My mother had her hands full raising me. So I know that when she clasped them together in prayer, she must have been greatly relieved to set aside the trouble and tasks of motherhood and hold on to her faith.

The poem continues to describe the events of childhood, closing with, "Mother, I always knew I was in good hands." A parent who prays for a child is comforted by the child's acknowledgment of the source of strength and power.

God promises us continuing divine presence in our lives, sustained by the inscription carved on God's palms. Such assurance is life's greatest gift. It is the good news we share with others as we invite them into the community. Invite People to Christ.

Prayer for Peace

We rest in the palms of your hands, God, assured that you will not forget us. Assure us of your love. Assure us of your promise of peace for us to share.

Spiritual Practice: Hand Ministry

Place your hand on a piece of paper and trace around it to create an outline. Add details of fingernails, wrinkles, or skin color if desired. Look at your hand and meditate on what you do with your hands each day. Ask God to direct your thoughts to a person in need of blessing, kindness, or healing touch. Pray for wisdom about the specific act needed by this person and discern how and when you will use your hands to complete this ministry.

Peace Covenant

Today, God, I will ponder my hands as representing all who have gone before, sharing Christ's peace.

17
Saturday
August

Learn and Discern

By Andrew Bolton, Council of Twelve Apostles

> *...so we, who are many, are one body in Christ, and individually we are members one of another. We have gifts that differ according to the grace given to us: prophecy, in proportion to faith; ministry, in ministering; the teacher, in teaching; the exhorter, in exhortation; the giver, in generosity; the leader, in diligence; the compassionate, in cheerfulness.*
>
> —Romans 12:5–8

Christianity began as a teaching movement. Church leaders throughout the Asia Mission Field have the opportunity to take part in Ministerial Education and Discipleship Studies (MEADS). Here they can expand their knowledge of Christ's message.

It is a joy to teach those who are eager to learn: 10 staff members in the Philippines, 15 full-time and volunteer leaders in Sri Lanka; and 50 in Kathmandu, Nepal. In Orissa, India, where there are about 150 Community of Christ congregations, MEADS classes include 100 leaders, most of whom are volunteers in their villages.

Your contributions to world mission tithes provide resources such as MEADS classes that help make mission real throughout the world. Thank you for responding generously.

Prayer for Peace

God of wisdom, open our minds to the message of Christ. Envelop those who are eager to learn with your discerning Spirit. Guide us in ways to share Christ's peace with the world.

Spiritual Practice: The International Community

Find (or imagine) a globe or map of the world. Look at all the nations and find a country other than your own where you know someone. Notice the geographic distance between your homeland and theirs. Pray for this person. Sense God's love connecting you just as the oceans connect the continents. Thank God for the connection you have with this person and with all of God's people around the globe. Ask a blessing on the church as a community sharing Christ's peace, drawing all into the family of God.

Peace Covenant

Today, God, I will study and learn and share.

18
Sunday
August

Shattering the Status Quo

By Wim van Klinken, director of International Headquarters

"I came to bring fire to the earth, and how I wish it were already kindled! I have a baptism with which to be baptized, and what stress I am under until it is completed! Do you think that I have come to bring peace to the earth? No, I tell you, but rather division!"

—Luke 12:49–51

In the scripture passage from Luke, Jesus makes clear that division within families is one possible experience and result of being in mission with Christ. The road to shalom, eternal peace for all creation, challenges us to uproot all evil and injustice and to "bring fire to the earth."

This is confirmed in our call to challenge "cultural, political, and religious trends that are contrary to the reconciling and restoring purposes of God" (Doctrine and Covenants 163:3b).

Challenging these trends requires a change of heart, repentance, and decision. It asks for commitment to the journey of "restoring persons to healthy or righteous relationships with God, others, themselves, and the earth" (Doctrine and Covenants 163:2b).

God's reign is something happening among us, if only we are willing to see it and willing to address the forces obstructing its presence. It needs us to be different, to shatter our status quo, and to become "a true and living expression of the life, sacrifice, resurrection, and continuing presence of Christ" (Doctrine and Covenants 164:4c).

Prayer for Peace

Creator God, give us courage to make the changes in our lives that will further define our path to shalom. Allow us to release preconceptions that hinder our understanding. Give us the strength to overcome any fears we might have in sharing Christ's peace.

Spiritual Practice: Embodying God's Shalom

Find a way to express and embody God's shalom. Begin by prayerfully listening to your longing for peace. Become silent and imagine you can hear the groaning of the Earth's people, nations, and creatures. Prayerfully open yourself to what needs to be changed to find peace and the divine vision of shalom.

What images, feelings, and words come to you? What prayer for peace comes to you from your time of listening? Speak or write this prayer. What act of justice, kindness, healing, or peacemaking does God invite you to consider this day?

Peace Covenant

Today, God, I will reexamine and adjust my agenda for Christ's mission.

19
Monday
August

"Pardon Me, Telephone Pole"

By Flo McDonald of Lee's Summit, Missouri, USA

> *And there came a voice to them, a pleasant voice, as if it were a whisper, saying "Peace, peace be to you because of your faith in my well beloved, who was from the foundation of the world."*
>
> —Helaman 2:112

In 1962, before clean-air laws were enacted, our family lived in Santa Monica, California, near Los Angeles. Smog could be a problem. One day our 12-year-old son, Joe, left early for school. The usual understanding was that he would come straight home after school. This particular day he had permission to stay at school and play basketball. This is his story in his words:

> As I approached the basketball courts I noticed the sky was beginning to turn gray, and the air was difficult to breathe. After we'd played about 30 minutes, the smog thickened. The coach told us to check in our equipment and get home. I had more than a mile to walk up a busy street. I knew my parents would worry, so I hurried as fast as I could.
>
> I started walking in the direction I thought would get me home. It was hard to tell. I walked slowly until I heard the sounds of traffic. I thought I had come to Ocean Park, the street we lived on. Cautiously I walked up the street, trying not to run into anyone or anything. It was taking much longer than the usual 20 minutes.
>
> All I remember is that I prayed all the way that I would get home safely. After stumbling and running into telephone poles, I finally saw our apartment building. I was so happy I could have cried. My parents were happy and relieved to see me. After answering a lot of questions I thanked God for my safe return.

Mom talking: Our family realized that day how blessed we were, and we were thankful. In difficult times, relying on the power of God is a wonderful way to cope with and work through our fears.

Prayer for Peace

Tender Shepherd, may we listen carefully for your whispering voice and find light for the journey in your presence. May we place our fears in your hands. Increase our faith in Christ, whose peace we share.

Spiritual Practice: Light

Close your eyes, and become centered with your breath. Reflect on the statement, "The light of God is in all things," as you breathe gently in and out. Sense or see a point of light in the distance, coming gradually toward you. With each breath it comes closer, growing in size and brightness. The light has a bright, soft beauty and radiates loving peace. The light of God reaches you and permeates you with a deep sense of peace. Rest in the light as it surrounds and fills you. Thank God that you live in God's light and it lives in you.

Peace Covenant

Today God, I will pray for direction through the fog and confusion in my life.

20
Tuesday
August

There's a Rock in My Shoe... Where's God?

By Louita Clothier of Lamoni, Iowa, USA

Learn of me, and listen to my words; walk in the meekness of my Spirit and you shall have peace in me.

—Doctrine and Covenants 18:2n

It was a beautiful summer day in the countryside. A mix of forests and pastures covered the hills, typical of southern Iowa. The grasshoppers had not yet taken over the fields. The big, round hay bales made interesting patterns on the landscape. Yet as I walked along, I saw only ordinary trees, ordinary fields. I probably didn't even notice the birds singing. I did notice a pain in my knee and a rock in my shoe.

Fast forward two or three days, walking down that same road. Somehow my spirit had awakened, and this time God surrounded me with loving presence. I looked at the wide sky stretching over me from horizon to horizon and peeked through several layers of clouds to the deep blue beyond. I felt like I saw into all eternity.

Every leaf on every tree and every bird that sang—even every spinning spider—was a manifestation that God's love is in all and through all creation. Everything seemed such a miracle, and my heart was full. I wanted to skip!

My thoughts turned to prayer, and I found myself a mile down the road, not remembering how I got there. What was the difference between these two days? Why was I able to see—see and experience that second day? Wasn't God there the first day?

Of course, God's Spirit was there both days. It's just that I wasn't ready. I wasn't aware. God was there, but I was "out to lunch." When we prepare ourselves for the presence of God, we receive a deep awareness of the beauty, blessings, and miracles present all day, every day.

Prayer for Peace

Eternal Presence, eternal Creator, thank you for what we experience from horizon to horizon—evidence of your loving presence. As we become aware of your gift of inner peace, may we share it with others.

Spiritual Practice: Caring for God's Sacred Creation

Choose a way to notice, give thanks, and care for God's sacred creation. Prayerfully consider one of the following practices or create your own. Walk in nature with a spirit of gratitude while looking and listening for God in all things. Write or pray a psalm of praise for the Earth's beauty or a prayer of healing and blessing for its wounds.

Learn about and engage in an act of Earth-keeping such as recycling, simple living, or fasting from over-consumption of resources. Notice the diversity of the planet's creatures and be gentle to plants, animals, trees, and people! Fall in love with the vast, intricate wonder of God's creation and give thanks.

Peace Covenant

Today, God, I will walk with an awareness of creation—an awareness of you.

21
Wednesday
August

The Heart of the Piano Player

By John Bonney of Springfield, Oregon, USA

Sing to him a new song; play skillfully on the strings, with loud shouts.

—Psalm 33:3

I remember speaking to a nearby congregation. There was an older couple, both of whom have since passed on, but I must tell you about the wife and her piano.

She didn't just tickle the ivories, she brought them into full submission. She played hymns with more gusto than most. The thing was, she missed many notes. That didn't dampen her enthusiasm or slow her down.

She also included many notes that were not part of the musical arrangement. It was a little difficult to know what she was playing. However, in her rapture at producing music, she knew that if she hit enough notes, the ones she aimed for would be in there. So she did a high-energy rendition that included grabbing handfuls of notes on both the left and the right and, by golly, she always included some of the right ones. We singers just had to find them.

Some people amuse me. But other people, animals, places, and things act as a muse *for* me. I find myself compelled to tell their stories. There are also flowers, dogs, cats, sunrises, sunsets, ocean waves, water running in a narrow channel, and singing. Somehow, God's words make me want to sing like the water.

Singing God's praises reminds me of the singing water. It is sacred and fun at the same time. I hope God hears it that way. I'm sure the heart of the piano player pleased God.

Prayer for Peace

Help us capture the spirit of the piano player, God, and sing your praises with joy. May we also shout joyfully the peace of Jesus Christ from the mountains and the hills.

Spiritual Practice: Honoring God's Call to Others

Reflect on God's call in your life. Quietly reflect on the moments when you have experienced God's presence and invitation. Write in your journal or quietly reflect on images and insights that come. When have you experienced God through the calling and gifts of others. How do your gifts connect with the call of God you notice in your family, friends, congregation, or community?

Peace Covenant

Today, God, I will sing with joy, even if I hit the wrong notes.

22
Thursday
August

At the Table

By Janné Grover of Lee's Summit, Missouri, USA

> *The mission of Jesus Christ is what matters most for the journey ahead.*
>
> —Doctrine and Covenants 164:9f

The table in our kitchen is about 100 years old. It originally belonged to my great-grandma. I have fond memories of gathering around that table when it was in my grandma's kitchen, then my parents', and now mine.

The table never received a formal blessing. It is plain, not ornate. It is not a holy relic. It is special to *me* because of the sentiment it holds and the rich family story it tells. What makes the plain, old table sacred, however, is the life and love lived and shared around it.

When we experience God through ordinary family meals, they become times of worship and ministry. Mealtime is more than just eating. It is the time when our family lifts joys and concerns. We connect with one another and in so doing connect even more closely to the Divine.

I will not try to portray our family meals as perfect, reverent, or even always peaceful. But I have learned to appreciate stressful times as opportunities to extend and receive grace, learn from one another, and grow together in faith.

In my home congregation's evangelist blessing, we were counseled to "…throw the door wide and invite all to come inside."

We can apply this in our homes. Hospitality has a wonderful way of bringing us in touch with the Divine through acts of serving and sharing, breaking bread, and being present in the lives of others. Time shared with others and with God is so important.

Prayer for Peace

Welcoming God, may we "throw the door wide and invite all to come inside." May we make room at the table for the unseen guest. May we share our time and the peace of Christ.

Spiritual Practice: Offering Blessings of Community

Receive and share Blessings of Community. Begin with a prayer of gratitude for the relationships in your life. See and feel connections with family members, spiritual friends, people in your congregation and community, and people and creatures in God's sacred web of life. What blessings flow to you from these circles?

Reflect, pray, or write in your journal about the call to be "Community of Christ." Go deeper each day as you discern what act of blessing you are invited to complete.

Peace Covenant

Today, God, I will invite a lonely person to the table.

23
Friday
August

Which One Fits?

By Chris Lasley of Vancouver, Washington, USA

> *"The Spirit of the Lord is upon me, because he has anointed me to bring good news to the poor. He has sent me to proclaim release to the captives and recovery of sight to the blind, to let the oppressed go free, to proclaim the year of the Lord's favor."*
>
> —Luke 4:18–19

Here's a story about Stan, a hardware store owner who *is* good news to the poor. A few years ago he received a phone call from an older woman named Anna. She wanted to know if he knew any good plumbers.

Stan replied, "I know they will charge you US$80 for walking up your sidewalk and knocking on your door. What seems to be the problem?" Anna replied, "I don't have any hot water."

Stan asked if she had anyone who could look at her water heater, but Anna couldn't think of anyone. So Stan wrote down her address and told her he would be off work at 5:00 p.m. and would drop by.

When Stan arrived at Anna's house she showed him the water heater. He pushed the reset button, and Anna had hot water again. That's all it took.

He asked, "How long have you been without hot water?" She replied, "About four years now. I've been heating the water on the stove." She told him she had family coming from California and wanted to make sure they had hot water.

A few years passed, and Stan thought he would stop by to see how Anna was doing. When he knocked on her door, a young man answered. Two small children and a young mother looked on curiously. Stan recognized the man, who had been in his store before, but didn't know his name. Stan asked if Anna still lived there.

"No," the young man replied. "She went to a nursing home and then passed away." Stan was surprised and then asked, "How's your water heater doing?" "Not so well" the young man replied, "The water is only lukewarm."

"Well," Stan said grinning, "I just happened to bring two different thermostats with me. Let's see which one fits." Stan had a gift to give—to whoever needed it.

Prayer for Peace

Generous God, thank you for guiding us to be the hands of Jesus whenever needed. Thank you for inspiring us to have our gifts and talents ready and tuned for your use. May we always be ready to share Christ's peace.

Spiritual Practice: Shaping into Wholeness

Hold (or imagine holding) a glass cup, bowl, or vase. Explore its shape, texture, and color. Let the container symbolize your life as it is being formed. Write on strips of paper (or in your journal) the things that are not yet just and whole in your life. Place the strips in the glass container and hold it in your hands. Pray a prayer of confession and petition, asking God to continue to breathe in and on you, shaping you into a just and compassionate person.

Peace Covenant

Today, God, I will look for people who need my gifts.

24
Saturday
August

Life Is Better than Before

By Jeanne Marie Kalaba Kiwele of Lubumbashi, Congo

> *...for during a severe ordeal of affliction, their abundant joy and their extreme poverty have overflowed in a wealth of generosity on their part...they voluntarily gave according to their means, and even beyond their means,...and this, not merely as we expected; they gave themselves first to the Lord and, by the will of God, to us...*
>
> —2 Corinthians 8:2–5

In our community, we had a sister named Mambwe. She had a child named Mary, who was 2 years old. Mambwe was living in Village Poland. They stayed in a house made of bricks, with a grass roof.

Mambwe's husband was not working. He had lost his job a long time before. Sister Mambwe's daughter was very sick, but she did not decide to take the child to the hospital until a member of the Kafwa (HealthEd Connect volunteers) encouraged her.

When they arrived, the doctor examined the child and found she had malaria and anemia. She was admitted to the hospital for almost one week. They received a prescription for medicine, but they had no money. The Kafwa took the prescription and used its group money. Mary was discharged from the hospital and recovered completely.

Their life in the past had been bad from illness and poverty. Now, since the child has recovered, life is better.

HealthEd Connect helped because it did not wait for problems but prepared the Kafwa, who always have the heart to help people in time of need.

This family appreciated so much the assistance. They are good friends now. Life now for sister Mambwe and her daughter, Mary, is better. Praise God.

Prayer for Peace

Compassionate God, who weeps for the poor, may we always be aware of those in need around the world. We are thankful for volunteers who help when we are too far away. May we be generous in support of efforts to Abolish Poverty, End Suffering. In this way we share the peace of Christ.

Spiritual Practice: Making Responsible Choices

Offer yourself to God with the prayer of Teresa of Avila: "God, what do you want of me today?" Sit prayerfully with this question as you review the day again. Be aware of images, thoughts, names, or actions that come to you. Ask for a blessing to live this day responsibly and compassionately in the Spirit of Christ.

Peace Covenant

Today, God, I will show my appreciation for all that I have by sharing.

25
Sunday
August

Be Compassionate

By Becky Savage, First Presidency

> *. . . She was bent over and was quite unable to stand up straight. When Jesus saw her, he called her over and said, "Woman, you are set free from your ailment." When he laid his hands on her, immediately she stood up straight and began praising God.*
>
> —Luke 13:11–13

The judge ordered me to train the parents of a kidney patient in the hospital where I was working. The court ruling took the baby into protective care shortly after delivery. The baby had multiple physical anomalies, and the medical professionals believed the parents could not meet the baby's needs.

The first time I met the parents the father swaggered in with the mother lagging behind. She was bent nearly double with her eyes looking at the floor. She did not rise, make eye contact, or speak.

The father boasted he could care for the child and would get the child's Social Security money for his efforts. But he did not follow directions and acted bored. His breath smelled of alcohol, and he slurred his words. After two sessions he quit coming.

The mother continued to come, and gradually her posture and behavior changed. She learned to take a blood pressure and temperature, measure medications, apply a special body cast and splints, and to count sodium and protein in foods. By the end of the lessons, she had learned to care for her child.

In addition, her body was restored to a straight posture, and this once-mute woman had found her voice. She bravely left the father and found a safe place for her and her child.

Jesus compassionately called the woman bent double forward, touched her, and released her from physical deformity. God asks us also to see those burdened by life circumstances. We are to share the message of Christ's peace and healing touch. Most importantly, our open eyes, healing hands, soothing words, and active feet can make a difference in people's lives.

Those bent double under burdens and oppression can stand upright when healed by hands serving with healing touch.

Prayer for Peace

God of compassion, may we find those who suffer and share the message of Christ's healing. May we find those who are voiceless and bring justice as we share Christ's love.

Spiritual Practice: Tears of Compassion

Offer a silent prayer for the gift of God's compassion. Cup your hands and ask God to make you aware of the suffering that causes the Earth and its inhabitants to groan and weep. Be open to faces, places, sounds, voices, and feelings of connection with those who suffer.

Imagine catching and holding the tears of those you see. Listen for prayer images or words God may give you. Discern any active responses of ministry or healing you are invited to complete for those who weep.

Peace Covenant

Today, God, I will listen for the nearly voiceless and respond compassionately.

26
Monday
August

In Touch

By Barrie Fox of Kirkby-in-Ashfield, Nottinghamshire, England

Let us then pursue what makes for peace and for mutual upbuilding.
—Romans 14:19

Our congregation holds a monthly meeting called "In Touch." The agendas vary, but the purpose stays the same: to keep people in touch with one another and to remember and pray for those who have fallen out of touch with the congregation. We seek to keep Jesus Christ at the center of our personal lives and the life of the congregation.

These evenings bring good experiences and bless us with companionship and common support. We also seek to stress the importance of being a caring community that practices faith in God.

When we think about it, we can become even more aware that life consists of a multitude of everyday acts of faith. When we plant bulbs in a garden, we plant with faith they will grow. When we set out on a journey, we expect to arrive. When we post a letter, we have faith it will arrive safely. Faith is a staple ingredient of our lives.

People say it is our faith, and how we use it, that settles whether our lives are "scared" or "sacred." We use the same letters to spell both words, but they have different meanings. Many people do become scared, for good reason, but it is the sacred influence of God and our faith community that restores our faith.

We are all made from the same alphabet, just arranged differently by the influence of our faith. I heard someone once say saints are just sinners who do not give in to their fears.

Prayer for Peace

Alpha and Omega, help us transform our everyday faith into a sacred trust. Help strengthen our resolve to pursue the peace of Christ by sharing it.

Spiritual Practice: Develop Disciples to Serve

Read and reflect on Psalm 42:1–2. As disciples of Jesus Christ, God calls us to respond to people and their needs. The call to journey inward can restore us in times of physical or spiritual depletion. Imagine you can feel a vessel at the center of your being (a clay jar, a crystal vase, a metal bucket, or other container).

Imagine drawing something from the vessel to share with another person, but as you reach inside you find only a tiny pool of stagnant liquid. You are thirsty and dry; empty. Listen prayerfully again to the psalm, "As a deer longs for flowing streams, so my soul longs for you, O God. My soul thirsts for God, for the living God." As you feel restored, thank God for the opportunity to be a responding, serving disciple while you move into the outward journey. Remember this exercise as you drink water throughout the day.

Peace Covenant

Today, God, I will rearrange my life so Christ's mission matters most.

27
Tuesday
August

Encouragement for the Journey

By Gary McDonald of Blue Springs, Missouri, USA

Open your hearts and feel the yearnings of your brothers and sisters who are lonely, despised, fearful, neglected, unloved. Reach out in understanding, clasp your hands, and invite all to share in the blessings of community created in the name of the One who suffered on behalf of all.

—Doctrine and Covenants 161:3a–c

My wife, Clare, and I made many car trips from Ohio to the Kansas City, Missouri, area to see our family. A trip would take about 12 hours one way. We made these jaunts to remain connected.

We suffered one hot summer day, driving through the farmlands of Indiana. We pulled off the road to take advantage of a rest area. I was tired and needed a break. Walking to the restroom, we passed an older man who had raised the hood of his car and was peering inside. The urge to stop and help tugged at me, but I overrode it and went my way. "Besides" I thought. "There are plenty of people here who can help."

On my return, I passed the old man again and plainly could see nobody was paying any attention to him. Reluctantly, I engaged him in conversation. I asked if he was having engine trouble; I could help if it was something minor.

He said, "No. It's just so hot I'm worried about my car." He worried about the risk of being stranded in the heat. I inspected hoses and so forth but saw nothing wrong. I told him everything looked fine. He looked relieved continued his journey.

Later I shared this story with a friend because the meaning puzzled me. My friend suggested that sometimes in life people just need reassurance and encouragement to continue their journey.

We need to feel we are not alone.

Prayer for Peace

God who leads us on our journeys, as we go let us be aware of companion travelers and their needs. Let us offer help when we can and share Christ's love and peace with those who are alone.

Spiritual Practice: Invite People to Christ

Read and reflect on Doctrine and Covenants 162:3b and 163:2b. Pray to be aware of people who might be receptive, and therefore blessed, by your sharing of the message of the Living Christ. Imagine being in relationship with them and inviting them to Christ. In preparation, discover your personal testimony of Christ. "Be persistent in your witness and diligent in your mission to the world." Repeat this mantra throughout the day: "Christ's mission, our mission, my mission."

Peace Covenant

Today, God, I will map out a plan to Invite People to Christ.

28
Wednesday
August

Tree Talk

By Carol Norris Vincent of Independence, Missouri, USA

For you shall go out in joy, and be led back in peace; the mountains and the hills before you shall burst into song, and all the trees of the field shall clap their hands.

—Isaiah 55:12

I have tried various meditative and spiritual practices, trying to experience what I sense others are experiencing. However, I realize each of us is unique, and our experiences will be unique to us.

My mother, for whom nature was a great joy, nurtured a love of nature in me. I often express my love of nature in how I rejoice over trees and birds. Now that I am retired and disabled, I find myself with time to sit on my patio and enjoy nature.

A beautiful, old elm tree, which survived the Dutch elm disease so prevalent many years ago, stands at the edge of the pond behind my home. One beautiful summer morning I was sitting outside "talking" to my tree. I began to sense a response to me, my comments about the tree's beauty, and the joy I received.

Just then an eastern bluebird landed a few feet away. I felt all the power of God's gift to me in that moment. I rejoiced because of the pure, spiritual joy I was feeling. Since then, bluebirds have visited my backyard, and the elm tree still "talks" to me. I praise God for the joy I receive. Whether it's called *meditation* or not, I see it as a gift from God.

As I reflect on that experience, I can't help but think of the beautiful old hymn, "This Is My Father's World." It reminds us that this is God's world, where all nature sings and we can hear the music of the spheres. The second verse is what I experienced that day, "…the birds their carols raise, the morning light, the ocean's might Declare their Maker's praise. This is God's wondrous world, God shines in all that's fair; in rustling grass or mountain pass; God's voice speaks everywhere."

God does indeed speak to me!

Prayer for Peace

Creator God, we hear you passing close to us and we are thankful for your presence. We praise you for the trees and mountains, bursting with joy. We hear the carols of the birds and have no doubt this is your creation. We rest in peace and know it is the peace of Christ.

Spiritual Practice: Trees

Watch the trees outside your window for a few moments. Close your eyes and meditate on Alma's words about seeds and trees. If you were to plant and grow the Word of God in your heart, what kind of tree might symbolically represent this process? Envision a *seed* as it grows into a tree of life and blessing. Ask God to show you how to begin (see Alma 16:152–173).

Peace Covenant

Today, God, I will go out in joy and be led back in peace.

29
Thursday
August

Good-bye Letters

By Lu Mountenay of Independence, Missouri, USA

Do not be discouraged. You have not been promised an easy path, but you have been assured that the Spirit that calls you will also accompany you.

—Doctrine and Covenants 162:3a

My dear hummingbirds,

At the end of summer I ask, "Is this my last day with you? Will you come again tomorrow?" My fear of you leaving corrupts our time together.

Each morning I sit on the patio, expecting, hoping, and yet aware of the possibility you won't come. But I didn't say good-bye! And then again, saying good-bye would have been too final, would have meant giving you up.

I *must* say good-bye and wish you safe journey. I'll be at peace with it…and what a surprise if you *do* show up for another visit to the feeder. Blessings—I'll be waiting for you in the spring.

* * * * *

I write this as I sit in my son's hospital room during the last week of his life. We had so much faith that he would survive, but now we finally believe the doctor when he says Zac will be gone any day.

So I listen to him breathe. We keep talking to him, even though we aren't sure he can hear us. If there is the slightest possibility he can, I want him to know we are here and how much we love him.

So with every ragged breath he takes, I ask God, "Is this my last day with him? Will he still be here tomorrow?"

My dear, dear son,

My fear of you leaving corrupts my time with you, and so I didn't say good-bye while you were still conscious. I didn't want to see the fear in your eyes when you saw what we knew. It would be too final. However, now I must say good-bye and wish you safe journey. I have no choice. I'll try to be at peace with it, even though I know you won't return in the spring. My darling son, wait for me in my winter. Go with God.

Prayer for Peace

Comforter God, be with us in our dark night of the soul. Lift us to your healing light. Send companions for our journey. Thank you for our community of peace.

Spiritual Practice: Tears of Compassion

Offer a silent prayer for the gift of God's compassion. Cup your hands and ask God to make you aware of the suffering that causes the Earth and its people to groan and weep. Be open to faces or places, sounds or voices; feelings of connection with those who suffer. Imagine catching the tears of those you see and holding them in your hands. Listen for prayer images or words God may give you. Discern any active responses of ministry or healing you are invited to complete for those who weep.

Peace Covenant

Today, God, I will seek someone who needs comforting.

30
Friday
August

From the Diversity Team: The Differences that Bless

By Karolyn Chapman Sharp of Kenmore, Washington, USA

...pursue righteousness, faith, love, and peace, along with those who call on the Lord from a pure heart.

—2 Timothy 2:22

I met Mike in a seventh-grade aerospace class. He is politically independent and a faithful member of a conservative faith community. I am politically liberal and a member of Community of Christ. We connected right away.

Over the years, we have seen each other's personal challenges and triumphs. Mike joined the Air Force and later did a tour in the Middle East. I prayed and prayed. No matter what was going on, when he called, I answered. The world would just have to wait.

We have struggled with our faith, found our respective spouses, married, and become parents. Mike and I each grew our own faith. As our political views developed, they drifted further apart. So now, our friendship is between a conservative and a liberal, each in faith communities that are distinct. Or simply, it's between Mike and Karolyn.

When I learned I was pregnant, I was thrilled...and terrified. My emotions hadn't yet settled when we learned something was wrong with the pregnancy. I was losing the baby, and there was nothing we could do. It devastated me.

My world blew apart. My pain trapped me under its rubble. Grief is a delicate process. Often there is an effort to make sense of our loss—to create an environment that will make it easier to bear. After my miscarriage, whenever anyone tried to comfort me, their words landed like blows. It was Mike who showed me a path out of the rubble. His words brought comfort when no one else's could.

In the depths of pain, it was not "someone like me" who had the power to reach me. Rather, it was someone I loved, despite and because of our differences, who offered me one of the most intense blessings of my life. He offered hope amid despair. Our friendship is a testimony to Unity in Diversity. Had we let our politics or our theologies divide us, I would have lost a treasured friend. And, as it turns out, one of the greatest sources of blessing.

Prayer for Peace

We call on you, God, in different ways. Yet Christ is our connection, and it is his peace we share.

Spiritual Practice: Welcoming Unity in Diversity

Meditate on Unity in Diversity. Create a large circle with your arms. See and feel the diverse people God invites inside the sanctuary of Christ's peace represented by this circle.

Who is easiest to welcome? Whom do you struggle to include? Confess the dividing walls between you and people too different or "dangerous" to invite into your spiritual home. Ask God to forgive and heal barriers that keep us from loving one another.

Peace Covenant

Today, God, I will open myself to a blessing from my brothers and sisters who call on the Lord in different ways.

31
Saturday
August

Acute Need in Horn of Africa

By Alex Kahtava of Raymore, Missouri, USA

> *How does God's love abide in anyone who has the world's goods and sees a brother or sister in need and yet refuses help?*
>
> —1 John 3:17

A Community of Christ World Hunger grant of US$20,000 provided relief to many suffering from drought in the Horn of Africa. More than 11 million people are in acute need of food assistance. The United Nations has called it the world's worst humanitarian disaster.

A declaration of famine in parts of southern Somalia has been issued. The crisis extends across parts of Djibouti, Ethiopia, Kenya, and Uganda.

World Church leaders are working with church leaders in Kenya, where Community of Christ has a strong presence.

As we strive to love one another, there is concern the famine will spread. Many people rely on livestock, which are dying in massive numbers because of lack of feed and water. The world's largest refugee site, Dadaab, is overcrowded with more than 465,000 displaced people in camps originally designed for 90,000.

Because of your contributions to the Abolish Poverty, End Suffering Mission Initiative, which includes World Hunger, Community of Christ can respond as an international church to the famine in East Africa.

Thank you for responding generously to this acute need.

Prayer for Peace

God who weeps for the hungry, may we who weep with you turn our tears into tangible love. May we use our finances as funds of compassion. May we share food for the body and Christ's peace for the soul.

Spiritual Practice: Abolish Poverty, End Suffering

Read and reflect on John 21:15–17 as a meditation. Let your mind be drawn to places where people have no homes. Think of refugees whose homes were destroyed by war or natural disaster. Be aware of the hungry and homeless, who wander the streets or live in shelters. Let the images fill your mind. Offer a prayer for those who suffer. Imagine Christ tending those sheep. Think of ways you might end their suffering as part of your mission. Throughout the day, carry in your mind the voice of Christ saying: "Feed my lambs…tend my sheep…feed my sheep."

Peace Covenant

Today, God, I will not reach for more bread than I need. May I rather reach out to those in need of the bread of life.

1
Sunday
September

All Are Welcome

By Jim Poirier, Presiding Bishopric

"When you are invited by someone to a wedding banquet, do not sit down at the place of honor…go and sit down at the lowest place…For all who exalt themselves will be humbled, and those who humble themselves will be exalted." He said also to the one who had invited him, "When you give a luncheon or a dinner, do not invite your friends or your brothers or your relatives or rich neighbors, in case they may invite you in return, and you would be repaid. But when you give a banquet, invite the poor, the crippled, the lame, and the blind. And you will be blessed, because they cannot repay you, for you will be repaid at the resurrection of the righteous."

—Luke 14:8, 10–14

Much of who I am and what I do I learned at my grandmother's table. She invited and welcomed everyone to her table. There was always more than enough food.

We greeted each first with a smile that said, "Welcome to our table…we are so happy you joined us." It was there that I learned the value of gathering at the table. There were lively discussions, but most of all there were joy and laughter. No matter what problems you carried to that table, they were lessened before you left.

And so when you come to my house today, we will welcome you at a large kitchen table where we will feed you, laugh with you, and help you feel free to smile. You will learn that others are welcome at our table, too.

In my office is a print of a painting titled "The Trinity." Andrei Rublev painted it in the 15th century. It is a story of three wanderers who visited Abraham and found hospitality. Abraham welcomed and gave them the best of what he had. There are three personages sitting around a table. The empty place at the front of the table is where the artist invites the viewer to sit.

This painting reminds me I am to welcome everyone to the table because my grandmother wouldn't have it any other way. Neither would Jesus.

Let us remember not only to invite, but to bring out our very best and add to the blessings of community for family, friend, and stranger.

Prayer for Peace

Host of the universe, may we share your hospitality with all we meet. May we always invite people to the table and to Christ.

Spiritual Practice: Welcoming Unity in Diversity

Meditate on Unity in Diversity. Create a large circle with your arms. See and feel the diverse people God invites inside the sanctuary of Christ's peace represented by this circle.

Who is easiest to welcome? Whom do you struggle to include? Confess the dividing walls between you and people too different or "dangerous" to invite into your spiritual home. Ask God to forgive and heal barriers that keep you and others from being one in Christ's peace.

Peace Covenant

Today, God, my door, my table, and my heart will be open to all.

2
Monday
September

Seek First Christ's Mission

By Donna Boyd of Independence, Missouri, USA

> *...and indeed your heavenly Father knows that you need all these things. But strive first for the kingdom of God and his righteousness, and all these things will be given to you as well... "Ask, and it will be given you; search, and you will find; knock, and the door will be opened for you. For everyone who asks receives, and everyone who searches finds, and for everyone who knocks, the door will be opened."*
>
> —Matthew 6:32–33, 7:7–8

We were seeking the home of friends. They gave us directions, and we started out confidently. We looked for landmarks along the way to assure us we had taken the right road. As we looked for the signs they told us to expect, we knew we were on the right road to the home of our friends.

When we choose baptism, we enter the mission of Christ. The Holy Spirit's presence in our lives reassures us that we are on the path of discipleship, the right road. We continue in faith as we develop in relationship with God.

Sometimes we become confused as the way seems long. We may seek direction from those who do not understand Christ's mission and get conflicting advice. We may fail to ask for God's guidance and become discouraged, ready to turn back. We may meet someone who tries to persuade us to change our course, to seek fame or pleasure instead of seeking Christ.

Through all the trials of the journey, we can remember to seek divine guidance. God has given us the Holy Spirit so we need not wander in darkness or confusion.

We remember that we ought to seek first the kingdom of God. When faith wavers, we need to open ourselves to the reassuring presence of God's Spirit.

Prayer for Peace

We are searching, God. We are knocking and asking. We have faith the doors will open. We have faith that you will guide us in the ways to share the peace of Christ.

Spiritual Practice: Praying for Leadership of the Church

An important spiritual practice for disciples is praying for members of the body of Christ, particularly those who carry leadership responsibilities. Ask God to guide your awareness of people who lead the community of faith in congregations, mission centers, and the World Church. Pray for God's outpouring of grace on each servant leader who comes to mind.

Peace Covenant

Today, God, I will not hesitate to call on you for direction in Christ's mission.

3
Tuesday
September

A Scripture Reflection from the Diversity Team

By Cathi Cackler-Veazey of Independence, Missouri, USA

> *...for in Christ Jesus you are all children of God through faith... There is no longer Jew or Greek, there is no longer slave or free, there is no longer male and female; for all of you are one in Christ Jesus.*
>
> —Galatians 3:26–28

There has been a growing awareness in the church that as a people we are one in Christ. Though different in the ways we look, worship, and experience culture, Community of Christ members value the Enduring Principle of Unity in Diversity. As disciples of the Christ who embraced all people, we have a challenge to follow Christ's example. Sometimes we fail; sometimes we succeed.

Mark A. Scherer, Community of Christ church historian, wrote a paper several years ago tracing the church's treatment of African Americans in earlier days. Mark told of faithful members who were treated unfairly in many ways, a treatment reflecting American culture at the time. Some Caucasian members showed prejudice based on skin color. Even church leaders made choices that created "second-class" membership for African Americans.

The church is blessed today because many of those members stuck with the church, forgiving those who ignored the counsel in Galatians.

Gradually, the church has become more unified in its diversity. Over the last few years, diversity teams, task forces, subcommittees, and councils have worked to help the church become more inclusive. The church is leaping forward in efforts to embrace diversity. At other times progress toward inclusion and acceptance has seemed slow.

Community of Christ is making progress. Church leaders regularly host an International Leaders Council that gives voice to diverse perspectives.

Recently, Stephen M. Veazey, president of the church, and I had the opportunity to be with a group of church members who embraced inclusiveness and acceptance.

Congregations, whose members were from mostly white communities and mostly African American communities, came together. It was a blessing to see the honest love and acceptance between all present. We can follow the example of the Christ and be one in Christ Jesus.

Prayer for Peace

Universal God, Creator of all, may we recognize the worth of every person. May we value the rich diversity of the community as we become one in Christ's peace.

Spiritual Practice: Welcoming Unity in Diversity

Meditate on Unity in Diversity. Create a large circle with your arms. See and feel the diverse people God invites inside the sanctuary of Christ's peace. Who is easiest to welcome? Whom do you struggle to include? Confess the dividing walls between you and "different" people. Ask God to forgive and heal barriers to loving one another.

Peace Covenant

Today, God, I will open my arms and my heart to embrace the diversity of your creation.

4
Wednesday
September

"Check the Babies!"

By Lu Mountenay of Independence, Missouri, USA

You hold precious lives in your hands. Be gentle and gracious with one another. A community is no stronger than the weakest within it. Even as the One you follow reached out to those who were rejected and marginalized, so must the community that bears his name.

—Doctrine and Covenants 162:6c

My married sister returned to our childhood family home to live for a short while. She had two toddlers, Mark and Guy. Because she and her husband worked outside the home, we four other sisters became live-in, babysitter aunties.

Most of the time no one auntie was assigned watch-care duties; we all were responsible for these two precious lives in our big house.

When we heard crying, someone would yell, "Check the babies!" And, someone would respond, "They're OK," or "Mark's OK, how about Guy?" When we heard Guy was good, too, we would all relax.

In a while it would get suspiciously quiet, and someone again would yell, "Check the babies!" And one or two aunties would put down their homework and solve the mystery of the quietness. So "check the babies" became our family community signal.

One day during nap time, we heard a faint, but frantic voice. "Check the babies! Check the babies!" We ran upstairs and found Guy precariously draped between his crib and Mark's crib, which stood about three feet away.

Guy's little fingers were clinging mightily to the rails of Mark's crib, and his toes were barely perched on his own rail. Panic was in his voice as he repeatedly called, "Check the babies!"

We didn't even know Guy could talk, much less understand what we had been saying! Yet, this was a phrase he trusted to bring help. We snatched him up and held his shaking body while he sobbed. In his mind, he had risked life and limb to be with his brother.

When we finally laid him back in his crib, he was smiling. I could imagine him thinking, "I knew they would come."

What is our signal to God that we need help? Do we recognize the signals of others in need of our serving? How fast do we respond?

Prayer for Peace

Tender Shepherd, we know you are with us, even before we call. We trust in you to guide us to sanctuary. As you care for us, may we attend to others who cry for help. May we share with them the assurance and peace of Jesus Christ.

Spiritual Practice: Listening to Children

Sit in your quiet place and center your heart and mind on God's presence. Spend several minutes asking God to bring into your awareness the names and images of children in your life. You may see their faces or hear their voices as you receive these impressions. Listen deeply to the unique gifts and needs of the children who come to mind. Offer a prayer of blessing for each child and the needs you perceive. If you feel led, you also may want to write a note or card and give a message of affirmation and love to each child.

Peace Covenant

Today, God, I will be mindful of the precious spirits in my care.

5
Thursday
September

Yearning for Justice

By Barbara Howard of Independence, Missouri, USA

Who is wise and understanding among you? Show by your good life that your works are done with gentleness born of wisdom…But the wisdom from above is first pure, then peaceable, gentle, willing to yield, full of mercy and good fruits, without a trace of partiality or hypocrisy. And a harvest of righteousness is sown in peace for those who make peace.

—James 3:13, 17–18

An old rabbi once asked his pupils how they could tell when the night had ended and the day had begun. "Could it be," asked one, "when you can see an animal in the distance and tell whether it's a sheep or a dog?" "No," answered the rabbi. "It is when you can look on the face of any man or woman and see that it is your sister or brother. Because if you cannot see this, it is still night."

—A rabbinic story.

In the 1960s, society in the USA made efforts to bring about greater justice for minorities and women. I was a substitute junior-high teacher. A girl in one class was the object of ridicule and prejudice. She was overweight and often came to school unkempt and dirty. I wanted to help her but didn't know where to begin. Because I did not see the class regularly, dealing with the problem seemed impossible.

One day, however, I had a conversation with one of the most popular boys in the school. He brought up the girl's situation. "I wish I knew how to keep the kids from making fun of her," he said. "It's so unfair."

His yearning for justice touched me. He said, "If I got a bunch of the students to make friends with her, maybe that would make a difference."

Several weeks passed before I was back at the school. The students astonished me. Our once-unhappy girl came into the classroom with her hair clean and shiny, neatly dressed, and smiling. She had a circle of friends who refused to bow to their peers.

In befriending her, they benefited, as did the young woman.

The student who had begun the transformation had taken the initiative to pursue peace.

Prayer for Peace

God of wisdom, as we learn from our young, may we carry forward our pursuit of Christ's peace and share it with the world.

Spiritual Practice: Honoring the Worth of All Persons

Imagine God watching you grow in your mother's womb. What thoughts and feelings do you have about being "fearfully and wonderfully made" (Psalm 139:14)?

Be aware of the sacred worth of each person. Weep with God over the soul-wounding forces and events that rob people of dignity and worth. Pray for compassion.

Peace Covenant

Today, God, I will be aware of someone who needs Christ's transforming peace, and take the initiative to make it happen.

6
Friday
September

Temple Encounter

By Karen Moreland of Independence, Missouri, USA

> *Become a people of the Temple...who encounter broken spirits and find pathways for healing...Open your hearts and feel the yearnings of your brothers and sisters who are lonely, despised, fearful, neglected, unloved...invite all to share in the blessings...*
>
> —Doctrine and Covenants 161:2a, 3a

Working as a receptionist at the Temple in Independence, Missouri, has been a joyful experience. People representing various life experiences come to the Temple. I never know the burdens that some carry in their hearts when they walk in and ask to see the Sanctuary.

Three young adults walked down the grand staircase and up to the reception counter. "What kind of crazy-looking building is this?" one asked. I explained it was the Community of Christ Temple, dedicated to the pursuit of peace. It is a sanctuary. When one asked, "Can we climb to the top?" I explained they could walk up the Worshiper's Path to the Sanctuary—a sacred space.

Two of the young adults kept apologizing for their friend, who kept asking questions, "You will let us see inside the spiral-shaped building?" "Yes," I replied, as I handed them the brochure with the map. Surprised, he said, "Even me?" "Yes, even you. All are welcome to come and experience the presence of God."

All three walked up the Worshiper's Path.

The Daily Prayer for Peace had just ended, and Cathy from Visitor Services met them in the Sanctuary. The building impressed all three, but so did the hospitality they received. They respected the sacred space and wanted to know more about Community of Christ. They said they had never experienced such loving peace and welcome.

They asked if they could come back in a couple of days. On their next visit they spent much time and asked many questions. They accepted information about Community of Christ. They accepted the invitation.

Prayer for Peace

God of hospitality, help us welcome strangers and invite them to return. Help us open our hearts and love them unconditionally. May we share Christ's peace with strangers and friends.

Spiritual Practice: Invite People to Christ

Read and reflect on Doctrine and Covenants 162:3b and 163:2b. Pray to be aware of people who might be receptive, and therefore blessed, by your sharing of the message of the Living Christ. Imagine being in relationship with them and inviting them to Christ. In preparation, discover your personal testimony of Christ. "Be persistent in your witness and diligent in your mission to the world." Repeat this mantra throughout the day: "Christ's mission, our mission, my mission."

Peace Covenant

Today, God, I will open my mind, my heart, answer questions, and invite.

7
Saturday
September

HealthEd Connect at Peacemakers Summit

By Sherri Kirkpatrick of Lee's Summit, Missouri, USA

> *You are called to create pathways in the world for peace in Christ to be relationally and culturally incarnate. The hope of Zion is realized when the vision of Christ is embodied in communities of generosity, justice, and peacefulness.*
>
> —Doctrine and Covenants 163:3a

My husband, Jac, and I had the privilege of attending the Peacemakers Summit at the Temple in Independence, Missouri, in September 2011. The gathering's purpose was to bring together leaders of the church and church-affiliated groups to discuss justice and peacemaking. Invigorating energy and stimulating ideas permeated the event.

One theme that recurred throughout the day was the need to involve young adults in internships to develop academic and practical skills of how to create justice and peace.

We felt the organization we lead, HealthEd Connect, was on the cutting edge of this effort. We arranged two internships for young adults to go to Zambia. One as a teacher-mentor to help the schools move forward in continual progress toward higher academic standards; the other as a guide for the emotional-support groups organized to help orphans work through their grief.

The idea is to match skills of young adults with needs in the field.

Your contributions to world mission tithes help make this possible. This effort to help Abolish Poverty, End Suffering excites us. Additionally, this project helps Develop Disciples to Serve.

That's a "win-win" approach!

Prayer for Peace

Generous God, inspire us with ways we can share Christ's peace. Infuse our programs with new ideas and give us strength to succeed.

Spiritual Practice: Praying with a Partner

Pray with a partner if possible, or imagine Christ sitting with you. The heart is a center of compassion and spiritual connection. Stand or sit across from your partner with hands open and palms up. Invite your partner to place hands, palms down, on your hands. Close your eyes and be aware of the connection between your heart and your partner's heart. What needs, feelings, or longings do you sense? Invite God's peace to flow into you and move from your heart to the heart of your partner. Feel or see God's healing light and love flowing between your hearts. After a period of silent prayer, thank God and your partner. Say amen. (You also may pray this prayer by envisioning a particular person across from you.)

Peace Covenant

Today, God, I will join my peacemaking skills with a partner to make a greater impact.

8
Sunday
September

Formed By God

By Becky Savage, First Presidency

> *The vessel he was making of clay was spoiled in the potter's hand, and he reworked it into another vessel, as seemed good to him. Then the word of the Lord came to me: Can I not do with you, O house of Israel, just as this potter has done? says the Lord. Just like the clay in the potter's hand, so are you in my hand, O house of Israel.*
>
> —Jeremiah 18:4–6

It is captivating to watch an artist take a lump of clay and form it into a beautiful vessel. How do the steps of throwing a clay pot reflect God forming us?

First, the artist wedges or kneads the clay to remove air pockets. Air bubbles may cause the vessel to blow up in the kiln. "Unity in Diversity" is one of our Enduring Principles. When we talk together we can remove misunderstandings that cause separation.

Next the artist centers the clay on the wheel. The artist wraps wet hands around the clay. This step requires a firm hold, focus, and stillness. This quiet step is essential or the clay loses its foundation and shape. *Be still and know that I am God.* We are at our best when we spend quiet, focused time with God.

This time may include studying scriptures, meditation, prayer, or other spiritual disciplines. When we skip this spiritual connection, our lives are more easily misshaped.

Water is essential for molding clay. The artist uses wet hands to smooth, shape, and remold the clay. The waters of baptism cleanse us. We remember and reclaim our baptismal covenant during the sacrament of the Lord's Supper.

To form the vessel the artist pulls the clay upward into a cylinder. The cylinder has form and space. The artist then forms the cylinder into a new shape. The walls offer form and stability. Then the potter opens the form into a useful, shapely vessel.

God forms each of us to be unique. We choose how our lives reflect God's grace and generosity.

How is God forming your life? Is there space for God's Spirit? Will you receive and respond faithfully?

Prayer for Peace

Molder and Shaper of the universe, we are yours to do with as you will. May we respond to your creative touch with grace. May we be vessels accepting of your Spirit and willing to carry and share the peace of Christ.

Spiritual Practice: Vessel for Living Water

Visualize or feel a vessel at the center of your being (a clay jar, a crystal vase, a metal bucket, or other container). Imagine drawing something from the bucket to share with someone, but as you reach inside you find only a tiny pool of stagnant liquid. You are thirsty, dry, empty. Then something clear and cool begins to pour over you. It fills the vessel to the brim. The living water of Christ pours on and in you, blessing your body and soul. Commit yourself to share living water with others.

Peace Covenant

Today, God, I will not shrink from Christ's mission, or swell with pride. I will hold the shape you envision for me.

9
Monday
September

♫ Hymn of the Month: "Hoy Queremos"

By V.L. Ben Peterson of Bella Vista, Arkansas, USA

> *"Behold, I say to you, and I would that you should remember, that God is merciful...therefore he desires, in the first place, that you should believe, even on his word. ...And this is not all; little children have words given to them many times which confound the wise and the learned."*
>
> —Alma 16:144, 146

I lost many papers in the great tornado in Joplin, Missouri, in 2011. I have only my memory to access the words to "How Gentle God's Commands!" But I can recall that I wanted that same warm, thoughtful, and tender sense of appreciation shown to God in that hymn for "Hoy Queremos."

Therefore, I hope people sense this in my text about the blessing of little children. I hope they feel the divine attribute of the Spirit of God in my words: "Hoy queremos presentarte nuestros niños, oh Señor..." I hope those who sing become fully aware of God's ability to bless children. I wanted this trust in God to be implicit in my words. Here are the first and last stanzas in English and Spanish:

Lord, we bring to you our children for a blessing here today;
and we ask for your protection o'er their lives, O Lord, we pray.
May you watch them and protect them with your great abiding love,
and each child receive your blessing. Send your Spirit as a dove!

> Into loving arms, O Jesus, gather all and call their names!
> Lay on hands to show your caring; guide their lives toward worthy aims.
> As on old Judea's hillside, so we, too, in this same way
> here do dedicate these children to the Master's heavenly reign.

Hoy queremos presentarte nuestros niños, oh Señor;
te pedimos que les seas un amigo protector,
que les cuides y les guardes con tu espiíritu de amor
y que cada niño tenga tu perfecta bendición

> En sus brazos, Jesucristo a los niños los tomó;
> demostrándo les cariño, con sus manos los tocó.
> Hoy también, igual que Cristo, deseamos dedicar
> estos niños que traemos, a tu reino celestial.

Prayer for Peace

For young miracles like these, God, we thank you on our knees. We know the children in our care portray the kingdom yet to be. May we reflect Christ's peace as we share with children everywhere.

Spiritual Practice

Contemplate this hymn as a poem (or sing to CROATIRAS DEL RENO tune).

10
Tuesday
September

Inner Buoyancy

By Barrie Fox of Kirkby-in-Ashfield, Nottinghamshire, England

The salvation of the righteous is from the Lord; he is their refuge in the time of trouble.

—Psalm 37:39

Take an empty bottle and put a cork in it so it's airtight. Fill a bucket with water. Put the empty bottle in the water and hold it down. Then let it go. Of course you know what happens. The bottle bobs back to the surface.

However long and hard you press down on the bottle, the moment you release it, up it comes.

We might say our lives sometimes are like this. At times, worries and trials press us down and hold us there. At times this pressure is overwhelming. But no matter how strong the pressure, no matter how horrific the circumstance, we know that Jesus is there with us.

Jesus Christ transforms us with his message of forgiveness and love, light and truth. When we feel times of trouble are drowning us, we can let God be our refuge.

Prayer for Peace

Lord, our refuge and salvation, help us build faith into the foundation of our lives. May we remember to draw on the light of Christ when we only see darkness. May we share the love and peace of Christ with those who feel oppressed.

Spiritual Practice: Light

Close your eyes, and become centered with your breath. Reflect on the statement: "The light of God is in all things," as you breathe gently in and out. The light has a bright, soft beauty and radiates loving peace. The light of God reaches you and permeates you with a deep sense of peace. Rest in the light as it surrounds and fills you. Thank God that you live in God's light, and it lives in you.

Peace Covenant

Today, God, I will light a candle and take refuge in your presence.

11
Wednesday
September

Open Your Eyes

By Peggy Michael of Cantonment, Florida, USA

> *O Lord, our Sovereign, how majestic is your name in all the earth! You have set your glory above the heavens. ... When I look at your heavens, the work of your fingers, the moon and the stars that you have established; what are human beings that you are mindful of them, mortals that you care for them? ... the birds of the air, and the fish of the sea, whatever passes along the paths of the seas. O Lord, our Sovereign, how majestic is your name in all the earth!*
>
> —Psalm 8:1, 3–4, 8–9

Darkness cloaks the land as mounds of rain clouds blot out the light. Thunder resounds across the hills, and people scurry for shelter from the deluge that follows. After a time, a timid ray of sunlight pierces the tattered, worn-out clouds. And then another ray of sunlight breaks through, followed by another.

The cowardly storm retreats, and all creatures come out of hiding to celebrate the cleansing of the earth.

Close your eyes and imagine there are no trees; there are no lakes where fish swim or lumpy tadpoles fatten in the shallows. What if dragonflies did not hover atop the grass to wait for prey? How sad it would be if there was no doe to lead her unsteady fawn into a sunlit patch in the thicket.

Open your eyes now. Awaken your senses. Listen to the wind whisper from pine to pine, and to the woodpecker hammering at the tree. Stoop to see the tiny orchids peeking through the grass.

Now, imagine the pleasure our Creator sees when we experience the various and particular beauty around us. How majestic is God's name in all the Earth!

Prayer for Peace

God of glory, God of wonder, every fiber of my being yearns to know you—to do your bidding, to dwell in your Holy Presence. Forgive me for times when my eyes were closed. Forgive me for time I wasted on shallow concerns and for trying to shape my pitiful life with my own hands. Still, you call me and urge me onward. O God of the ages, please reflect your glory in this fragment of flesh and use me to share Christ's peace.

Spiritual Practice: Psalm Writing

The psalms are prayers of honesty and trust. The psalmist trusts God's presence in times of fear and failure, joy and plenty, growth and change. Write a short psalm-prayer expressing to God the truth about your physical, emotional, and spiritual state. What are your deepest feelings, longings, and needs? What prayer of praise, intercession, or petition flows from you as you consider your life and the life of God's world?

Peace Covenant

Today, I will hear God's voice as whispered to the grasses beneath my scurrying feet. I will slow down and respond.

12
Thursday
September

Continuing Education

By Evelyn Spence of Council Bluffs, Iowa, USA

Keep on doing the things that you have learned and received and heard and seen in me, and the God of peace will be with you.

—Philippians 4:9

My husband and I attended two Community of Christ-sponsored events last fall—a retreat and a tour. Both enriched our spirituality and further equipped us for Christ's mission.

In September, we attended our congregational weekend retreat at the Guthrie Grove Retreat Center in Iowa. Our daughter, her 11-year-old son, and two great-grandsons, ages 9 and 11, accompanied us. We enjoyed classes, indoor and outdoor games, campfires, and worship. Everything was intergenerational. We witnessed remarkable spiritual growth in one of our great-grandsons.

In October, we joined the Community of Christ Historic Sites Foundation's tour. We were in the company of David Ettinger, Barbara Walden, and about 50 other Community of Christ learners.

We had 10 days of sightseeing, bus riding, visiting, and lessons taught by Barbara and David. We introduced ourselves to church tourists from all over the country.

We visited Frankenmuth, Michigan; Niagara Falls, Ontario; and Shaker, Amish, and Oneida communities. For fun, we dropped by the Baseball Hall of Fame and saw other sights.

Best of all, we visited Palmyra, New York; Kirtland, Ohio; Nauvoo, Illinois; and Lamoni, Iowa—all places dear to our hearts and full of church history. The meals and worship services prepared for us by the congregations we visited are now treasures to our souls.

How great it was to immerse ourselves in meditation and learning, while seeking a deeper connection to God. How great it is to join with companion disciples!

Prayer for Peace

God of Wisdom, may our minds always be open to learn of you. Help us continue learning as you continue to reveal yourself to us. May we join in community to share Christ's lessons and peace.

Spiritual Practice: Develop Disciples to Serve

Read and reflect on Psalm 42:1–2. As disciples of Jesus Christ, we are called to respond to people and their needs. The call to journey inward can restore us in times of physical or spiritual depletion. Imagine you can feel a vessel at the center of your being (a clay jar, a crystal vase, a metal bucket, or other container).

Imagine drawing something from the vessel to share with another person, but as you reach inside you find only a tiny pool of stagnant liquid. You are thirsty and dry; empty. Listen prayerfully again to the psalm, "As a deer longs for flowing streams, so my soul longs for you, O God. My soul thirsts for God, for the living God." As you feel restored, thank God for the opportunity to be a responding, serving disciple on the outward journey. Remember this exercise as you drink water throughout the day.

Peace Covenant

Today, God, I will review what I have learned and seen in Christ to become a better disciple.

13
Friday
September

Peace "Alive!"

By Danny Belrose of Independence, Missouri, USA

> *These are portentous times. The lives of many are being sacrificed unnecessarily to the gods of war, greed and avarice...*
>
> —Doctrine and Covenants 150:7

For generations the word "Peace" has dangled at the feet of a lion, a lamb and a child—the symbol and seal of Community of Christ. Each Sunday, I am grateful the "lighting of the peace candle" is a feature in my congregation's worship.

Next week, September 21, we will celebrate the International Day of Peace. That said, we are just *beginning* to understand what it means to be a people who incarnate peace personally and within diverse communities. There is a difference between "being at peace" and being "AT" peace.

More than a word or sleepy slogan, the letters P E A C E, *dangling* at the feet of a lion, a lamb, and a child, paradoxically remind us that peace is something we must *stand on* and *live for*.

Prayer for Peace

"Peace! Peace! Peace!"—so *easily* its slips off our tongues, God.
Peace—robbed of meaning, wrapped in familiarity,
tucked tightly away in narrow folds of understanding.
We confess, O God, a peace born of myopia—a peace that sees only the daylight
of saccharine sensibilities spun by soft summer breezes,
morning mist, lemonade and lazy afternoons free of care.
Peace—devoured by apathy—its brief life spent on slogans said
and banners blown on winds of hope—its voice heard but for a moment.
A peace betrayed by deception's subtle lie that to *talk* peace is to *do* peace.

May we see its resurrection, God. Let peace invade us and transform us.
Let it find meaning beyond hymns sung, prayers prayed,
sermons preached.
May we give it heart, heads, hands, and feet as well as lips.
May the peace of this strange man, Jesus, awaken within us new resolve
to move from slogans to deeds, from hope to reality.
Peace, ALIVE across the breakfast table. Peace, ALIVE and color blind.
Peace, ALIVE for saint, for sinner—for all who sing God's many names.
For only then, do we truly take your name upon us.

—Danny Belrose

Spiritual Practice: Daily Prayer for Peace

The Daily Prayer for Peace takes place year-round in the Independence and Kirtland Temples and weekly in many congregations. Each day we pray for a different country. Go to the front of this book and identify the country for today. Research information about the country and ask God for insights about the needs of the people. Pray for this country.

14
Saturday
September

The Blessing of Language

By Andrew Bolton, Council of Twelve Apostles

There are many lives waiting to hear the redeeming words of the gospel, or to be lifted from hopelessness by the hands of loving servants. But they will be lost to you without the generous response of disciples who share from their own bounty that others may know the joys of the kingdom…The call to respond is urgent…look also beyond your walls to the far-flung places where the church must go. Each disciple needs a spiritual home. You are called to build that home and care for it, but also to share equally in the outreaching ministries of the church. In that way the gospel may be sent to other souls also yearning for a spiritual resting place.

—Doctrine and Covenants 162:7

Those in English-speaking nations have many church resources (books, lessons, study guides, etc.). However, for those who speak a different tongue, such as the Asian languages, few church resources exist. To meet this serious need, the church is making a significant investment in translations.

In October 2010 Steven L. Shields, from International Headquarters, worked with a team in Andra Pradesh, India, to review a translation of *The Priesthood Manual* from English into the Telugu language. The project was an important milestone in the church's continuing effort to provide printed resources to the Asia Mission Field.

The team referenced key church words and phrases, then discussed what the best word or phrase to translate the fullest meaning in Telugu would be. For example, *evangelist* does not easily translate into Telugu, so the team decided to translate the priesthood office as *blessing giver.*

Your contributions to world mission tithes help make mission real by providing printed texts of church resources in many languages. Thank you for responding generously to this need.

Prayer for Peace

God of all nations, peoples, tongues, and tribes, let us not take our language for granted. May we speak to the people of far-flung places with a mutual spirit of understanding, communicating Christ's message of peace for all.

Spiritual Practice: Honoring Unity in Diversity

Meditate on Unity in Diversity. Create a large circle with your arms. Can you imagine a circle wide enough to include the world? See and feel the diverse people God invites inside the sanctuary of Christ's peace represented by this circle.

Who is easiest to welcome? Whom do you struggle to include because they are far away? Confess the dividing walls between you and people of other languages. Ask God to heal communication barriers that keep you and others from sharing in Christ's peace.

Peace Covenant

Today, God, I will reflect on a word or phrase that is important to me, and learn to speak it in another language. *Namaste.*

15
Sunday
September

Rejoice! The Lost Is Found!

By Jane Gardner, High Priest Quorum president

"Which one of you, having a hundred sheep and losing one of them, does not leave the ninety-nine in the wilderness and go after the one that is lost until he finds it? . . . And when he comes home, he calls together his friends and neighbors, saying to them, "Rejoice with me, for I have found my sheep that was lost." Just so, I tell you, there will be more joy in heaven over one sinner who repents than over ninety-nine righteous persons who need no repentance."

—Luke 15:4–7

One morning before sunrise I arrived at the Temple in a hurry to prepare for an early worship gathering. As I reached the front doors, I heard a voice call, "Hey lady!" I was alone and debated whether I should go ahead and enter the building and be safe. But I decided to turn and engage the person calling to me.

He ran down the hill and asked if he could go into the Temple and use the phone. I told him the building wasn't open yet, but if he would give me the number he could use my cell phone. He said he needed to call his boss to tell her he would be late because the buses were running late. He proudly showed me his work shirt and said he was just starting a new job.

He had a short phone conversation with his new boss, asking that she be patient—he really was trying to get there. She must have encouraged him, and he hung up. Then he said, "Could I make one more call?" Again, I dialed the number and handed him the phone.

He began, "Mom, I have a new job and a new shirt, and I want to stop by and show it to you." His next statement broke my heart, "Please, Mom, can I just stop by? I won't stay long, I promise. I just want to show you my shirt." She must have relented.

He said as he handed back the phone, "Lady, I don't know who you are or anything about this place, but today you have been my angel."

There are times in our lives and in our congregations when human boundaries get in the way of ministry. There are times when we, too, feel like the least, the last, or the lost. The good news of today's scripture is that when we feel unworthy or when others label us as unredeemable, God's grace still pursues us, like the shepherd searching for the lost sheep.

As disciples of Jesus, we are called into mission outside the boundaries, sometimes needing to make choices that, in the end, are a cause for celebration. Who knows? You may be somebody's angel.

Prayer for Peace

Tender Shepherd, we praise you for never taking your eyes off us when we wander. We rejoice when your sheep are found. Share Christ's peace with your sheep.

Spiritual Practice: Honoring the Worth of All Persons

Sense the intimate knowledge God has of you and every child. Be aware of the sacred worth of each person. Weep with God over soul-wounding forces that rob people of dignity and worth. How are you invited to notice, protect, heal, and affirm the spiritual identity of all God's beloved people today? Pray for God's compassion.

Peace Covenant

Today, God, I will search for your lost sheep and rejoice when they are found.

16
Monday
September

Lost in Omaha

By Cindy L. Korf of North Platte, Nebraska, USA

> *...If a shepherd has a hundred sheep, and one of them has gone astray, does he not leave the ninety-nine on the mountains and go in search of the one that went astray? And if he finds it, truly I tell you, he rejoices over it more than over the ninety-nine that never went astray. So it is not the will of your Father in heaven that one of these little ones should be lost.*
>
> —Matthew 18:12–14

I was in Omaha, Nebraska, and though I was unfamiliar with the city, I thought I knew where I was going. I was confident I could drive to a store and back to the hotel by myself. I did not need a map or guidance. But after an hour on roads that led to I don't know where, I knew I had lost my way.

As I waited at a red light, surrounded by cars and traffic moving quickly in the opposite direction, the realization that I was lost engulfed me and drained the life from me.

I thought, "I'm only lost in a large city. How does one cope with losing their way in life? How does one travel the perilous roads of life without God?"

We might fool ourselves into thinking we know the way, but without God, we really are lost.

Thankfully, we have God. We have the scriptures, Jesus Christ, and the Holy Spirit to direct, guide, and escort us on our journey of life. We need never be alone.

Prayer for Peace

Tender Shepherd, we thank you for searching for us when we lose our way. Thank you for your comfort and guidance on our journey. Help us never to lose sight of Christ's mission. May we faithfully share Christ's peace with those who lose their way.

Spiritual Practice: Praying with a Partner

Pray with a partner if possible, or imagine Christ sitting with you. The heart is a center of compassion and spiritual connection. Stand or sit across from your partner with hands open and palms up. Invite your partner to place hands, palms down, on your hands. Close your eyes and be aware of the connection between your heart and your partner's heart. What needs, feelings, or longings do you sense? Invite God's presence to flow into you and move from your heart to the heart of your partner. Feel or see God's healing light and love flowing between your hearts. After a period of silent prayer, thank God and your partner. Say amen. (You also may pray this prayer by envisioning a particular person across from you.)

Peace Covenant

Today, God, I will open myself to your Spirit and focus on what matters most.

17
Tuesday
September

Moon Trilogy (Three Moments)

By John Bonney of Springfield, Oregon, USA

. . . You have set your glory above the heavens. . . When I look at your heavens, the work of your fingers, the moon and the stars that you have established...

—Psalm 8:1, 3

1: Nature allowed me the wonderful sight of an obscured moon—a soft glow in darkened clouds. In the overcast was an area of limited brightness, drawing the contours of the surrounding clouds with silver. As usual, I was at a loss to hold onto it, to grasp it. I was taken out of myself for a few moments and sensed once more unity with creation. I was able only to stand in awe and fascination, beholding the sight. The creative ability of the Divine always astounds me.

2: The full moon was so bright one morning! It blazed in cool silver low in the western sky. I had to catch my breath, compelled to stand astounded. I had not seen the full moon for months. When I emerged into the open it hit me in the eye like molten silver. In biblical talk I would say it "smote" me in the eye. I stood there, transfixed. I wanted to grasp it, to reach the unreachable. I wanted to find words, yet none formed in my mind. I wanted to give glory to Presence, and to string together words of praise and honor. I could only stand there and be awed by that image. All I could say was, "Thank you, God."

3: There was that moon! "Wow." For days, despite clear skies, I did not see the moon. It wasn't time yet. Then today, there it was—bright and gorgeous. There were no clouds or haze. The sky was clear, and the moon was full.

It appeared to hang motionless in the western sky just above the horizon—a molten drop in a liquid sky. Only my walking allowed trees to enter the view, and then it moved among the leafy filigree. Flitting in and out of sight like a child playing peek-a-boo or hide-and-seek. And, seek it, I did.

After a long, cold month, the moon inserted itself again, reminding me of a hymn text, "Sometimes a Light Surprises." Praise for my Creator was on my lips, and joy was in my heart. A great wave of thanksgiving swept over me.

Prayer for Peace

Creator God, we praise you for the light you provide in the darkness.

Spiritual Practice: Sea of Light

Quiet and center yourself. Ask for God's healing and guidance as you enter this time of prayerful presence. Close your eyes, breathing deeply and calmly. Imagine that you are floating in a beautiful sea of light that rises and falls with each cycle of your breath. The golden light of this sea buoys you up, so you float effortlessly. Waves of light carry and wash over you, bringing wholeness and peace. Rest in the sea of God's love, then offer a prayer of gratitude.

Peace Covenant

The next time I see the moon, God, I will pray in its light.

18
Wednesday
September

What's in a Name?

By Dorene Kilburn of Stratford, Ontario, Canada

> *"And blessed is this people who are willing to bear my name; for in my name shall they be called; and they are mine."*
>
> —Mosiah 11:125

In my years of working as a dental receptionist and assistant, I had seemingly countless opportunities to attend conferences and workshops. Some lecturers were forgettable; some were gifted educators. Often I heard simple but profound truths.

One such statement in a workshop on communication skills was this: "The sweetest sound to any person is the sound of one's own name."

When a casual acquaintance calls me by name, I am impressed! That is, if it's someone I haven't seen for a long time or someone I didn't think knew me. When someone calls us by our name, we instantly feel important. It boosts our self-esteem. Our face registers surprise and delight. We have seen that same delight in another person's face when we can call a person by name.

God said, "...I have called you by name, you are mine" (Isaiah 43:1 NRSV). Can we understand what this means? What a blessing to know God does indeed call each of us by our name; that God cares about who we are and who we can become.

With a friend like this, we can move forward on our spiritual journey, confident of a worthy identity and opportunities to support our companion travelers along the way...Jim, Mary, Lauren, David, Judith, Jane, Steve—all are God's, every one.

Prayer for Peace

God of many names—Creator, Elohim, Gitche Manitou, Mother, Father, Holy Spirit, Deity, I Am, Tender Shepherd, Comforter, and others beyond count, we are yours. We follow your Son, Jesus. We promote and share his peace.

Spiritual Practice: The Many Names of God

In many languages, God's name contains the sound "Ahhh," a sound we make when we are breathing out or sighing. Our prayer will use the Ahh names for God with a gentle arm movement that opens us to God's presence. Begin with hands in front of you at chest level and move them up and in a large arc or circle as you breathe out each name for God. You may either speak the name of God or find a single musical note to hold or chant as you sing God's name. Pray or sing each name several times as you call on the God of many names: Yahweh, Adonai, Jehovah, Yeshua, Sophia, Allah, Alpha, Omega. Say or sing "amen" to close.

Peace Covenant

I will hear you when you call; I am yours, God.

19
Thursday
September

The Present Moment

By Darrell Belrose of Calgary, Alberta, Canada

"Blessed are the peacemakers, for they will be called children of God."

—Matthew 5:9

I arrived two hours early for Coley's celebration of life. I stationed myself in the lobby of a downtown hotel to get out of the cold. To fill time, I read from Thich Nhat Hanh's book, *Discovering the Magic of the Present Moment.* Noises and commotion barraged me from the lobby. I felt frustrated and annoyed by the many voices.

I realized that in a few short moments hundreds of people would be gathering for the duality of emotions—grief and joy. We would be celebrating the gracious and brave life of a 17-year-old. Coley lost her fight with cancer but gained the true meaning of life, living it to its fullest!

I began to reflect on what I was reading, "don't be judgmental of my surroundings" but lovingly "embrace what is." Accepting this sense of awareness, my inward turmoil quieted, and I prepared myself to celebrate Coley's short, but full life.

This celebration was an experience of great joy, laughter, admiration, and uninhibited tears. Most of all we expressed our appreciation to God. I had the privilege of experiencing those times when I basked in the presence of earthly angels in the form of Coley!

I want to take time always to appreciate and celebrate my connection with all of God's creation. I praise God for this awareness of living in the moment and for the beauty of all the Coleys of this world!

Prayer for Peace

Creator God, for lives lived to the fullest we praise you. For our awareness of the present moment, we thank you. From the lives of children who teach us so much, may we learn to share Christ's peace.

Spiritual Practice: Honoring the Worth of All Persons

Read Psalm 139:13–18. After each reading sit quietly and let the words sink deeply into your mind, heart, and body. Imagine God watching you grow in your mother's womb. What thoughts and feelings do you have about being "fearfully and wonderfully made" (Psalm 139:14)?

Sense the intimate knowledge God has of you and every child. Be aware of the sacred worth of each person. Weep with God over the soul-wounding forces and events that rob people of dignity and worth. How are you invited to notice, protect, heal, and affirm the spiritual identity of all God's beloved people today? Pray for God's compassion.

Peace Covenant

Today, God, I will not be frustrated by the noise of the crowd, for I know in its voice is your voice.

20
Friday
September

A Thousand Voices

By Becky Willis Shantz of Lamoni, Iowa, USA

"You are the light of the world. A city built on a hill cannot be hid. No one after lighting a lamp puts it under the bushel basket, but on the lampstand, and it gives light to all in the house. In the same way, let your light shine before others, so that they may see your good works and give glory to your Father in heaven."

—Matthew 5:14–16

I often work as a substitute teacher. This gives me a good opportunity to work with children and youth, a passion for me.

I didn't realize I would be blessed in unexpected ways. Hardly a day goes by that I don't receive inspiration that is just what I need in my life at that moment. I glean from sources such as posters on a classroom or hall wall, items on a teacher's desk, or even subject matter for students.

Recently I subbed for a high school English teacher. Some students gave speeches, using inspirational stories they had chosen. As I listened, I felt awe. Here I was again…blessed and uplifted at a most unexpected time. I asked for copies of the stories. Not only were the words encouraging, I thought they were perfect to contribute to a book of devotional readings my sister was compiling. This was a double blessing!

One quote from the stories jumped at me: "It takes a thousand voices to tell a single story" (Native American proverb).

Thank you, again! As we travel life's journey together, we can never know from where the voice of help and inspiration will come. We connect to a spiritual community that reveals itself to us continually. I can't help thinking this was God pouring out blessing after blessing that day.

Each of us has the potential to be the voice that inspires and gives strength to others at moments when most needed.

Let your light shine!

Prayer for Peace

God whose story we tell through the ages, thank you for sending your Son that we might better understand you. Help us share the peace that he taught us.

Spiritual Practice: Teacher-learner

The first disciples of Jesus followed to hear his words, to be taught, to learn a new way of living, to practice what they learned in daily life. Prayerfully consider your role as a teacher-learner, disciple-apprentice, a people cultivator in Community of Christ. In your journal, write the names of several persons you discern as teachers or mentors and several you feel called to nurture and encourage in specific ways. Ask God's blessing on you and your congregation as a community of learners.

Peace Covenant

Today, God, I will share my story and invite someone to Christ.

21
Saturday
September

Children Explore Peace (United Nations International Day of Peace)

By Andrew Fox of Chesterfield, Danesmoor, British Isles

> *Do not neglect the smallest among you, for even the least of these are treasures in God's sight. Receive the giftedness and energy of children and youth, listening to understand their questions and their wisdom. Respond to their need to be loved and nurtured as they grow.*
>
> —Doctrine and Covenants 161:4a

Children throughout the British Isles Mission Centre now have a unique opportunity to explore peace through the Peace Mobile, a set of 20 interactive displays. The Peace Mobile is designed to help children discover the power of peace through play. Peace Mobile themes include increasing self-esteem, holding respect for others, celebrating diversity, and caring for the planet.

A Tangible Love grant, funded through the Mission Initiative of Abolish Poverty, End Suffering, helped to create a second set of displays and employ a part-time coordinator to meet the Peace Mobile's demand. The grant enabled 12 schools to participate in the program in the last year. The project recently added two more displays, one based at the British Isles Mission Centre church campground and the other in a community school for children with social, emotional, and behavioral difficulties.

Your contributions to world mission tithes make it possible for children to have a fun, hands-on way to learn peacemaking skills that will benefit them throughout their lives. Thank you for responding generously to this need to Pursue Peace on Earth.

Prayer for Peace

God of justice and peace, may we follow the teachings lived by Christ. May we live them as examples to our children. Help us learn new ideas for peacemaking *from* our children. May we, as adults and children together, share the peace of Christ as we live it in the world.

Spiritual Practice: Embodying God's Shalom

Find a way to express and embody God's shalom. Begin by prayerfully listening to your longing for peace. Become silent and imagine you can hear the groaning of the Earth's people, nations, and creatures. Prayerfully open yourself to God's yearning for peace and the divine vision of shalom.

What images, feelings, and words come to you? What prayer for peace comes to you from your time of listening? Speak or write this prayer. What small act of justice, kindness, healing, or peacemaking does God invite you to consider this day?

Peace Covenant

Today, God, I will treasure and support young peacemakers.

22
Sunday
September

Serve God

By Robert Adie of Kisumu, Kenya

No slave can serve two masters; for a slave will either hate the one and love the other, or be devoted to the one and despise the other. You cannot serve God and wealth."

—Luke 16:13

Many years ago in my village in Kenya, my wife and I visited an old woman who was living alone in her small, two-room house. When we approached the door I called to ask whether someone was in the house. There was no response, but the door was half open.

We entered, and I called again. She responded with low, deep voice, "Enter, I am not feeling well."

When we entered the bedroom, which was dark and without proper ventilation, we called her, and she recognized my voice. "Karibu, my son" (this is a Swahili word for welcome). The smell was not pleasant. I opened the window and went closer to the bed to hold her hands and listen to her.

When I approached I saw many bedbugs trying to hide in the bedding. I prayed for courage and found myself having to take a deep breath. Without thinking I managed to get her out of bed and carry her outside to bask in God's sunlight.

My wife and I realized as we looked at her, that she could not go back to that bed without further action.

As my wife continued to talk with her about Christ, who she knew very much about, I went in to remove the bed and all the bedding, taking them into the sun. My wife took charge of the mattress, sheets, and blankets, cleaning them with soap and water and placing them on shrubs to dry. I went in the house and cleaned the entire place with insecticide powder, leaving no chance for the bedbugs to live.

When we finished and went back to the woman, she told us she had been sick for a week, and nobody had come to see her. On the night after our visit, she felt Christ promised she would get well. We prepared food for her, and my wife bathed her. She healed.

She told us how she had a good, peaceful sleep, and she offered a blessing prayer. She testified of this to everybody she met. She always encouraged us to do good to everybody in need. I felt I had met a challenge as part of my walk with Christ. I felt I had served God.

Prayer for Peace

Tender Shepherd, may we work to serve Christ's mission of compassion.

Spiritual Practice: Abolish Poverty, End Suffering

Read and reflect on John 21:15–17 as a meditation. Let your mind be drawn to places where people have no homes. Be aware of the insufferable conditions of poverty. Let the images fill your mind. Imagine Christ tending those sheep. Think of ways you might end their suffering as part of your mission. Throughout the day, hear the voice of Christ saying: "Feed my lambs…tend my sheep…feed my sheep."

Peace Covenant

Today, God, I will not be repulsed by poverty's infestations but will bring them into your healing light.

23
Monday
September

A Kind and Compassionate Voice

By Don Streeter of Dallas, Oregon, USA

Then he shouted, "Jesus, Son of David, have mercy on me!"

—Luke 18:38

(*Inspired by scripture*)

"You are beautiful!"

You might wonder why a stranger would say this to you. But you must understand—until three days ago I was blind. I lost my sight as a child and lived as a beggar on the road outside Jericho.

For many days recently as people passed, I heard them talking about a preacher named Jesus. He traveled the area, teaching and preaching. I learned he was a descendant of David. He had the gift of healing. Some said he might even be the prophesied Messiah. But what do I know of prophets and Messiahs? Blind beggars aren't welcome in the synagogues.

What I wanted more than life itself was to see—to see flowers and faces, sunrises and sunsets. I wanted to see even the dirt upon my feet. If only this Jesus could heal me. But how could I find him? Who would take me to him?

Then my life changed. As I sat on the road begging, I heard a crowd approaching. "What is this? Who passes by?" A person joyfully answered, "It's Jesus of Nazareth. Come." My heart leapt. Jesus, the one who could make me see again. In my soul I knew he could heal me. I had no doubt. I cried out, "Jesus, Son of David, have mercy on me!" He just had to hear me!

Someone from the crowd told me to hold my peace, that Jesus had important things to do. He had no time for me. But I knew he could heal me if he could just hear me. I called again, "Son of David, Son of David, hear me. Have mercy on me!"

Through the crowd's noise I heard Jesus ask that I come to him. I could feel a strong presence, and I knew Jesus must be near. I feared I might collapse. But a kind and compassionate voice said to me, "What do you want me to do for you?" I calmly answered, "Lord, let me see again."

Then he said to me, "Receive your sight; your faith has saved you." Immediately I could see. The first person I saw was a man who, despite great fatigue, carried an uncommon strength. As my newly opened eyes met his I saw a depth of love and compassion I had never known.

I praised God right there. I blessed God for my wholeness. Your bodies may not be blind, crippled, or sick; but your spirit may be blind to God's love, crippled with hate, or sick with loneliness.

Call to him as I did, "Jesus, Son of God, have mercy on me!" Ask him as I did, "Have mercy on me!"

Prayer for Peace

Open our eyes, God, that we may see your love.

Spiritual Practice: The Jesus Prayer of Mercy

Silently enter prayer. Greet God and take up the prayer phrase: Lord, Jesus Christ (as you breathe in)...have mercy on me (as you breathe out). Prayerfully repeat these words several times. Breathe in the transforming presence of Christ.

Peace Covenant

Today, God, I will be transformed as I accept your mercy.

24
Tuesday
September

Zion's Gate

By Glenn Johnson of Covina, California, USA

> *Heed the urgent call to become a global family united in the name of Christ, committed in love to one another, seeking the kingdom for which you yearn and to which you have always been summoned. That kingdom shall be a peaceable one and it shall be known as Zion.*
>
> —Doctrine and Covenants 161:6b

On a recent business trip to Israel, I asked a colleague for a ride to Jerusalem. He dropped me by the Jaffa Gate. When I arrived it was dark. It had been a few years since I had navigated the narrow streets, but I managed to find my way past the Cardo to the Western Wall. A crowd had recently dispersed after some sort of concert or rally. I felt I had missed something important.

On my way back, I made a wrong turn. The Jaffa Gate was not in sight. I turned right. I came to another gate. I went through and read the sign: "Zion's Gate." My mind raced as I considered whether this hill really was "Mount Zion," a beacon of the present and future kingdom of God for my faith community.

I explored the streets nearby and found Hagia Zion, or Holy Zion Church, and the Jewish Yeshiva Institute for the Preservation of Holy Mount Zion. Beyond a barbwire fence, I saw the minaret of a mosque. Despite all hopes for peace, Jerusalem remained a city divided. Yet from this new vantage point on Zion's holy hill, the city's outer walls were an apparition in golden light.

Jesus spoke of *basileia tou theou*, the kingdom of God, as a present reality and a hoped-for future. My unexpected nighttime discovery of Zion helped me to understand better Jesus' teachings. As we work together as an imperfect yet transforming community, let us always see the cause of Zion as tangible, real communities to be celebrated and experienced, as well as future ideals toward which we can strive.

Prayer for Peace

Gather us in, O God, in closeness to your peaceable kingdom. Help us become a community that embraces Christ's mission of peace.

Spiritual Practice: The International Community

Find (or imagine) a globe or map of the world. Look at all the nations and find a country other than your own. Notice the geographic distance between your homeland and this one. Picture a person living there. Pray for this person. Sense God's love connecting you just as the oceans connect the continents. Thank God for the spiritual connection you have with all of God's people around the globe. Ask a blessing on the church as a community sharing Christ's peace, drawing all into the family of God.

Peace Covenant

Today, God, I will work for the reality of the peaceable kingdom.

25
Wednesday
September

Reshaping Our Lives

By Rosemary Holmes of Clay Cross, Derbyshire, England

Create in me a clean heart, O God, and put a new and right spirit within me. Do not cast me away from your presence, and do not take your holy spirit from me.

—Psalm 51:10–11

With some sadness, I recently witnessed the gardener pruning heavily three 80-year-old lime trees in our garden. They had become too tall and overpowering. When in full leaf they kept out the light. This not only caused some of their lower limbs to die, it stunted the flowers and shrubs beneath them. Though I felt sad, I knew in the spring the trees would branch out again toward their former glory.

Pondering this, I thought about our own lives and our influence on others. As the years go by our thoughts and ideas, if biased and outdated, not only affect our own growth but may stifle the development of those around us. May we have the grace to let go of stale precepts. And, may we have the generosity to share God's continuing truth.

We should try always to be sensitive to the needs of others. We periodically should reevaluate and reshape our own formation. As we gain new perspective, those with whom we associate will encourage us to grow spiritually.

Prayer for Peace

God of all growing creation, help us find the time to reevaluate our perceptions of your truths. Give us courage to prune those ideas that stifle our own growth and the growth of those around us. Build into our lives an inner strength that influences others for good. Renew us as we grow toward the light and reach for higher levels of spirituality and understanding. Renew in us the will to share the peace of Jesus Christ.

Spiritual Practice: Weeding the Garden

Inner transformation can take place amid daily activities and work. Try cultivating the spiritual discipline of grace and acceptance while weeding the garden. As you pull each weed, offer a short prayer. Tug. (*God remove from my heart all prejudice and fear.*) Tug again. (*God, keep me from making unjust judgments.*) As you remove the weed, continue praying. (*Plant in my heart the seeds of your love.*) If you don't have a garden, try this kind of transforming prayer today while doing repetitive activities or work (cleaning out a closet, washing dishes, cleaning the floors, mowing the lawn).

Peace Covenant

Today, God, I will be aware of how I might help Develop Disciples to Serve.

26
Thursday
September

Kindred Spirit

By Shirley Remmenga of Fort Collins, Colorado, USA

> *And you will not have a mind to injure one another, but to live peaceably, and to render to every one according to that which is their due.*
>
> —Mosiah 2:24, adapted

One fall morning, I was standing at my kitchen sink, looking out toward the lawn between my house and the house next door. A slender-nosed, bushy-tailed red fox came around the corner of the house.

She carried something white in her mouth. She went directly to a big flowerpot on the neighbor's sidewalk, jumped up, dug a hole, and dropped it in. She covered it up, jumped down, loped around the house, and was gone.

She tempted me to go see what she had buried. I started to leave the sink, but another thought halted me. Do I have the right to invade her privacy? Why do I need to know what it is? Why can't I accept the mystery?

That beautiful creature deliberately had hidden something of value to her that she would unearth later. If I disturbed it, she would know, and perhaps it wouldn't be of any use to her then. So, I left it there.

I never saw her return for it, but I'm sure she did. I enjoyed seeing her occasionally after that, just running along the greenbelt next to the houses. She and I shared the same space, so to speak. She didn't threaten my life, and I didn't want to leave footprints in her habitat. We had a kinship in a sense.

It was a good feeling and a blessing for me to have this peaceful connection with one of God's beautiful, clever creatures.

Prayer for Peace

Creator God, thank you for the creatures that share our world. We learn about you and see your mystery in them. We would leave them in peace. We would share Christ's peace, which teaches us to restore right relationships with creation.

Spiritual Practice: Caring for God's Sacred Creation

Choose a way to notice, give thanks, and care for God's sacred creation. Prayerfully consider one of the following practices or create your own. Walk in nature with a spirit of gratitude while looking and listening for God in all things. Write or pray a psalm of praise for the Earth's beauty or a prayer of healing and blessing for its wounds.

Learn about and engage in an act of Earth-keeping such as recycling, simple living, or fasting from over-consumption of resources. Notice the diversity of the planet's creatures and be gentle to plants, animals, trees, and people! Fall in love with the vast, intricate wonder of God's creation and give thanks.

Peace Covenant

Today, God, I will leave the stone unturned and bless what lies beneath.

27
Friday
September

Lost Words

By Sara Parkin of Midland, Michigan, USA

Let me hear what God the Lord will speak, for he will speak peace to his people, to his faithful, to those who turn to him in their hearts.

—Psalm 85:8

(Part 7 of My Journey with Alzheimer's Disease)

Doctors told me earlier that I had dementia with memory loss. *Words* were what I lost. It is hard to talk with words when you can't speak the words that won't come from your mouth.

I told my pastor a year and a half ago that I would not stand up in a service to speak. I was leading the Lord's Prayer, and in the middle of the prayer, I lost my words. Thankfully, someone in the first row saw what was happening, picked it up, and kept it going.

When I was diagnosed with Alzheimer's disease, God put me to work remembering that I am alive, and God is with me. It is not just the words now as I learn there is help. I realized my pride was in the way. I did not want people to know what was going on in my life. I cannot do it alone, not any more. Now I ask for help.

Many words mean a lot to me. I am sure we all have words that have meaning in our lives. I have made a list of more than 30 words that mean a lot to me: God, Jesus Christ, Holy Spirit, surrender, will, love, peace, joy, hope, prayers, family, friends, laughter, care, free, accept, change, courage, new, alive, share, kind, today, now, feel, Alzheimer's, help, focus, smile.

In the next journal entry, I will share what these words mean to me as a person with Alzheimer's disease. I will start the list with God.

Prayer for Peace

We turn to you in our hearts, God. We listen for your words. We try to find the words to Invite People to Christ, to share his peace.

Spiritual Practice: Tears of Compassion

Offer a silent prayer for the gift of God's compassion. Cup your hands and ask God to make you aware of the suffering that causes the Earth and its inhabitants to groan and weep. Be open to faces or places, sounds or voices; feelings of connection with those who suffer. Imagine catching the tears of those you see and holding them in your hands. Listen for prayer images or words God may give you. Discern any active responses of ministry or healing you are invited to complete for those who weep.

Peace Covenant

Today, God, I may lose the right words, but I will not lose my faith in you.

28
Saturday
September

"Something Is Happening in Spain"

By Keith McMillan of Waltham Cross, England

God is calling for a prophetic community to emerge, drawn from the nations of the world, that is characterized by uncommon devotion to the compassion and peace of God revealed in Jesus Christ. Through divine grace and wisdom, this faith community has been given abundant gifts, resources, and opportunities to equip it to become such a people. Chief among these is the power of community in Christ expressed locally in distinctive fashions while upholding a unity of vision, foundational beliefs, and mission throughout the world.

—Doctrine and Covenants 163:11a

"Something is happening in Spain!" I heard this many times on recent visits to Madrid and Barcelona. Many people are asking about Community of Christ. Several have chosen baptism. The church is beginning to recognize its potential in that nation.

Recently, about 25 members and friends of the church gathered in Madrid to celebrate Communion, the first time in many years for some of them. A wonderful spirit prevailed as the group sang hymns, prayed, and shared in companionship. This is just one example of how the Spirit of God calls us into new places to share the good news of Jesus Christ.

Your contributions make Christ's mission a reality throughout the world. Thank you for responding faithfully to the Mission Initiative of Invite People to Christ.

Prayer for Peace

Welcoming God, may we send the sound the Earth around, inviting people to Christ. May we take Christ's message of peace and share with all who might hear.

Spiritual Practice: Ongoing Revelation

One Enduring Principle of Community of Christ is Continuing Revelation. We are a people always in process, becoming shaped by God's interaction with us. In prayer, listen deeply to the name, "Community of Christ." Write or say a prayer asking God to continue to form us through our name. Listen deeply to what it would mean to live in community, following and sharing the way of Christ. Become comfortable with sharing who we are.

Peace Covenant

Today, God, I will do what I can to expand Christ's mission beyond borders.

29
Sunday
September

God Is with Us

By Lackings Banda of Lilongwe, Malawi

Those who love me, I will deliver; I will protect those who know my name. When they call to me, I will answer them; I will be with them in trouble, I will rescue them and honor them. With long life I will satisfy them, and show them my salvation.

—Psalm 91:14–16

I tell this story of Christmas, but it is for all the year. Many are the times when people in prisons, orphan-care centers, and hospitals do not have hope of a merry Christmas and a happy New Year. Good food, a little merrymaking, and a message of Emmanuel (God with us) mostly symbolize celebration for the newly born baby.

Prisoners, orphans, and patients expect little from the outside world at Christmas time.

This year it has been different in Lilongwe. People in prisons, orphan-care centers, and hospitals were cheered on Christmas day. Many disciples showed their love by sharing Christmas gifts. Some went to the prisons and hospitals with food and clothing. Others went with the good news of the gospel.

Love and sharing was at the heart of the message of Christmas. Radios, televisions, and homes displayed the heart of a sharing people who cheered up those who least expected to be remembered.

Jesus Christ was a gift first given by God for our salvation. Let us show the same spirit of sharing with the less privileged before and after Christmas. Hope and comfort to the needy is not needed only during Christmas, but always.

Remember, individually and cooperatively as a church, the Lord needs us to bring hope and show love by sharing with those in need.

You can do something. Do not underrate the help you can offer them. People in the hospitals, prisons, and orphan-care centers need our prayers and comfort to bring back lost hope.

Sharing at Christmas can be the starting point of sharing what matters most. God will protect us. God is with us!

Prayer for Peace

Generous God, may we learn to share the spirit of Christmas throughout the year. May we not wait for a special time of the year to give to those in need. May we remember that Christ lives and that you, our God, are with us. May we celebrate every day as an opportunity to give and share the peace of Christ.

Spiritual Practice: Growing a Gracious, Generous Heart

Open your heart to God's grace and generosity with a "breath prayer." Let your breathing slow and deepen. Be aware of God's breath moving in and out of your heart. Spend several minutes focusing on breathing in God's generosity. With each breath, silently name one gift for which you are thankful. Let your heart expand to contain God's gracious outpouring of love. With each breath out, name one gift you want to share from the overflow of your heart.

Peace Covenant

Today, God, and every day, I will remember the prisoner, the orphan, and the patient.

30
Monday
September

Peace Then…Peace Now

By Ramona Seeley of Leeton, Missouri, USA

All this is from God, who reconciled us to himself through Christ, and has given us the ministry of reconciliation; that is, in Christ God was reconciling the world to himself, not counting their trespasses against them, and entrusting the message of reconciliation to us.

—2 Corinthians 5:18–19

I was working for the Red Cross in San Francisco in 1945 as the Second World War drew to a close. Down the block and across the street from the Red Cross building was the place where the United Nations began.

During my lunch break, I would watch as men and women from different nations came and went. What a feeling of hope it gave me to see people involved in peace and soldiers coming home! I thought peace and harmony were possible.

Today the United Nations has not yet fulfilled all our hopes and dreams of a world without war. It has made a beginning, and I still have hope that someday we may learn to live in peace with one another and through Christ be reconciled.

Can you imagine what a blessed world this would be if we could understand, appreciate, and accept the differences and diversities among us? If only we would realize that one God created all of us.

At the same time, I need to remember that peace begins with me and with what I do. The words I use affect not only the community in which I live, but the world.

Prayer for Peace

Reconciling God, we long to be a peaceful people. We long to be close to you. Bless us with a resolve to reconcile with one another and Christ, so we may share his peace.

Spiritual Practice: Peace Action

Community of Christ is called to ministries of peace, reconciliation, and healing of the spirit. PeacePathways is a church-sponsored website sharing justice and peace ministries, resources, and opportunities. Visit *www.peace-pathways.org* and prayerfully discern one ministry that speaks to you or captures your attention. Offer a prayer of blessing on the peace ministry you have selected. Listen quietly to see if God is calling you to additional responses to this ministry or another ministry of peace, reconciliation, or healing. If you cannot visit the website, offer a prayer of blessing on all peace ministries.

Peace Covenant:

Today, God, I will remember that peace on Earth begins with…the next thing I do.

1
Tuesday
October

The Roommate

By Cindy L. Korf of North Platte, Nebraska, USA

> *We…are one body in Christ, and individually we are members one of another. We have gifts that differ according to the grace given to us: prophecy, in proportion to faith; ministry, in ministering; the teacher, in teaching; the exhorter, in exhortation; the giver, in generosity; the leader, in diligence; the compassionate, in cheerfulness.*
>
> —Romans 12:5–8

When my dad lived in a nursing home, his roommate, David, was recovering from a brain tremor.

David's condition limited his speech to three expressions—arms thrown in the air with a giant smile and a shout, "OK!"; a stare straight through you and the word, "Bummer"; and a slow walk toward you after which he'd wrap his arms around you and say, "I love you."

My dad, a tough, retired US Air Force sergeant, was uncomfortable with David's strange mannerisms and expressions. He avoided this "crazy man."

Yet, on my visits I noticed how David could correctly express the full gamut of emotions my dad was feeling—loneliness, pain, happiness, or self-pity.

On the day of my dad's release from the nursing home, I told David, "My dad is getting better."

David threw his arms in the air and yelled, "OK!"

"So, he's going home. He won't be your roommate anymore," I said.

David put his arms down. "Bummer."

My dad whispered something under his breath about his crazy roommate.

David shuffled over to my dad, wrapped his arms around him and said, "I love you."

I have thought often how David was like the voice and presence of Jesus. He expressed the needs, sorrows, and joys my dad had while away from home and family. I feel like David looked out for my dad. It is revealing how God can use any person to show divine love and concern. All Are Called.

Prayer for Peace

Bless our various gifts, God, so that we may use them for what matters most.

Spiritual Practice: Examining God's Call to Me and to All

Reflect on God's call in your life. Begin by prayerfully asking to recall particular moments when you have experienced God's presence and invitation. Write in your journal or quietly reflect on images and insights that come.

When has God seemed most real in your life? How and when has God called you to use your energies and gifts? When have you felt God's love in your life? When have you felt disconnected or resistant to God's call? How do your gifts and callings connect with the call of God you notice in your family, friends, congregation, or community?

Peace Covenant

Today, God, I will give my gifts with compassion and cheerfulness.

2
Wednesday
October

Ministers of Reconciliation

By Carolyn Brock of Redmond, Oregon, USA

> *All this is from God, who reconciled us to himself through Christ, and has given us the ministry of reconciliation.*
>
> —2 Corinthians 5:18

It was a good day. The district conference in Nigeria ended with a joyous Communion service.

The more than 800 attendees had begun to leave the church when we heard shouts from outside. Chaos invaded the church as youths entered with a friend who had been "wounded in battle." Sunday Charlie Akpan, then the national minister, escorted the youths into a small room with instructions to attend to the cut. Then he hurried outside to restore calm.

Young people from rival clans had exchanged insults and then started flinging rocks, resulting in a head wound for one, a deep cut on the hand of another.

Reconciliation took time, patience, respect, and listening to all parties. It took wisdom. It took assessment of damages and several trips to the hospital to bind wounds. It took a soothing voice among angry ones. It took the oil of grace poured over the results of destructive actions. It took a skilled minister of reconciliation; it took a disciple.

While perhaps few of us heave rocks at each other after a Communion service, have we launched unkind words and acts with intent to wound? Have we at times divided ourselves into rival camps? Are there yet divisions that absorb our attention and sap our energy?

How do we yet need to restore peace with one another? How can we embrace each other and our differences in the spirit of patience, respect, wisdom, listening, and healing? Who among us will offer soothing words and become anointers of wounds and skilled ministers of reconciliation? Who will be disciples?

Prayer for Peace

Reconciling God, help us break down barriers, real and imaginary. Help us lose our attitude of rivalry. Help us experience Unity in Diversity.

Spiritual Practice: The International Community

Find (or imagine) a globe or map of the world. Look at the nations and find a country other than your own. Notice the geographic distance between your homeland and this one. Picture a person living there. Pray for this person. Sense God's love connecting you just as the oceans connect the continents. Thank God for the spiritual connection you have with all of God's people around the globe. Ask a blessing on the church as a community sharing Christ's peace, drawing all into the family of God.

Peace Covenant

Today, God, I will tear down dividing walls and build bridges of invitation. I will unlock doors that restrict listening and throw away the key.

3

Thursday October

Patient and Persistent Spirit

By Shirley Remmenga of Fort Collins, Colorado, USA

> *The Lord is exalted, he dwells on high; he filled Zion with justice and righteousness; he will be the stability of your times, abundance of salvation, wisdom, and knowledge; the fear of the Lord is Zion's treasure.*
>
> —Isaiah 33:5–6

As my day began, the thought came to me that I ought to call Dalene. It was too early to make the call, so I dismissed the feeling. But the thought kept coming back all morning. Finally, after lunch, I made the call.

She wasn't there. I left a message on her answering machine that I had called just to say hello and would try again.

Dalene called back about an hour later. "I can't believe you called me," she said. "How did you know I needed to talk with someone? I'm having one of the worst weeks of my life. I am wracked with pain, I can hardly walk, and I'm scheduled for back surgery this Friday. I have to have surgery, but I'm dreading it because my last surgery was such a terrible experience!"

We talked for a few minutes. I listened, consoled her, and assured her God would be with her all the way. I promised to see her at the hospital before surgery.

Why did I call? I called because the Holy Spirit was persistent. The Spirit would not let me ignore the thought of calling my friend. I'm so glad that I listened and responded.

I had the opportunity to share God's love in a tangible way. Thank you, God, for being patient and persistent with me. Thank you for your generous mercy for my friend.

Prayer for Peace

Just and righteous God, don't give up on us if we don't respond right away. Please call again. We don't want to miss opportunities to share Christ's comfort and peace.

Spiritual Practice: Intercessory Reflection

Sit quietly with your eyes closed as you enter intercessory reflection and prayer. Ask God to bring persons to your mind and heart who need prayer. Be open to images of the persons or spiritual insight into their needs. Listen for signals from their lives and let the depth of God's love for them become powerful and real to you. Write, speak, or think a prayer of blessing and healing for these much-loved disciples and friends. Ask God to help you see ways to affirm and support them when you meet them in daily life.

Peace Covenant

Today, God, I will respond without hesitation to your gentle whisper.

4
Friday
October

Discovery

By Evelyn Spence of Council Bluffs, Iowa, USA

Let us then pursue what makes for peace and for mutual upbuilding.

—Romans 14:19

I tutor new readers in our congregation's program, where I teach kindergarteners. What fun! Many days I witness children involved in discovery.

Recently, a little girl said, "I can't read."

I responded, "Oh yes you can. Just try this book, and you'll see. You'll be surprised at how many words you already know. If you come to a hard one, I'll help you figure it out."

The book had encouraging repetition and colorful pictures that gave clues to the appealing story.

When she finished the 10-page book with just a little help, she looked at me with pride and gleaming eyes.

"This book is fun. Can we read it again?" she asked.

I thank God that I was part of the formation of a young disciple. I thank God that I was blessed to be a blessing.

Curiosity killed the cat?
We'll have none of that!
Curiosity skilled the child
And so the child smiled.
—Lu Mountenay

Prayer for Peace

God of discovery, surprise, and curiosity, may we always search for new understandings of your creation. May we always search for new ways to teach your word and share Christ's peace.

Spiritual Practice: Listening to Children

Sit in your quiet place and center your heart and mind on God's presence. Spend several minutes asking God to bring into your awareness the names and images of children in your life. You may see their faces or hear their voices as you receive these impressions. Listen deeply to the unique gifts and needs of the children who come to mind. Offer a prayer of blessing for each child and the needs you perceive. If you feel led, you also may want to write a note or card and give a message of affirmation and love to each child.

Peace Covenant

Today, God, I will ask "how?" and "why?" I will let my eyes gleam with a new awareness.

5
Saturday
October

Do Not Turn Away

By Andrew Bolton, Council of Twelve Apostles

> *God, the Eternal Creator, weeps for the poor, displaced, mistreated, and diseased of the world because of their unnecessary suffering. Such conditions are not God's will. Open your ears to hear the pleading of mothers and fathers in all nations who desperately seek a future of hope for their children. Do not turn away from them. For in their welfare resides your welfare.*
>
> —Doctrine and Covenants 163:4a

The people of the Philippines are no strangers to devastating typhoons. Yet Typhoon Megi's destruction in October 2010 was overwhelming, crippling the province of Isabela.

The storm damaged three Community of Christ buildings and their surrounding villages: Simimbaan, Damsite, and Tumauini.

Community of Christ staff, members and friends were the first relief workers of any organization to arrive at the typhoon-struck locations. The Mission Initiative of Abolish Poverty, End Suffering provided emergency food, medical supplies, and the services of volunteer nurses.

Your contributions to World Mission Tithes make a difference in times of disaster. Almost 2,000 Typhoon Megi victims, about 334 families, received help to rebuild the Damsite church. Your generosity will ease their burden. Thank you for responding generously.

Prayer for Peace

Creator God, we will weep with you for the displaced and suffering people in the world. May we open our ears and respond. May we support rebuilding lives and restoring hope and peace.

Spiritual Practice: Praying with the Doctrine and Covenants

For this body prayer, we will use simple postures with phrases from Doctrine and Covenants Section 163. Create a bowl with your hands, close your eyes, and meditate with the phrase, "*God the Eternal Creator weeps.*" Imagine your bowl catching God's tears. End this posture by emptying the container over your head and being anointed by God's tears.

Create a large circle with your arms as if hugging someone and meditate with the phrase: "*God yearns to draw you close so that wounds may be healed.*" End by placing your hands over your heart. Now create your own body posture of openness to God and meditate on the phrase: "*Do not turn away from them. For in their welfare resides your welfare.*" Say amen by bowing to God with palms together.

Peace Covenant

Today, God, I will act on the awareness that welfare comes to your people when I share Christ's justice and peace.

6
Sunday
October

Increase Our Faith

By Linda Booth, Council of Twelve Apostles

The apostles said to the Lord, "Increase our faith!" The Lord replied, "If you had faith the size of a mustard seed, you could say to this mulberry tree, 'Be uprooted and planted in the sea,' and it would obey you."

—Luke 17:5–6

Sometimes we think that our faith is too small. However, Jesus told his disciples that even faith as small as a mustard seed can bring amazing results.

I spent five days with the Mayfield Congregation in Kentucky. This band of faithful people puts its faith into action and daily lives Christ's mission. As a result, the members invite many people to Christ, baptizing and confirming them. They become his disciples and go out to have an impact on the lives of others.

During my time there, I met a young father who told me his family's story. His parents made and sold crystal meth—a dangerous and illegal drug. When he was 10, he began to use drugs. When he was 20, he decided to escape his family's influence.

He moved to Mayfield, met a young woman, and their new daughter arrived. His girlfriend knew a little about Jesus, so they began to attend a Bible-based church. They enjoyed going to church as a family until one Sunday the minister pointed to them during his sermon and used them as an example of sin.

This young family left and never returned. They yearned for a community that would love them and teach them about Jesus.

Someone from Community of Christ heard their story and invited them to a church event. The young father said these folks cared about his family. As a result, for the first time he felt he was worthy of God's love. The couple married in the church, became fully engaged with the congregation, and experienced the Blessings of Community. Their 4-year-old daughter said to me, "I love Jesus so very much."

Prayer for Peace

Responsive God, learning of the life of your Son has caused our faith to grow. Worshiping among your loving, accepting community has developed us as disciples who care. May we respond as disciples who share Christ's peace.

Spiritual Practice: Welcoming Unity in Diversity

Meditate on Unity in Diversity. Create a large circle with your arms. See and feel the diverse people God invites inside the sanctuary of Christ's circle of peace.

Who is easiest to welcome? Whom do you struggle to include? Confess the dividing walls between you and people too different or "dangerous" to invite into your spiritual home. Ask God to forgive and heal barriers that keep you and others from being one in Christ's peace.

Peace Covenant

Today, God, I will search for those outside the peace and invite them into the embrace of the community.

7
Monday
October

♫ Hymn of the Month: "The Peace of the Earth"

Introduction by Lauren Hall of Kansas City, Missouri, USA

> *And there came a voice to them, a pleasant voice, as if it were a whisper, saying, "Peace, peace be to you because of your faith in my well beloved, who was from the foundation of the world."*
>
> —Helaman 2:112

"The Peace of the Earth" (*La Paz de la Tierra*)

This beautiful text is a traditional Guatemalan blessing. "The Peace of the Earth" is an affirmation of the peace that is inherent in creation, "falling over us" and unconditionally available to us. The hymn reminds us that this peace is God's peace and, as in creation, grows within us.

This Guatemalan blessing was written down by Christine Carson, a former musician at Iona Abbey and member of the Wild Goose Worship Group. She worked for a year in Guatemala. The text, though, is similar in many ways to words found in the ancient Celtic tradition.

Enjoy the blessing of "The Peace of the Earth."

The Peace of the earth be with you,
the peace of the heavens too;
the peace of the rivers be with you,
the peace of the oceans too.
Deep peace falling over you;
God's peace growing in you.

Prayer for Peace

God of the rivers and oceans, thank you for your peace that falls over us. We praise you for the blessing of peace wherever we find it. As we seek peace and find it, so may we share it with all of creation.

Spiritual Practice

Contemplate this hymn as a poem. Repeat it as a chant several times.

Peace Covenant

Today, God, I will listen for the music of your voice of peace in all of creation.

8
Tuesday
October

Singing…Unafraid

By Peggy Michael of Cantonment, Florida, USA

Rejoice in the Lord, O you righteous. Praise befits the upright. Praise the Lord with the lyre; make melody to him with the harp of ten strings. Sing to him a new song; play skillfully on the strings, with loud shouts. For the word of the Lord is upright, and all his work is done in faithfulness. He loves righteousness and justice; the earth is full of the steadfast love of the Lord.
—Psalm 33:1-5

Trees and marsh grasses framed the serene lake, and a perfect October sky illumined the scene.

I stood, drinking in the beauty and studying the perfect painting of God. As I reflected, I noticed birds darting from a menacing swamp to the lake and back.

They were singing…unafraid. I wondered why *I* was so anxious.

O Lord of grandeur, you have given me a remnant of heaven for my habitation and bid me preside over it. How can I? I do not know the language of the birds, the wind, or the seasons. And who can improve on the beauty of patchwork meadows and the endless waves that break at my feet? I cannot even understand it.

Yet your Spirit rests on me, and I sing… unafraid.

Prayer for Peace

My Creator, my Redeemer, awaken my senses so I may honor the ways you bless me. Melt my heart until I tremble at your holy Presence. You hold the Earth in your hands and bid it be still. Will you calm my frightened heart, make me brave enough to sing? Bid me to live fearlessly, sharing Christ's peace, sharing what matters most.

—Peggy Michael, adapted

Spiritual Practice: Music for Meditation

Identify a form of music for meditation. If hearing music is not an option, choose a song you can sing or play on a musical instrument. Choose music that carries a soulful, spiritual, or healing quality for you. Sit quietly and soak in the melody and resonance. Allow healing waves of sound to pierce body, spirit, and emotions. What do you feel or see as you listen? Does the music have colors? What spiritual message comes? How are you being restored, nurtured, healed, or moved to compassionate response?

Peace Covenant

Today, God, I will sing of your steadfast love.

9
Wednesday
October

Surrender

By Sara Parkin of Midland, Michigan, USA

> *Do not turn away in pride, fear, or guilt from the One who seeks only the best for you and your loved ones. Come before your Eternal Creator with open minds and hearts and discover the blessings of the gospel anew. Be vulnerable to divine grace.*
>
> —Doctrine and Covenants 163:10b

(Part 8 of My Journey with Alzheimer's Disease)

Surrender your will to God. All my life I struggled with these words. To me it meant to give up, follow the leader, don't have a mind of my own, or do it another way.

In 2005 I learned a new word: vulnerable. "Be vulnerable to divine grace." Because of my disease, I was struggling with my body, my brain, my emotions, and my spiritual life, and I did not know what to do. I was led to go on my knees and to say: "God, I can't do this anymore. I will do anything you tell me to do. I surrender. I am vulnerable."

I made a promise to follow the Lord's will for the rest of my life. I don't always want to do what God wants me to do, but if I don't, I mess up. When I do what God wants me to do, it is a blessing.

God lets us use our will freely, and we can make Responsible Choices. I pray every morning, sometimes on my knees, in a chair, or in bed, and I want to end the prayer by saying: "Lord, help me remember your will, not mine."

Sometimes, I forget to pray. Just now I had a nudge to remember that Christ had a choice to walk away or walk to the cross. I don't want to walk away, but at times I choose to do my own will, not God's will, and I feel like I am on my own. But then I know what I did wrong. I pray for forgiveness, and God forgives me. Thank you, Lord!

Prayer for Peace

Eternal Creator, you seek only the best for us. It is ours to take or leave. May we always choose to follow you. May we not walk away from the decision to share the peace of Christ.

Spiritual Practice: Making Responsible Choices

Prayerfully seek God's guidance in your choices. Discernment invites us to orient our lives toward God and God's vision for us and creation. Begin by reviewing the responsibilities and opportunities in the day before you. Take these choices into prayer, asking God for wisdom and insight about what matters most.

Offer yourself to God with the prayer of Teresa of Avila: "God, what do you want of me today?" Sit prayerfully with this question as you review the day again. Be aware of images, thoughts, names, or actions that come to you. Ask for a blessing to live this day responsibly and compassionately in the spirit of Christ.

Peace Covenant

Today, God, I will open my mind and heart to your guidance for Responsible Choices.

10
Thursday
October

I Will Lift up Mine Eyes

By Jimmie Kurtz of Fulton, Mississippi, USA

> *I lift up my eyes to the hills—from where will my help come? My help comes from the Lord, who made heaven and earth. He will not let your foot be moved; he who keeps you will not slumber. He who keeps Israel will neither slumber nor sleep. The Lord is your keeper; the Lord is your shade at your right hand.*
>
> —Psalm 121:1–5

This scripture became real to me as a young man. I had walked to the grocery store two blocks from our home one Saturday morning to get a gallon of milk. I had a terrible headache. Walking home, I looked at the ground in front of me, downcast, with my total attention on my pounding head.

I was about a half block from home when I heard a still, small voice within me say, "Look up." I looked to the sky, focusing on the horizon. I saw one of the most beautiful sights I ever had seen.

The sunlight was bursting through the clouds, creating a brilliant scene, shining over the panoramic view.

I immediately began praising and thanking God for what I beheld as a blessing. I thanked God for all of creation. With my eyes no longer fixed on the ground and my step lighter, I reflected my joy the rest of the way home. When I arrived a few minutes later, to my surprise, my headache was gone.

Where we focus our attention makes a difference. God blesses us when we attend to things that matter. God enlightens us and helps us make Christ's mission our mission.

Prayer for Peace

Creator of sunrises, we lift our eyes to your creation. You lift our spirits and reward us with what we find there. You bless us to continue our journey. May we choose to journey where we can share peace with companion travelers and with those beyond the horizon.

Spiritual Practice: Time with God

Sit quietly and let your breathing become calm and deep. Ask God's Spirit to rest on you. See or sense the Spirit anointing you in the form of light, a dove, wind, color, or other images that might come. Ask to be made aware of God's love. Listen to the ways in which God wants to flow from your heart as living water. Give thanks that your name is "beloved," that our name is Community of Christ.

Peace Covenant

Today, God, I choose to seek what matters most.

11
Friday
October

The Creator's Rhapsody

By John Bonney of Springfield, Oregon, USA

For just as the body is one and has many members, and all the members of the body, though many, are one body, so it is with Christ…If one member suffers, all suffer together with it; if one member is honored, all rejoice together with it. Now you are the body of Christ and individually members of it.

—1 Corinthians 12:12, 26–27

One October day, I was driving into town and had just rounded the corner. Suddenly I saw what God wanted me to see. A stiff breeze was blowing, and the autumn leaves seemed to follow the lyrics and melody of a song as they fell to the ground.

The leaves were small, glowing like gold as they floated earthward. Before my eyes was a blizzard of yellow-orange leaves, dancing through the air on the wings of the wind, heading toward their final resting place.

I became aware of two brief periods of my life journey. I thank God for the early spring and middle autumn. In the spring fling, the flowering trees bloom. It doesn't last long, but it's breathtaking and wonderful in shades of pink, white, yellow, and lavender. And in the fall, suddenly the leaves turn color. I can't improve on the rhapsodies writers have woven about the colors of fall leaves. But I can enjoy the moment when God gives them one last chance to shine with the spectacular colors of their crowning death.

The elderly and the young alike are part of the body of Christ.

I like to think that I bloomed adequately in the springtime of my life. I pray that I have given someone a lift like the wind that inspires blossoms to fly in spring. And I hope to glow, however briefly, like the brightly colored leaves of fall as they move toward their final and eternal sleep while nourishing the Earth.

Prayer for Peace

Creator God, may we dance in every season of our lives. May we inspire one another with our colorful spirits. May we lift someone from darkness by sharing the peace of Jesus Christ.

Spiritual Practice: Honoring the Worth of All Persons

Read Psalm 139:13–18. After each reading sit quietly and let the words sink deeply into your mind, heart, and body. Imagine God watching you grow in your mother's womb. What thoughts and feelings do you have about being "fearfully and wonderfully made" (Psalm 139:14)?

Sense the intimate knowledge and love God has of you and every child. Be aware of the sacred worth of each person. Weep with God over the soul-wounding forces and events that rob people of dignity and worth. How are you invited to notice, protect, heal, and affirm the spiritual identity of all God's beloved people today? Pray for God's compassion.

Peace Covenant

Today, God, I will be aware of my season and rejoice in it.

12
Saturday
October

The Far-flung Places

By Kenny Wilson of Nevada, Missouri, USA

> *There are many lives waiting to hear the redeeming words of the gospel, or to be lifted from hopelessness by the hands of loving servants. But they will be lost to you without the generous response of disciples who share from their own bounty that others may know the joys of the kingdom…The answers you seek are not inherent in the things of this world but in a faith that places its trust in the promises given to all who would follow Jesus Christ…The call to respond is urgent. Look to the needs of your own congregations, but look also beyond your walls to the far-flung places where the church must go. Each disciple needs a spiritual home. You are called to build that home and care for it, but also to share equally in the outreaching ministries of the church. In that way the gospel may be sent to other souls also yearning for a spiritual resting place.*
>
> —Doctrine and Covenants 162:7a–b,d

Mary Ann had a mission: to help children in Nevada, Missouri, make a difference through the World Hunger Fund for those dying of starvation caused by severe drought and famine in Africa.

The plan included a bake sale at a family owned store. Grandparents and grandchildren throughout the congregation baked cookies, brownies, muffins, and cupcakes.

The project, Cookies for Kids, was a success, raising a generous amount of money! The project enabled children and adults in the Nevada Congregation to engage in the Mission Initiative of Abolish Poverty, End Suffering.

Your contributions to this initiative, which includes the World Hunger Fund, enable Community of Christ to respond as a worldwide church to those in need.

Thank you for responding faithfully to a generous God.

Prayer for Peace

Generous God, give us eyes to see past our immediate surroundings to the needs of those across the world. Let our communication technology tell us of conditions in places we cannot go ourselves. May we share with those who are out of sight but not out of mind. May we share Christ's peace.

Spiritual Practice: Abolish Poverty, End Suffering

Read and reflect on John 21:15–17 as a meditation. Let your mind be drawn to places where people have no homes. Think of refugees whose homes were destroyed by war or natural disaster. Be aware of the hungry and homeless, who wander the streets or live in shelters. Let the images fill your mind. Offer a prayer for those who are suffering. Imagine Christ tending those sheep. Think of ways you might end their suffering as part of your mission. Throughout the day, carry in your mind the voice of Christ saying: "Feed my lambs…tend my sheep…feed my sheep."

Peace Covenant

Today, God, I will open my eyes to see the need. I will open my ears to hear the cries.

13
Sunday
October

Get up and Go

By Stassi Cramm, Council of Twelve Apostles

> *Then [Jesus] said to him, "Get up and go on your way; your faith has made you well."*
>
> —Luke 17:19

On our kitchen counter is a pair of hands sculpted from concrete, open to hold birdseed or candy. Next to the hands is a bowl of hand-polished gemstones. When I receive prayer requests or I have prayer concerns of my own, I go to the hands. I place a gemstone in the hands for each prayer I offer as I picture myself placing my prayer concerns in God's hands.

Often I pick a certain color gemstone that reminds me of the person I pray for. Each time the hands start to fill up, I move the gemstones back to the bowl, restarting the cycle.

Recently, as I was moving the gemstones back to the bowl, I realized that almost all of my prayers were intercessory prayers or prayers asking for God's help. I was missing the opportunity to say thanks for God's blessing.

I continue to place my prayer concerns in God's hands, but now I offer thanksgiving prayers for God's blessing as I move the gemstones from the hands back to the bowl. I have found that adding a focused action for thanksgiving prayers in addition to intercessory prayers has deepened my faith.

When Jesus healed the 10 lepers only the Samaritan leper returned to thank Jesus. Jesus sent the Samaritan leper on his way, affirming how the leper's faith had made him well.

My testimony is that when I go beyond asking for God's help by also opening my eyes, seeing God's blessing, and giving thanks, I experience a faith that makes me more whole.

Try it. Open your eyes, look for God's blessing, and give thanks!

Prayer for Peace

Healing God, thank you for hearing our prayers. Thank you for holding us in your holy hands. Thank you for giving us Christ's peace to share.

Spiritual Practice: Open Hands

Stand or sit with your hands extended in front of you. Prayerfully ponder all that you hold in your hands that makes you feel too full, busy, drained, or tight. Spread your hands up and apart to release these burdens, then hold them open and empty them again. Thank God for relationships that fill and feed your spirit. Pray for a generous heart and open hands that reach out to make room for all in the circle of Christ's community.

Peace Covenant

Today, God, when I pray for your healing touch, I will thank you for your comfort.

14
Monday
October

Your Creation Calls to Me

By Darrell Belrose of Calgary, Alberta, Canada

The Lord is a stronghold for the oppressed, a stronghold in times of trouble. And those who know your name put their trust in you, for you, O Lord, have not forsaken those who seek you. Sing praises to the Lord, who dwells in Zion.

—Psalm 9:9–11

The Hills of Peace reunion directors challenged campers to express their thoughts on Doctrine and Covenants 163:7a: "…Scripture has been written and shaped by human authors through experiences of revelation and ongoing inspiration of the Holy Spirit…"

The leaders then asked if we could be sensitive to the Holy Spirit's guidance and write a psalm to the glory of God, telling how we experienced God. One group wrote:

I stand alone, bathed in your love.
I listen—
I hear the trembling leaves
that whisper my name.
I hear the birds sweetly singing
your praises.
The wind caresses my soul;
The waters sparkle with joy at my feet.
Your creation calls to me,
and I am here—
reluctant, yet welcomed,
unworthy, yet loved,
sinful, yet forgiven.
I stand in your presence, O Lord.
I praise your name!

I am eternally grateful for the challenge to be mindful, to live in the present moment and experience a creating and inspirational God!

Prayer for Peace

Hear our prayer, O Lord. Forgive us when we do not respond to your presence. May we always listen for your voice in trembling leaves and answer when your creation calls. We praise your name for Christ's peace, which we may share.

Spiritual Practice: Caring for God's Sacred Creation

Choose a way to notice, give thanks, and care for God's sacred creation. Prayerfully consider one of the following practices or create your own. Walk in nature with a spirit of gratitude while looking and listening for God in all things. Write or pray a psalm of praise for the Earth's beauty or a prayer of healing and blessing for its wounds.

Peace Covenant

Today, God, I will write a psalm, singing my gratitude for creation.

15
Tuesday
October

Bird Hospitality

By Dorene Kilburn of Stratford, Ontario, Canada

> *"'. . . for I was hungry and you gave me food, I was thirsty and you gave me something to drink, I was a stranger and you welcomed me, I was naked and you gave me clothing, I was sick and you took care of me, I was in prison and you visited me.'"*
>
> —Matthew 25:35–36

There is no end to the lessons we can learn from nature. Almost every year Baltimore orioles stop in our backyard. How long they stay depends on what they find.

They like to build their hanging nests in trees with dense clusters of leaves. If they like their surroundings, they will stay. Fruit attracts the birds, and they quickly will pick the pulp from orange halves we set out for them.

We have not always succeeded in keeping orioles around long enough for them to raise young ones and allow us to enjoy their brilliant colors. This year, the moment we saw the first flash of orange feathers, we lost no time halving an orange and setting it out. It wasn't long until they found it. It seems they liked the habitat and food, and this delighted us!

I wonder if I am always as quick to provide inviting surroundings for someone visiting our home for the first time. As our guest shares a meal with us, is a sense of being fed by the Divine experienced, too?

God calls us to community—to a *new vision* of community. God calls us to welcome the stranger and feed the hungry, whether in our homes or our congregations. As we respond to the needs of others in Christ's name, we not only give, but receive.

Prayer for Peace

Welcoming God, may we respond to the needs of others and provide inviting surroundings to make them feel welcome. May our lives be lived in a way that lets your Spirit feel welcome. May we live our lives in a way that shares Christ's peace.

Spiritual Practice: Offering Blessings of Community

Receive and share Blessings of Community. Begin with a prayer of gratitude for the relationships in your life. See and feel connections with family members, spiritual friends, people in your congregation and community, and people and creatures in God's sacred web of life. What blessings flow to you from these circles?

Reflect, pray, or write in your journal about the call to be "Community of Christ." Go deeper each day as you discern what act of blessing you are invited to complete.

Peace Covenant

Today, God, I will break out the good china to welcome a stranger.

16
Wednesday
October

A Note of Appreciation

By Janné Grover of Lee's Summit, Missouri, USA

> *Collectively and individually, you are loved with an everlasting love that delights in each faithful step taken. God yearns to draw you close so that wounds may be healed, emptiness filled, and hope strengthened. Do not turn away in pride, fear, or guilt from the One who seeks only the best for you and your loved ones. Come before your Eternal Creator with open minds and hearts and discover the blessings of the gospel anew. Be vulnerable to divine grace.*
>
> —Doctrine and Covenants 163:10

A young boy received a note in the mail from an adult member of our congregation. The note expressed how much it meant that the boy took time to talk with the adult after church. It also meant a great deal to the boy that the man took time to send him a note.

When I became aware of this, I realized how wonderful it is to have a church family with opportunity for nurturing companionship across all ages and interests.

There is great potential for ministry to all people, regardless of age. We have only begun to realize this. It has nothing to do with a personal call or response to priesthood or even a person's life circumstances.

Some of the best Blessings of Community are taking time to be present in the lives of others, being a loving and welcoming presence, and allowing ourselves to receive hospitality extended by others.

Prayer for Peace

Eternal Creator, we come to you with open minds and hearts, ready to receive your grace presented from unexpected places and across all ages. May we be present for all as we share the peace of Christ.

Spiritual Practice: Growing a Gracious, Generous Heart

Open your heart to God's grace and generosity with a "breath prayer." Let your breathing slow and deepen. Be aware of God's breath moving in and out of your heart. Spend several minutes focusing on breathing in God's generosity. With each breath, silently name one gift for which you are thankful. Let your heart expand to contain God's gracious outpouring. With each breath out, name one gift you want to share from the overflow of your heart.

Peace Covenant

Today, God, I will reflect on a kindness done to me and respond with a call or note of thanks.

17
Thursday
October

Bridge the Gap...Prevent the Gulf

By Donna Boyd of Independence, Missouri, USA

> *"But I say to you that listen, Love your enemies, do good to those who hate you, bless those who curse you, pray for those who abuse you...But love your enemies, do good, and lend, expecting nothing in return. Your reward will be great, and you will be children of the Most High; for he is kind..."*
>
> —Luke 6:27–28, 35

How much heartache could we prevent if we lived in the spirit of reconciliation? Many times we let a chance remark, which strikes us in the wrong way, fester. It becomes coldness amid the warm companionship of the community. Often a healing comment could bridge the gap before it becomes a gulf in the relationship.

We would likely forgive if our companions reassured us they intended no offense.

One of the most precious gifts of the gospel is the love and unity found in the companionship of the community. We each can take our share of responsibility in preserving this precious gift of peace, reconciliation, and healing of the spirit.

The Healing Touch

In anger I cried out,
"I am offended by my enemy."
A quiet voice whispered to me,
"Do not judge them—love them instead."
I then insisted,
"I tried to teach truth but
they refused to listen,
so I went away."
But my Lord pleaded,
"Bring them to me
and I will heal *both* of you."
—Peggy Michael

Prayer for Peace

Great Healer, we would take care with the sensibilities of others. We would forgive as you forgive us. Thank you for that part of Christ's mission, which includes reconciliation and healing of the spirit. Thank you for helping us bridge gaps by sharing the peace of Christ.

Spiritual Practice: Weaving a Life

Hold (or imagine) a piece of patterned cloth. Examine it carefully. Notice the overlapping threads, the mingling of colors to form the design. Write a journal entry or meditate about the threads and patterns of your life. What design do you see? How does the life pattern you weave create justice and wholeness in God's world? What new pattern is God calling you to weave?

Peace Covenant

Today, God, I will mend the small tear, before the garment is destroyed.

18
Friday
October

A New Response

By Karen Moreland of Independence, Missouri, USA

> *These are the things that you shall do: Speak the truth to one another, render in your gates judgments that are true and make for peace…*
>
> —Zechariah 8:16

"You will be a peacemaker." I paused as I reflected on those words from my evangelist blessing. "Me, a peacemaker? Me—the one other children always picked on in grade school? The first one to run and hide when conflict emerges? Me, a peacemaker?" I only knew two ways to cope with conflict: battle it out orally or quickly retreat. I did not *make* peace.

I remember the year I taught a class at reunion (family camp). The lesson was how to deal with a bully who had stolen lunch money.

Again, I paused at my feelings of inadequacy. Cautiously I had the children act out the scene. The message to resolve issues peacefully got across and pleased me. Then a boy raised his hand and said, "You just don't understand what it's like at school. You have to *deck them* first and then demand the money back."

I briefly was speechless and then glibly explained we are to be peacemakers, not fighters. I did not address his frustration or pain.

Several years later, my own son was in middle school and facing bullies. I knew he was home by the sound of a door slamming. He angrily tossed his books around and shoved items off the table, sending them crashing to the floor.

Instead of our usual argument, I responded in a soft voice, "I'm sorry if my work was in your way." I picked the items off the floor and said, "I'll keep them somewhere else."

He stood, mouth agape, and finally stammered, "You weren't supposed to say that!" Then he went quietly to his room. Later, when he was calm, we discussed his frustrations.

Finally, I was a peacemaker! I had learned from the adage, "If you always respond the same way, you will always get the same results." The evangelist was *right on* with his inspired words. Today I work at the Temple reception desk in Independence, Missouri. I greet those who enter to learn ways of peace.

Prayer for Peace

God, teach us the ways of peace. May we be examples of calm to those who are frustrated. May we respond with love when we face a hateful action. May we "listen" for pain and have compassion. In doing this, we share the peace of Christ.

Spiritual Practice: Teacher-learner

The first disciples of Jesus followed to hear his words, to be taught, to learn a new way of living, to practice what they learned in daily life. Prayerfully consider your role as a teacher-learner, disciple-apprentice, a people cultivator in Community of Christ. In your journal, write the names of several persons you discern as teachers or mentors and several you feel called to nurture and encourage in specific ways. Ask God's blessing on you and your congregation as a community of learners.

Peace Covenant

Today, God, I will respond to hate and violence in a new way—Christ's way.

19
Saturday
October

When Did We See You in Argentina?

By Adam Yeargin of Independence, Missouri, USA

> *"And when was it that we saw you a stranger and welcomed you…And when was it that we saw you sick and in prison and we visited you? And the king will answer them, 'Truly I tell you, just as you did it to one of the least of these who are members of my family, you did it to me.'"*
>
> —Matthew 25:38–40

Traveling to another part of the world can be frightening. However, the lifelong friends I found as a World Service Corps volunteer in Argentina recently made my service there a time I will never forget.

Ernesto, Pablo, Mario, Maria, Jose, and Dolores are just a few of my brothers and sisters in Christ who I have come to love as part of my family. The culture of the church in Argentina is open and welcoming, filled with energy and a love unlike anything I have ever experienced.

Brandon, my associate volunteer, and I lived in the church building with Ernesto, the pastor, and his family. We experienced what it is truly like to live in community. Living in the church meant our door was always open to members of the community. Neighborhood children often visited just to share a gentle smile.

Often, we heard their voices at the front door, asking if they could join us for lunch. We never turned them away. Instead, everyone received a warm welcome. We shared companionship and our many blessings.

Your contributions to the Mission Initiative of Experience Congregations in Mission enable volunteers to share the gospel through World Service Corps. Thank you for your generous response.

Prayer for Peace

God, who turns no one away, may we open our arms as you do. May we embrace diversity as your Spirit transforms it to unity. May we look upon strangers and see you and an opportunity to share Christ's peace.

Spiritual Practice: The International Community

Find (or imagine) a globe or map of the world. Look at all the nations and find a country other than your own. Notice the geographic distance between your homeland and theirs. Picture a person living there. Pray for this person. Sense God's love connecting you just as the oceans connect the continents. Thank God for the connection you have with this person and with all of God's people around the globe. Ask a blessing on the church as a community sharing Christ's peace, drawing all into the family of God.

Peace Covenant

Today, God, I will expand my family to include the stranger.

20
Sunday
October

Justice for All

By Barbara Borkowski of Lee's Summit, Missouri, USA

And will not God grant justice to his chosen ones who cry to him day and night? Will he delay long in helping them?

—Luke 18:7

Too often we accept the status quo.˙ We believe life should remain settled and unchallenged so we can remain comfortable with our stereotypes and prejudices.

Throughout the scriptures we find examples of a God who continues to demand justice by shifting and challenging our ideas about power.

God challenged the right of the firstborn son to inherit the larger blessing through Jacob and Esau.

The story of Jonah and his call to Nineveh taught us about a God who loved all people, even those Jonah considered less worthy and sinful.

Our views of a Savior dramatically shifted when Jesus came into the world as a helpless baby born in poverty instead of the conquering prince in charge of a powerful army.

The parable of the unjust judge and the persistent widow uses stereotypes that are old and familiar—the nagging woman without any power and the uncaring man who holds all the power. We traditionally understand this parable as viewed through this familiar cultural lens.

What if the uncaring judge represents *us*, and God is the persistent widow demanding justice? God asks us to readjust our thoughts and helps us see the injustice around us. Prayer is the avenue and source of a connection with God that helps us see with new eyes and hear with new ears. So Jesus asks us, his disciples, to pray unceasingly, day and night.

Prayer for Peace

Is it we, God, who remain unjustly comfortable with our values? Even when we don't want to see it, God, show us the truth. Thank you for parables that point the way to justice. Thank you for pointing the way to share Christ's peace.

Spiritual Practice: Encountering Scripture as Continuing Revelation

Read and pray with Doctrine and Covenants as Continuing Revelation of God's vision for the church and creation. Choose a favorite section or focus on counsel in Sections 156—164. Read a few selected paragraphs slowly three or four times. Pause to pray for deep understanding after each reading.

Pray for the opening of your heart and emotions. Prayerfully ask to hear the phrase or word that speaks to you or touches your life. Stay with this word or phrase. Listen as fully and openly as you can. What sense of divine presence or invitation comes? What is revealed?

Peace Covenant

Today, God, I will allow myself to be uncomfortable and learn anew Christ's peace.

21
Monday
October

Emma's Church

By Lillian Kirby of Blue Springs, Missouri, USA

You who are my disciples must be found continuing in the forefront of those organizations and movements which are recognizing the worth of persons and are committed to bringing the ministry of my Son to bear on their lives.

—Doctrine and Covenants 151:9

At times, we might wonder why we spend time attending Temple School classes, studying the scriptures, and engaging in corporate and personal meditation.

Like the Apostle Paul, challenges test our faith for what is yet to come.

While serving as a chaplain at the Temple in Independence, Missouri, I sat at my desk reading the "Basic Beliefs." The connection between them and the Enduring Principles captured my interest.

Soon I received a phone call from a woman in California who wanted to talk to a chaplain about "Emma's church," a reference to Emma Smith, the wife of the church's founder and the mother of the church's second president.

I was surprised to hear her call Community of Christ "Emma's church." Her way of honestly questioning the history and beliefs of the church challenged me.

God was my partner throughout our conversation. With spiritual guidance, I responded to her questions. I drew from my studies and experiences to try to carry truth to a waiting, seeking soul. After our hour-long discussion, she wanted to know more. I was physically, mentally, and spiritually drained.

Several days later, she asked for a copy of the Doctrine and Covenants. I mailed her a complimentary copy. I also sent her the address and phone number of the nearest congregation to her home.

May God reward her faith journey with insight and peace of mind. May I continue study and prayer to be a ready and willing witness. May I make Christ's mission my mission.

Prayer for Peace

God of wisdom, make us ready and willing witnesses of your love. Prompt us to study and learn the history of our faith, the Enduring Principles, and Mission Initiatives. Equip us for sharing Christ's love and peace.

Spiritual Practice: Invite People to Christ

Read and reflect on Doctrine and Covenants 162:3b and 163:2b. Pray to be aware of people who might be receptive, and therefore blessed, by your sharing of the message of the Living Christ. Imagine being in relationship with them and inviting them to Christ. In preparation, discover your personal testimony of Christ. "Be persistent in your witness and diligent in your mission to the world." Repeat this mantra throughout the day: "Christ's mission, our mission, my mission."

Peace Covenant

Today, God, I will be ready to share the Living Christ with a neighbor or someone far away.

22
Tuesday
October

Make a Difference Day

By Eleanor St. Clair of Oak Harbor, Ohio, USA

"For my yoke is easy, and my burden is light."

—Matthew 11:30

Donnella is the most generous person I know. Because of her concern for others, she is the neighborhood repair/recycle center. Nothing is thrown away if someone can benefit.

She washes and bleaches clothing until it is sparkling white. She collects and delivers furniture to bare homes. She even takes care of the trash from our congregation. Her daughter, Kristine, is at her side in much of this ministry.

Donnella is generous in her encouragement and support as well. Joyous laughter often comes with her exclamation, "Wonderful!" She spends many hours caring for children, without charge.

She helps people find jobs. She is on her knees for those in need of prayer, and she finds pleasure in filling her offering envelope on Saturday night.

Is this a young whirlwind? No, she is a diabetic senior citizen who has bad days with aches, pain, and fatigue. But she spends her healing time planning for tomorrow. Her heart also knows spiritual pain from poor choices of loved ones, but it doesn't affect her joyous response to the community.

Many take part in the Make a Difference Day in October. Donnella makes a difference every day, and her joy is evident. In her way, she busily engages in the Mission Initiative of Abolish Poverty, End Suffering. She inspires the neighborhood to be part of it, too. What an example of doing Christ's mission!

Prayer for Peace

Burden-sharing God, we thank you for the gift of Christ, who lightens our burdens. Thank you for your everyday community disciples, who show they care. Thank you for all those who share the peace of Christ.

Spiritual Practice: Abolish Poverty, End Suffering

Read and reflect on John 21:15–17 as a meditation. Let your mind be drawn to places where people have no homes. Think of refugees whose homes were destroyed by war or natural disaster. Be aware of the hungry and homeless, who wander the streets or live in shelters. Let the images fill your mind. Offer a prayer for those who are suffering. Imagine Christ tending those sheep. Think of ways you might end their suffering as part of your mission. Throughout the day, carry in your mind the voice of Christ saying: "Feed my lambs...tend my sheep...feed my sheep."

Peace Covenant

Today, God, and every day, I will try to make a difference.

23
Wednesday
October

Quiet Overcomes the Noise

By Donald Kirby of Blue Springs, Missouri, USA

He shall judge between the nations, and shall arbitrate for many peoples; they shall beat their swords into plowshares, and their spears into pruning hooks; nation shall not lift up sword against nation, neither shall they learn war any more.

—Isaiah 2:4

The church in England set up Dunfield House as a retreat center in the 1960s. The grounds were large with classroom space, meeting halls, and a dining area that could seat 300 or more. The US Air Force stationed me at a nearby base.

On summer days we often met at Dunfield House in open-air rooms with breezes blowing through. One day during a pouring rain, it was too noisy to hear what was going on in the worship service. The tin roof magnified the sound of the rain. One minister stood and went to the front. As he began to speak, the rain suddenly stopped.

The speaker told us he was inspired to share a special message. During this 30-minute pause in the rain we clearly heard his message. He shared what God had put in his heart.

He spoke about how the United Nations had just sent 5,000 troops to Beirut, Lebanon. The world feared another war. He told us not to worry.

We were to work harder for peace. He assured us the Holy Spirit would be with us always.

The Lord was preparing us to become a community of peace. During this message, it was so still you could hear a baby's breath. The quiet overcame our noisy fears. The Holy Spirit moved and comforted the congregation.

Prayer for Peace

Holy Presence, by all you have revealed to us, we know you continually prepare us to be a community of peace. Hear our prayers for peace. Be glad in what we do for peace. Prompt us to do more. Prompt us to share Christ's peace in places far and near.

Spiritual Practice: Peace Action

Community of Christ is called to ministries of peace, reconciliation, and healing of the spirit. PeacePathways is a church-sponsored website that shares justice and peace ministries, resources, and opportunities. Visit *www.peace-pathways.org* and prayerfully discern one ministry that speaks to you or captures your attention. Offer a prayer of blessing on the peace ministry you have selected. Listen quietly to see if God is calling you for additional responses to this ministry or another ministry of peace, reconciliation, or healing. If you cannot visit the website, offer a prayer of blessing on all peace ministries.

Peace Covenant

Today, God, I will set aside time for quietness amid my noisy fears, and I will take comfort in your peaceful Spirit.

24
Thursday
October

Peaceable Sports

By Lu Mountenay of Independence, Missouri, USA

But the wisdom from above is first pure, then peaceable, gentle, willing to yield, full of mercy and good fruits, without a trace of partiality or hypocrisy.

—James 3:17

One crisp day near the autumn harvest, our extended family and friends gathered for a turkey dinner. We expected about 40 people, so we reserved the dining hall at a campground.

Recovering from a fractured tibia in my right leg, I was "forced" to rest while several others cooked and served the meal (too bad... so sad).

My husband set up a lawn chair for me outside, and I spent this waiting-for-dinner time watching the children play. Soccer was on the agenda for ages 4 to 18—boys and girls, big and small.

No, the 18 children did not divide into separate teams—they were all together. They didn't *choose* players for teams or *leave anyone out*. Everyone cheered and encouraged everyone else. Kicks from older to younger were gentle. Usually fast players ran in slow-motion so little legs could keep up. Goalies "accidentally" allowed younger children the GOOOOOOAL! Usually competitive youth were willing to yield points to build confidence in others. They naturally honored the worth of each person.

This scenario did not sacrifice the fun, but rather increased it by the spirit of sharing. The two oldest boys, Wesley and J'Cole, heads taller than the rest, were right in the mix—coaching and teaching as they played. The rest of the children were excited to have them there.

You see, these two boys are members of the Sporting Kansas City Team Juniors. The professional team calls them up to play occasionally.

Part of this program is doing community service. Wesley and J'Cole did not flaunt their skills. They didn't patronize the younger ones. They didn't play "around" them—they played "with" them. And they had as much fun as the little rookies. It was a heart-warmer on a cool day.

Prayer for Peace

Coach of our lives, may we sometimes set aside our need to win, to share winning moments with others. May we honor the Worth of All Persons by sharing the spotlight and Christ's peace.

Spiritual Practice: Develop Disciples to Serve

Read and reflect on Psalm 42:1–2. As disciples of Jesus Christ, we are called to respond to people and their needs. The call to journey inward can restore us in times of physical or spiritual depletion. Listen prayerfully again to the psalm, "As a deer longs for flowing streams, so my soul longs for you, O God. My soul thirsts for God, for the living God." As you feel restored, thank God for the opportunity to be a responding, serving disciple while you move into the outward journey. Remember this exercise as you drink water throughout the day.

Peace Covenant

Today, God, I will play and share with others without keeping score.

25
Friday
October

There Was a Knock at the Door…

By Robert Glenn of Evansville, Indiana, USA

The Spirit of the One you follow is the spirit of love and peace. That Spirit seeks to abide in the hearts of those who would embrace its call and live its message. The path will not always be easy, the choices will not always be clear, but the cause is sure and the Spirit will bear witness to the truth, and those who live the truth will know the hope and the joy of discipleship in the community of Christ. Amen.

—Doctrine and Covenants 161:7

A new family bought a house three doors from me. I had been looking for someone outside the house so I could stop the car and offer a welcome to the neighborhood. But the weather was cold and snowy for about two months, so no one had been outside.

One night, just after dark, there was a knock at the door. I opened the door and saw a little child and her father. They were my new neighbors, and she was selling Girl Scout cookies. I told her she was the first Girl Scout to knock on my door in four years.

Her father was friendly. In our brief conversation I learned he grew up on a farm in northern Indiana. He said the neighbors depended on one another. His nearest neighbor lived two miles away, and they had to work together to survive. He could tell I was elderly (88 years young), and he said if I ever needed anything, it was his habit to do whatever needed doing. He would like to be a helpful and friendly neighbor.

That's what community is all about. When I think about Community of Christ, I think about people worshiping and working together—all doing their parts to fulfill the mission of Christ, all sharing the peace of Christ with their neighbor.

Our community and our congregation work well together. The younger ones among us see how we depend on one another. They see how the name of the church comes alive.

Prayer for Peace

Welcoming God, we knock at any hour, and you are there. May we experience Christ as the one who embodies your shalom. Help us share Christ's peace with our community.

Spiritual Practice: Offering Blessings of Community

Receive and share Blessings of Community. Begin with a prayer of gratitude for the connections in your life. See and feel connections with family members, spiritual friends, people in your congregation and community, and people and creatures in God's sacred web of life. What blessings flow to you from these circles?

Reflect, pray, or write in your journal about the call to be "Community of Christ." Go deeper each day as you discern what act of blessing you are invited to complete.

Peace Covenant

Today, God, a knock at the door will not disturb me. I will answer expecting new friends.

26
Saturday
October

Enabling Us to Emulate Christ

By Joanne Kramer of Onaway, Michigan, USA

"But who am I, and what is my people, that we should be able to make this freewill offering? For all things come from you, and of your own have we given you.

—1 Chronicles 29:14

The couple entered my office in tears. They had paid their rent on time, but the water company had turned off their water without notice. Their landlord had been taking the rent, which included water, but wasn't paying the water department.

A neighbor called Child Protective Services, which took the couple's two children. The caseworker said they would not return the children until the family had running water.

Barberton Area Community Ministries (BACM) helped this family with emergency shelter so the children could come home, and it provided food for the week.

This is one demonstration of the power of the grants offered under the Mission Initiative of Abolish Poverty, End Suffering. Our ministries first received a World Hunger grant in 2009, and since then we have served thousands of residents. The grant enables BACM not only to feed the most vulnerable among us, but to share the love of Christ with people in need. Thanks to your generous response, we can respond to this Mission Initiative.

Prayer for Peace

Generous God, may we be generous with our many blessings. May we be mindful of the victims of poverty and injustice. May we share with them the peace of Christ.

Spiritual Practice: The Chalice Prayer

The chalice prayer is a form of intercession. Create a cup or chalice with your hands in front of your heart. Open your heart to God's concern for the Earth and human family as you hold them in your chalice. See beauty and suffering as you lift the chalice and release the creation (open hands) to be blessed and healed by God. Form the chalice again and hold persons who have particular needs—friends, loved ones, strangers. Lift them and release them for God's blessing. Place yourself inside the chalice as you confess your deepest needs. Lift and release yourself to God to be a blessing to others. "Thank you and amen."

Peace Covenant

Today, God, I will be mindful of the many blessings I have to share.

27
Sunday
October

Serve Humbly

By John Wight, senior president of seventy

> *..."'God, be merciful to me, a sinner!' I tell you, this man went down to his home justified rather than the other; for all who exalt themselves will be humbled, but all who humble themselves will be exalted."*
>
> —Luke 18:13–14

I had known this man as an apostle and as the presiding evangelist of Community of Christ. People regarded him favorably in these prominent leadership roles. Thus, I was a bit surprised to see brother Everett Graffeo rolling around on a gym floor in a local Boys and Girls Club.

He was laughing and playing with children in the Hawthorne Place Jesus and Me Club.

As I thought more about it, the surprise quickly disappeared into an understanding that Everett, now retired from full-time church service, was exactly where one would expect to find him—serving humbly.

Despite his years of service in church leadership, this gentle, loving servant of Jesus Christ was again living out his understanding of humble service.

This was not a onetime experience. Week after week, I would see Brother Graffeo sitting on that gym floor, sharing the love and peace of Jesus Christ with children who came from difficult family environments. He communicated to them how important they were and how much worth they had—a message different from what they heard at home.

Most weeks he eventually would end up carrying little David from activity to activity because the 6-year-old would fall asleep in his arms. David didn't know that "Mr. Everett" had been a church leader. All he knew was that his friend, a humble servant of the Lord, loved and cared about him.

I am grateful for this living example of humble service. It is a wonderful model for me to emulate in my own efforts to serve humbly.

Prayer for Peace

Tender Shepherd, we thank you for sending Christ to find us when we lose our way. We thank you for models of generous and humble natures that we may understand how to share the peace of Christ.

Spiritual Practice: The Jesus Prayer of Mercy

The Jesus Prayer is an ancient spiritual practice from Orthodox Christianity. It is a way of connecting with the gracious spirit of Christ as we ask to receive his mercy. The prayer comes from the scripture of the blind man calling Jesus to heal him. Silently enter prayer and let your breath become slow and even. Greet God and then take up the prayer phrase: *Lord, Jesus Christ* (as you breathe in)...*have mercy on me* (as you breathe out). Prayerfully repeat these words for several minutes (or 40 times). Breathe the humble presence of Christ into your mind, heart, and body. Be transformed as you receive the humble, peaceful heart of Jesus.

Peace Covenant

Today, God, I will reflect on a disciple whose humble nature I might emulate.

28
Monday
October

Stitched with Loving Hands

By Betty Batzli of Chino Valley, Arizona, USA

> *...uphold the worth and giftedness of all people and...protect the most vulnerable.*
>
> —Doctrine and Covenants 164:6a

We lived on a small farm in the Southwest. We played host to many transient people walking across the country looking for work. They had no permanent homes and carried all they owned, living from one meal to the next. As a young girl, I saw the superficial differences between them and myself, and I assumed they must be different on the inside, as well.

When the bolls of cotton were bursting and ready to harvest, these seasonal workers moved in to pick. Migrant workers stayed as long as there was work. All who were old enough worked in the fields. The younger children came to school for a while but soon moved on. They never felt at home with the local students.

Late in the fall, a new girl came into our class. She wore a faded dress that hung from her skinny shoulders as if draped over a fence post. Her ragged hair hid her face as she looked at the floor, trying to hide.

At noon we saw her go outside, stand uncertainly for a while, and sit alone on a bench. She carefully pulled a crumbling piece of cornbread from her bag. She took small bites as crumbs fell to her lap. We asked her to eat with us, and we found we liked her. We were sorry that she had to wear the same clothes day after day. We wondered whether she owned only one dress.

One day she entered the classroom with a broad smile and a new dress. This dress had puffed sleeves that fit her shoulders and hid their smallness.

We surrounded her at recess, admiring the dress, and she proudly proclaimed that her mother had made it. I told her my mother was making me a dress, too, but she had broken the needle on her sewing machine and couldn't finish it now.

"My mother doesn't have a sewing machine," the little girl shared sheepishly. At first we didn't believe her. We looked closely and saw the dress was hand-stitched. We asked her how long it took. She told us her mother worked on it at night after she came home from picking cotton all day, fixed their supper, and the rest had gone to bed.

That memory revisits me often, and I'm impressed that no matter how different we appear on the surface, we have much in common underneath. Whether wealthy or poor, mothers and fathers love their children. God creates each of us with the potential to love unselfishly. We all are loved and of worth to God.

Prayer for Peace

Loving God, as we are of worth to you, may we find worth in one another.

Spiritual Practice: Honoring the Worth of All Persons

Sense the intimate knowledge and love God has of you and every child. Be aware of the sacred worth of each person. Weep with God over the soul-wounding forces and events that rob people of dignity and worth. How are you invited to affirm the worth of persons?

Peace Covenant

Today, God, I will find ways to protect and affirm the vulnerable.

29
Tuesday
October

Planting Trees... Planting Foundations

By Louita Clothier of Lamoni, Iowa, USA

> *Listen to its teachings and discover anew its principles. Do not yearn for times that are past, but recognize that you have been given a foundation of faithful service, even as you build a foundation for what is yet to be.*
>
> —Doctrine and Covenants 162:2b

Among the many times I feel grateful to my father is when I look at the giant pin oak tree in front of our home.

Besides being a majestic beauty, it shelters squirrels and birds and provides shade for the bench where I sit and gaze on the lake across the street. Dad planted that young tree as a gift for the new house in 1958. How could he have known his daughter would live in that house and draw such pleasure from his generosity a half-century later?

Dad, a chemistry professor at Graceland University, loved growing plants and trees. He was a gifted landscape architect. From 1955 to 1985, Dad gave and planted a high-quality tree in the yard of every new house built in Lamoni. He landscaped three new churches built in Lamoni during those years and every new Community of Christ church building in the mission center. He transformed Graceland's west campus from a cornfield into a park-like sanctuary. At age 80, he designed and helped plant the Old, Old Path Memorial Park at the corner of West Main and State streets.

Lamoni would look different without Dad's artistry, generosity, and willing work.

Lucy, in the "Peanuts" comic strip, said, "The planting of a tree shows faith in the future." Dad chose the best trees—the slowest-growing and longest-lived—knowing he would never see them in their maturity. He was more than a planter of trees; he was a nurturer of the generations to come. He left a foundation for the future—a legacy of lasting beauty.

Prayer for Peace

Creator of seeds, saplings, and trees, help us plant a firm foundation in fertile soil, so we may become well-formed disciples, generously sharing the peace of Christ.

Spiritual Practice: Trees

Watch the trees outside your window for a few moments. Close your eyes and meditate on Alma's words about seeds and trees (see Alma 16:152–173). If you were to plant and grow the Word of God in your heart, what kind of tree might symbolically represent this process? Envision a *seed* as it grows into a tree of life and blessing. Ask God to show you how to begin.

Peace Covenant

Today, God, I will invest in the future with faith.

30
Wednesday
October

From the Diversity Team: Jesus Knows Best

By Nanette Chun-Ming Ward of Ashland, Missouri, USA

> *So he came and proclaimed peace to you who were far off and peace to those who were near; for through him both of us have access in one Spirit to the Father. So then you are no longer strangers and aliens, but you are citizens with the saints and also members of the household of God...*
>
> —Ephesians 2:17–19

As a child living in Hawaii in the 1960s, I watched "Father Knows Best" on television. This classic American family comedy series was about loving parents and their three children.

Kathy, the daughter about my age, always (in my memory) wore a dress, socks, and shoes. She didn't look like me, a girl of Chinese ancestry, and she didn't dress like me. Shorts, shirt, and slippers were my typical island wear.

Most characters on popular shows didn't look like me because they were white, like the "Father Knows Best" family.

One day after watching the show, I wanted to be like Kathy. So, I put on a dress, socks, and Sunday shoes and went outside to play. My mom spotted me in the front yard and immediately called me back in to change. I remember feeling embarrassed.

Years later I recognized my need to mirror Kathy was about cultural identity. I was out of sync with the dominant white culture presented to me on TV, a powerful, influencing medium then and now. I wanted to be different. That, in my young mind, was somehow better. After all, Chinese people on TV then were bucktoothed, spoke broken English, wore drab clothes, and were low-paid workers.

However, trying not to be who I truly was didn't feel right. I was neither Kathy nor the Chinese worker. I was Nanette Chun-Ming, living a great life as a kid in Hawaii with a loving family that looked like me. I had my own identity.

I am grateful that my parents and my church family loved me, and others, in all the beauty of our diversity. They assured me in my early years that Jesus loves all the children of the world, just as the song says.

I also am grateful for the lesson from that childhood experience. The lesson was to be sensitive to those who feel different. It is important not only to affirm their worth and Jesus' love for them, but to recognize and make room for their offerings of love and service.

Prayer for Peace

Loving God, we come as your children, knowing you love us for our diverse characteristics and gifts. Help us use our varied abilities to share the peace of Christ.

Spiritual Practice: Welcoming Unity in Diversity

Meditate on Unity in Diversity. Create a large circle with your arms. See and feel the diverse people God invites inside the sanctuary of Christ's peace represented by this circle. Who is easiest to welcome? Whom do you struggle to include? Confess the dividing walls between you and people too different or "dangerous" to invite into your spiritual home. Ask God to forgive and heal barriers.

Peace Covenant

Today, God, I will be myself, knowing I am loved by you just as I am.

31
Thursday
October

I Am Here

By Ramona Seeley of Leeton, Missouri, USA

I will make a covenant of peace with them; it shall be an everlasting covenant with them; and I will bless them and multiply them, and will set my sanctuary among them for forevermore. My dwelling place shall be with them; and I will be their God, and they shall be my people.

—Ezekiel 37:26–27

His Footsteps

I cannot help but know there is a God.
I have seen the footsteps where he has trod.
They left their mark on valley, hill, and sea,
On hearts and minds and souls—and me.

It was a gloomy day outside and I was feeling despondent. I was 18 and still feeling the loss of my mother, even though she had been gone for six years. Suddenly, the clouds parted, and a beam of light landed directly on my desk. It felt like God was saying to me, "I am here." I immediately penned this poem.

When I think back, I know God has been with me many times when I wasn't aware of the divine presence. I am blessed with joy when I write my experiences. I hope you know God is with you always.

Prayer for Peace

Covenant God, we see evidence of your presence all around. You bless us with your presence. We are indeed your people as we share Christ's peace.

Spiritual Practice: God's Healing Light

Today's intercessory prayer is adapted from the Quaker tradition. Become still and turn your attention to God. Prayerfully identify a person who is in need of healing, blessing, or guidance. Close your eyes and imagine God's presence surrounding the person. See or sense the person being held in God's light. Continue holding the person in the light and release the person into whatever blessing God knows is needed. Words are not necessary. Trust the Spirit to see and penetrate more deeply than human awareness. Thank God and close with "amen."

Peace Covenant

Today, God, I will hold another to your healing light.

1
Friday
November

Led to Prayer

By Jean Webb of Ridgefield, Connecticut, USA

Humble yourselves, and continue in prayer to him; cry to him when you are in your fields, and over all your flocks; cry to him in your houses, and over all your household, morning, midday, and evening...But this is not all: you must pour out your souls in your closets, and your secret places, and in your wilderness.

—Alma 16:219, 221

Like many others, I suffer from age and health issues. I don't feel I can serve God and God's people the way I used to. Often I talk to God about this and wonder how I can serve.

Recently, during our morning prayers, my husband and I felt urged to pray for a young couple in our congregation. We did not know of any special need or problem. We just prayed as we felt led.

We prayed for many days before the couple shared about their problem. The problem was still developing, and we knew then that God had led us to them. They were going to need guidance.

After watching a video sermon by Steve Veazey, Community of Christ president, from the church website, we felt we should share our experience with the young couple.

It affirmed to them that God's love is greater than we can imagine. God's love is always available to us.

This experience reminds me that regardless of age and health, God can use us if we allow it and are open to the divine Spirit.

Prayer for Peace

Listening God, may we always follow the guiding of your Spirit and pray without hesitation. May we always be open to your promptings to share our witness with those who may be waiting for hope. Lead us from the wilderness to where we might find opportunities to share Christ's peace.

Spiritual Practice: Praying for Leadership of the Church

An important spiritual practice for disciples is praying for members of the body of Christ, particularly those who carry leadership responsibilities. Ask God to guide your awareness to persons who lead the community of faith at congregational, mission center, and World Church levels. See or sense these persons and ask for insight into any particular physical, emotional, or spiritual needs they may have. Pray for God's outpouring of grace on each servant leader who comes to mind.

Peace Covenant

Today, God, I will remember that you are available 24 hours a day, seven days a week, 365 days a year to hear our prayers.

2
Saturday
November

Teachers in Zambia

By Sherri Kirkpatrick of Lee's Summit, Missouri, USA

> *Therefore, continue to be strong in faith. To you who hear my voice and know my promises I will reveal myself and give my peace, even in the midst of your uncertainties.*
>
> —Doctrine and Covenants 158:11a

Many good events are happening at the school in Chipulukusu, Zambia!

The enrollment is 291 students. The school capped registrations, knowing it could not handle more children. The staff holds two sessions every day—one in the morning and one in the afternoon.

The way the teachers organize the program impresses me. They give the children an exam at the end of each term. In the past, a 50-percent pass rate allowed the child to progress to the next term. The teachers have determined a 50-percent standard is too low. They plan to raise it to 60 and eventually 70 percent. They created a clear form to track each student's test results.

They weigh and measure all the children for the next term. In reviewing the report I noticed most children had gained 1 or 2 kilograms (2.2 pounds=1 kilogram). Several, however, had lost 3–5 kilograms—a huge drop! The children who had lost weight had been seriously sick. However, they have returned to school and are recovering.

I often hear sad stories. One teacher told me some orphans must stay home from school to work and make money.

Their supervisors tell them they can't have food if they don't work. Those children especially want to come to school because they know they will receive a good lunch.

The World Hunger and Tangible Love funds are great sources for helping to Abolish Poverty, End Suffering.

Prayer for Peace

God, you have revealed your peace in Jesus Christ. We look to him to model our justice and peacemaking efforts. We are thankful for the teachers around the world.

Spiritual Practice: Open Hands

Stand, if possible, with arms outstretched. Imagine God filling your arms with all that you have: family, friends, and possessions. Hold out your arms until they feel tired. Now, bring your arms across your body. Place your hand over your heart and thank God for the abundance that fills your life. Sit for a time aware of that abundance. Then ask God to help you open your heart in gratitude and share freely with others in deepest gratitude.

Peace Covenant

Today, God, I will be aware of those in need. I will focus on how I can respond.

3
Sunday
November

Respond to Grace

By Dave Brown, Presiding Bishopric

> *He [Zacchaeus] was trying to see who Jesus was, but on account of the crowd he could not, because he was short in stature. So he ran ahead and climbed a sycamore tree to see him, because he was going to pass that way.*
>
> —Luke 19:3–4

One of my favorite television shows, "Friday Night Lights," was about a high school football team and its community. An important cast member was the coach. While he obviously had interest in helping his team win games, I liked him because he took more interest in helping the team members develop character and the traits needed to grow into responsible young men.

A recurring phrase he used in pre-game pep talks was, "Clear eyes, full hearts, can't lose." When he said this, he was not predicting the outcome, but encouraging the players in how to approach the game. He was saying that if they played without regard for the scorekeeping and with gratitude for taking part, they would be transformed.

Regardless of the final score, they could not lose if they expressed their gratitude for being able to enjoy playing football and finding ways to share with others.

Because Zacchaeus wanted to see who Jesus was, he put himself in a position to receive God's grace. He then said he intended to give half of his possessions to the poor and repay those whom he had defrauded by four times as much. This giving did not reveal how thankful he was for Jesus' invitation as much as it expressed how thankful he *wanted* to be.

Our giving isn't only to express gratitude for how God has transformed our lives. It is to say to God, "I know my transformation isn't over, and I'm going to put my treasure (money, time, talents) where I *want* my heart to be."

Prayer for Peace

Generous God, we respond to your grace with gratitude. We want so much for Christ's mission to be our mission. We want to share our treasure and Christ's peace.

Spiritual Practice: Growing a Gracious, Generous Heart

Open your heart to God's grace and generosity with a "breath prayer." Let your breathing slow and deepen. Be aware of God's breath moving in and out of your heart. Spend several minutes focusing on breathing in God's generosity. With each breath, silently name one gift for which you are thankful. Let your heart expand to contain God's gracious outpouring of love. With each breath out, name one gift you want to share from the overflow of your heart.

Peace Covenant

Today, God, I will be open to receive your transforming power in my life.

4
Monday
November

From the Diversity Team: Unity in Diverse Communities

By Markie McCoy (Red Feather) of Edmond, Oklahoma, USA

God is calling for a prophetic community to emerge, drawn from the nations of the world, that is characterized by uncommon devotion to the compassion and peace of God revealed in Jesus Christ... Chief among these is the power of community in Christ expressed locally in distinctive fashions while upholding a unity of vision...and mission throughout the world.

—Doctrine and Covenants 163:11a

Through the years, contact with Community of Christ has blessed me. My life is different because of the gospel of Christ and the Christian ministry I received.

I felt loved by my Native American family, but my mother's illnesses sent our lives in a different direction. I was 5 when my mother passed away. Conditions worsened after that.

My father tried to raise my brother, sister, and me with the help of my two older sisters.

An abusive stepmother, Indian boarding school, and separation from my family for many years while in foster homes affected my self-esteem and outlook on life. My father, unable to both work and care for us, finally sought help from Community of Christ families who responded to us with care.

As a child and as an adult, I have developed many fond memories of church members. I recall learning in Sunday school as a teen what we now call the Enduring Principles. Guest ministers also blessed us by sharing many wonderful stories of their experiences in ministry. Kind people from our congregations, youth retreats, and family reunions loved and accepted us.

Because of these contacts, I grew to trust people again, and I grew spiritually closer to God. Since age 16 I have read my scriptures intensively and sought to be of help to others. I feel God has given me a Christ-like heart that loves people beyond color or station in life.

Being on the Community of Christ Diversity Team allows me to pass forward the blessings I have received.

Because of my new direction in life, I have the opportunity as a psychoanalyst–psychotherapist, and most of all as a Christian, to give back to the community and beyond.

Prayer for Peace

Universal God, help us break down the walls that divide us. Help us see beyond skin color to colorful souls within. May we accept and embrace the diversity of your creation. May we respond by sharing Christ's love and peace.

Spiritual Practice: Welcoming Unity in Diversity

Meditate on Unity in Diversity. Create a large circle with your arms. See and feel the diverse people God invites inside the sanctuary of Christ's peace represented by this circle.

Who is easiest to welcome? Whom do you struggle to include? Ask God to forgive and heal barriers that keep us from loving one another.

Peace Covenant

Today, God, I will study the history of another culture.

5
Tuesday
November

Watch Where You Sow, Watch How You Grow

By Donna Boyd of Independence, Missouri, USA

And he told them many things in parables, saying: "Listen! A sower went out to sow. And as he sowed, some seeds fell on the path, and the birds came and ate them up. Other seeds fell on rocky ground, where they did not have much soil, and they sprang up quickly, since they had no depth of soil. But when the sun rose, they were scorched; and since they had no root, they withered away. Other seeds fell among thorns, and the thorns grew up and choked them. Other seeds fell on good soil and brought forth grain, some a hundredfold, some sixty, some thirty. Let anyone with ears listen!"

—Matthew 13:3–9

God has entrusted Community of Christ with "sacred seeds" as expressed in the Mission Initiatives. Some people respond more readily than others. The gospel bears more fruit in some lives than in others.

Until I reread the parable of the sower, I had been casting seeds randomly—in all directions—with little knowledge of the condition of the soil on which they landed. In my eagerness to share the fruits of the Spirit with everyone, I didn't take the time to follow up. I didn't find out what became of my work.

We once lived in a desert community where much work went into preparing the ground for the seed and in keeping the growing crop watered, weeded, and protected.

This has helped me realize my responsibility to those with whom I try to share the gospel.

Experienced planters prepare each heart for the seed and nourish it until it bears fruit. Love gives the stony ground depth—a place where roots can thrive. With gentle hands, they pull out the thorns that otherwise would choke the Word.

These planters help guide disciples to Invite People to Christ.

Prayer for Peace

Creator God, help us grow in our discipleship of invitation. Help us make the necessary preparation so souls can fully receive the gospel. Help us share Christ's love and peace.

Spiritual Practice: Deepening Roots

A tree with superficial roots will wither during drought or be uprooted by severe storms. A tree whose roots go deep is stable and draws from deep waters. Imagine yourself as a tree by a river or stream. Sense your roots extending deep into the earth in search of God's Spirit. Reflect or pray about what you hope to find as your spirit searches for deeper identity in God.

Peace Covenant

Today, God, I will make a plan and prepare the soil to spread the Word.

6

'ednesday
lovember

Sanctuary

By Cindy L. Korf of North Platte, Nebraska, USA

> *"Peace I leave with you; my peace I give to you. I do not give to you as the world gives. Do not let your hearts be troubled, and do not let them be afraid."*
>
> —John 14:27

A colleague was having increasing marital problems. One morning she arrived at work with a suspected broken arm and bruises from beatings. She confided in me and expressed fear of her husband and of returning home. She refused to go to a safe house for battered women, and she refused to stay with me at my house.

"My husband will look there and find me," she reasoned. Instead, she decided to spend the night at the office, though I said her husband would look for her there.

Late in the evening, I felt strongly that my friend was not safe. I knew her husband would find her at the office. I drove there and told her to come with me because I was going to take her to a true safe house, a sanctuary.

It was a place where she could sleep in peace—something she hadn't done for three days. I took her to the church.

At times, we each need a place of peace and safety—a sanctuary. To me, no sanctuary is better than the arms of Jesus.

Prayer for Peace

Compassionate God, we cry out to you for peace and justice for those in need. Help us bring your healing light into their lives. Help them pass from the dark night of the soul into your presence. Help them find their way to your sanctuary.

Spiritual Practice: Healing for Broken Spirits

Begin with quiet prayer. Ask God to help you discern some "sore places" in the body of Christ and in God's creation. Become aware of people who feel separated, wounded, or left out. Reflect on or write a short journal entry of healing words to at least one person who comes to mind. Ask God for words that will touch this person's broken spirit like healing ointment. Keep this person in your heart and prayers today and act on any ideas that come to bring blessing and wholeness.

Peace Covenant

Today, God, I will be a sanctuary for a hurting soul.

7
Thursday
November

How Can I Keep from Singing?

By John Bonney of Springfield, Oregon, USA

Listen to its teachings and discover anew its principles. Do not yearn for times that are past, but recognize that you have been given a foundation of faithful service, even as you build a foundation for what is yet to be.

—Doctrine and Covenants 162:2b

I was a young music student, and music was my life. It was how I could use my gifts and find fulfillment. I loved being able to perform and lead others in music.

Although I played many instruments and conducted musical groups, singing was my primary joy. I felt a deep satisfaction in sharing my voice with others.

I earned a doctorate in music education and vocal performance. Some of my most satisfying and deeply felt moments of singing came within the church. Music and singing were my identity.

When I left the field of professional music I still had my ability to sing! My voice came with me. With passing years my hearing suffered, and it became difficult to hear some consonants. But I still could sing! Then chronic asthma slowly developed. Some medications reduced my voice to a rasping whisper. New medications restored part of my voice. I no longer had much of a lower range, but I still could sing!

I was the speaker one Sunday morning when the theme was "Consecrate Your Blessings." We sang a few hymns as I sat on the rostrum waiting to speak. In singing those hymns, I began coughing and realized I no longer had the strength of voice I had before. I no longer enjoyed singing as I once did. I realized it was over. The blessing I wanted to "consecrate" was gone.

I realize now I still can serve and minister in other ways. I still can listen to music and to others singing. I still can wonder at the sky, the moon, the silhouette of a winter tree, and the sweet vulnerability of a child's face. I still have my wonderful companion of 50 years, good friends, and neighbors.

I look forward to continuing adventures. So yes, I'm thankful to my God. I hope every day allows you to say "thank you for this day."

Prayer for Peace

Creator God, we are thankful for blessings that come and go in our lives. We consecrate them to you. May we use the gifts we have to share the peace of Christ.

Spiritual Practice: Music for Meditation

Identify a form of music for meditation. If hearing music is not an option, choose a song you can sing or play on a musical instrument. Choose music that carries a soulful, spiritual, or healing quality for you. Sit quietly and soak in the melody and resonance. Allow healing waves of sound to pierce body, spirit, and emotions. What spiritual message comes? How are you being restored, nurtured, healed, or moved to compassionate response?

Peace Covenant

As long as I have stewardship of a gift, God, I will use it to share Christ's peace.

8

Friday

November

"Supper and a Sunset"

By Becky Willis Shantz of Lamoni, Iowa, USA

The mission of Jesus Christ is what matters most for the journey ahead.

—Doctrine and Covenants 164:9f

Winter in Florida can be comfortably warm or a little chilly. On my last visit with my family there, the weather turned from beautifully warm to beautifully nippy!

For many years, I have made it my goal to drive the 10 minutes to the beach for a few minutes at least every-other day. If I don't reach that goal, then I wish I had nourished myself with the beauty of the beach more often. I like to time it so I can see the sunsets.

One day we decided to have a chili-to-go picnic on the beach. Better than "dinner and a movie" was "supper and a sunset."

We bundled up in coats and hats. We wrapped Mom's steamy pot of chili in newspaper to keep it warm.

As we filled our plates, the sun set—right on time. It was a feast for the soul. Vibrant colors spread across the clouds near the horizon, lasting well beyond the visual drop of the sun. The blues in the sky turned darker until stars appeared. The canopy of an Australian pine tree framed our moment.

We wondered if many others would head to the beach in such cool weather for a picnic. Yet by choosing to do so, a devotional experience enveloped us as we sat in the crisp, cool air surrounded by God's glorious wonders.

Though often unnoticed, moments like these renew my devotion—when I take time to admire all that is good and pure around me.

May we devote ourselves to Jesus' call to live life anew, to love deeply, to be kind, to bear each other's burdens, to forgive, to affirm one another—to engage in Christ's mission is what matters most.

Prayer for Peace

Revealing God, we see you in sunsets and in one another. May we clearly see Christ's mission so it may become our mission.

Spiritual Practice: Sacredness of Creation

Choose a way to notice, give thanks, and care for God's sacred creation. Prayerfully consider one of the following practices or create your own. Walk in nature with a spirit of gratitude while looking and listening for God in all things. Write or pray a psalm of praise for the Earth's beauty or a prayer of healing and blessing for its wounds.

Learn about and engage in an act of Earth-keeping such as recycling, simple living, or fasting from over-consumption of resources. Notice the diversity of the planet's creatures and be gentle to plants, animals, trees, and people. Fall in love with the vast, intricate wonder of God's creation and give thanks.

Peace Covenant

Today, God, I will choose watching your sunset over watching a movie.

9
Saturday
November

The Snowplow Lesson

By Karin Franklin Peter of Adrian, Missouri, USA

> *...So we, who are many, are one body in Christ, and individually we are members one of another. We have gifts that differ according to the grace given to us: prophecy, in proportion to faith; ministry, in ministering; the teacher, in teaching; the exhorter, in exhortation; the giver, in generosity; the leader, in diligence; the compassionate, in cheerfulness.*
>
> —Romans 12:5–8

Last winter my sister came from the Pacific Coast to visit us in Missouri. One night we had a significant snowfall.

She awoke to the sound of our neighbor and his teenage son plowing our driveway and shoveling our sidewalk. After they completed our yard, they surprised my sister by clearing the sidewalks and driveways of the entire neighborhood. As she watched them shovel and plow, she noted their generosity.

"Your neighbors," she said, "could have cleared their own driveway and yours and then gone home to a warm house. Instead they expanded their giving to those they didn't personally know." She likened this to sharing equally through local and world mission tithes.

"When we give locally we take care of the needs in our own congregation and our local community. When we contribute to worldwide ministries we help ministry to take place in neighborhoods, villages, and cities that are down roads we may never travel."

As I plan my financial giving for next year, I will remember the "snowplow lesson" and generously share my resources in both local and world ministries.

Thank you for your generous response, near and far.

Prayer for Peace

We thank you, God, for our many gifts and abilities. May we use them to glorify you by helping those in our community. May we widen our community by reaching out with our generous response to places of need around the world. May we reach out and share the peace of Christ.

Spiritual Practice: Generosity and Discipleship

Bring a basket or other container to your place of prayer. Meditate on the link between generosity and discipleship. Write a prayer of commitment in which you name specific acts of generosity and sharing to which you feel called. Fold the paper and place the prayer in the offering container. Close by singing a hymn of gratitude or praise as you offer your gift to God.

Peace Covenant

Today, God, I will plan a generous financial response for the coming year.

10
Sunday
November

Bless God's Name Forever

By Dale Luffman, Council of Twelve Apostles

I will extol you, my God and King, and bless your name forever and ever. Every day I will bless you, and praise your name forever and ever. My mouth will speak the praise of the Lord, and all flesh will bless his holy name forever and ever.

—Psalm 145:1–2, 21

The Psalms have always appealed to me. The capacity of these liturgical texts to express the range of human emotions—from lament to praise—has always intrigued me. One topic of the Psalter is the praise of God. Psalm 145 gives exquisite expression to the Psalter's concern to give praise to the character of the God of Israel.

Psalm 145 is unique. In it, speech bursts forth: "I will extol you…I will bless you…I will declare your greatness." What claims my attention is that not only human speech, but all God's works bless, honor, and adore God.

One is ushered into speech, giving voice to an unbroken chain of praise—praise throughout all time and space. Praise, according to this psalm, is to fill the life of the worshiper.

The creation becomes for the worshiper "the theater of God's glory" (John Calvin). The splendor of the sound of praise acknowledges God's majesty and marvelous works, enabling me to "speak the praise of the Lord" (Psalm 145:21), joining others in worship in blessing God's holy name.

This is why gathering for worship with God's people is important.

Language is a powerful thing. Language creates our sense and understanding of the world. It creates our way of seeing and believing, and it is why inclusive language is important!

The language of this psalm speaks of the goodness of God and the power of God in the world. God is God; the One worthy of praise! God's rule, God's reign, cannot be equaled. It takes precedence over all other powers and authorities.

The praise of God, in fact, is a political act. It is a political act that refuses to grant praise or allegiance to lesser rulers. The praise of God reflected in the psalm is intended to acknowledge God's sole, sovereign reign. It is a witness against all forms of idolatry, and it's an affirmation of Israel's God through the voicing of heartfelt praise to the One who alone is worthy of such praise.

Let all gather in worship today and bless God's name forever!

Prayer for Peace

Forever God, we will praise your name. We worship you alone. We honor your presence with our attention. We respond with unbroken gratitude. We lament that we have not always shared Christ's peace. We praise you for your free-flowing grace.

Spiritual Practice: Psalm Writing

The psalms are prayers of honesty and trust. The psalmist trusts God's presence in times of fear and failure, joy and plenty, growth and change. Write a short psalm-prayer expressing to God the truth about your physical, emotional, and spiritual state. What prayer of praise, intercession, or petition flows from you as you consider your life and the life of God's world?

Peace Covenant

Today, God, I will give voice to the praise that resides in my heart.

11
Monday
November

♫ Hymn of the Month: A Favorite Hymn Carried Forward

By Lauren Hall of Kansas City, Missouri, USA

The Spirit of the One you follow is the spirit of love and peace. That Spirit seeks to abide in the hearts of those who would embrace its call and live its message.

—Doctrine and Covenants 161:7

I have always loved the hymn "Touch Me, Lord, with Thy Spirit Eternal" (*Hymns of the Saints* 409).

The sincere longing and constant companionship of the Holy Spirit is timeless. It is personal and invitational.

The Russian melody makes the hymn even more evocative.

At the time I write this, this hymn speaks to me for another reason. I used to have frequent conversations with my friend, Roy Schafer, about two hymns being in the next hymnal. This was one of them. We shared a mutual love for the beautiful melody and text: "stir my soul…take my love…hear my prayer." "Teach me…fill me" and "I shall serve thee with all of my soul."

We discovered we both used this text in our personal spiritual practices. As followers of Jesus, it was our response to the *other* hymn that was also special to us, "Jesus Loves Me."

As Roy would say, "The Good News doesn't get any more complicated than that!"

Touch me, Lord, with thy Spirit eternal;
Stir my soul to respond to thy call.
Take my love, for I offer it freely;
Hear my prayer as I thank thee for all.
Hear my prayer as I thank thee for all.

Teach me, Lord, to walk humbly before thee;
May I hasten thy will to obey.
Make me wise to see clearly thy purpose;
Keep me true to my calling, I pray.
Keep me true to my calling, I pray.

Fill me, Lord, with thine infinite power;
Make me firm, make me pure, make me whole.
With thy Spirit to strengthen and guide me,
I shall serve thee with all of my soul.
I shall serve thee with all of my soul.

—R. Romanov

Prayer for Peace

Hear our prayer, Lord, as we thank thee for all.

Spiritual Practice

Contemplate this hymn as a prayer or poem, or sing it to the tune *Russian Melody.*

Peace Covenant

Today, God, I will allow my soul to be stirred by your Spirit as I seek to respond to what matters most.

12
Tuesday
November

Expect Joy…"The Lord Is Near"

By Dwight Barnhard of Independence, Missouri, USA

> *See, I have inscribed you on the palms of my hands; your walls are continually before me.*
>
> —Isaiah 49:16

Next month we begin our Advent journey in preparation for the coming of the Christ child.

I begin my journey early. I find myself expectant of the week that focuses on *joy*. We set it apart to remind our souls to expect joy in knowing, "The Lord is near."

It is human, at least for me, to get *happiness* and *joy* confused. Happiness is an emotion that depends on life circumstances. Because human conditions magnify the noise of the world, life's events don't always happen the way I would like.

When life doesn't happen according to my plan, discouragement and fear can become the attitude of the day. *Happenings* influence *happiness*—and these temporary conditions can change on a whim.

Joy, on the other hand, is a spiritual constant built on lasting principles. If you have joy, it is ever-present and as close as God's love no matter what life's happenings bring.

God has placed examples of spiritual joy throughout my life. One example was my grandfather, who modeled a spiritual joy amid life's complexity. He taught me the simple parts of my life, like doing chores and fishing. He also taught me to build deep joy based on faith, hope, trust, grace, and love.

Grandpa built his faith on his bedrock belief that God's grace is always as close as the palms of our hands. He found true joy in trusting God's plan for his life.

Developing spiritual joy is a soul-building journey. Knowing God's loving grace and the Spirit of Christ are always with us, we can trust God's plan for our lives. We can "find joy in all things." I'm a little early, but for me Advent starts today. It is every day that is full of joy and expectation.

Prayer for Peace

Holy Parent, we thank you for the gift of your Son. He is the reason for our joy. His was not a temporary life, but life everlasting. He is our Living Water, constant and true. We have joy in our expectation of sharing the joy and peace of Christ.

Spiritual Practice: Joy

Prepare room in your heart for the Christ child. Prepare room in your heart for joy. Think of the many ways you might *experience* joy in the coming Advent season: bells, candles, lights, carols, special food, gift giving, time spent with family and friends, celebrations of the birth of Christ. Reflect on the many ways you can *share* joy in the Advent season: giving to those in need, making a place for everyone at the table, greeting strangers, helping others, being a presence. Continue your own list. Thank God for the joy you experience and the opportunities to share it throughout the year.

Peace Covenant

Today, God, even if unhappiness occurs, I will have faith and expect joy will continue.

13
Wednesday
November

Rest Assured

By Dorene Kilburn of Stratford, Ontario, Canada

> *"For the mountains shall depart and the hills be removed; but my kindness shall not depart from thee, neither shall the covenant of my peace be removed, saith the Lord that hath mercy on thee."*
>
> —3 Nephi 10:18

A very special servant of the Lord passed on recently, a sad loss for those of us who knew him well. We sang Leighton's favorite hymns at his memorial service. They brought back many memories. You see, no one sang hymns like Leighton. With his strong voice, he sang every word with gusto.

Every word held deep meaning for him. Every word was a prayer of thanksgiving to the God who carried him. His whole body showed his enthusiasm.

A few days after attending Leighton's memorial service, on a day that wasn't going well for me, suddenly I "heard" Leighton singing "Great Is Thy Faithfulness." In my mind's eye, I could see the joy he radiated. He exuded God's assurance and grace. Before I realized it, I was smiling spontaneously!

God reminded me of the continual presence of the Divine, even when the road gets bumpy. This wasn't an isolated incident. When I need encouragement, Leighton's singing of that hymn comes to me, assuring me of God's covenant of peace with us. The journey ahead, with my husband's seriously declining health, will not be easy, but I know there is no need to fear because God is with us.

That is an assurance we all can count on!

Prayer for Peace

God of music and harmony, God of words of deep meaning, you bring us peace. May we radiate your assurance of love as we share Christ's peace.

Spiritual Practice: Praying with the Doctrine and Covenants

For this body prayer, we will use simple postures with phrases from Doctrine and Covenants Section 163. Create a bowl with your hands, close your eyes, and meditate with the phrase, "*God the Eternal Creator weeps.*" Imagine your bowl catching God's tears. End this posture by emptying the container over your head and being anointed by God's tears.

Create a large circle with your arms as if hugging someone and meditate with the phrase: "*God yearns to draw you close so that wounds may be healed.*" End by placing your hands over your heart. Now create your own body posture of openness to God and meditate on the phrase: "*Be vulnerable to divine grace.*" Say amen by bowing to God with palms together.

Peace Covenant

Today, God, I will express faith in your covenant of peace.

14
Thursday
November

The Spirit among You

By Don Richardson of Nauvoo, Illinois, USA

> *You are a good and faithful people, but sometimes you fail to see the power that is resident in your own story and fellowship. Look carefully, listen attentively, and sense the Spirit among you.*
>
> —Doctrine and Covenants 162:8a

During the harvest season of thankfulness, the service planner asked me to offer the benediction for the Sunday worship. In preparation, I thought about what I should include in the prayer. I wanted it to express thankful, hopeful, and joyful feelings.

I rehearsed this prayer in my mind several times. When I offered the prayer, it flowed well. Afterward, I thought about the prayer I had prepared in my mind and the prayer I had spoken. I realized I used phrases I usually do not use. I then realized the Holy Spirit was guiding me as I offered that prayer.

In Doctrine and Covenants 162:8a, God promises that when we "look carefully, listen attentively" we will sense the Spirit. May each of us be ready and willing to serve wherever we can. May we keep ourselves open and receptive to the message of the "still small voice."

An old hymn expresses this reflection, "Breathe on me, breath of God." May we let that same Holy Spirit breathe in our lives as we serve our Creator.

Lord, in Christ's name I ask you to help us sense your Holy Spirit leading and guiding us whenever we prepare to serve you. Amen.

Prayer for Peace

Revealing God, help us be open to your guiding Spirit. We trust you, God, to help us express our faithfulness and willingness to serve. May we follow your call to share the peace of Jesus Christ.

Spiritual Practice: Voices of God

What is the voice of God saying to us? Do we hear the whispers of God's longing for shalom; God's dream of beauty and wholeness for all creation? Do we hear the "voice" of God calling to us in faces and eyes, in the sounds of suffering and joy, in scripture and sacred word, in tears and laughter, in silence and noise? Spend a few moments reflecting on when and how God's voice has spoken to you. When did you first feel called to join God in the pursuit of peace and justice? How does that call to shalom continue to come to you through the many "voices" of God?

Peace Covenant

Today, God, I will be quiet and listen for you.

15
Friday
November

Sanctuary in a Messy Room

By Janné Grover of Lee's Summit, Missouri, USA

> *... the Temple calls the entire church to become a sanctuary of Christ's peace, where people from all nations, ethnicities, and life circumstances can be gathered into a spiritual home without dividing walls, as a fulfillment of the vision for which Jesus Christ sacrificed his life.*
>
> —Doctrine and Covenants 163:8c

If each person were to share the first word or image that comes to mind when thinking of sanctuary, the responses would be broad and varied. Maybe you think of home, a place in nature, a safe harbor, a moment of peace, or a feeling of safety.

For me, my home is my sanctuary. It is the place where the people I love the most share my life. It is the place where we feel safe enough to express who we are—the good and the bad.

Home and family are two areas of ministry for which I have a passion. We make our closest connections to God through our connections with one another. We have this wonderful opportunity to nurture and minister to the people who live in our homes as well to those we invite into our homes.

When you think of sanctuary, I'm sure the image of a messy bedroom shared by two young boys is not what comes to mind. Normally it would not be my first thought either. However, several months ago Dillon, our 7-year-old, insisted we meet in the boys' room to have prayer.

In a hectic, take-your-bath time of day, we come together for a few peaceful moments when we take turns in prayer at the end of our day.

In the messiest room of our house, we find sanctuary. Most of the time, I am the one who receives—more than the one who offers—nurturing and ministry. It causes me to remember that in the busyness and messiness of life, I need to take the time to let the Spirit of God breathe in and through me.

I need to pause and *find* sanctuary so I can *be* sanctuary.

Prayer for Peace

We find our sanctuary in you, God, and in your people. We would be sanctuaries for our families, congregations, and communities. May all people find sanctuary and feel welcome within our doors and through our ministries. May we not wait to invite until conditions are perfect. May we serve while we develop as disciples who share the peace of Christ.

Spiritual Practice: Encountering Scripture as Continuing Revelation

Read and pray with Doctrine and Covenants as Continuing Revelation of God's vision for the church and creation. Choose a favorite section or focus on counsel in Sections 156–164. Read a few selected paragraphs slowly three or four times. Pause to pray for deep understanding after each reading.

Pray for the opening of your heart and emotions. Prayerfully ask to hear the phrase or word that touches your life. Stay with this word or phrase. Listen as fully as you can. What sense of divine presence or invitation comes? What is revealed?

Peace Covenant

Today, God, I will Invite People to Christ.

16
Saturday
November

Perfection Not Required

By Brandon Bennett of Verona, Wisconsin, USA

> *Do nothing from selfish ambition or conceit, but in humility regard others as better than yourselves. Let each of you look not to your own interests, but to the interests of others.*
>
> —Philippians 2:3–4

I have to admit, I'm not a perfect person. My greatest fault is that I'm conceited. This creates a barrier for me to grow as a person.

I signed up for World Service Corps because I had a need to gain a deeper knowledge of myself. I wanted to understand a different culture and develop a better connection with God.

I had a need to change.

Through World Service Corps, I now have a home and family in a different country. I understand my deeper calling—to recognize the need of all of God's creation, even the part that is not right in front of me.

My experience with World Service Corps changed my thoughts and actions for the rest of my life.

Your contributions to the Mission Initiative of Develop Disciples to Serve enable volunteers in World Service Corps to share the gospel throughout the international community. Thank you for responding to this Mission Initiative.

Prayer for Peace

Just as we are, God, use us to realize Christ's mission. For Christ's mission is our mission. As we respond and seek to understand our call, may we develop into disciples who serve—disciples who share the peace of Christ.

Spiritual Practice: Weaving a Life

Hold (or imagine) a piece of patterned cloth. Examine it carefully. Notice the overlapping of threads, the mingling of colors to form the design. Write a journal entry or meditate about the threads and patterns of your life. What design do you see? How does the life pattern you are weaving create justice and wholeness in God's world? What new patterns is God calling you to weave?

Peace Covenant

Today, God, I will pray and discern my call. I will make Christ's mission my mission.

17
Sunday
November

Rejoice in God's New Creation

By Dave Schaal of Independence, Missouri, USA

> *For I am about to create new heavens and a new earth; the former things shall not be remembered or come to mind. But be glad and rejoice forever in what I am creating... The wolf and the lamb shall feed together, the lion shall eat straw like the ox... They shall not hurt or destroy on all my holy mountain, says the Lord.*
>
> —Isaiah 65:17–18, 25

It was a difficult month. Unpleasant circumstances that I could not control surrounded me, and the whirlwind of events and the demands of life seemed unrelenting. In times like this, it's easy to lose track of ourselves as we pour our lives into addressing what demands our attention.

So, one morning I decided to drive into the countryside and spend some time in the woods. As I did, I gradually felt my stress decrease. My breathing became deeper, and for the first time in several days I felt as though I was becoming myself again.

It's often been my experience to find renewal through immersing myself in God's natural creation. Whether it's the woods, a stream, my yard, or walking in the city under the night sky, nature restores my soul. If I spend enough time in nature, God mends my spirit, calms my mind, and helps me find my bearings.

It's more than just nature's beauty that does this. In nature, everything is simply "being" what it's intended to be. Trees don't try to be squirrels, and clouds don't compete with the grass.

I think that if we spend enough time immersed in settings where creations simply "are" as they ought to be, it's possible for us to reacquaint ourselves with whom God wants us to be. Nature strips away the facades of life.

I rejoice in God's new creation. This includes what God is creating in us as we make ourselves available to God. Sometimes that availability comes more readily when we surround ourselves by creatures living in peace. Creatures fulfilling their divine intent.

Prayer for Peace

Creator God, may we take time to surround ourselves with your nature and learn of peace in the holy places. May we share what we learn with the world.

Spiritual Practice: All that Lives

Take a walk and find a tree where you can sit. (Or imagine walking and sitting beneath a tree.) Lean against the tree and feel the texture of the bark. Listen to the wind move through the leaves. Sit quietly and sense God's presence flowing through the tree and all creation. Offer a prayer of gratitude for your connection to all that lives. Ask for grace to discern and carry out one small act of justice or healing that creates greater wholeness for the plants, animals, trees, waters, air, and land that are part of the community of creation.

Peace Covenant

Today, God, I will leave my busy life behind, pause in your presence, and know peace.

18
Monday
November

The Mercy of God

By Richard Howard of Independence, Missouri, USA

"No one has greater love than this, to lay down one's life for one's friends (and enemies)."

—John 15:13, adapted

Elsa Brändström-Ulich stood at a window of her father's suite of rooms in the Swedish Embassy in St. Petersburg, Russia, in 1915. Looking down into the snow-covered streets, she saw a long file of bleeding, ragged German prisoners of war, inching toward the railroad terminal under heavy guard.

Filled with pity she realized their future: slavery in Siberia. Bitter, lonely death awaited many of them, who were separated forever from home and friends. These unpleasant thoughts flooded her mind.

She was born into wealth, position, and a life of cultured refinement. But she already had rejected part of what those privileges meant by training as a nurse.

As a child, she had read of the great work of Florence Nightingale during the horrors of the Crimean War. What she saw in that street below affected her deeply.

She snatched up her shawl and plunged into the darkening street. She heard men's groans, curses, and sobs. She felt their sense of fear and hopelessness. She entered *their* valley of the shadow of death, and she made it her *own* all the way to Siberia.

It was in that bleak, snowbound wilderness that she became known as the "Angel of Siberia."

She spent many months binding the wounds of victims of a brutal war. She gave a healing ministry of hope to forgotten men. She never vocalized the name of Christ as Savior, but it was Christ she served, doing his work, laying down her own life in the breach inflicted by warring madness.

Prayer for Peace

May our hands be your hands, God. May our love be your love. Help us see and sense the needs of others and respond with the compassion shown by Jesus in his ministry. Help us respond by sharing the Peace of Christ in deed and word.

Spiritual Practice: Embodying God's Shalom

Find a way to express and embody God's shalom. Begin by prayerfully listening to your longing for peace. Become silent and imagine you can hear the groaning of the Earth's people, nations, and creatures. Prayerfully open yourself to God's yearning for peace and the divine vision of shalom.

What images, feelings, and words come to you? What prayer for peace comes to you from your time of listening? Speak or write this prayer. What act of justice, kindness, healing, or peacemaking does God invite you to consider this day?

Peace Covenant

Today, God, I will be the love of Christ for someone in need.

19
Tuesday
November

The Voice of the Suffering City

By Peggy Michael of Cantonment, Florida, USA

> *But seek the welfare of the city where I have sent you into exile, and pray to the Lord on its behalf, for in its welfare you will find your welfare...For surely I know the plans I have for you, says the Lord, plans for your welfare and not for harm, to give you a future with hope.*
>
> —Jeremiah 29:7,11

I cry for those who have no voice—for children who do not sleep in warmth or cuddle a ragged bear. I yearn to dry the tears of the neglected, forlorn, battered, and lonely.

I want to feed the ones who have no choice of what they eat, or *if* they eat. I long to speak for those who play among the debris of the wealthy.

I will wait beside those who have no one to greet them after school. Yes, Lord, I will speak for those who have no voice. But, what if I fail?

Bid me be silent so I may hear the cries of my neighbors. Make my heart pure so I will not injure or bear false witness against another. Teach me to reason and restore when differences would separate. When I question my purpose, bid me be silent, until I gather courage to speak and act on behalf of the suffering city.

Prayer for Peace

Creator God, I hear, I see, I feel the pain. Now let me speak, respond, and help heal. May I be part of your plans of a future with hope. May I be one who shares the peace of Christ.

Spiritual Practice: Hunger Action

Compassion is a fruit of the spiritual life. When we open a space for God, we become vessels and channels for the flow of God's justice and healing. Enter into quiet prayer and ask God to open your heart to those who are hungry. Of what spiritual and physical hungers do you become aware? What persons or groups come into your mind and heart? What responses are you being invited to make? Pray about and write down the response or action you choose to complete. Is it a phone call, a pantry donation, a check to support the World Hunger Fund or Outreach International, a visit? Move into completing this action as you leave your prayer space.

Peace Covenant

Today, God, I will respond to voices of pain.

20
'ednesday
lovember

Noisy, but Nice, Neighbors

By Louita Clothier of Lamoni, Iowa, USA

"'...you shall love the Lord your God with all your heart, and with all your soul, and with all your mind, and with all your strength.' The second is this, 'You shall love your neighbor as yourself.' There is no other commandment greater than these."

—Mark 12:30–31

We remember well the "ice storm of the century" in southern Iowa. It was soon after my husband, Dick, had major surgery, leaving his left hand and forearm in a thick, white bandage.

The forecast was for freezing rain, but we never expected anything like this.

Soon after midnight, a one-inch coating of ice began collecting on every twig, limb, and electric wire. We awoke in the night to sounds like rifle shots as limbs snapped. The fields became like frozen battlefields as limbs fell, echoing *crack-bang*. A huge limb from our giant oak tree crashed onto our roof over an unused bedroom.

The light of dawn revealed the extent of the strangely beautiful destruction. Glistening limbs hung dangerously from grotesquely disfigured trees. Every foot of our yard became a sparkling fallen jungle.

We were helplessly wondering how we would deal with the frozen chaos with Dick's unusable hand, when a friend knocked at the door. She asked how his surgery went and if it would be OK if they worked on clearing our yard.

"Would it be OK!" we said with gratitude. We stepped outside and saw five men already cutting fallen limbs with chainsaws and dragging them to the curb. Soon, another friend and teenage son showed up to find out if the limb on the roof had done any damage. That was a dangerous task—with his son on the sloping, ice-coated roof, the father carefully removed the trunk piece by piece with his chainsaw.

When the swarm of generous workers had finished, they had piled a wall of ice-covered debris along the entire front curb. Our property looked like a medieval fortress! Then they moved on to help another neighbor. Did you know—angels sometimes carry chainsaws?

Prayer for Peace

God of the storm and quiet snow, we thank you for neighbors to love and to help. We thank you for neighbors with whom we can share Christ's peace.

Spiritual Practice: Offering Blessings of Community

Receive and share Blessings of Community. Begin with a prayer of gratitude for the relationships in your life. See and feel connections with family members, spiritual friends, people in your congregation and community, and people and creatures in God's sacred web of life. What blessings flow to you from these circles? How have you felt the love of the community?

Reflect, pray, or write in your journal about the call to be "Community of Christ." Go deeper each day as you discern what act of blessing you are invited to complete.

Peace Covenant

Today, God, I will gather my tools and love my neighbor by offering help.

21
Thursday
November

These Are My Disciples

By Gary McDonald of Blue Springs, Missouri, USA

> *Let me hear what God the Lord will speak, for he will speak peace to his people, to his faithful, to those who turn to him in their hearts…Faithfulness will spring up from the ground, and righteousness will look down from the sky…Righteousness will go before him, and will make a path for his steps.*
>
> —Psalm 85:8, 11, 13

I am sitting quietly in church when the Holy Spirit becomes visible through the loving actions of those around me.

An elderly gentleman named Dean decides to part with a treasured possession, an antique Boy Scout knife he has owned for over 60 years. He gives it to a young man honored as an Eagle Scout. A grandmother named Wanda shares how her granddaughter likes our church because we think she's beautiful. A priesthood member visits with a frail, elderly woman and gives her a hug.

A man stands to sing a touching song during worship, and it brings tears. Our speaker of the morning apologizes. She is under medication that dries out her mouth. Someone in the congregation provides her with a cup of water. Our granddaughter attends church because it is here she finds love and acceptance.

Our Enduring Principles capture all of these actions. They are voluntary. They come from the hearts of those who turn to God. I am humbled, and my heart is full.

There are times when my critical, cynical nature takes these people to task. Sometimes these moments are private, and other times they are public. Unkindly I have privately criticized them for being "unspiritual." Now I must take my words back and confess I know nothing about them or about what it takes to be a spiritual people. Yet, I am forgiven. God knows Christ's disciples and moves among them.

Prayer for Peace

All-knowing God, we turn our hearts to you. We know your Spirit speaks to us. We see you in the Christ-like actions of the community. We feel humble. Allow us to be disciples who share the peace of Christ.

Spiritual Practice: Develop Disciples to Serve

Read and reflect on Psalm 42:1–2. As disciples of Jesus Christ, we are called to respond to people and their needs. The call to journey inward can restore us in times of physical or spiritual depletion. When you are thirsty, dry, empty, listen again to the psalm, "As a deer longs for flowing streams, so my soul longs for you, O God. My soul thirsts for God, for the living God." As you feel restored, thank God for the opportunity to be a responding, serving disciple while you move into the outward journey. Remember this exercise as you drink water throughout the day.

Peace Covenant

Today, God, I will recognize Christ in peaceful actions.

22
Friday
November

Coming out of Hibernation

By Evelyn Spence of Council Bluffs, Iowa, USA

And the peace of God, which surpasses all understanding, will guard your hearts and your minds in Christ Jesus.

—Philippians 4:7

This cold morning, in an otherwise warm winter, I seek tranquility. I feel compelled by the Spirit to seek a quiet hibernation from the din of my busy world. I go to the scriptures for counsel and spiritual help. I go from one reference to another, searching for a message.

The hostile world presented by the news media affects my usually optimistic outlook on life. I cannot do much about the violence and greed in our world. I often need to escape and seek assurance from the Lord.

As I read encouraging passages of scripture, I regain courage and peace of mind. God reaffirms my need to continue working in the ministries of our congregation, where I find comfort chatting with my friends. Studying with my church school classmates enlightens me. Reaching out to the community blesses me.

I even find satisfaction as I clean the church bathroom. And, I gather more strength in worship.

Learning and doing are blessings for mind and body. I thank the Lord that I still can learn and do things.

I am thankful for my congregation, where I can experience Christ's mission.

Prayer for Peace

God of wisdom, we seek you for assurance that what we do matters for Christ's mission. We can always learn more and share more of the peace of Christ.

Spiritual Practice: Experience Congregations in Mission

Read and reflect on Doctrine and Covenants 164:9a–d. Re-read the sentence, "If you truly would be Community of Christ, then embody and live the concerns and passion of Christ." Make a list of the issues you feel matter most to Christ. Make another list of issues that matter to your congregation. Reflect on the similarities and differences. How can you help align the lists? Throughout the day, as issues arise, ask yourself, "Would this matter to Christ?"

Peace Covenant

Today, God, I will find a place to rise above the clamor and learn from you.

23
Saturday
November

Mittens, and Scarves, and Boots, Oh My!

By David Ettinger and Nick Moore of Council Bluffs, Iowa, USA

> *Do not withhold good from those to whom it is due, when it is in your power to do it. Do not say to your neighbor, "Go, and come again, tomorrow I will give it"—when you have it with you.*
>
> —Proverbs 3:27–28

In the winter of 2011 in Iowa, we had below-freezing temperatures, blizzards, and ice. The Community of Christ thrift store in Council Bluffs, Iowa, became involved in giving new cold-weather clothing to needy, elementary-age schoolchildren. A letter to the thrift store from teacher Nick Moore expressed the overall gratitude of the young recipients.

> I hope that you know the impact you are having on these children. When there may not be as much to celebrate as we would like, services like this matter most. The mother of one of my students came to school the next day and told me how her daughter interrupted their bedtime routine because she would not take off her new boots! They were her "most special and prized possession," and she wanted to sleep in them. She has worn them to school every day since.

Your contributions to the Mission Initiative of Abolish Poverty, End Suffering help provide Tangible Love grants that make mission possible through ministries such as Council Bluffs' thrift store and pantry. Thank you for responding generously and helping to equip the children for winter.

Prayer for Peace

Loving God, we know the smallest among us sometimes can have the greatest needs. Help us nurture them and keep them warm. May we always witness to them that they will be safe in your loving arms. May we be generous and share Christ so the children may be at peace.

Spiritual Practice: Listening to Children

Sit in your quiet place and center your heart and mind on God's presence. Spend several minutes asking God to bring into your awareness the names and images of children in your life. You may see their faces or hear their voices as you receive these impressions. Listen deeply to the unique gifts and needs of the children who come to mind. Offer a prayer of blessing for each child and the needs you perceive. If you feel led, you may want to write a note or card and give a message of affirmation and love to each child.

Peace Covenant

Today, God, I will do something to provide love and warmth to a child.

24
Sunday
November

God's Chosen One

By Jane Gardner, Hymnal Steering Team

> *One of the criminals who were hanged there kept deriding him and saying, "Are you not the Messiah? Save yourself and us!"*
>
> —Luke 23:39

On "Christ the King" Sunday, there is paradox in this scriptural account of Jesus' last hours. Jesus is mocked by the leaders, soldiers, and a criminal being crucified next to him. "Save yourself," they said. But, as we know from this account, he doesn't save himself. Instead, the world is offered peace through his sacrifice. Take time to reflect on this paradox and many others present in Jesus' ministry as voiced in this hymn text, "You, Lord Are Both Lamb and Shepherd," by Sylvia Dunstan.

1. You, Lord, are both Lamb and Shepherd.
You, Lord, are both prince and slave.
You, peacemaker and sword-bringer
of the way you took and gave.
You, the everlasting instant;
You, whom we both scorn and crave.

2. Clothed in light upon the mountain,
stripped of might upon the cross,
shining in eternal glory,
beggar'd by a soldier's toss,
You, the everlasting instant;
You, who are both gift and cost.

3. You, who walk each day beside us,
sit in power at God's side.
You, who preach a way that's narrow,
have a love that reaches wide.
You, the everlasting instant;
You, who are our pilgrim guide.

4. Worthy is our earthly Jesus!
Worthy is our cosmic Christ!
Worthy your defeat and victory.
Worthy still your peace and strife.
You, the everlasting instant;
You, who are our death and life.

—Sylvia G. Dunstan © 1991 GIA

Prayer for Peace

Help us understand, God, the complex nature of Christ. Help us know to serve the servant. Help us share his radical peace.

Spiritual Practice

Reflect on this hymn as a poem, or sing to the PICARDY tune.

25
Monday
November

I Will Be with You

By Sara Parkin of Midland, Michigan, USA

"…And remember, I am with you always, to the end of the age."

—Matthew 28:20

(Part 9 of My Journey with Alzheimer's Disease)

I have been struggling for two to three weeks to write this. I know what I want to do with my words, yet I can't put them where I want them. I have about three different messages in my mind, waiting to deliver to you.

I start on one, and I can't remember the words or where they go. The letters don't look right. I want to scream. I need help. I need focus. I need patience. I need rest. I need God. I know that God is here all the time. I start to think that God does not want me working on this project and wants me to rest.

The word "focus" comes into my mind. I need to sit down and take on one thing at a time. Then I say to myself, "Sara, you have to get the bulletin ready for the service on August 29." The instant I saw the theme, "I Will Be with You," it hit my heart hard, and I went looking for the pastor to claim it. I wanted to preside. Then I started to doubt.

I know there is no bad service. If only one person is blessed by God, it is good.

I had two months to be ready. I read the scriptures, the music, the readings, and all the things that were laid out that week. Then, I took a break and made time to feel it in my soul.

Then it was August; got to get going. About that time I slowly was getting tired, and I was getting upset, angry. Why am I not able to work on my writing? I am not laughing or smiling. Why? Why? Why?

I went back on my knees and again asked, "Why, what is wrong, when will it get better?" I know it will get better. Ah! Your will! O Lord, I am sorry. I have been focusing at the wrong times, not taking rests.

It was OK. Lying on my bed, I took the time to listen to God as I kept my mouth shut. God answered my questions in my prayer: Focus on the next two weeks, and you will be able to preside at the service if you keep focusing. Can I focus? Yes, I can, as long as I walk side by side with God.

Praise God, who was with us at our service on Sunday. "I Will Be with You." What a beautiful day! And the Lord gives us one beautiful day at a time.

Prayer for Peace

Ever-present God, may we always feel you beside us. We have so many questions and frustrations. Give us patience. Give us strength to share Christ's peace.

Spiritual Practice: Spiritual Hunger

Jesus discerned hungers of body and spirit, and he fed those hungers through a physical, verbal, spiritual ministry of presence. In a time of listening prayer ask God to help you discern physical or spiritual hungers of people in your congregation, community, and global family. Invite the Spirit to move you to one hospitable act that "feeds" someone's hunger today.

Peace Covenant

Today, God, I will focus on what matters most.

26
Tuesday
November

God Speaks in the Wee Hours

By Karen Moreland of Independence, Missouri, USA

> *God, the Eternal Creator, weeps for the poor, displaced, mistreated, and diseased of the world because of their unnecessary suffering. Such conditions are not God's will. Open your ears to hear the pleading of mothers and fathers in all nations who desperately seek a future of hope for their children. Do not turn away from them. For in their welfare resides your welfare.*
>
> —Doctrine and Covenants 163:4a

Working the night shift, I would arrive home in the wee hours of the morning. It was hard to unwind. Watching television was one way to relax. One night I watched a documentary about children living in poverty. My heart ached for their plight. I decided to respond to the plea and sponsor a child. I marked my money to be applied "where needed most."

Soon a picture arrived of a young girl in Ethiopia named Tigist. Two years later, my own daughter suddenly passed away, and I decided to sponsor a second child. I kept dreaming about a young infant crying and crying. I felt many emotions when I received the information packet and a picture of a young Ethiopian boy named Dessalegn. This was the child I had known in my dreams.

Shortly after, one of my co-workers had an opportunity to visit Africa with his church group. They were going to Addis Ababa, Ethiopia. I was eager to talk to him when he returned. I asked if my dollars were specifically helping the struggling families and children in Ethiopia. The young man planned to stay three weeks in Africa but returned after one.

He explained that he never had seen such poverty, and food was so scarce he could not cope in those living conditions. I asked, "Is my support needed?" His reply was, "Oh yeah, they need all the help they can get."

I feel blessed that God led me to share my plenty with children in far-off lands so they, too, would find blessings. That was 13 years ago, and I still sponsor both children in Ethiopia. I feel led to continue Christ's mission of compassion.

Prayer for Peace

Open my heart, God, to feel compassion for your suffering children. Open my ears to hear their cries.

Spiritual Practice: Abolish Poverty, End Suffering

Read and reflect on John 21:15–17 as a meditation. Let your mind be drawn to places where people have no homes. Think of refugees whose homes were destroyed by war or natural disaster. Be aware of the hungry and homeless, who wander the streets or live in shelters. Let the images fill your mind. Offer a prayer for those who are suffering. Imagine Christ tending those sheep. Think of ways you might end their suffering as part of your mission. Throughout the day, carry in your mind the voice of Christ saying, "Feed my lambs...tend my sheep...feed my sheep."

Peace Covenant

Today, God, I will respond to Christ's mission of compassion.

27
Wednesday
November

Developing a Disciple to Serve

By Barbara Howard of Independence, Missouri, USA

Do not neglect the smallest among you, for even the least of these are treasures in God's sight. Receive the giftedness and energy of children and youth, listening to understand their questions...Respond to their need to be loved and nurtured as they grow."

—Doctrine and Covenants 161:4a

We are communities in time...Our lives are touched by those who lived centuries ago, and we hope that our lives will mean something to people who won't be alive until centuries from now. It's a great "chain of being."

—Dorothy Day, as quoted in *Dorothy Day* by Robert Coles

Hands were a significant part in the sacramental blessing of our friend, Brian, who is now an adult. Members of his parents' congregation gathered to celebrate his birth, a new life in their community.

As part of the blessing service, each person received a hand, made of felt, on which to write his or her name and a blessing for Brian. The congregation placed the hands on a banner that hung in Brian's room for years.

Those hands represented people who were significant in Brian's development in this faith community. Some held him when he was an infant in the nursery. Others helped him cut out his craft work in church school; others held his hands at campfires during church retreats.

Some people who shared in that early blessing service are no longer living. The community has changed, but the strength of those hands still touches and nurtures Brian's life.

Because Brian was a warm, loving child, his own hands brought ministry to others. One woman in the congregation still tells the story of the time when he was 4 and he sat with her in church. She was grieving over the death of a friend, and he kept rubbing her arm, touching her face, and whispering, "It will be all right."

When our congregations equip us for Christ's mission, we equip our children for Christ's mission. Brian's hands will continue to serve, to love, to heal. He learned from a caring community that helped develop a disciple to serve.

Prayer for Peace

Nurturing God, as we serve and love our children, may they continue to serve and love others. May they, with us, share the peace of Christ.

Spiritual Practice: Hand Ministry

Place your hand on a piece of paper and trace around it. Add details of fingernails, wrinkles, or skin color if desired. Look at your hand and meditate on what you do with your hands each day. Ask God to direct your thoughts to a person in need of blessing, kindness, or healing touch. Pray for wisdom about the specific act needed by this person and discern how and when you will use your hands to complete this ministry.

Peace Covenant

Today, God, I will hold a child with loving arms, and reflect on their future as a disciple.

28
Thursday
November

Revealing Steps

By Lu Mountenay of Independence, Missouri, USA

Collectively and individually, you are loved with an everlasting love that delights in each faithful step taken…

—Doctrine and Covenants 163:10a

Moses stepped down from the mountain
confronted by God's mystery
challenged by God's authority
changed by God's love.
Tablets enfolded in strong arms—
Heavy. Heavy on his heart.
Disappointed by the people…
broken covenant
broken hearts
broken tablets.
Moses stepped back up the mountain
into the Presence.
Brokenness reflected
people atoned
covenant renewed
Mosaic law restored
and God said,
"It is an awesome thing
I will do with you."
And the people were healed.

If we look closely at a piece of mosaic art we might see rough, ragged edges. The artist breaks individual pieces into irregular shapes and sizes—no two exactly alike. They don't fit with perfect and precise margins. We find the pieces varying in color and we might not see how they matter to the big picture. **Step back.**

Now we see. The difference in colors is what it's all about. This light shade brings the figure forward; this dark shade takes it back, creating a shadow, lending depth. The artist groups like-colored shapes together forming an image—perhaps a figure or a landscape. Placing contrasting colors next to each other defines a new shape. The varied surfaces of the tiles, glass, or other pieces help define the artist's theme and give it texture. **Step closer.**

We lose the intended shapes once more. The image disappears. We see chaos again. The artist created this piece with a certain perspective in mind. The various colors, textures, and shapes have a purpose—they *do* matter. **Step back.**

The image comes back into focus. The fragments work together to complete the whole when we don't try to judge each piece's worth. When compelled to judge, we need to step back and pause. Now, reflect on one particular tile, one life.

If we left it out because of its flaws, the creation would not be complete. All Are Called. Diversity unifies us. We are whole.

Prayer for Peace

Creator God, may we always find Unity in Diversity.

Spiritual Practice: Honoring Unity in Diversity

Meditate on Unity in Diversity. Create a large circle with your arms. See and feel the diverse people God invites inside the sanctuary of Christ's peace. Ask God to forgive and heal barriers of unfamiliarity that keep you and others from being one in Christ's peace.

Peace Covenant

Today, God, I will **step back** to get a better perspective on what matters most.

29
Friday
November

Like the Tide

By John Bonney of Springfield, Oregon, USA

> *For everything there is a season, and a time for every matter under heaven: a time to be born, and a time to die; a time to plant, and a time to pluck up what is planted…a time to break down, and a time to build up; a time to weep, and a time to laugh; a time to mourn, and a time to dance; a time to throw away stones, and a time to gather stones together…*
>
> —Ecclesiastes 3:1–5

I love this time of year. November is my favorite month. In the Pacific Northwest, it's cool, damp, and dark—somber, cloudy, and gray. The day darkens early in the afternoon; by 3 o'clock, it is dark enough to put one in the mindset of evening. For me, there's something peaceful about evening. It is a time for rest. It seems the demand to *do* something, anything, is reduced in this cycle of the year.

My wife, Pat, and I conducted a memorial service for a distant relative Sunday afternoon, followed by a meal together. We carried the bulk of the planning and officiating. We met with the family that evening. They cremated his body. A cycle completed.

That day I also introduced myself to a baby. He was about 100 hours old. His mother and grandmother both called him by a nickname already. The baby's grandfather had died a few years before, and his name was the baby's nickname. So it is with memories; we continue the cycle.

Interestingly, here was this newborn baby, just beginning life, still trailing wisps of living in creative Presence. The one we honored at the memorial service had finished the race and moved on. He had passed through the portal of life fewer than 100 hours before. One goes out, and one comes in. And so it goes. Praise God for the awesome cycle.

Prayer for Peace

We pray, God, our sharing will take us past the time for weeping and bring about a time for peace.

Spiritual Practice: Breathing with the Ocean

Sit or lie in a relaxed posture. Pay attention to your breathing. Let the rhythm become calm and even. Imagine sitting or lying on a warm, sandy beach with ocean waves rolling in and out near your feet. Listen to the waves as they "exhale" and "inhale." Begin to breathe in time with the waves. Become aware of the ocean as the presence of God washing onto the shore to touch your body and spirit. With each breath receive what the ocean of God brings you. Let go of what is carried into the sea of God's presence. Offer a prayer of thanksgiving. Ask how you can share God's healing and peace today.

Peace Covenant

Today, God, I will not question your timing. I will look for what matters most under heaven, and I will respond.

30
Saturday
November

A Good Problem

By Maria Glushkovetska and Anatoliy Huralskyy of Kiev, Ukraine

God is calling for a prophetic community to emerge, drawn from the nations of the world, that is characterized by uncommon devotion to the compassion and peace of God revealed in Jesus Christ. Through divine grace and wisdom, this faith community has been given abundant gifts, resources, and opportunities to equip it to become such a people. Chief among these is the power of community in Christ expressed locally in distinctive fashions while upholding a unity of vision, foundational beliefs, and mission throughout the world.

—Doctrine and Covenants 163:11a

The Kiev-Borispol Congregation used to meet in a home. Over the years, as we grew, there was often not enough room for everyone.

What a good problem to have.

Now, thanks to your contributions to the Mission Initiative of Experience Congregations in Mission, we rent an apartment. We have enough room for everyone to come together for worship and youth programs.

Our weekly ministries include Bible study, singing, crafts, and English lessons. Many new people attend our activities. We are very thankful that this is now possible in Kiev, the capital of Ukraine.

We commit ourselves to sharing the good news with as many as we can. Thank you for responding generously so we might continue to grow.

Prayer for Peace

Generous God, go ahead—give our congregations problems. We'd like some over-crowded parking lots, please. We'll have too many people for the chairs in our worship and classes. We'll have too many services and projects to fit in the bulletin, too much giftedness to use in our congregations. Go ahead, God, we can take it. With your help, we'll figure it out. With your help, we'll share Christ's peace from the joy and peace overflowing in our hearts.

Spiritual Practice: Praying for Leadership of the Church

An important spiritual practice for disciples is praying for members of the body of Christ, particularly those who carry leadership responsibilities. Ask God to guide your awareness to persons who lead the community of faith at congregational, mission center, and World Church levels. See or sense these persons and ask for insight into any particular physical, emotional, or spiritual needs they may have. Pray for God's outpouring of grace on each servant leader who comes to mind.

Peace Covenant

Today, God, I will assess my blessings. Because there are so many, if I have time, I will count them all.

1
Sunday
December

Pray for Peace

By Jan Marshall of Independence, Missouri, USA

I was glad when they said to me, "Let us go to the house of the Lord!"... "Peace be within your walls."...For the sake of my relatives and friends I will say "Peace be within you." For the sake of the house of the Lord our God, I will seek your good.

—Psalm122:1, 7–9

The Israelites probably sang a psalm-song as they trekked to Jerusalem for a festival. Their journey began with an invitation, "Let us go..." They would end their journey standing inside Jerusalem's gates.

The Israelites joyfully sang their gratitude after arriving at a place sacred to them. In this place where they peacefully sought their God, they prayed for peace for the city and the people. I understand the powerfully compelling feeling of sanctuary, a place of peace and not fear. That search for inner peace is one reason I joined Community of Christ.

The focus of this first Sunday in the season of Advent, the beginning of the Christian liturgical year, is peace. These four Sundays before Christmas are a time of expectation and preparation to celebrate Jesus' birth. Yet let us not skip too quickly to the end of the story (Jesus' birth). Rather, consider the journey of all God's people toward the peaceable reign of God. It is a time to ask ourselves serious questions.

How does the peace of Jesus Christ impact my life? What am I doing to help others experience this peace? To whom will you extend an invitation "to go to the house of the Lord?" When was the last time you intentionally sought the good of someone else, without thought for yourself? The joy of celebrating Christ's birth is made more real through serious questions about peace.

Someone extended an invitation to me when I was a teenager. Someone "sought my good." I learned that peace does not come easily, especially in family difficulties. The peace that God provides may come to us in a different way than we expect. Yet this scripture compels us to accept the invitation to seek the good of *all.* May your journey through Advent be filled with Christ's peace.

Prayer for Peace

We thank you God, for this time of expectation and for all that happens on our journey to the stable. We celebrate Christ's peace during our time of waiting.

Spiritual Practice: Daily Prayer for Peace

The Daily Prayer for Peace is a spiritual practice that takes place year-round at the Temples in Independence, Missouri, and Kirtland, Ohio, and many Community of Christ congregations throughout the world. Each day we pray for a different country or group. Go to the front of this book to identify the group or country for today. Listen and ask God for images and insights about the people, environment, and needs of this country. Speak or write a prayer of blessing and peace for this part of God's world.

Peace Covenant

Today, God, I will seek the good of another.

2
Monday
December

♫ Advent Carol: "Jesus, Our Brother, Strong and Good"

By Lauren Hall of Kansas City, Missouri, USA

> *And she gave birth to her firstborn son and wrapped him in bands of cloth, and laid him in a manger, because there was no place for them in the inn.*
>
> —Luke 2:7

Also called *The Friendly Beasts*, this 12th-century French carol was most special to me as a child. It filled my mind with wonder and the sounds and smells of the nativity story. It drew me intimately close to the small community of creatures that story says were a part of our Savior's birth.

More than any other song, it shaped my early understanding of the sacredness of all creation. When I read or sing this carol now, it continues to have a distinctive hold on me, as it captures in such a humble way our understanding of generosity and the giftedness of each person. Certainly, my inner child is happy that this "children's" hymn may be included in the next hymnal collection.

Jesus, our brother, strong and good, was humbly born in a stable rude,
and the friendly beasts around him stood, Jesus our brother, strong and good.

"I," said the donkey, shaggy and brown, "I carried his mother uphill and down,
I carried his mother to Bethlehem town; I," said the donkey, shaggy and brown.

"I," said the cow, all white and red, "I gave him my manger for his bed,
I gave him hay to pillow his head; I," said the cow, all white and red.

"I," said the sheep with curly horn, "I gave him my wool for his blanket warm,
he wore my coat on Christmas morn; I," said the sheep with curly horn.

"I," said the dove, from the rafters high, "I cooed him to sleep that he should not cry, we cooed him to sleep, my mate and I; I," said the dove, from the rafters high.

Thus all the beasts, by some good spell, in the stable dark were glad to tell
of the gifts they gave Emmanuel, the gifts they gave Emmanuel.

Prayer for Peace

As we prepare to celebrate the birth of your son, God, we ready our humble gifts. May they be used to carry, to pillow, to warm, and to soothe those in need. As we share our gifts with Emmanuel, may we share his peace with the world.

Spiritual Practice

Contemplate this hymn as a poem. Share it with a child. Use it as a children's pageant in a worship service this Advent season.

Peace Covenant

Today, God I will sing a song of joy as I prepare to receive the Prince of Peace.

3
Tuesday
December

Christmas Blessing

By Julie Conway-Sword of Gainesville, Florida, USA

Are any among you sick? They should call for the elders of the church and have them pray over them, anointing them with oil in the name of the Lord.

—James 5:14

The voices of the carolers floated down the hall to my hospital room, filling my 8-year-old head with wonderful thoughts as I looked forward to Christmas. "*Joy to the world, the Lord is come.*"

I would soon be home for Christmas with my parents and my sisters—or so I wished. "*Let Earth receive its King.*"

It was 1941, and the radio stations in our city of Minneapolis were reporting many cases of spinal meningitis. So when I developed a deep chest cough, and my temperature spiked, my parents immediately hospitalized me.

The doctor did a painful spinal tap while Mother held my hand. Then two elders entered my room—one was Brother Keairnes from our congregation, and the other was Apostle George G. Lewis. "We've come to anoint and pray for you," said Brother Lewis. "*Let every heart prepare him room.*"

Tears filled my eyes as brother Lewis' beautiful, heartfelt prayer echoed in my room. My fears slipped away, my heart rejoiced. The report was negative for meningitis, but positive for pneumonia. In a few days I was well enough to return home for continued healing. I was going home for Christmas! "*And heaven and nature sing.*"

Laying on of hands for the sick is a beautiful sacrament, one we readily can invite as a blessing for all ages. I praise the Lord for marvelous blessings given through humble servants all along our journey of life. "*And heaven, and heaven, and nature sing!*"

Prayer for Peace

Healing God, the expectation of the gift of your son makes us want to sing. Celebration, praise and thanksgiving fill our hearts. Joy shines from faces, and bells call us to worship. If only, if only we could know peace this Advent season.

Spiritual Practice for Advent: Peace

Pause amid this busy season and open yourself to be mindful of the source of your life-giving breath. Reflect on where that breath blows you. Pray it leads you to Pursue Peace on Earth. In this short time of reflection, close your eyes, close out the din of the Christmas crowds, and prepare yourself for the coming of the Messiah. If your mind wanders to the commercial clamor, allow God to pull you back to focus on Christ, the center of Christmas. Expose your soul to God's signature and the writing of the covenant of Christ's peace on your heart.

Peace Covenant

Today, God, I will answer the sigh of *if only,* with a covenant that I will pursue peace.

4
Wednesday
December

Finding Beauty in Inconvenience

By Janné Grover of Lee's Summit, Missouri, USA

> *"And blessed are all the peacemakers, for they shall be called children of God."*
>
> —3 Nephi 5:56

December brings snow to Missouri. When fresh, sparkling snow blankets the landscape, serenity and peacefulness abound. We recognize a gift from God.

Watching children play and enjoy the snow is a treat. It's fun to see a group gather to build a snow fort or snowman, or to gather at a favorite hill for a ride on a sled. These are the moments that draw us together. Then we come inside to warm ourselves with hot chocolate and conversation. In these moments it is easy to thank God for snow.

Snow also can be a huge inconvenience. It can create isolation because of limited travel and be cold and uncomfortable. As it starts to melt, and as we drive on it, snow turns into something messy. Then it's harder to see beauty in snow.

Recently our children enjoyed the "beauty" of an extra week of holiday. Many of us were snowed-in for several days, missing the opportunity to gather for worship. For days, we didn't leave the house.

It was a chance for me to rest from the frantic pace of holiday preparations, to draw apart from regular routine, and to prepare for the Christ child. We enjoyed lazy mornings, reading, and family game time. We welcomed a time of relational healing.

Sometimes it takes a snowstorm to remind us that it is healing to slow down and enjoy one another. We focus on the joy of being together and know the presence of God more fully in ourselves and others. We can't always rely on God's gifts of nature to make renewal and peaceful reconnection possible, but we can make efforts to take time to embrace the Sacredness of Creation…together.

Prayer for Peace

As we gather with our families, God, may we remember those who are alone. May we include them in our companionship and worship. As we prepare for the coming of your son, may we share his peace.

Spiritual Practice for Advent: Peace

Pause amid this busy season and open yourself to be mindful of the source of your life-giving breath. Reflect on where that breath blows you. Pray it leads you to Pursue Peace on Earth. In this short time of reflection, close your eyes, close out the din of the Christmas crowds, and prepare yourself for the coming of the Messiah. If your mind wanders to the commercial clamor, allow God to pull you back to focus on Christ, the center of Christmas.

Peace Covenant

Today, God, I will find someone who is alone and invite them to build a snowman. If we have no snow, we will prepare a meal together.

5
Thursday
December

Ho! Ho! Ho!

By Don Richardson of Nauvoo, Illinois, USA

Lift up your eyes and fix them on the place beyond the horizon to which you are sent. Journey in trust, assured that the great and marvelous work is for this time and for all time.

—Doctrine and Covenants 161:1a

I hung the Christmas banner on our front porch in preparation for the holiday season. It had a seasonal image on it with the words "Ho! Ho! Ho!" across the top. Because Advent is a time of joy, as well as hope, love, and peace—it seemed fitting.

However, as I stepped behind the banner, the words became "oH, oH, oH" from the back. These words, unfortunately, often express how some experience Advent. We feel stress because of the expectations we place on ourselves to meet the secular events of the Christmas season. Gifts for everyone, crowds in the malls, extra expenses of the season, expectations of Christmas dinner, and pressure of work all add worry to our lives.

We instead can focus on the "Ho! Ho! Ho!" happy, joyful part of the season. We celebrate what the birth of Jesus Christ, the Son of God, the Hope of the world means to our individual lives and all of creation.

Keeping our eyes fixed on Christ not only lessens the stress of the season, it allows us to experience the joy, hope, love, and peace that Jesus Christ brings to our lives. Let's make it a "Ho-pe! Ho-pe! Ho-pe!" season.

Prayer for Peace

Bringer of Emmanuel, set us free from shallow tradition so we may our honor our covenant tradition with you. Let our minds journey to the manger and share Christ's peace.

Spiritual Practice for Advent: Peace

Pause amid this busy season and open yourself to be mindful of the source of your life-giving breath. Reflect on where that breath blows you. Pray it leads you to Pursue Peace on Earth. In this short time of reflection, close your eyes, close out the din of the Christmas crowds, and prepare yourself for the coming of the Messiah. If your mind wanders to the commercial clamor, allow God to pull you back to focus on Christ, the center of Christmas. Expose your soul to God's signature and the writing of the covenant of Christ's peace on your heart.

Peace Covenant

Today, God, I will place Christ at the center of my celebration.

6
Friday
December

Reinventing Advent

By Carol Norris Vincent of Independence, Missouri, USA

Therefore my people shall know my name; therefore in that day they shall know that it is I who speak; here am I.

—Isaiah 52:6

My husband died a week before Christmas. This changed forever the way I observe the holy day. As we approached Advent season in 2004, we knew my husband's death would come soon. His acceptance of his illness and eventual death witnessed deeply to many as he waited expectantly for his new life in God's presence.

The Advent season celebrates the joy of Christ's birth. In that one season, I was anticipating both birth and re-birth—of my Lord and of my husband. I now look at Christmas differently.

The days following my husband's death were surprisingly peaceful, yet the traditional celebration activities of Christmas changed. I felt a different kind of joy. Because I was not yet ready to mingle with friends at my large Methodist church—and receive all the hugs and murmurs of sympathy—I went to a service at another church. The quiet, peace, and reflection I found there calmed my soul.

I limited Christmas decorations at home to a small crèche. We omitted gift giving. Everyone respected this change in my life.

I have celebrated in this quiet, reflective way since. My family and friends know I was changed in that Advent season, and I feel I am a better person for it. My joy in the gift of God's son to us is more complete, more focused, more serene. I know God speaks—here am I!

Prayer for Peace

Generous God, may we feel your presence as we prepare the way. May we share the peace, hope, love, and joy of Jesus Christ.

Spiritual Practice for Advent: Peace

Pause amid this busy season and open yourself to be mindful of the source of your life-giving breath. Reflect on where that breath blows you. Pray it leads you to Pursue Peace on Earth. In this short time of reflection, close your eyes, close out the din of the Christmas crowds, and prepare yourself for the coming of the Messiah. If your mind wanders to the commercial clamor, allow God to pull you back to focus on Christ, the center of Christmas. Expose your soul to God's signature and the writing of the covenant of Christ's peace on your heart.

Peace Covenant

This year, God, I will change the way I celebrate Advent to ensure Christ is at the center.

7
Saturday
December

God Is the Potter, We Are the Clay

By Laurel Eisler of Blue Springs, Missouri, USA

> *Yet, O Lord, you are our Father; we are the clay, and you are our potter; we are all the work of your hand.*
>
> —Isaiah 64:8

I can sum up my World Service Corps experience in Peru in a six-word sentence: "Yes, I would go back again!"

My time there made me think about how God is the potter and we are the clay. On Tuesdays and Fridays, we led Bible study for adults in the Monte Sión Congregation. Saturdays included teaching classes for children and young adults, followed by a short worship service. We traveled to the Filadelfia Congregation for services on Sundays. Our last day in Monte Sión included a clothing-donation project for the community. It was a significant and joyous day.

Adjusting to life after World Service Corps has been a challenge. I live differently now. The people, places, and new experiences I encountered in Peru had a deep impact on me. I feel I have discovered traits that I never would have known if not for the amazing opportunity World Service Corps offers.

Your contributions to the Mission Initiative of Develop Disciples to Serve enable volunteers in World Service Corps to share the gospel throughout the worldwide community. Thank you for responding to this Mission Initiative so generously.

Prayer for Peace

God who shapes us, form us into disciples who serve. Mold us into faithful servants who share Christ's peace.

Spiritual Practice for Advent: Peace

Pause amid this busy season and open yourself to be mindful of the source of your life-giving breath. Reflect on where that breath blows you. Pray it leads you to Pursue Peace on Earth. In this short time of reflection, close your eyes, close out the din of the Christmas crowds, and prepare yourself for the coming of the Messiah. If your mind wanders to the commercial clamor, allow God to pull you back to focus on Christ, the center of Christmas. Expose your soul to God's signature and the writing of the covenant of Christ's peace on your heart.

Peace Covenant

Today, God, I will support development of young disciples working in the world community.

Prepare the Way

By Charmaine Chvala-Smith of Independence, Missouri, USA

In those days John the Baptist appeared in the wilderness of Judea, proclaiming, "Repent, for the kingdom of heaven has come near."

—Matthew 3:1

Today, many people seem allergic to the word, "repent."

Perhaps it's been abused and yelled at us from the television or pulpit. Perhaps we think ourselves perfect with no need to repent. Perhaps we don't like the idea of a creator to whom we are responsible. Or perhaps we just want to ignore the fact we are imperfect, greedy, or mean-spirited.

Whatever the reason, it's a shame so many resist the word and what it offers, because the word "repent" is an invitation. It means to *turn* or *turn back to*.

John is saying, "Look! Turn around, don't miss it. The kingdom is about to come near. You'll need to turn from other preoccupations and *life as usual* to see or experience the one who will "baptize you with the Holy Spirit and fire."

For John the kingdom of heaven, God's reign, is synonymous with Jesus, and they are about to make an entrance.

So why is this *turning* needed today—by us? We already know the story of Jesus. Isn't that enough? I think John would ask us, "Where is your life focused? Is it on what God's loving presence is doing near you? Is it on practicing the radical acceptance and love that Christ taught? If not, then I invite you to turn. Turn from the things that would consume you and...Look! There is another way to live life that brings you near God's presence!"

John's role was to prepare people to see what was happening among them—to give a message of hope. That is also the purpose of Advent. We are invited to a time of honest self-reflection; a time when we turn from our over-full lives and create a manger-sized space where we will let God's reign of hope come near. Prepare yourselves...prepare the way!

Prayer for Peace

We accept your invitation, God, to turn toward your peaceable reign. As we turn from our crowded place and make room for Jesus, we have hope. May we share that hope and Christ's peace with the waiting world.

Spiritual Practice: Hope

Close your mind to troubling thoughts from the past by placing them in God's generous hands and letting them go. Let God speak to your fearful heart. Think of your hope for the future—open windows in your mind through which you can see compassionate actions. Reflect on the approaching hope of the Christ child. What is your part in the reason for that hope? Rejoice in the Hope of the world.

Peace Covenant

Today, God, I will create a manger-sized space in my life.

9
Monday
December

We Are Innkeepers

By Dorene Kilburn of Stratford, Ontario, Canada

> *"And you will not have a mind to injure one another, but to live peaceably, and to render to every man according to that which is his due."*
>
> —Mosiah 2:24

It's the time of year when colored lights begin to adorn houses and front lawns. Amid the Christmas shopping frenzy, we hear carols. The Advent season is upon us, and churches all over our city are leading worshipers to Bethlehem to celebrate Christ's birth.

A congregation here displayed more than 300 nativity scenes. The leaders set the display on long planks that stretched across the pews from the front to the back of the sanctuary. This allowed observers to walk up and down the aisles to view these wonderful creations.

Some were made of wood, others clay. All drew us to the baby in the manger, whose coming as Messiah was prophesied.

That's a very comforting thought. However, I recently read a short comment that challenged my thinking. It said, "Each of us is an innkeeper who decides if there is room in the inn for Jesus."

Suddenly I wasn't just a passive observer. This was about me and my commitment. I ask myself, "Have I rendered to Jesus that room in my life, which is his due?"

As I think back over the years, there have been times when I haven't had room for Jesus. Regrettably, I can't change that, but I hope these words continue to remind me that real joy and fulfillment come only when I make room for Jesus.

Prayer for Peace

Creator God, help us blur from our eyes the sparkling garland and let them instead reflect the light of Christ. Raise our hearing above the clamor of commerce, and let us listen to the bells of freedom and justice. Let us make room in our lives for Christ and sharing his peace.

Spiritual Practice for Advent: Hope

Close your mind to troubling thoughts from the past by placing them in God's generous hands and letting them go. Let God speak to your fearful heart. Think of your hope for the future—open windows in your mind through which you can see compassionate actions. Reflect on the approaching hope of the Christ child. What is your part in the reason for that hope? Rejoice in the Hope of the world.

Peace Covenant

Today, God, I will not count shopping days until December 25; I will count preparation days for the coming of the Christ Child.

10
Tuesday
December

The Boss

By Lu Mountenay of Independence, Missouri, USA

The eyes of the Lord are on the righteous, and his ears are open to their cry... When the righteous cry for help, the Lord hears, and rescues them from all their troubles. The Lord is near to the brokenhearted, and saves the crushed in spirit.

—Psalm 34:15, 17–18

Pam was the middle sister of the five of us girls. She was not only in the middle age-wise, she was our center. She was the center of our sister-family structure.

All five of us went on a trip. While in the car, I told my sisters I had read somewhere that most siblings had a leader, or a boss, among them. When I said "boss" all four of us said, "Pam!" She indignantly said, with the map on her lap, "I am not the boss! Turn left at the next corner." We burst out laughing, even Pam.

We always asked her advice. And she gave it! She's the one who dragged us to church as kids. She's the one who wouldn't let me swing my legs while sitting in the pew. I asked her how she would like it if her legs couldn't reach the ground. I'd give anything to hear her call me "shorty" one more time.

Pam was there when we struggled through the death of our mom—she was our rock. She was the keystone of our family structure. When we lost Pam, our hearts broke. Each one of us is strong, but we had been stronger together. We will rebuild, but we'll never be the same. We are different because Pam was part of our lives. We miss her today on the anniversary of her death.

Christ is the center of my community structure. He is the keystone. Without him, I would be different. He is my rock, my compass. He carries the map. He is the reason I can laugh.

Prayer for Peace

Sometimes we feel unworthy, God, for your eyes to be on us. And yet you do not even question our worth. You hear our faintest cry. You are near when our spirits are crushed. Thank you for sisters and brothers and Community of Christ, who are instruments for sharing Christ's comfort and peace.

Spiritual Practice for Advent: Hope

Close your mind to troubling thoughts from the past by placing them in God's generous hands and letting them go. Let God speak to your fearful heart. Think of your hope for the future—open windows in your mind through which you can see compassionate actions. Reflect on the approaching hope of the Christ child. What is your part in the reason for that hope? Rejoice in the Hope of the world.

Peace Covenant

Today, God, I will invite people to Christ, who is our center.

11
Wednesday
December

Waiting for the Visitors

By Evelyn Richardson of Nauvoo, Illinois, USA

> *Do not be defined by the things that separate you but by the things that unite you in Jesus Christ.*
>
> —Doctrine and Covenants 162:5a

It is the day of the Christmas Walk in old Nauvoo. At the Joseph Smith Historic Site, we are ready and waiting.

The Christmas tree brightens the foyer, and Christmas carols play softly in the background. My husband and I wait for our first visitors.

Who will they be—a family on vacation, travelers wanting directions, or those with little children needing a restroom break? Maybe they will be folks who saw our sign and wanted more information.

Some may be well versed in Restoration history. Others might ask searching questions such as, "Who was Joseph Smith Jr.? Why did the Mormons settle in this area? What happened here? What are your Basic Beliefs?"

The questioners might catch us off guard—like the gentleman who asked me to briefly tell him the differences between Community of Christ and other denominations.

My mind quickly went to Section 162:5a of the Doctrine and Covenants where it says "Do not be defined by the things that separate you but by the things that unite you in Jesus Christ."

I responded that it was a matter of interpretation on many things, but Christian faith communities believe in Jesus Christ; he is our foundation, our cornerstone. We discussed several other doctrinal topics, but Jesus Christ *is* the factor we have in common. In our faith, we proclaim his message—a message of joy, hope, love, and peace.

Yes, many come "seeking." Some knock on the door, some call on the phone or send a card or letter. What will be our response? What will we tell them matters most to us?

Oh, a blue car just drove into the Visitors Center parking lot. Who will it be? Let all be ready, Lord. It's a lone gentleman. He immediately asks for a tour.

Our day begins…

Prayer for Peace

Living Presence, give us faith in our identity, so we may fulfill Christ's mission—our mission. May we know the peace of Christ so we may share with others.

Spiritual Practice for Advent: Hope

Close your mind to troubling thoughts from the past by placing them in God's generous hands and letting them go. Let God speak to your fearful heart. Think of your hope for the future—open windows in your mind through which you can see compassionate actions. Reflect on the approaching hope of the Christ child. What is your part in the reason for that hope? Rejoice in the Hope of the world.

Peace Covenant

Today, God, I will be ready for the next visitor who comes seeking.

12
Thursday
December

Trust and Hope

By Becky Willis Shantz of Lamoni, Iowa, USA

Those of steadfast mind you keep in peace—in peace because they trust in you.

—Isaiah 26:3

Though I had planned carefully to miss the storm, the Kentucky highway was treacherous with snow and ice. The few others on the road and I drove slowly. After battling icy ruts on the interstate during the night, I finally decided to get some rest. I would wait and try the road again in daylight.

We passed many cars stuck on the side of the road. Some had passengers waiting for help. My heart was heavy with the pain of my own family problems.

As dawn broke, I resumed my drive. Daylight brought many drivers out, and traffic was stopped because of accidents. Not far away was a familiar family restaurant. I looked forward to a hot breakfast in front of the fireplace.

As I walked in, I noticed a woman in the gift shop. During my meal, I looked across the room and again saw her sitting only a few tables away. As I stood in line after my meal to pay the cashier, the same woman came up behind me. Just before my turn to pay, she asked, "Are you going to Nashville?"

I turned to her. "I'm going through there, but I'm headed to Florida to be with my family for Christmas." She suggested I take an alternate route, parallel to the interstate highway, and gave me directions.

"It will also be covered with snow, but at least you will be moving." I was skeptical to leave my known route but decided to try this alternative rather than sit on the interstate highway indefinitely.

She was right. Snow still covered most of the route. But I was moving! And the scenery was awesome! As the sun shone in a bright blue sky, it revealed the after-effects of the storm—sparkling ice covered trees and bushes. After about two hours, I joined the interstate highway at Nashville, and the road was clear from there.

That woman was an angel for me. Out of nowhere she had come and directed me to a path of great beauty and blessing. I trusted her. I trusted God. I felt the assurance that God was with me. I felt full to overflowing with strength, hope, and gratitude.

Prayer for Peace

Thank you, God, for sending helpers, comforters, and guides. May we guide others as we share Christ's peace.

Spiritual Practice for Advent: Hope

Close your mind to troubling thoughts from the past by placing them in God's generous hands and letting them go. Let God speak to your fearful heart. Think of your hope for the future—open windows in your mind through which you can see compassionate actions. Reflect on the approaching hope of the Christ child. What is your part in the reason for that hope? Rejoice in the Hope of the world.

Peace Covenant

Today, God, I will be someone's earthly angel.

13
Friday
December

Spiritual Energy

By John Bonney of Springfield, Oregon, USA

> *Therefore, continue to be strong in faith. To you who hear my voice and know my promises I will reveal myself and give my peace, even in the midst of your uncertainties. Indeed, I am longing to pour out greater blessings than you have ever known, if you, my people, will open yourselves through preparation, study, and prayer.*
>
> —Doctrine and Covenants 158:11a–b

The Spirit impinges on me. For a moment I am brought to a different level of awareness, and my response is emotion—tears.

It may be the moon, a sunset, or water in its various forms. It may be that overwhelming sense of the curvature of Earth, the all-encompassing circumference defined by water and sky, and the indistinct border between the two. It may be a bird song or J.S. Bach.

I also have noticed this strong, inspiring, and uplifting effect brought to me by people. I notice it when they charge the air with energy of expectation.

It happened again last Sunday at our annual children's Christmas program. The congregation at first responded with smiles to the whimsy of the kids and their antics. These smiles then became tears of awareness. The redeeming feature of the whole production by the kids was because *of* the kids. They were so dear, uninhibited, and earnest. But this Sunday was a little different for me.

It was the *just beforehand* that affected me most. People gathered in expectation. I sensed a spiritual presence emanating from the hundred-plus people. The spirit of the season caught them up; the spirit of celebration, love, and being companions on the journey.

I do not want people to see me weeping in public. "Men don't cry!" So it hurts to throttle it down, swallow hard, and not let the tears creep forth too obviously. The energy of love and hope emanating from the room just lifted me to another level—a blessing for me.

I came to an awareness that I was responding to the spiritual energy of the people around me. I will not forget that lesson. So whether the hair stands up on the neck, a sweat breaks out, the breathing comes faster, or we let ourselves cry, we respond when the Spirit touches us. We encounter a thin place and rise in our sensitivities to a greater association with reality beyond reality. Is it redundant to say, "I was moved to tears?" I was moved with eternity.

Prayer for Peace

We are expectant, God, of your spiritual blessings. We open our hearts to receive them.

Spiritual Practice for Advent: Hope

Close your mind to troubling thoughts from the past by placing them in God's generous hands and letting them go. Let God speak to your fearful heart. Think of your hope for the future—open windows in your mind through which you can see compassionate actions. Reflect on the approaching hope of the Christ child. What is your part in the reason for that hope? Rejoice in the Hope of the world.

Peace Covenant

Today, God, I will tune in and listen.

14
Saturday
December

Christmas Gift for the Fire Station

By Karin Peter of Adrian, Missouri, USA

All are called according to the gifts of God unto them; and to the intent that all may labor together, let those that labor in the ministry and those that toil in the affairs of the people of business and of work labor together with God for the accomplishment of the work entrusted to all.

—Doctrine and Covenants 119:8b, adapted

Most folks in the Jackson Congregation in Mississippi don't live in the same neighborhood as their church building. They wanted a way they could be good neighbors.

They learned about the ministry of the Atlanta North Congregation with a nearby Georgia fire station. They learned the firefighters work in three rotating shifts.

"We decided we could pray for each shift on the day they work and take them goodies once a month," Julie Wright explained. That's when the congregation members learned that when a call came, the firefighters looked at a large wall map to pinpoint the location. The firefighters did not have global-positioning systems (GPS) in the trucks.

By the following spring, the Jackson Congregation had raised enough money to buy GPS units and accessory kits for both fire trucks. It might not be the direction members expected their ministry to go, but they are responding to challenges and opportunities wherever they can.

They're trying to relieve physical and spiritual suffering, build healthy connections with those who serve their community, and ensure a timely response for people in crisis. They are experiencing their congregation in mission.

Prayer for Peace

God of wisdom, point us in a new direction. Help us search for and find new ways to help and serve our communities. Help us find new opportunities to share the peace of Christ.

Spiritual Practice for Advent: Hope

Close your mind to troubling thoughts from the past by placing them in God's generous hands and letting them go. Let God speak to your fearful heart. Think of your hope for the future—open windows in your mind through which you can see compassionate actions. Reflect on the approaching hope of the Christ child. What is your part in the reason for that hope? Rejoice in the Hope of the world.

Peace Covenant

Today, God, I will partner with the people of the community for the mission you have entrusted to us.

15
Sunday
December

Tell What You Hear and See

By Kris Judd of Kansas City, Missouri, USA

> *When John heard in prison what the Messiah was doing, he sent word by his disciples and said to him, "Are you the one who is to come, or are we to wait for another?" Jesus answered them, "Go and tell John what you hear and see: the blind receive their sight, the lame walk, the lepers are cleansed, the deaf hear, the dead are raised, and the poor have good news brought to them. And blessed is anyone who takes no offense at me."*
>
> —Matthew 11:2–6

Have you ever been called to testify in a court of law about something you've witnessed? I have nervously gone to court several times, ready to share my story, but have never had to speak. The standard instruction given to witnesses is, "tell the court what you saw or heard." Witnesses are not to persuade the jury or judge; they merely are to tell the truth and let the truth speak for itself.

In today's scripture passage, Jesus challenged John's disciples to be witnesses of what they experienced of Christ's ministry. They were not asked to quote scripture or share a list of beliefs, but to tell what their own eyes had seen and what their ears had heard. Their lives were to speak of what Christ was doing through them and among them.

Like the early disciples who spent time with Jesus, we are called to be witnesses of what *we* have seen and heard. Are we watching and listening for how God's Spirit is at work in our world? Are we paying attention to what the Spirit of the Living Christ is doing through us and within us?

We are not called to persuade, merely to tell the truth, and the truth will speak for itself.

Prayer for Peace

God of truth, make us witnesses of our experiences with Christ. May we share the joy of our life with him. May we share Christ's peace.

Spiritual Practice: Love

Reflect on the love of God. How is it that God sent Christ to be "all our loves exceeding"? How do you see God's love revealed in Christ? How is God's love revealed in your own life? Think of ways you can express that love as you prepare for the Son of God—love's pure light. Thank God for the supreme gift of love: Jesus Christ.

Peace Covenant

Today, God, I will witness of what I know, not of what I think others want to hear.

16
Monday
December

Best Friend (for a Day)

By Deb Crowley of Charlotte, Michigan, USA

Heed the urgent call to become a global family united in the name of the Christ, committed in love to one another, seeking the kingdom for which you yearn and to which you have always been summoned. That kingdom shall be a peaceable one and it shall be known as Zion.

—Doctrine and Covenants 161:6b

Reflecting on the Advent theme of love from church yesterday, I thought of my grandson. My heart turned to mush while embraced in 3-year-old Tyson's bear hug. It didn't matter that the day before I had denied him a second cookie, scolded for hitting, set him in time out for throwing a tantrum, or lectured about why we don't use "bad" words.

As his little arms squeezed my neck, he uttered words that set the world in order, "Grammie, you are my best friend!" Wow!

It would be easy to allow my grandson's "best friend" declaration to make me too prideful. However, on arriving home and asking him to repeat to his mommy who his best friend was, he exclaimed, "Bryce and Max!" I figured the response was environmental, but it kept me humble.

However, for one poignant, unexpected moment, I felt loved and special—not to exclude anyone, but included *with* everyone important in Tyson's world.

I imagine God's love this same way. God may be saying, "My child, you are my finest creation!" Despite disobedience, selfishness, stubbornness, or failure to listen, God never fails to forgive and offer second chances. And while I am made whole by God's love, God extends love to everyone—it is not mine alone.

The memory of Ty's declaration warms my heart daily even though he is 500 miles away. God's embracing love extends across the universe. God sent Jesus to Earth as a visible expression of love and then blessed the world with the Holy Spirit that continues to breathe in and through all of life. We understand God's love from experiencing nature, through kindness, through other people, or answered prayers.

And, sometimes, God's love reaches us through bear hugs from 3-year-olds.

Prayer for Peace

Loving God, thank you for sending the Christ child to teach what love is. May this love, as we have received it, spread throughout your global village and bring peace.

Spiritual Practice for Advent: Love

Reflect on the love of God. How is it that God sent Christ to be "all our loves exceeding"? How do you see God's love revealed in Christ? How is God's love revealed in your own life? Think of ways you can express that love as you prepare for the Son of God—love's pure light. Thank God for the ultimate gift of love: Jesus Christ.

Peace Covenant

Today, God, I will let love lead me through Advent.

17
Tuesday
December

Proof Positive

By Talitha Pennington of Sterling Heights, Michigan, USA

> *An account of the genealogy of Jesus the Messiah, the son of David, the son of Abraham… and Jacob the father of Joseph the husband of Mary, of whom Jesus was born, who is called the Messiah.*
>
> —Matthew 1:1, 16

My husband, like his mother, is one of millions of people who love genealogy. He has traveled to cemeteries, courthouses, and libraries, as well as doing online research. He is trying to trace his ancestry back as far as possible. For some, it is just a hobby of interest; for others it's important to find out where they came from. Having proof of heritage may provide needed medical history or links for membership in certain organizations.

The opening verses of the gospel of Matthew begin with a genealogy for Jesus. Many times this text is glossed over. Matthew connects one generation to the next from Abraham to Joseph. For Matthew, who was writing for the early Christian community, showing that Jesus was a "son of David" was important. After all, they believed prophets had declared the Messiah would come from David's lineage.

Do we need proof that Jesus is the Christ? The only real proof comes when we open our hearts to "Emmanuel—God with us." May his extraordinary love fill your heart to overflowing this Christmas and beyond.

Prayer for Peace

God of ages past and ages to come, allow us to open our minds and hearts to speakers across time. May we look back with respect for tradition, and look forward with joyful expectation. May Christ remain in our hearts as evidence of your love.

Spiritual Practice for Advent: Love

Reflect on the love of God. How is it that God sent Christ to be "all our loves exceeding"? How do you see God's love revealed in Christ? How is God's love revealed in your own life? Think of ways you can express that love as you prepare for the Son of God—love's pure light. Thank God for the ultimate gift of love: Jesus Christ.

Peace Covenant

Today, God, I will be aware of where I come from and where I am going on the joyful path to peace.

18

ednesday
ecember

Sanctuary

By Peggy Michael of Cantonment, Florida, USA

> *...receptive congregations in the areas around the Temple and throughout the world will be revived and equipped for more effective ministry. Vital to this awakening is the understanding that the Temple calls the entire church to become a sanctuary of Christ's peace, where people from all nations, ethnicities, and life circumstances can be gathered into a spiritual home without dividing walls, as a fulfillment of the vision for which Jesus Christ sacrificed his life.*
>
> —Doctrine and Covenants 163:8c

In the middle of winter, the angry wind clawed the last leaf from the maple tree. Slowly its life fed the farthermost root. The last wedge of geese winged southward, and below, a pheasant scurried through the ragged cornfield.

Brave willows lashed at the ice tyrant, but it would not retreat. Nearby, the sleepy turtles said goodnight and hid deep in the muddy pond. I, too, retreated with my coat clutched tightly about me. I headed inside for my chair beside the warm fire. Was my work done for the winter?

From my window I saw a lonely pine tree silhouetted by the moonlight. I thought, "Your work is not done. You must stand on the rocky ledge and brace yourself against the savage wind. You cling to the uneven rocks with living roots.

"Strong and secure, you do not exist for yourself alone. You offer a resting place, a sanctuary for tired birds. Season after season you point the way across the deep valley toward nurturing fields. Oh pine tree, like you, I want to provide sanctuary for the weary. Let them rest on me for a time, and I will bless them on their way."

Prayer for Peace

God, as a tree is sanctuary for a bird, and as you are sanctuary for me, I pray I might be sanctuary for another. Perhaps as a community we might be sanctuaries for those who share Christ's peace.

Spiritual Practice for Advent: Love

Reflect on the love of God. How is it that God sent Christ to be "all our loves exceeding"? How do you see God's love revealed in Christ? How is God's love revealed in your own life? Think of ways you can express that love as you prepare for the Son of God—love's pure light. Thank God for the supreme gift of love: Jesus Christ.

Peace Covenant

Today, God, I will employ ministries of the Temple to become sanctuary for another.

19
Thursday
December

Alleluia Everywhere and Always

By Elizabeth Else of St. Thomas, Ontario, Canada

> *Jesus Christ, the embodiment of God's shalom, invites all people to come and receive divine peace in the midst of the difficult questions and struggles of life. Follow Christ in the way that leads to God's peace and discover the blessings of all the dimensions of salvation.*
>
> —Doctrine and Covenants 163:2a

Recently I viewed a video showing adults and children of a Native Alaskan village holding signs with the words of Handel's "Hallelujah Chorus." While sung by an unseen choir, a community member held up the matching syllable or word on a large card. It was a creative video done as a school computer project involving many people in the village.

The people were all ages, and the sequence was filmed in many venues. Children came down slides with syllable cards; people in stores held word cards. People—old, young, and in between—held cards in churches, schools, houses, fields, and on the streets. They were in the post office, in cars, trucks, and buses. Even in the snow with dogsleds. Some were in a boat, in a stairwell, and in Dumpsters. Each time a word was sung, someone popped up, card in hand, with the right word, at the right time.

On the surface, it was a fun and even amusing project, full of expectation. However, as I thought about it further, I was touched by how it showed Unity in Diversity.

People of all ages and skills joined in this presentation.

It also was symbolic of the ever-present God of all. Divinity is in all places and times of our lives: schools, home, and the outdoors. God is not just in our times of worship, but in all moments of our busy lives: learning, playing, even doing chores.

"King of Kings, Lord of Lords, Prince of Peace; forever and ever. Alleluia! Alleluia! (Quick, hold up your card) Al—le—lu—ia!"

Prayer for Peace

Thank you, God, for the gift of your Son. May we be expectant of his coming wherever we are and whatever we're doing. May we be ready with joy and peace in our hearts to share.

Spiritual Practice for Advent: Love

Reflect on the love of God. How is it that God sent Christ to be "all our loves exceeding"? How do you see God's love revealed in Christ? How is God's love revealed in your own life? Think of ways you can express that love as you prepare for the Son of God—love's pure light. Thank God for the supreme gift of love: Jesus Christ.

Peace Covenant

According to the order of your word, God, I will be ready to respond at the right time.

20
Friday
December

No Time Like the Present

By Karen Smith of Ludington, Michigan, USA

And those who know your name put their trust in you, for you, O Lord, have not forsaken those who seek you. Sing praises to the Lord, who dwells in Zion. Declare his deeds among the peoples.

—Psalm 9:10–11

Two days after Christmas is an excellent time to shop for bargains. As I searched the department store shelves I found a cute teddy bear holding a bottle of my mother-in-law's favorite perfume. "You should get that for Mother," a little voice said. I thought it was a good idea, but I had to watch my budget. I walked away and continued to shop.

Every time I strolled past that shelf, the little voice became more insistent. "You need to get that for Mother. Bev loves that perfume and little bears, too!"

I reached for the bear and its gift. At the same time, across town in the nursing home, a discouraged Bev prayed, "Help me, God. What will I do? Please, please send somebody!"

She had arranged for a Bible study for her residents and had just learned the leader wasn't coming.

I wheeled the cart to my car when a new thought came to me, "Don't wait for her birthday or next Christmas; take your gift to Mother right now!" No time like the present for a present. I drove to the nursing home. When I walked in the front door, Bev greeted me, beaming with joy. She said, "You are an answer to my prayer!"

I was afraid. I had never led a Bible study, much less one for seniors. But as I prayed I was assured Christ would be with us. We had a beautiful time with prayers for those in need being our main focus. The Holy Spirit filled the room and inspired our prayer and study.

As I looked around the room, warm smiles greeted me. Wherever God takes us, whatever God asks of us, we can trust we will be led in our ministry. Just remember to take a moment to pray and let God in. I received a gift also—I have a new testimony of how God can guide us even while shopping for bargains.

Prayer for Peace

Loving God, thank you for your guiding spirit. We trust in you. Thank you for your presence among us when we are afraid. Lead us to share Christ's peace.

Spiritual Practice for Advent: Love

Reflect on the love of God. How is it that God sent Christ to be "all our loves exceeding"? How do you see God's love revealed in Christ? How is God's love revealed in your own life? Think of ways you can express that love as you prepare for the Son of God—love's pure light. Thank God for the supreme gift of love: Jesus Christ.

Peace Covenant

Today, God, I will not hesitate to respond when I feel led by your Spirit.

21
Saturday
December

Responsible Choices, Responsible Giving

By Donna Boyd of Independence, Missouri, USA

> *The Spirit of the One you follow is the spirit of love and peace. That Spirit seeks to abide in the hearts of those who would embrace its call and live its message. The path will not always be easy, the choices will not always be clear, but the cause is sure and the Spirit will bear witness to the truth, and those who live the truth will know the hope and the joy of discipleship in the community of Christ. Amen.*
>
> —Doctrine and Covenants 161:7

As we prepare to celebrate the birth of Christ, we face many decisions. If we take part in the gift-giving tradition, we have to decide who gets what. If we are hosting guests we have to decide who to invite and what food to serve. How do we spend our time—all party and decoration or in worship and centering on Christ?

Even in everyday tasks we find guidance from God. We know the Divine cares for us by the direction we receive. Our lives are richer when we let the model of Christ guide us in all matters.

When we face a major choice, which may change our lives and the lives of others, we are more likely to pause for guidance. We don't try to consult God like an oracle or expect an answer as tangible as we might find in a fortune cookie. God is not our decision maker, but a spiritual guide. With prayer and discernment, we can expect broadening insight to make more Responsible Choices.

Sometimes the Spirit of God makes us aware of the wisest choice. Sometimes the facts become clearer for us to analyze. We learn to take responsibility for our choices. We rejoice that we have the freedom to choose for ourselves. We are thankful that engaging in Christ's mission guides us toward right decisions "and the Spirit will bear witness to the truth..."

Perhaps we'll feel led to choose to invest in the growth of others—perhaps helping them put Christ at the center of their Christmas. We praise God for the light shed on our learning, growing, and decision making.

Prayer for Peace

Generous God, lead us to generosity. May we choose to follow the star and lay our gifts at the manger of grace.

Spiritual Practice for Advent: Love

Reflect on the love of God. How is it that God sent Christ to be "all our loves exceeding"? How do you see God's love revealed in Christ? How is God's love revealed in your own life? Think of ways you can express that love as you prepare for the Son of God—love's pure light. Thank God for the supreme gift of love: Jesus Christ.

Peace Covenant

Today I am deciding to choose love, God—love to the world!

22
Sunday
ecember

Jesus Is Born

By Kris Judd of Kansas City, Missouri, USA

Now the birth of Jesus the Messiah took place in this way. When his mother Mary had been engaged to Joseph, but before they lived together, she was found to be with child from the Holy Spirit. Her husband Joseph, being a righteous man and unwilling to expose her to public disgrace, planned to dismiss her quietly...An angel of the Lord appeared to him... "...Do not be afraid to take Mary as your wife, for the child conceived in her is from the Holy Spirit. She will bear a son, and you are to name him Jesus, for he will save his people from their sins."

—Matthew 1:18–21

I have many children, all of whom belong to other mothers. I never had the privilege of giving birth but have been blessed to love and care for children from my family, friends, and church. A few years ago I had the opportunity to witness the birth of a special baby, Jasmine, the daughter of two good friends.

Jasmine was not an expected pregnancy. Neither mother nor father was ready to welcome her into the world. Her father was not sure she was even his but vowed to raise her and treat her as his own. I was in the hospital room with Jasmine's mother, father, and grandmother the day she arrived. It had been a long night, filled with discomfort and fear.

On her arrival, the world seemed different, more alive, more real. God opened my eyes with a sense of wonder and possibility that I had not experienced. I fell in love with the world and with a baby whose life changed forever the lives of two unprepared but willing parents.

Perhaps that is how Joseph and Mary were feeling when their son arrived. They did not plan, nor were they ready for this baby. But the baby that arrived changed not only their lives but millions of lives around the world.

His birth continues to change lives every moment.

Two thousand years ago, the birth of Jesus Christ ushered in a new possibility of a kingdom for which the faithful had been waiting for way too long. The world is still waiting to see it in its fullness. It is here, and it is coming. Hallelujah! Jesus is born!

Prayer for Peace

Generous God, let us be the ones who bring good news to the poor, joy to the brokenhearted, hope to those who wait. Let us share the news of the Christ child and his peace.

Spiritual Practice: Joy

Prepare room in your heart for the Christ child. Prepare room in your heart for joy. Think of the many ways you *experience* joy in the Advent season: bells, candles, lights, carols, special food, gift giving, time with family and friends, celebrations of the birth of Christ. Reflect on the many ways you can *share* joy in the Advent season: giving to those in need, making a place for everyone at the table, greeting strangers, helping others, being a presence. Continue your own list. Thank God for the joy you experience and the opportunities to share it.

Peace Covenant

On this joyous day, God, I will share the joy of the coming of the Christ Child.

23
Monday
December

The Blessing of Size-12 Slippers

By Cindy L. Korf of North Platte, Nebraska, USA

> *You will be enriched in every way for your great generosity, which will produce thanksgiving to God through us; for the rendering of this ministry not only supplies the needs of the saints but also overflows with many thanksgivings to God. Through the testing of this ministry you glorify God by your obedience to the confession of the gospel of Christ and by the generosity of your sharing with them and with all others, while they long for you and pray for you because of the surpassing grace of God that he has given you. Thanks be to God for his indescribable gift!*
>
> —2 Corinthians 9:11–15

At the nursing home's annual Christmas party, each resident received a package especially for them. One resident, Mark, a middle-aged man staying there while recovering from an accident, showed elation at his package, which contained a box of chocolate candy, a blanket, and a pair of size-12 slippers.

When I wheeled Mark and his bounty of food, cookies, hot chocolate, and presents back to his room, I asked him if he enjoyed the party.

"Oh, yes," he responded. "It was an answer to my prayer."

"Oh?"

"I have wanted badly to give Brian a gift, but I had nothing to give him or any way to buy something—until today. I wear a size 7 shoe. Brian wears a size 12, and he had no slippers."

He looked up at me and smiled. "I gave him my slippers!"

I don't know who received more of a blessing—Mark for giving the gift, Brian for receiving, or I for witnessing the true joy in giving and receiving.

Prayer for Peace

Thank you, God, for the joy we receive when we give. Thank you for the peace we receive when we share Christ's peace.

Spiritual Practice for Advent: Joy

Prepare room in your heart for the Christ child. Prepare room in your heart for joy. Think of the many ways you *experience* joy in the Advent season: bells, candles, lights, carols, special food, gift giving, time with family and friends, celebrations of the birth of Christ. Reflect on the many ways you can *share* joy in the Advent season: giving to those in need, making a place for everyone at the table, greeting strangers, helping others, being a presence. Continue your own list. Thank God for the joy you experience and the opportunities to share it.

Peace Covenant

Today, God, and all through Advent, I will express my joy in your gift of the Christ child.

24
Tuesday
December

Cold Feet on Christmas Eve

By Chris Lasley of Vancouver, Washington, USA

Praise the Lord, all you nations! Extol him, all you peoples! For great is his steadfast love toward us, and the faithfulness of the Lord endures forever. Praise the Lord!

—Psalm 117

When I was little, the worst gifts I got for Christmas were socks and underwear. Underwear was embarrassing, and socks, well, just plain boring. Try getting excited over a pair of socks—not something I looked forward to with great expectation.

A woman in our congregation works with hard-living students who are homeless or in foster care. Their goal is to graduate, but they struggle because of their living conditions. Each year Vanessa makes a "giving tree" at church. She lists the students' names, gifts they need, and gifts they want. Some gifts are cool, like skateboards, and others are just downright necessary, like bath towels or…socks!

The girl and boy we drew from the tree *chose* socks as their necessary item. My husband said, "If you ask for socks for Christmas, you must need socks." I had to agree, though it never would have been on *my* list as a child.

As I wrapped the socks I thought, "This is a boring gift." However, Vanessa shared with me that the girl really was looking forward to getting socks. Vanessa explained that these two teens were couch surfers, meaning they were homeless. They slept on friends' couches from house to house. The girl and her friend shared one pair of socks between them.

Some days when I'm sitting at my desk and my feet are cold, I put on as many as three pairs of socks. What if I had only one pair and had to share them—sometimes going a day with bare feet?

Now, when I open my over-stuffed sock drawer, I think about how those in need might look forward to Christmas. I realize how blessed I am to have so much joy to look forward to.

I am blessed to have in my heart the expectation of the Christ child—a needed *and* wanted gift.

Prayer for Peace

Generous God, may we always have the joy and peace of Christ in our heart to share with others.

Spiritual Practice for Advent: Joy

Prepare room in your heart for the Christ child. Prepare room in your heart for joy. Think of the many ways you *experience* joy in the Advent season: bells, candles, lights, carols, special food, gift giving, time with family and friends, celebrations of the birth of Christ. Reflect on the many ways you can *share* joy in the Advent season: giving to those in need, making a place for everyone at the table, greeting strangers, helping others, being a presence. Continue your own list. Thank God for the joy you experience and the opportunities to share it.

Peace Covenant

Today, God, I will prepare for the Christ child by giving a generous gift.

25
Wednesday
December

(What Child is This?)

By Karen Moreland of Independence, Missouri, USA

> *Make a joyful noise to the Lord, all the earth; break forth into joyous song and sing praises. Sing praises to the Lord with the lyre, with the lyre and the sound of melody. With trumpets and the sound of the horn make a joyful noise before the King, the Lord.*
>
> —Psalm 98:4–7

Christmas is a time for caroling. I always looked forward to my congregation's annual caroling tour. Some years ago, shortly after the birth of one of my sons, I took him caroling with me. One place we went was the Washington State School for the Blind.

The children gathered in the hallway as we joyfully sang familiar Christmas carols. After the singing, some children were huddling close and whispering. The supervisor approached me and said, "Some of the children *can* see a little and told the others that you are holding a baby. Many of the children have been blind since birth and have never seen a real baby. They only have dolls to play with."

They wanted to know if I would let them "see" my child. I looked at their hopeful faces and quickly said all right.

I knelt as the woman and several small children gathered around me. The woman guided them as they reached out and touched the tiny hands and feet of my squirming baby. Then they brushed their hands across the soft hair on my son's head.

They were in awe at the tiny, cooing baby I held in my arms. They smiled and giggled at this opportunity to see with their gentle, touching hands.

My thoughts wandered to what Mary must have felt when the throng of visitors came to see her infant son, Jesus. My heart pounded with joy as I saw the smiles and joyful faces of those children gathered around me. The words from "Silent Night" ran through my head, "... mother and child, Holy Infant, so tender and mild..." The Christmas story came alive as we shared the joy and peace of this holy night. I will never forget that Christmas.

Prayer for Peace

Creator God, thank you for the many ways we can share the story of the Christ child with others. Thank you for silent nights, gentle infants, and hopeful children. Thank you for your Son and his peace that we can share.

Spiritual Practice for Advent: Joy

Prepare room in your heart for the Christ child. Prepare room in your heart for joy. Think of the many ways you *experience* joy in the Advent season: bells, candles, lights, carols, special food, gift giving, time with family and friends, celebrations of the birth of Christ. Reflect on the many ways you can *share* joy in the Advent season: giving to those in need, making a place for everyone at the table, greeting strangers, helping others, being a presence. Continue your own list. Thank God for the joy you experience and the opportunities to share it.

Peace Covenant

Today, God, I will help someone "see" Christ by my actions.

26
Thursday
December

Terrible and Wonderful

By Michelle McGrath of Mission Viejo, California, USA

> *A voice cries out: "In the wilderness prepare the way of the Lord, make straight in the desert a highway for our God. Every valley shall be lifted up, and every mountain and hill be made low; the uneven ground shall become level, and the rough places a plain."*
>
> —Isaiah 40:3–4

It was both terrible and wonderful. They had to leave at night. In the utter darkness rough terrain becomes rougher. Unseen contours and loose rocks cause sudden trips and falls. The sharp desert vegetation snags and rips clothing and pierces sturdy footwear. Venomous creatures creep and run across the desert floor.

The way is easy to lose; yet life depends on finding the way.

There was no guiding star left in the utter darkness of this cold desert night. One can navigate by the other stars, if one knows how, and if they are visible. For a family seeking to avoid discovery, night was the only time to travel. The cold was a relief to the brutal heat of the day. It was both terrible and wonderful.

"The desert is no place for a baby!" people would say. But life depended on *not* drawing attention. Not yet, anyway. Not here. They followed the voice that said if you want to live you have to go—away from oppression and violence, toward a new life, the life God promises all God's beloved children. It was both terrible and wonderful.

I wonder if this holy immigrant family hummed the promise of Isaiah as they undertook this risky journey. Did they dream of a straight pathway through the desert, where the uneven places are level, and the rough places are like a plain—a direct route to the kingdom of God? Did they dream of a welcoming home? I wonder, does every holy immigrant family dream of this? Do we?

Prayer for Peace

God of the desert and highway, God of the mountain and border, help us cross to a new life in you. Thank you for Emmanuel, our bridge, our peace, our hope for the world.

Spiritual Practice: Honoring the Worth of All Persons

Read Psalm 139:13–18. After each reading sit quietly and let the words sink deeply into your mind, heart, and body. Imagine God watching you grow in your mother's womb. What thoughts and feelings do you have about being "fearfully and wonderfully made" (Psalm 139:14)?

Sense the intimate knowledge and love God has of you and every child. Be aware of the sacred worth of each person. Weep with God over the soul-wounding forces and events that rob people of dignity and worth. How are you invited to notice, protect, heal, and affirm the spiritual identity of all God's beloved people today? Pray for God's compassion.

Peace Covenant

Today, God, I will see the immigrant family and recognize the holy family in them.

27
Friday
December

The Need to Be Heard

By Sara Parkin of Midland, Michigan, USA

> *Finally, brothers and sisters, farewell. Put things in order, listen to my appeal, agree with one another, live in peace; and the God of love and peace will be with you.*
>
> —2 Corinthians 13:11

(Part 10 of My Journey with Alzheimer's Disease)

I was at a walk in Saginaw, Michigan. It was a gathering of people who care. They care enough to share their lives, give support, and listen to those who need hearing—those with Alzheimer's disease.

I heard and saw laughter, joy, happiness, dancing, sharing, tears, helping, and walking. It was an amazing day. People were there to show many kinds of support: some to remind us that we are still alive, some to help with fundraising, and some to share their stories.

When I arrived I saw a lot of volunteers setting things up for the walk, caregivers, family, friends, and those with forms of Alzheimer's disease.

God bless them all!

After that walk, I was a speaker at the Alzheimer's Walk in Midland, Michigan. You can speak, too. If you have a form of Alzheimer's disease and are still lucid, please know that God is with you and will walk with you every day. Share your stories. Caregivers: You can speak for them also. Everyone is a child of God, and if you are afraid to speak, God will help you. God gives me the words that I need when I falter.

After reading my blog, someone asked to interview me for the *Daily News*. I was scared, but I remembered God would let it happen or not. I said yes. Once I found out that I have a form of dementia, I could start to find what I can do. It has been a challenge. Not easy! I learned that if I am stressed, my brain slows me down. When I start to think that I failed the challenge, I remember my brain is still working. I am tired, but I say, the end of Alzheimer's starts with me and you! Thank you for being part of my journey. Go in peace.

Prayer for Peace

God of love and peace, help us remember you are with us every step of our journey. Help us understand how frustrating it is for those who suffer loss of memory, speech, and recognition. Help us encourage them and let them know we will be with them also. We will help them share Christ's peace.

Spiritual Practice

Pray with a partner if possible, or imagine Christ sitting with you. The heart is a center of compassion and spiritual connection. Stand or sit across from your partner with hands open and palms up. Invite your partner to place hands, palms down, on your hands. Close your eyes and be aware of the connection between your heart and your partner's heart. What needs, feelings, or longings do you sense? Invite God's presence to flow into you and move from your heart to the heart of your partner. Feel or see God's healing light and love flowing between your hearts. (You also may pray this prayer by envisioning a particular person across from you.)

Peace Covenant

Today, God, I will be present with someone who may not know who I am, or even that I am there.

28
aturday
ecember

Follow a Worthy Example, *Be* a Worthy Example

By Paul McCain of Oklahoma City, Oklahoma, USA

The Spirit of the One you follow is the spirit of love and peace. That Spirit seeks to abide in the hearts of those would embrace its call and live its message.

—Doctrine and Covenants 161:7

I have a co-worker who I try to emulate. Many times she has left a coupon, a piece of chocolate, or some other item on a colleague's desk—perhaps something found at a garage sale that uniquely fits a co-worker's need or fancy. She lives her life thinking of others, sharing selflessly.

I saw her recently at a community garage sale, and she had a bag of goodies. Suspecting the reason for the bulging bag, I asked her about the contents. One item was for a woman she had befriended—one who, like the woman at the well with Christ, had a bad reputation. Her list of gifts went on to include one whom many had scratched off their list of friends, one who struggles with a mental illness, one who continues to need friends.

I shared about her kindness in a Disciples' Generous Response moment, encouraging those present to set good examples like hers, or at least, find one to follow. My co-worker is one who teaches me about sharing, grace, and caring.

The spirit of love abides in her heart and she lives its message.

She sets an example to follow. May we find a good example to follow and then set an example of life-affirming generosity.

Prayer for Peace

Generous God, help us take our minds off ourselves, at times, and think of others. Our everyday acquaintances may need a life-affirming gift, word, or gesture to show we are aware of their needs. May we also be aware of our brothers and sisters around the world, who need life-sustaining gifts—who need the peace and justice of Christ.

Spiritual Practice: Teacher-learner

The first disciples of Jesus followed to hear his words, to be taught, to learn a new way of living, to practice what they learned in daily life. Prayerfully consider your role as a teacher-learner, disciple-apprentice—a people cultivator in Community of Christ. In your journal write the names of several persons you discern as teachers or mentors and several you feel called to nurture and encourage in specific ways. Ask God's blessing on you and your congregation as a community of learners.

Peace Covenant

Today, God, I will think of a person and a gift that might give them a lift.

29
Sunday
December

Listen to the Voice

By David Brock, presiding evangelist

> *...an angel of the Lord appeared to Joseph in a dream and said, "Get up, take the child and his mother, and flee to Egypt, and remain there until I tell you; for Herod is about to search for the child, to destroy him."... "A voice was heard in Ramah, wailing and loud lamentation, Rachel weeping for her children; she refused to be consoled, because they are no more." When Herod died, an angel of the Lord suddenly appeared in a dream to Joseph in Egypt and said, "Get up, take the child and his mother, and go to the land of Israel..." Then Joseph got up, took the child and his mother, and went to the land of Israel... And after being warned in a dream, he went away to the district of Galilee.*
>
> —Matthew 2:13, 18–21

There are two important voices to listen to in this well-known passage. The first is the voice of the angel of the Lord that speaks to Joseph in dreams: "Get up, take the child and his mother and flee to Egypt." "Get up...and go to the land of Israel." Get up...and go to Galilee." (Note throughout the scriptures the multitude of times dreams are the means God uses to reveal truths to humankind!)

As with Joseph, God can speak in our dreams. In our hectic, waking lives, we often miss the Voice that speaks deepest truths, that provides guidance beyond our own intellect... as essential as human reasoning is. As the voice of God guided Joseph in dreams for Jesus' well-being, so are we as the body of Christ called. We read in the Doctrine and Covenants, "Listen to the Voice that echoes across the eons of time and yet speaks anew in this moment."

The other voice in this passage is the voice of loud weeping; the anguished voice of Rachel mourning the death of her children. We, too, must hear the God weeping in Rachel and weeping "for the poor, displaced, mistreated, and diseased of the world." We must open our ears to hear the Rachel of old as well as "the pleading of mothers and fathers...who desperately seek a future of hope for their children."

Rachel's voice is the voice of God. The angel speaking to Joseph in the dream is the voice of God. "Listen to the Voice, for it cannot be stilled, and it calls you once again to the great and marvelous work of building the peaceable kingdom, even Zion...."

Prayer for Peace

Holy Voice, we listen through the voices of the mistreated. We listen to those in need of justice and the peace of Christ. We will respond by hearing and sharing.

Spiritual Practice: Voices of God

What is the voice of God saying to us? Do we hear the whispers of God's longing for shalom; God's dream of justice and wholeness for all creation? Do we hear the voice of God calling to us in faces and eyes, in the sounds of suffering and joy, in scripture and sacred word? Reflect on when and how God's voice has spoken to you. When did you first feel called to join God in the pursuit of peace and justice?

Peace Covenant

Today, God, I will listen for your voice. I will hear. I will consider. I will respond.

30
Monday
December

♫ Year End Hymn: "Here from This Place"

By Lu Mountenay of Independence, Missouri, USA

> *...Open your ears to hear the pleading of mothers and fathers in all nations who desperately seek a future of hope for their children. Do not turn away from them. For in their welfare resides your welfare.*
>
> —Doctrine and Covenants 163:4a

I have always enjoyed Marty Haugen's hymn, "Gather Us In." I wanted to write a hymn with matching gusto to *send us out* after gaining strength at the center. To me, these two hymns represent the journey inward and the journey outward. I combined these thoughts with language from Doctrine and Covenants 163. We are transformed from the *lost and forsaken* in "Gather Us In" to the *found and forgiven* in the new hymn. With hope, a hymn to journey into a new year.

1) Here from this place, a journey beginning,
Here from the center, outward we go.
Divinely inspired by breath of the Spirit,
To share Christ's Shalom by the love that we sow

Refrain:
Send us now forth the found and forgiven,
Seek those in need and burdens they bear.
Aware of our calling, our mission, our purpose,
Send us now forth as disciples to share.

2) As we now leave this space that is sacred,
Make of us sanctuaries, we pray.
Turn not away from fathers and mothers,
Who plead for the lives of their children each day.

3) From silence of prayer and deep meditation,
Carry the awe and wonder abroad.
As the Divine has graced us with presence,
We will be present to others for God.

Prayer for Peace

God of beginnings and endings, let us gather in our worship community and journey out into the new year as one, to share the peace of Christ.

Spiritual Practice

Contemplate this hymn as a poem (or sing to the tune of "Gather Us In").

Peace Covenant

Today, God, I will seek to share the peace of Christ as you send me from my place of comfort.

31
Tuesday
December

Look Back—Remember… Look Forward—Envision

By John Bonney of Springfield, Oregon, USA

> *Lift up your eyes and fix them on the place beyond the horizon to which you are sent. Journey in trust, assured that the great and marvelous work is for this time and for all time.*
>
> —Doctrine and Covenants161:1a

I just won a game of solitaire and I'm happy. Oh, you think I should get a life? Now don't feel sorry for me just because I like to sit alone in front of my computer and play solitaire.

My solitaire game is leading up to my message. Do you know the feeling, "I've been here and done this before?" I don't mea*n déjà vu.* I mean, "I've gone this way so often I can almost see myself returning."

I'd be on the road, heading somewhere. I'd have an agenda, see the same highway, meet the same people, drive thousands of miles, and I imagined I could see myself returning. I would leave in the morning for my destination and think, "There I am coming back later." I don't know if others feel this way.

I am not comfortable in the present. I don't do *now*. I spend much time in the past because I thrive on nostalgia. I like to look back and remember.

But I also look forward and envision. Entering the new year is a good time for this.

I live in a world of creativity and imagination. I like people but prefer to be alone.

I enjoy music, poetry, and the visual arts. These venues may be common ground for you and me, but in other ways I feel I have a different personality than most. The Enduring Principle of Unity in Diversity allows me to fit into my community. I am happier than when winning a game of solitaire, knowing I am accepted and loved the way I am—by God and you.

Prayer for Peace

We thank you, God, for the familiarity of the past and the mystery of the future. Walk with us into the new year.

Spiritual Practice: Ongoing Revelation

One Enduring Principle of Community of Christ is Continuing Revelation. We are a people always in process, becoming shaped by God's interaction with us. In prayer, listen deeply to the name, "Community of Christ." Write or say a prayer asking God to continue to form us through our name. Listen deeply to what it would mean to live in community, following and sharing the way of Christ.

Peace Covenant

I commit myself anew to sharing Christ's peace in the fresh, new year.

DAILY BREAD 2013

Author Index

O

P

R

S

T

V

W

Y

DAILY BREAD 2013

Scripture Index

Your Future Stories for Daily Bread

Your Future Stories for Daily Bread

Your Future Stories for Daily Bread

Your Future Stories for Daily Bread

Your Future Stories for Daily Bread